PACIFIC
HARVEST

PACIFIC HARVEST

A Northwest Coast Foraging Guide

JENNIFER HAHN

SKIPSTONE

For all our relatives,
mountains to sea

SKIPSTONE

Published by Skipstone, an imprint of Mountaineers Books—an independent, nonprofit publisher
Skipstone and its colophon are registered trademarks of The Mountaineers organization.
Printed in China
28 27 26 25   1 2 3 4 5

Portions of this guide were originally published, in different form, in *Pacific Feast: A Cook's Guide to West Coast Foraging and Cuisine* (Mountaineers Books, 2010), by Jennifer Hahn.
Tamiflu is a registered trademark of Roche.
All photographs and illustrations by the author unless otherwise indicated.
Design: Jen Grable
Cover photographs, front, clockwise from top left: harvesting fucus, ostrich fern (*Photo by Gingerjohns, iStock*), Pacific blue mussels (*Photo by Katherine Palmer*), giant red sea urchin, and Oregon-grape; spine: mountain blond morel (*Photo by Fred Rhoades*); back: Wild Pile Salad (*Photo by Katherine Palmer*), grand fir tips, giant kelp (*Photo by Natalie Ruffing, iStock*)
Frontispiece: Harvesting beach asparagus

Disclaimer: Foraging for and eating wild foods is inherently risky. This is not a complete text on foraging and harvesting. It is incumbent upon the reader to assess their own skills and usage related to this guide and to foraging in general. Nothing substitutes for formal instruction, practice, and plenty of experience. Neither the author nor the publisher accepts responsibility for any mistakes in identification, personal reactions to consuming foraged foods, or other adverse consequences resulting directly or indirectly from information contained in this book. The author and publisher disclaim all liability.

Library of Congress Cataloging-in-Publication record is available at https://lccn.loc.gov/2024038638. The ebook record is available at https://lccn.loc.gov/2024038639.

Produced with support from the Port of Seattle Tourism Marketing Support Program

Printed on FSC-certified materials

MIX
Paper | Supporting responsible forestry
FSC® C188448

ISBN (paperback): 978-1-68051-668-5
ISBN (ebook): 978-1-68051-669-2

Skipstone
1001 SW Klickitat Way | Suite 201 | Seattle, Washington 98134
206.223.6303 | www.skipstonebooks.org | www.mountaineersbooks.org

LIVE LIFE. MAKE RIPPLES.

CONTENTS

Guide to Wild Morsels

Recipes for Foraged Foods

Foraging from hand-high blueberry bushes in a bog in Southeast Alaska

INTRODUCTION TO NORTHWEST FORAGING

There is something deep-down satisfying, almost mystical, about foraging for your dinner—or even a morsel of it. On my first winter foraging trip to Copalis Beach on the Washington coast, I remember kneeling, at sunset, in the damp sand of a surf-slammed beach, reaching into a gloppy shovel hole, and feeling for a soap-smooth razor clam. It was as cold as river stone but pulsed with life as I touched it, as if awakened from a long nap. The clam pulled away from my grip like a kite spool tugged ever deeper by forces beyond my reach. Remembering the pattern, I held tight to the upper half. Soon the clam's digging foot paused and drew in. The downward tug slacked. I lifted into the salt air a creature whose coastal roots go back millions of years. "Thanks," I said, wiping the sandy clam, long and tapered like an eyeglass case, across my pant leg. The razor clam's varnished surface reflected white surf, rose clouds, and my shadowed face and flying hair. It was a scene as ancient and immediate as hunger, one that had repeated thousands of times—and I was part of this continuum.

I could imagine a long feast table spanning from Yakutat Bay in Southeast Alaska right past my wave-sloshed rubber boots to Point Conception, California. I could see it rising from the Pacific Ocean to the crest of the Cascade Mountains and over the lip. Since the great Ice Age, that three-thousand-mile-long table is where Northwest coast Indigenous peoples traversed rainforests, clam-squirting beaches, wildflower meadows, muskegs, and river estuaries to gather all the food, medicine, and supplies they needed to live. From alder-smoked salmon to red huckleberries, Dungeness crab to sea vegetables, the flavors, textures, colors, and aromas of ocean and earth filled their canoes, cedar storage boxes, and communal feast dishes.

Since that first winter foraging trip, a lot of changes have affected our coastal table. I watched in angst, during three years of marine heat waves, as toxic algae bloomed to unprecedented levels, early-season oysters were tainted with vibrio (a bacteria that ramps up in warming salt water and can cause foodborne infections), and one million emaciated common murres started appearing on our shores. The murre—a seabird of Olympian proportions that can dive two football fields deep to chase herring, capelin, and sand lance—was like a canary in a *Silent Spring* sequel. (I *adore* these black-and-white "flying penguins." Dad murres raise their young to be exquisite fishers. My ocean-themed wedding dress even shows a diving murre—to honor my widowed father who raised me.)

Amid the heat waves, when a mysteriously large patch of warm ocean water oozed out of the Bering Sea toward Baja, Mexico, I was sampling and researching seaweed for my master's degree, trying to figure out if our local seaweeds were safe to eat. More than a dozen First Nations and Tribes generously allowed me to access their traditional harvesting areas. I kayaked, motorboated, walked, and once swam to collect seaweed from forty-three sites ranging from Quadra Island, British Columbia, to Squaxin Island in South Puget Sound. I lost count of how many times the boat drivers in South Puget Sound would say something like, "Wow, where did the bull kelp go? Gee, last year, in this spot, kelp was tangling in the prop, and we couldn't get close to shore." On the Fourth of July weekend, as the forests of Douglas-fir, cedar, and hemlock were burning in three locations on Vancouver Island, the waterways looked like electrified fur. Ash touched everything—the still, early morning sea, my nitrile sampling gloves. When I reached over the boat rail to knife loose five kelp blades, they were feathered in ash, as if from an infestation of wool moths.

That same year, up in Glacier Bay National Park and Preserve in Alaska, where I lead kayak and hiking trips for tourists off a small historic wood ship, park scientists were monitoring migratory humpback whales. These gentle, forty-ton grazers of the deep migrate three to four thousand miles from Hawaii and Mexico to Southeast Alaska, where they lunge through gazillions of shrimp-like krill, capelin, sand lance, and other forage fish glittering in the straits—fish that are crucial for building up fat reserves. But that summer, the whales were "skinny," in the words of my whale research friend Dr. Fred Sharpe. The next year, 140 whales went missing. The warm surface waters, which had grown to Goliathan proportions, now stretched from Baja, Mexico, to the Aleutian Chain. Nicknamed "the blob," the warm, oxygen-poor surface seas were pushing the forage fish to deep waters. I was astonished to see ribs when whales surfaced. It felt too painful to watch yet necessary to witness.

At my home in the Chuckanut Mountains of Washington, in the ancestral and traditional territories of the Noxws'áʔaq (Nooksack) and Lhaq'temish (Lummi) peoples, surrounded by tall cedars, fir, and bigleaf maples, I have recently noticed a lot of crown die-off and shriveled fists of leaves. The western redcedars are thinner too. I can see clear through the once-thick foliage to the upward swooping branches. A few summers back, the western hemlocks turned brittle and dry. If I touched the branches gently with my fingertip, a shower of needles would fall to the earth.

Sea lettuce in the intertidal zone in the Salish Sea

"The blob" and nasty marine heat waves eventually dissipated. I am happy to read reports that the bull kelp swaying in cool, deep waters with skookum-strong current in the Strait of Juan de Fuca, the outer coast of Washington, and Vancouver Island is holding on despite these climatic shifts. Research is underway to figure out why bull kelp beds are still declining in south and central Puget Sound. Just a couple years after the multiyear heat waves, the humpback whales were, according to Dr. Sharpe, "gloriously happy and fat!" And they counted 150 *more* whales in Southeast Alaska waters that summer—it was a record! In September, as we cruised south from Juneau through Frederick Sound to Ketchikan, I lost count of all the flukes and spouts and flippers and backs swirling about as we floated, motor silenced, in our 1941 vessel. We leaned over the gunnels, practically looking down twin blowholes as big as grapefruits that showered us in glorious, krill-scented, sulfurous whale breath from humpbacks clear to the horizon in every direction. *I took a breath.*

So much more seems at stake now than when I wrote my first foraging book almost two decades ago. Animals, plants, places, and people have experienced unprecedented

Harvesting beach asparagus with friends

changes. As a well-salted Northwest-coast naturalist—having studied the animals and plants, casually and in depth, for nearly half a century now—I take extra special care when I am foraging for even a morsel of my delicious dinner.

———

This is a time of unprecedented restoration, too. A movement to renew wild and traditional food systems shimmers across the Pacific rim. It shines through in innumerable hands-on restoration projects. Take, for instance, the Swinomish Indian Tribal Community's clam garden project—an ancient form of aquaculture being resurrected on Kiket Island in the Salish Sea. Rock by rock, hand by muddy hand, the community is building a sturdy, two-hundred-foot-long, knee-high rock wall across the throat of a low-tide beach. According to radiocarbon analysis of ancient barnacle scars in a clam garden in British Columbia, the practice dates back four thousand years. The wall looks like a stone necklace that repeats the arc of the shore at the lowest watermark. Over tides and lifetimes, sediment will fill in landward of the wall. In this rich environment, littleneck and butter clams will grow faster and more plentiful. Recent research in British Columbia shows that "clam gardens contained four times as many butter clams and over twice as many littleneck clams relative to non-walled beaches." That's a big bow to millennia of Indigenous stewardship practices!

Meanwhile, a blue wave of kelp farms and tank-based seaweed aquaculture start-ups is growing from Alaska to Baja. Hundreds of ephemeral seaweedy habitats are sprouting up from anchor lines and cables. Where there was once vacant seawater, golden acres of lush bull kelp, winged kelp, and sugar kelp now attract herring, ling cod, and salmon. It's easier than ever to stock your kelp kitchen. Sea vegetables surpass most land vegetables in nutrient density and culinary flexibility, don't require fresh water or a land base, and can reduce acidification in local oyster farms. In California, the Yurok Indigenous people are revitalizing their ancient huckleberry harvesting sites through controlled burns. In overgrown, fire-suppressed forests, they use selective burning to open clearings that provide shade from the overstory and enough sunshine for berries to prosper—as well as all the creatures, including us, who eat them.

Embracing an old-growth Sitka spruce (Photo by Chris Moench)

Yes, indeed, good things are happening all up and down the Pacific Northwest coast. In the words of Jared Qwustenuxun Williams, Indigenous chef from the Cowichan Nation, it's all about connection: "We need to appreciate that we're all related . . . eating locally, wild harvesting, eating whole foods isn't only our Indigenous way. *Everyone* is indigenous from somewhere. . . . Wherever you're from, well, they look after the land there too! We just don't remember. . . . If we learn how to eat where we are, we can eat a lot healthier." Williams explains how important this connection is to our survival: "We could be looking after the land. Why? Because we want to be able to return there to harvest year after year. Reconnecting is really the answer." We're still here.

This book is all about reconnecting. When you're out foraging, engage all your senses. Notice the aromas, the birdsong, the hush of the water or wind as it travels though the landscape around you. Take your kids with you, or someone else's kids. Help the sprouts grow deep and wild roots.

To help you connect the forest to your plate and the tide to your table, in Recipes for Foraged Foods and sprinkled throughout the book you'll find dozens of recipes, pairings, and loads more ideas featuring foraged goodies. My far-flung foraging friends and I have developed recipes ranging from camp-friendly, no-fuss delights you can pull off with a little forethought—like Salal Berry Scones, Porcini Camp Scramble, and Kelp-Wrapped Steamed Salmon—to kitchen comfort foods such as Fiddlehead Fern Quiche, Ginger Rice with Foraged Greens, and Wild Mushroom Stroganoff. You'll find decadently sweet recipes from Chocolate Ocean Pudding to Evergreen Tree Cookies, thirst quenchers from Oregon-Grape Infused Water to Cuppa Berry Leaves Tea, as well as homemade seasonings to wow your taste buds, including Pickleweed Salt, Spruce-Tip Salt, and Popcorn SEA-sonings with umami-rich sea veggies.

In this book you'll connect with six foragers who are teachers, chefs, and herbalists. Muckleshoot Tribe member Val Segrest is a traditional foods teacher. Tlingit Elder Naomi Kaasei Michalsen founded the Kayaaní Sisters Council—a group of seven Tlingit Elders who conceived foraging guidelines to help care for the plants, animals, and people. Indigenous chef Jared Qwustenuxun Williams shares stories of teaching traditional foods and culture to his two young boys. Alaskan forager Judy Brakel guided kayak tours until she was almost seventy years old; she continues her lively work still—gathering beach greens by sea kayak. Herbalist and forager Linda Quintana tends chickweed and keeps a special spot in her garden just for dandelions. Myco-chef Patrick Hamilton knows mushroom foraging isn't so much about looking for the final prize but about knowing and preserving the forest.

In her rich trove of ethnoecology, *Ancient Pathways, Ancestral Knowledge*, Nancy J. Turner recounts that the Haida traditional stories tell how a red alder was formerly a woman, and so you should hug an alder tree before you cut it down. What if we hugged every tree or berry bush before we snipped its needles for tea or grabbed a big juicy blueberry? What if we hugged every salt-brimming oyster before we held it to our lips? Maybe a hug is a form of wordless grace when offered from the heart with gratitude and respect. When you speak the traditional languages of the place you inhabit, you show respect to the ancestors, to the plants and animals, to everyone around you. One summer, while sharing a bag of sea asparagus I'd picked in Icy Strait, Alaska, with friends, Ahl'lidaaw, a Tsimshian Elder and teacher of the Tsimshian language (Shm'algyack), taught me what you might say to plants when harvesting. She spoke the line very slowly: "Kam Goahl Waan." *Put grace in the air.*

HOW TO USE THIS BOOK

This book will help you get to know many edible Pacific Northwest foods from coast to crest. More importantly, it will help you connect in new ways with our beaches, meadows, and inland forests—even your own backyard. By enhancing your senses—learning by sight and taste the foods that nourished humanity for thousands of years—you may feel a deeper connection to your surroundings. I certainly have.

To help you connect more readily, this book features two main sections: **Guide to Wild Morsels** teaches you what to forage for, and **Recipes for Foraged Foods** showcases enticing recipes to help you discover ways to enjoy what you find. The foraging guide is divided into six sections: Wild & Weedy Greens, Berries & Roses, Trees & Ferns, Mushrooms, Seaweeds & Beach Vegetables, and Shellfish. Each **Featured Food Listing** includes a given species's most common names, taxonomy, primary location, and description, with a photograph to help you sharpen your skill. It is always prudent to cross-reference your field identifications, especially mushrooms, with a second regional guide or, better yet, a knowledgeable expert.

In each listing, a **Harvest Guide** details what to harvest, when, and how, followed by **Culinary Tips** that help you transition from wild table to kitchen table. If you hope to preserve some of your foraged goodies, you'll find DIY sidebars on processing and preserving seaweed, nettles, dandelion root, mushrooms, fennel pollen, and so forth. Select species listings call out a specific **Superpower**—nutrition and wellness benefits that have been discovered over time, or the latest research that demonstrates how a species survives or is helping the planet. To satisfy your hunger, dive into the second part of the book, **Recipes for Foraged Foods**, a robust collection of recipes that serve as springboards for your own creations.

With heightened awareness, and as you learn to locate more wild foods, you may find yourself seeing more signs of animals, birds, and insects. After all, the dining hall we are discovering is already occupied—just not usually when we're tromping through. To help you see who else may be foraging when people aren't around, each wild food entry ends by answering the question: **Who Eats and Shelters Here?** You may be surprised by just how many other creatures depend on the wild foods we harvest, not just for sustenance but for a home too. It's a good reminder to be generous and sometimes to take just a taste.

Not every wild food in this book is native to the Northwest. Some are invasive but delicious newcomers to this coast. Two examples are the mahogany or varnish clam—also called savory clam ("savoury" in Canada)—and Japanese knotweed, a delicious rhubarb-flavored invasive you will learn how to harvest very carefully to avoid spreading. The adage "If you can't beat it, eat it!" applies. Look for the **Caution** icon ❶ indicating that a food requires special harvesting, processing, or disposal.

In the next section, "Preserving Nature's Pantry," as well as in each of the six book sections, look for foraging guidelines on how to harvest with a gentle hand and with respect. As my friend Val Segrest, a member of the Muckleshoot Tribe, says, "It's a luxury to do the kind of foraging we are doing."

To ensure that you will find berries and mushrooms when you return to your favorite foraging spots, consider how you can help this wild food's future and your own foraging future in the process. Toward this end, look for the **Foraging for the Future** icon ❓ throughout this book. These notable sections offer scientific updates from the field to spur you to consider the well-being of the trees, ferns, berries, wild greens, mushrooms, seaweed, and shellfish, as well as the animals and insects who depend on them.

As people foraging in a time of climate upheaval, we must continually ask ourselves questions: What is my foraging footprint? What best practices support the well-being of native plants and animals at this moment? How can I minimize harm? What will I give back? We must keep our eyes wide open and monitor the places we visit for changes. We must get down on our knees and get dirty. We must work together to restore damaged and polluted areas. And if we commit to being stewards, to giving back more than we take, then the animals, plants, fungi, and seaweeds can do the work they were meant to do: share their gifts—not just with us, but with the more-than-human-world too.

PRESERVING NATURE'S PANTRY

stew·ard·ship *The conducting, supervising, or managing of something; especially: the careful and responsible management of something entrusted to one's care.*
—Merriam-Webster's Collegiate Dictionary, *11th edition*

When Captain George Vancouver sailed the HMS *Discovery* up the Inside Passage of British Columbia in the 1790s, his on-board surgeon and naturalist, Archibald Menzies, observed Indigenous women digging clover roots near one of the voyagers' anchorages. The Kwakwaka'wakw root diggers tended spring bank clover, as well as sweet potato and chocolate lily (also known as rice root). To help their "root gardens" flourish, the women tucked the tiniest rice-grain-sized bulbs and broken root ends back into the estuary mud so they would sprout into new plants. Fluffing the surrounding dirt with wood digging sticks, the women aerated the soil and weeded the beds of competing species. Similar care was given elsewhere to the prolific nori seaweed gardens festooning beach rocks at low tide. The Kashaya Pomo women of California purposely removed only part of each nori blade and left a bit anchored to the wave-washed rock. In a month, the tender new growth provided a second harvest. They've been gleaning nori annually from the same coastal boulders for centuries.

All along the West Coast, women were the keepers of the wisdom on plant harvesting. They tended the wild populations of berries, greens, medicinal herbs, and fiber-producing plants with an eye for sustaining the next seven generations. Leaving some huckleberries, salal berries, and rose hips untouched was standard practice so animals could eat and plants flourish. Grandmothers, mothers, and aunties passed on their skills to daughters, granddaughters, and nieces by example, as well as through stories, songs, and harvest ceremonies. Stewardship education started at an early age. The California Atsugewi children joined their parents to learn harvesting skills at eight years old, the age of a typical third grader in the twenty-first century.

First Nations men also practiced stewardship techniques while fishing, hunting, and trapping and instructed their sons, grandsons, and nephews in these vital arts.

Reef-net salmon fishing is a beautiful example. The men anchored two cedar dugout canoes parallel, with a net slung between, and an artificial reef made of cut bull whip kelp stalks and waving blades directed the salmon toward the net. This formation allowed most of the churning schools to swim around, but enough silvered the nets to feed the community all winter and, if the sea was generous, to provide the cherished smoked fish for trade too. Likewise, when these first fishermen constructed cedar weirs across small river channels, it was often customary to allow the biggest salmon to pass through the fencelike structure to spawn upstream.

Perhaps the most impressive testament of Indigenous sustainable harvesting practices involved forestry. Using yew wedges, mauls, and axes (adzes), the men could pry a thirty-foot house plank from a standing cedar without harming the tree, according to Hilary Stewart's book *Cedar*. "Culturally modified trees" still grow along the West Coast, a living tribute to First Nations stewardship.

After Captain Vancouver sailed his tall-masted ship up the Northwest coast and charted his course—renaming native landmarks after English diplomats and well-heeled financiers—entire traditional foodways and lifeways met troubled waters. The beautiful names that honored plants and animals, such as the Kwakwaka'wakw phrase sag'wadē ("having fern roots") or hē'ladē ("having many berries") or wasē las ("place for gathering herring spawn"), were swept aside. The Hudson Bay Company plopped trading posts on well-established Native trade routes. Soon, European settlers arrived with cattle, corn, and dreams of their own. In Washington State alone (then a territory), thirteen land-settlement treaties were rushed forward in the mid-1850s. The treaties were meant to disrupt the traditional fishing and foraging territories and relocate First Nations peoples to less desirable land to make way for more settlers and logging, fishing, and mining industries.

Reservation lands and farming implements were forced on canoe families who for millennia had made seasonal rounds for traditional foods from both their permanent village sites and summer camps. The seasonal rounds and teachings between Elders and youngers that took place for thousands of years—such as how to gather herring spawn, camas bulbs, salmonberry shoots, and seaweed in spring; salmon in summer; deer, mountain goat, seal, and migratory ducks in fall; and clams in winter—were replaced with commodity foods and boarding schools.

A heart-wrenching, conveniently gone-missing-chapter in US history, was recently illuminated in the 2024 *Federal Indian Boarding School Initiative Investigative Report, Volume II*. Between 1819 and 1969, more than eighteen thousand Indian children were forcedly taken from their families. Children were separated from parents, grandparents, aunties, and uncles and sent away to more than four hundred US government-funded boarding schools. (That figure doesn't include the more than one thousand private, often religiously run boarding schools.) Boys and girls as young as four were shorn of their long hair, which was sacred, forced to dress like European settlers, beaten for speaking their Native language, and abused in more horrific ways. All these children were switched to a diet of non-traditional foods.

One Alaska boarding schooled person shared this account in the report: ". . . we couldn't bring any of our traditional foods. We ate industrial Western processed foods and these huge industrials cans of salted meats and salted vegetables. There was powdered juice, powdered milk, powdered eggs. We were forced to eat all those kind of foods [sic], and of course, we all got violently ill because our bodies couldn't process changing our diet [sic] over from our traditional Native foods." Many children did not return home. (The report accounts for nine hundred documented deaths.)

"When the tide goes out, the table is set"
—a First Nations' saying.

In the blink of a grandfather clock, through treaties and unceded land grabs, outlawing Native customs and culture, dividing families, and forced schooling, the settlers gained land, rivers, and coastal waterways, but set in motion the erosion of perhaps ten thousand years of intimate observations and stewardship practices guided by generations of Elders, tides, moons, animals, and plants—all considered sacred gifts in their seasons.

I tell you this sidelined history, because, whether you knew it or not, Indigenous people's lifeways deeply inform much of what we know today about so-called "wild foods" of the Pacific Northwest Coast. We are blessed to the rim of our foraging basket that this knowledge was carried forward through some of the greatest heartbreaks, waves of disease, and assaults on family, culture, and homelands in our shared world. Let's move forward together to do the good work of deep reparation of people, places, plants, creatures—all that help sustain us.

Today our love affair with wild food is a good change of heart—and appetite. It also ushers in new challenges, such as overharvesting. Let me share a cautionary tale. In 1959, the Washington Department of Fish and Wildlife (WDFW) opened up recreational harvesting of xʷč'iɫqs—Lushootseed for pinto abalone (*Haliotis kamtschatkana*). Nontribal divers could harvest abalone with bag and shell size limits, but this culturally important animal—used for food, art, ceremony, and subsistence—was never opened for commercial harvest. However, in 1992, shellfish biologists became concerned that abalone in the San Juan Islands of Washington was disappearing. They set up ten monitoring stations. Two years later, after noticing more decline and evidence of illegal harvesting, the state shut down the fishery. At that time, 359 pinto abalone were surveyed in the stations. But by 2017, only 12 abalone were found—97 percent had disappeared! One illegal commercial harvester is known to have harvested hundreds, a crime that led to jail time. Recreational harvesters also likely caused the precipitous decline. Today, the Puget Sound Restoration Fund, the WDFW, the Seattle Aquarium, Western Washington University, the University of Washington, and other partners are raising pinto abalone for release into the wild. If this kind of devastation can happen to abalone, it can happen to other coveted wild foods.

When someone else does the harvesting for us, there's no knowing—without some third-party certification process—whether our food was foraged in a respectful and sustainable manner. A few years ago, two "recreational" seaweed harvesters filled twenty-gallon plastic trash bags with fresh-cut seaweed from a popular state park beach. (Washington law sets the daily limit at ten pounds wet weight per day—about one to two gallons, depending on the species.) The harvesters had ten times their limit and were planning to deliver their bounty to a restaurant when a ranger stopped them. A year or so before that, two fiddlehead fern harvesters were caught in the Cascade foothills hauling two trash bags through the forest. Turns out, they had intended to collect every last lady fern fiddlehead from a friend's forest and sell the trendy vegetables at Seattle's Pike Place Market.

Most people who forage want to do it right. They would like to return to their favorite chanterelle patch for decades. The scale of sustainability weighs in our favor precisely because many of us already have the attitude of a caretaker, but *sustainable* remains an enduring word with a soap-slippery finish. You can't grasp sustainability and hold on—it can change with elevation, season, the earlier visit of another forager, and climate disruption. We don't know how quickly ocean acidification will make it harder for sea urchins, mussels, and Dungeness crab larvae to build shells. We don't know how often marine heat waves will bake beaches and the acres of clams tucked beneath. We aren't sure when unseasonably early rains in Southeast Alaska will cause mushy berries with lower sugar content or why a furry coat of bitter diatoms—single-celled algae called Licmophora—are fouling a culturally treasured seaweed. In recent years, Tlingit subsistence gatherers in Hoonah, Alaska, and Metlakatla, British Columbia, are voicing such concerns more publicly. We must all pay attention.

GUIDELINES FOR SUSTAINABLE WILD FORAGING

As the popularity of foraging grows, the following guidelines for sustainable harvesting of wild foods, based on Indigenous and Western science, are essential to protect these foods from being overharvested. While there are guidelines and laws for recreational harvesters for shellfish (like Dungeness crab and razor clams), as well as for nontimber forest products (such as mushrooms, berries, and tree bark), in some national forests and Department of Natural Resources lands, many of the wild foods people gather are not monitored or protected under official regulations. Even when they are, there is little to no enforcement. Likewise, precious little scientific research exists evaluating the impacts of recreational or commercial harvesting of wild berries, evergreen needle tips, fiddlehead ferns, or of hardwood sap-tapping. This gap leaves us in the dark regarding how to responsibly collect many wild foods, especially in times of great change.

The guidelines offered in this book, which use the mnemonic STEWARDSHIP, are based on the limited research available and on traditional wisdom and common sense. You'll also find specific guidelines for harvesting shellfish, seaweeds, mushrooms, and other foods for the wild table in the appropriate chapters. But even these guidelines are a living document that must be adapted to the place and situation you find yourself in, each time you forage in the future:

- **S**ustain native wild populations.
- **T**read lightly.
- **E**ducate yourself.
- **W**aste nothing.
- **A**ssume the attitude of a caretaker.
- **R**egulations, restoration, and reciprocity.
- **D**on't harvest what you can't identify.
- **S**hare with wildlife.
- **H**arvest from healthy populations and unpolluted sites.
- **I**ndigenous people's traditional harvest sites deserve respect.
- **P**ause and offer gratitude before you harvest.

Sustain native wild populations. Wild plants face many challenges, including loss of habitat from development, introduced species, pollution, disease, and pathogens. Today, climate disruption is playing havoc with phenology. (*Phenology* is a fancy word for the perfect timing together of, say, flower blooms and pollinators.) Warmer springs cause earlier blooms, and in some cases, wild plants flower before pollinators arrive. If no official guidelines for sustainable harvesting of a specific native plant exist for your region, use the 1-in-20 Rule, also known as the Botanist's Rule of Thumb (developed by David H. Wagner of the University of Oregon's Department of Botany and James Grimes of the New York Botanical Garden). First, do a thorough area survey, and do not collect an entire plant until you have found at least twenty more. If there are fewer than twenty plants, take none. The rule works for collecting plant parts too. Remove no more than 5 percent (or $1/20$) from any one plant—for instance, 5 percent of a spruce tree's new tips or 5 percent of a blueberry bush's leaves.

Tread lightly on land and intertidal shores. For example, try not to step on low-tide seaweeds, such as rockweed (*Fucus*), a seaweed also known as "popweed" because it pops underfoot! Consider that sound your warning shot. Research shows rockweed does not recover well from trampling nor do the tiny creatures who shelter beneath. When harvesting mushrooms, try to minimize soil compaction (especially when raining or wet). Many forest mushrooms require soft, loose soil with pockets of oxygen to nourish their delicate, thread-like hyphae. Nettle patches, too, stop sprouting after soil is compacted. Over the last decade and a half, my forest patch has stopped sprouting on the hardening trail that visitors like myself have followed. Spread out your harvesting over a large area by moving about as you pick so that it looks natural—as if you've never been there.

Educate yourself. Learn how to identify edible plants, mushrooms, shellfish, and seaweed, as well as poisonous look-alikes, in all phases of their life cycle. Study field guides and apps. But the best teachers are people with years of experience who practice respectful harvesting. Join a Native Plant Society chapter or the North American Mycological Association or a regional mushroom club to learn from local experts through field trips and other educational resources. Learn what edible species in your area are native (ones that have inhabited this area for thousands of years), nonnative (introduced species, such as some weeds), and invasive (introduced species that quickly take over the habitat of native species). This knowledge will guide how much you take. You may pick buckets of weedy species! Learn what not to pick too. State Natural Heritage Programs (available online) often have information that can help you identify rare, threatened, and endangered plants. Learn when and how a species reproduces (by seed, rhizomes, spores, etc.) and whether it is a perennial or annual. Be observant of signs of mammals, birds, and insects. Learn what other species eat and shelter in and near the wild food you are foraging.

Waste nothing. Take only what you need and can process (dry, can, freeze, or otherwise use). Do not remove a whole native plant if you are using only the leaves or flowers or fruit. When possible, snip portions of a native plant instead of taking whole individuals. Think of harvesting as a hair trim—clip a little here and there. Learn how to remove plant parts without damaging roots, reproductive parts, or growth patterns. Your foraging tools are also important. For instance, know when to use your bare hands or a sharp knife, pruning shears, or scissors to remove, say, a nettle top or sea-

Caterpillar on nettle leaf

weed blade to avoid tugging at the plant and accidentally damaging roots or breaking the seaweed's anchor point. Sustainable foraging skills should enable the plants to grow and flourish after you depart. Before you begin a foraging outing, prepare, purchase, and organize the food processing gear and storage containers you'll need when you get home.

Assume the attitude of a caretaker. Stewardship involves caring for and managing something entrusted to you. Wild food is a gift. Assess the health of the plant or patch before and after foraging—and over time. Is the stand or population size shrinking, growing, or stable? Is any maintenance needed (e.g., weeding out invasive species or helping disperse a plant's seeds)? Are you leaving enough mature plants to produce seeds or mature mushrooms to create spores?

Regulations, restoration, and reciprocity. Regulations and laws are meant to prevent overharvesting. Get a license if needed. Submit required "catch" or "harvest" records so population size is monitored for conservation. Review state and provincial rules to understand the limits on size and amount of take, harvest times, and locations. Keep in mind that Bureau of Land Management (BLM) lands; national forests; and national, provincial, and state parks may have their own foraging laws. Don't trespass on private property. Reach out to landowners and ask permission first. Restoration and reciprocity go hand in hand. My friend Val Segrest told my "Wild Food" course students, "You have no business foraging if you don't help restore." We can come together, with our shovels, to plant more native species and weed out English ivy, Himalayan blackberry, Japanese knotweed—there is no shortage of invasives!

Afterward, we can gather around a table of local, nutritious food and have honest, kind, deep, sometimes challenging conversations. Delicious foods can be part of what draws us, what mends our relationships with each other, Indigenous and non-Indigenous, introduced species and native species, nettles and dandelions. Both groups carry strong medicine.

Don't harvest what you can't identify. If in doubt, leave it to sprout! If you can't ID a specimen in the field, take several photos showing a whole plant, individual leaves, flowers, fruits, and seeds, then submit them to iNaturalist.org. Here you can connect with other nature-curious folks, some of whom are experts who may be able to identify the plants, mushrooms, and animals you observe. Or try your old-school naturalist skills and make a sketch. If the plants are plentiful, take a cutting (including leaves and flowers) to practice identifying with field guides.

Share with wildlife. Leave behind enough berries, rose hips, mushrooms, and flowers for birds, bees, bears, and other animals. Humans have alternative food sources, but other animals don't. During droughts or after fire damage and flooding, there may be less food for wild animals. Bear in mind what other creatures may forage from the stand you are picking, and consider buying or using garden-grown substitutes when wild sources are scarce.

Harvest from healthy populations and unpolluted sites. Harvest leaves, flowers, seeds, and fruits from healthy, vibrant plants, and avoid diseased or insect-eaten ones. Over time you will develop an intuitive sense of what plants or sites are healthy, from monitoring plants in the field over years and becoming familiar with their growth cycles, including when nutrients are at their prime and the flavors taste best. During droughts, some plants are best left untouched. Minimize contamination by harvesting fifty feet or more away from roads. Avoid industrial sites (former or present), airports, military installations, power lines, railroads, and golf courses, where herbicides and pesticides may be used. Consider park lawns suspect unless you know the maintenance history. Seaweeds and shellfish can be magnets for potentially toxic levels of metals such as inorganic arsenic, lead, mercury, and cadmium, as well as carcinogenic substances like PCBs and PAHs, including BaP (benzo(a)pyrene). To reduce your exposure, harvest in high-current areas with a lot of tidal flushing and away from heavy industry, marinas, outfalls, and busy roadways. But truth be told, research shows that even our grocery store foods have chemical contaminants.

Respect Indigenous people's traditional harvest sites. We depend on millennia of First Nations wisdom to help us understand what is edible and medicinal and how to harvest sustainably with respect. Traditional ecological wisdom is being applied worldwide side by side with Western scientific methods to manage natural resources sustainably. To keep traditional ecological wisdom alive, these skills must be practiced and passed down to the next generations. Please defer to First Nations people—who use traditional foods for both subsistence and ceremonial purposes—when they are gathering in their time-honored locations, and find a different place to forage.

Pause and offer gratitude before you harvest. There's a beautiful Indigenous tradition that involves telling the plant or animal what you will use your harvest for and then leaving a gift. For instance, I've heard of some Coast Salish women offering a tiny woven basket to a cedar tree before they pull a strip of bark. From this perspective, we no longer stand at a summit of dominion but in a circle of connection. We are transformed from a mindset of taking to giving, asking what we can offer in return.

OPPOSITE: *Clockwise from top left: chickweed, salmonberries, fucus, fireweed, and heart cockles* (Photo of salmonberries by Katherine Palmer)

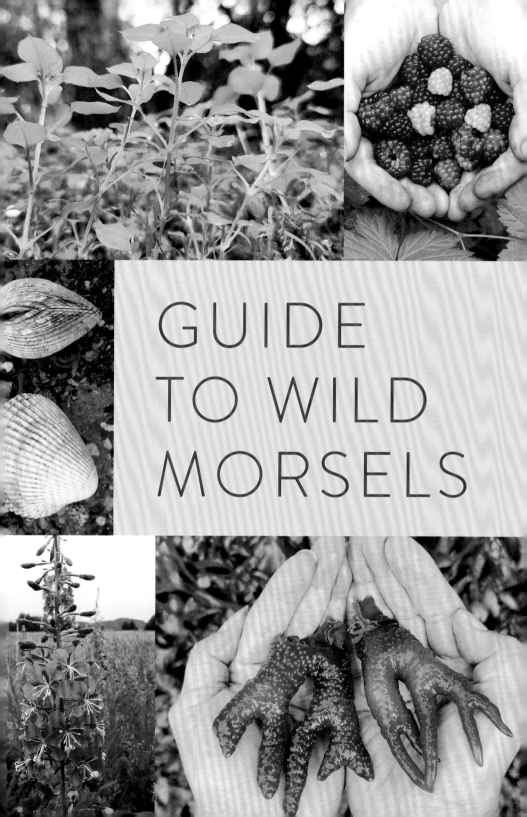

GUIDE
TO WILD
MORSELS

WILD & WEEDY GREENS

Pacific Coast foragers are fortunate to live in a maritime climate with a profusion of wild and weedy greens. From spring nettles to summer sorrel to fall fennel seeds to winter dandelion roots, Nature's pantry is closer than you think. If you know what to look for, you can enjoy a taste of these often-overlooked, nutrient-dense superfoods year-round. They hunker outside your house in the lawn and in abandoned fields and are tucked in patio cracks.

Better yet, if you can grow even a handful of the weeds you find in your neighborhood in your own yard or containers, you can be sure your stash isn't tainted. *Grow weeds—on purpose?!* Why not? They don't require a lot of fussing. Just dirt, a dousing of tap water, and daylight. A pot or garden box filled with soil will promote succulent chickweed, lemony purslane, or nutritious lamb's quarters. If you are fortunate enough to work a garden plot and dandelions keep troubling you, why not let wild and weedy nature be? You can have a dandy source of detoxifying roasted roots for chai tea, plus bone-strengthening greens! As herbalist Linda Quintana says, "You don't always need heroic herbs. The simple herbs that grow abundantly are also nourishing to people and animals."

Your mother was right when she said, "Eat your greens." Leafy greens are antidepressants in disguise, helping our brains make chemicals that lift our mood. Vitamins B9 (folic acid) and B6 (pyridoxine)—building blocks for serotonin, our "happiness" chemical—are latticed into the cells of leafy greens. Folic acid helps your body make red and white blood cells and the new genetic material in cells and is instrumental in the development of a healthy fetus. Leafy greens are rich in the essential minerals calcium, iron, and magnesium, as well as plant nutrients such as lutein, beta-carotene, and zeaxanthin, which nourish our eyes and fight against cataracts and macular degeneration. A diet rich in leafy greens can also cut the risk of stomach and colon cancer, help prevent diabetes, and fight osteoporosis.

The best part is that wild and weedy greens can be even more nutritious than their domesticated cousins. Nettles have more protein than almost any other green

Common fireweed (Photo by Katherine Palmer)

vegetable: 6.9 grams of high-quality protein per 100 grams of leaves. Purslane, a delicious salad succulent, contains more antioxidants and omega-3 fatty acids than other green leafy vegetables. Lutein, a skin tonic that slows the effects of skin aging, is especially abundant in nettles, dandelion leaves, and lamb's quarters.

Come spring, greens grow like the dickens. Fireweed sprouts in clearcuts. Stinging nettles shoot up like arrows from dead leaf litter. Dandelions and hairy cat's ear sunbathe shamelessly on lawns and athletic fields. Miner's lettuce, decked out in cotton-candy-pink blooms, brightens forests and stream banks. Bouquets of peppery western bittercress lace the sleeves of ditches, drives, and footpaths. Japanese knotweed proliferates on beaches, riverbanks, and too many places to list.

As summer settles in, native wild greens hit their stride. Wood sorrel carpets rainforests in a delightful profusion of shamrocks. Weedy introduced greens hit their stride too. Chickweed and lamb's quarters quietly trespass among neat garden rows of broccoli, lettuce, and sugar snap pea starts. Turn your back, and they've conquered all. Purslane puckers from sidewalk cracks. Common fennel flaunts its six-foot-tall feather tresses in abandoned lots and roadside ditches. In fall and winter, in milder climates, the hardiest weedy greens—such as dandelion, sheep sorrel, hairy cat's ear, nettle, and fennel—provide a continual garden of eating all year.

Like it or not, the weedy and the wild greens are here—and even more so with climate change, as weeds erupt across disturbed landscapes such as burned forestlands and chaparral. So pull out a chopping knife (or whir your food processor), then tuck in your dinner napkin. With a little familiarity, these common Pacific Coast greens are a forager's friend. In this section, you'll learn about nine pernicious yet delicious weedy greens and four wonderfully wild greens. (Note: Two "beach greens"—beach asparagus and goosetongue—are covered in Seaweeds & Beach Vegetables.)

STINGING NETTLE
Urtica dioica

FAMILY: Urticaceae (Nettle)
STATUS: Native (ssp. *gracilis*), introduced (ssp. *dioica*)
OTHER NAMES: California nettle (ssp. *gracilis*), hoary nettle (ssp. *holosericea*)

This tall, erect, and elegant plant grows up to 9 feet with opposite, coarse-toothed, heart-to lance-shaped leaves up to 5.5 inches long. *Urtica dioica* has three subspecie: *dioica* was introduced from Eurasia and has stinging hairs on both sides of the leaves, while subspecies *gracilis* and *holosericea* have stinging hairs mostly on the lower leaves. The nettle's long, creeping rootstock (called a rhizome) is perennial and sprouts annual stems and leaves. Young shoots may be tinged burgundy. Dense, hanging clusters of greenish bead-like flowers develop where leaves join the stem.

Found in moist, rich soils in forests, mountains, and sagebrush deserts, from sea level to subalpine, Alaska to California and across North America.

HARVEST GUIDE

WHAT: Leaves, stems, and seeds
WHEN: Young leaves and stems in spring (for food); after flowering (for tea)
Wear gloves and use scissors to cut off the young nettle leaves and tops before the flowers appear. If you cut only tops, you'll get a second and sometimes a third crop of new leaves. After flowering, leaves develop cystoliths (calcium carbonate crystals), a kidney irritant. The hollow stinging hairs covering the nettle leaf act like tiny hypodermic needles, releasing chemicals such as 5-hydroxytryptamine (serotonin), histamine, acetylcholine, and a bit of formic acid from glands in the leaf.

If you get stung while picking, rub a paste of baking soda and water over the welts. If you're far from home, try a handful of dock leaves, or use the counterintuitive remedy that works even better: Rub a couple of fresh leaves between your gloved hands until green juice appears. Dab the juice over the sting—nettle juice reduces the welt as well as the pins-and-needles prickling sensation.

CULINARY TIPS

For any dish you'd welcome spinach into, substitute blanched or steamed nettles. Nettles are lovely blanched and blended into pesto or curried nettle soup; layered with smoked salmon in quiche; tucked into lasagna, ravioli filling, spanakopita, or double-crust pizza; minced and kneaded into sage-green pasta sheets; simmered in Indian dishes such as palak paneer; dried and ground for gomashio—a Japanese condiment

How to cut nettles: a, cut the tops of young plants with scissors; b, the top will regrow two sprouts you can harvest later.

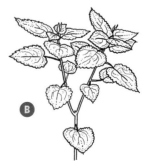

NETTLING NEWS

At the March equinox, I climbed the forested hillside behind our house to check for nettles—*are they here yet?* I eagerly scanned the leaf litter for tiny spears of green. Nothing. Three weeks earlier, my foraging pal Mac, who lives fifty miles southwest of us as the eagle flies, had phoned, elated: "Nettles are popping on the Olympic Peninsula!" A few days later, a friend emailed nettling news from his sunny seaside lot across town. "Jen, nettles carpet the ground everywhere!" I stopped hovering over the dimly lit hillside. Better to let Mother Nature nurture my nettle patch at her own pace.

By early April, I was hankering for wild greens like my husband craves chocolate. I walked up the hill for the third time, brazenly confident, armed with rubber gloves, scissors, and a grocery bag. Sure enough, the clearing had transformed into a green vista of stinging pagodas. In just twenty minutes I filled my paper bag with nettle tops, barely denting the twenty-by-fifty-foot patch. By wearing gloves and scissoring just the upper leaf clusters into the open bag, I avoided most of the walloping stings. The full bag was light—maybe two pounds—but heavy in vitamins C, B, K, A, beta-carotene, and lycopene, as well as the minerals calcium, iron, and magnesium. Ounce for ounce, nettles have twice the protein of spinach. Their protein is high quality due to loads of amino acids, such as lysine. Young leaves are a good source of omega-3 fatty acids, while older leaves and seeds contain omega-6s.

There are a lot of scientific studies that explain the potential benefits of consuming nettles. In fact, a study in a 2020 issue of the journal *Nutrients* found that nettle tea inhibits the cell growth of acute myeloid leukemia in lab-cultured cells. In the United Kingdom, scientists at the Warwick Cancer Research Center are experimenting with a chemical found in nettles and ants, sodium formate, for an innovative treatment for breast and prostate cancer. Apparently, sodium formate is a trigger for a chemical, JPC11, that attacks cancer cells. Nettle leaf extracts are rich in antioxidants and linoleic acid, a polyunsaturated fat found in nuts and vegetable oil, and they can improve insulin sensitivity and reduce inflammation and cholesterol in lab mice.

Historical records for nettle use date back to the Bronze Age—3000 to 2000 BC. As food, they've been forked up at tables from Rome to Russia since ancient times. Pliny the Elder praised a dish of spring nettles two thousand years ago in his *Naturalis Historia*. Steamed or boiled as a potherb, those first spring shoots were cherished by sourdough miners, settlers, and Pacific Coast First Nations. Hence the name Indian spinach. The folksy name is a culinary clue. Steamed nettle leaves taste a lot like spinach, only more feral and flavorful, with a mineral tang.

Besides providing delicious greens for centuries, nettles were fiber factories for pro-ducing a strong twine with flaxen softness. On the Pacific Coast, First Nations spun nettle fiber into cordage for making dozens of specialized fishing nets and harpoon

Blanching nettles in boiling water

lines. Even sleeping bags were painstakingly woven from nettle fiber and interwoven with bird down. The Old English word *netele* refers to the nets woven from nettle fiber and the needlelike sting.

Those notorious stings are used for their medicinal properties, too, such as aiding circulation. In her classic 1945 text *Ethnobotany of Western Washington: The Knowledge and Use of Indigenous Plants by Native Americans*, anthropologist Erna Gunther wrote this about *Urtica dioica*: "The medicinal value of this plant seems to be as great as its power of irritation." Gunther told how the Quileute, for instance, lashed nettles over limbs to reduce symptoms of rheumatism or paralysis. Even Hippocrates reported sixty-one remedies using the nettle, including "urtication"—using the sting of the nettle leaf to treat joint pain.

Upon returning to my kitchen, I chucked two large soup pots onto the stove, one topped with a strainer, the other filled with an inch of water and set to boil. As the pot began to bubble, I dropped in several giant tongfuls of fresh stinging nettles.

Within an hour and a half of picking nettles, we dipped our spoons into steaming bowls of curried nettle soup. We toasted with a refreshing tonic made by my Coast Salish "Seaweed Sisters"—nettle lemon-aid made by stirring the reserved nettle broth with fresh lemon and sweetener.

After stinging nettles grow flowers, use it only for tea. Emerging flowers look like tiny ferns (see inset).

of toasted sesame seeds and salt; or juiced for a nettle martini! In Denmark, my relatives use the leaves to smoke a cheese called rygeost. The uses are endless. Cook with fresh-blanched, steamed, frozen, or dry leaves and nettle tops. Seeds are edible and rich in linoleic acid. Young stems can be delicious too, just a bit fibrous and furry. But beware, stems can wind around processor blades like cordage.

Blanching, steaming, pulverizing, or drying nettles removes the sting:

- **To blanch nettles**, use tongs to place leaves or nettle tops in a pot with two inches of boiling-hot water. Turn over the leaves a few times with tongs until wilted (fifteen to thirty seconds). Drain into a colander, or remove to a bowl of ice-cold water to stop the cooking process. When cool, squeeze out the excess water with your hands into the cook pot to save the flavorful juice (blanching stops the sting), chop, and use. Drink the nutritious nettle "tea" remaining in the pot or use as stock.
- **To steam nettles**, use tongs to place leaves or nettle tops in a steamer basket over a pot with two inches of rapidly boiling water. Cover with a tight-fitting lid. Steam one minute, open lid, turn nettles with tongs, re-cover, and steam for one more minute or until wilted.

- **To freeze nettles**, pack chopped blanched or steamed leaves or nettle tops into ice cube trays. Store frozen nettle cubes in a freezer-friendly container.
- **To pulverize nettles**, place leaves in a processor and whirl with oil. While some folks use pulverized raw nettles in pesto, I prefer to blanch nettles first, or they can cause a choke-like dryness and a grassier flavor.
- **To dry nettle leaves**, use gloved hands to arrange on a cotton tablecloth or in food dehydrator racks. Process only when brittle dry. Crumble by hand (the sting disappears with drying). Store the leaf bits in an airtight jar. Use for tea. Sift to remove leaf stems before adding to soup, seasoning, or chimichurri. One cup of dry nettle leaf flakes plus one cup of boiling water equals one cup of blanched fresh leaves.

WHO EATS AND SHELTERS HERE?

Columbian black-tailed deer, wild horses, domestic sheep, snails, and rabbits eat the leaves of this so-called wildlife magnet. A whirlwind of butterflies lay eggs on the underside of nettle leaves so that emerging larvae can munch on whole-leaf dinners. Aphids pierce the plant tissue with their sharp stylus and sip up juices. Bug-eating birds frequent nettle patches in spring and summer, while seed-eating birds scarf up autumn seed clusters.

Lacewings, hoverflies, and aphids all hunker down in nettles.

COMMON DANDELION
Taraxacum officinale

FAMILY: Asteraceae (Aster)
STATUS: Introduced (weed)
OTHER NAMES: Swine snout, priest's crown, wild endive, blowball, yellow gowan, cankerwort, clock, piss-a-bed (due to its diuretic ability), and more. *Dent-de-lion* ("lion's tooth") is originally from old French.

Next to roses, dandelion may be the most easily recognized flower in the world. Long, deeply toothed, hairless leaves up to 15 inches long grow in a rosette and work like downspouts directing rain to a long taproot. Plush yellow flowers 1 to 2 inches across close up at night or when rain is near. White sap drips from all parts of this perennial when broken. Globe-like seed balls can launch 150 airborne "parachute seeds" for miles.

Grows all over the world from sea level to timberline. Rumor has it that colonists introduced the seeds to the Americas from the *Mayflower*.

ROASTED DANDELION ROOTS

Unearthed, scrubbed clean, sliced, roasted, and pulverized, dandelion roots make a delicious addition to hot chai. Just simmer one teaspoon of roasted roots with your favorite chai tea spice mix for two, strain, add milk of choice and honey, and enjoy warm or chilled. Roasted dandelion root ice cream is a wildly flavorful dessert with notes of peanut butter, coffee, and butterscotch.

To make your own roots, all you need is a big handful of uprooted dandelion, a sink, oven, and coffee grinder. Scrub your fresh-harvested roots thoroughly with a vegetable brush—rinsing repeatedly to remove grit—towel them dry, and chop into ⅛-inch discs. Spread fresh slices in a single layer on a large sheet pan. Oven roast your "dandy" discs at 250 degrees F for at least forty-five minutes, stirring every fifteen minutes. The cream-colored roots will shrink and turn golden brown when done—be careful not to burn them. A roasted dandelion root should "crunch" in your mouth and taste mildly of coffee or grain. Pulverize the roots in a coffee grinder and store in an airtight jar.

If you have only a small handful of fresh roots to show for your weed-pulling efforts, just scrub what you have, pat dry, and freeze in a plastic bag or jar. Keep adding scrubbed roots until you have a gallon bag full. Then you're ready to chop and roast.

If you can't find fresh dandelion roots, many natural food stores and online shops sell dried, cut, and sifted dandelion root in bulk. To roast the dried, store-bought root cuttings, spread 1½ cups of root pieces on a large sheet pan. Bake at 300 degrees F for fourteen to fifteen minutes. Stir at ten minutes to roast them evenly.

Chopping dandelion roots to dry, roast, and ground them.

Common dandelion in bloom

HARVEST GUIDE

WHAT: Blossoms, leaves, and roots

WHEN: Leaves in spring (harvest before flower buds appear to reduce bitterness), flowers from spring to summer, roots anytime (easier to dig after rains)

Pick leaves by hand or cut with scissors from basal cluster. Wash gently in a bowl of water. Pat dry. Pick flowers on a dry, sunny day around the time you will use them. Don't wash off debris—shake or brush it off. They perish quickly; store leaves or flowers in the fridge in a damp cotton cloth or place leaves upright in a jar with an inch of water.

For roots, use a shovel or weeding fork. Loose garden soil is an ideal place for digging taproots that can grow over a foot long, an inch thick, and sprout multiple side roots. Broken-off roots will regrow.

CULINARY TIPS

Although they are considered a weed across North America, in Europe dandelions are revered as haute cuisine. These delicious cultivars are honored with names like *Amélioré à Coeur Plein* and *Vert de Montmagny*. Add raw greens to kimchi, Caesar salad, or hot-bacon-dressed salads. Mix steamed greens with spinach or nettles for quiche, spanakopita, and lasagna. Process a few leaves in a food processor or blender for adding to a smoothie or a delicious cream of dandelion soup with a dash of nutmeg. Blanching the leaves makes them less bitter.

WILD SALAD

One June, my husband and I embarked on a midweek camping adventure from Bellingham, then across the Salish Sea by ferry, to explore low-tide beaches on the Olympic Peninsula—at least that was our intention. Foragers have a way of planning their movement by what's growing and where. Destinations and miles are soon forgotten in the thrill of the hunt.

"Did you shut off the drip hose in the garden?" Chris asked as he loaded the camp stove into our vehicle. I stuffed some wine into a red cooler brimming with all the accoutrements of a gourmet camp cupboard and dashed for the garden.

I was only planning to grab a handful of dandelion leaves for our salad. The mildly bitter greens would balance the avocados, blue cheese, and maple-glazed pecans I'd packed. These oft-neglected edibles contain more iron punch than Popeye's spinach, plus a hearty dose of calcium, and vitamins A, C, E, and K. As I was snapping greens off the bridal-sized bouquet of dandelion leaves, I remembered the roots offer culinary gifts too. Why not add some dandelion root to our chai tea mix? I decided to take the whole plant.

As I was unearthing the dandelion taproot from between neat rows of chard and romaine lettuce leaves, a scribble of chickweed caught my eye. This succulent weed has a lovely nutty flavor and snaps like a pea tendril. I broke off a few inches of the plant's uppermost new growth. The twisting stems can grow sixteen inches long and form garden-sized tangled mats. In maritime climates, chickweed can sprout, flower, and seed anytime, but the most succulent plants are found in spring and fall. Chickens love it, and wild birds too. I've eaten it since I was a kid growing up in rural Wisconsin.

I set a couple of handfuls aside for pesto. And that's when I noticed a new succulent creeping by the spinach starts, looking like a miniature jade plant with scarlet stems doing prostrations on the soil. Purslane! I was thrilled. True, it is a noxious weed—one of the ten worst in the world, in fact. One plant can carpet two feet, produce almost 240,000 seeds, which can still germinate four decades later! But hey, purslane makes a great salad mixed with beets and goat cheese. The juicy leaves have a refreshing lemony flavor with an excellent crunch factor. In Mexico it is called verdolagas and mixed with salsa verde and pork. It has been cherished as a food in India and Persia for two thousand years and cultivated in Europe as a salad green. Two cups of raw purslane pack in a whopping 8,000 IU of vitamin A. Overall, it was more nutritious than the spinach sprouting nearby.

"Jeennn?" Chris called from the driveway.

"Just a minute, honey. Just picking our salad greens."

"We're going to miss the ferry."

Chris was right. We missed the Keystone Ferry.

The underside of a wood sorrel leaf
(Photo by Katherine Palmer)

After crossing to Port Townsend an hour later, we meandered toward Sequim. Chris was singing to John Prine when I asked for a pit stop. As I bounded from the car into a patch of vegetation, an overwhelming licorice aroma rose, along with my excitement. Minutes later we were on our way again, as anise clouds from a feathery green bouquet of wild fennel wafted through our car.

Originally a garden herb from the Mediterranean, common fennel has naturalized from British Columbia to California and across much of the rest of North America, Asia, and Australia. (See the "Eat Heaps of Weedy Greens" sidebar in Lamb's Quarters later in this section). The anise-flavored stalks, leaves, and seeds have been used since Roman times, when fennel was cultivated for sweet and savory dishes and medicine. I made sure I wasn't taking any remnant seeds so I wouldn't spread this delicious but invasive pest. Wild fennel has drastically changed the diversity of plant communities in wetlands, grasslands, river corridors, and coastal scrub areas, including the open meadows of the Olympic Peninsula.

"We can roast some fish over fennel stalks tonight!"

Chris laughed. "If we get there by dinner."

Lucky for us, it was almost the longest day of the year. Sunlight filtered into our rainforest camp. This time it was Chris who found himself foraging far afield. He'd gone to photograph the sunset and returned with a bandana full of miner's lettuce and heart-shaped wood sorrel leaves.

"How's this for a fresh salad? I hear it's a love tonic."

He had been a good sport all along the winding journey to camp.

Use dandelion flowers for jelly or syrup for waffles and baklava. Mix petals into lemon-dandelion cheesecake or for festive salad toppings; use whole flowers in falafel balls or dandy apple-cinnamon fritters. Dry and roast the roots for a grainlike beverage. Powdered dandelion root added to vanilla ice cream mix transforms it into a velvety coffee-dulce frozen custard. My great-grandmother Rose was famous in her Midwest prairie-side town for her cellar shelves of dandelion wine.

SUPERPOWER

Scientific research links dandelion and formulas combining dandelion parts to the successful treatment of certain cardiovascular, gastrointestinal, and ovarian health disorders. Although the chemical taraxasterol was isolated from the roots in 1912, recent research links its protective effect against rheumatoid arthritis to its ability to modulate inflammation.

WHO EATS AND SHELTERS HERE?

Grizzly bears and black bears feast on dandelion leaves, stems, seeds, and flowers in summer. Bighorn sheep, deer, elk, and pocket gophers devour it spring through fall. When pocket gophers, furry "dandivores," were removed from Oregon's mountain grasslands in a scientific experiment, the population of dandelions exploded by half again in two years.

The ubiquitous bloom is visited by ninety-three different insects. It is often called the "bee's magnet," as it provides bees with pollen in early spring and with nectar after orchards are done blooming. Nectar and pollen in spring blooms are one of the first foods for emerging caterpillars, moths, flies, beetles, and butterflies. To protect itself from nibbling, the delectable dandy produces a factory of sticky latex that gums up the insects' mouthparts and digestive tracts. Sparrows and finches adore the seeds. Many butterflies and moths lay eggs and nourish their caterpillar offspring on the leaves.

CHICKWEED
Stellaria media

FAMILY: Caryophyllaceae (Pink)
STATUS: Introduced (weed)
OTHER NAMES: Winterweed, stitchwort, starweed, white bird's eye, chicken meat, chick wittles, clucken wort, satinflower, skirt buttons, common chickweed

This mat-like succulent has brittle greenish-white stems up to 16 inches long, opposite pairs of cat's-eye-shaped leaves with a wavy surface, and tiny white starry flowers with five deeply notched petals. A key characteristic is the singular row of white hairs running down the stem.

A common weed, this cosmopolitan traveler has spread from Eurasia to North America, South America, and Arctic and sub-Antarctic islands. Find it sprawling in lawns, cultivated ground, abandoned lots, and pastures.

HARVEST GUIDE

WHAT: Leaves, stems, flowers, seeds
WHEN: Spring and fall (most succulent, prime picking)

A single row of white hair on stem and five deeply notched petals make it easy to identify chickweed. (Photos by Katherine Palmer)

Chickweed uproots easily if you pull on it. To maintain a patch, simply snip it with scissors. If it is growing where you don't like it, uproot it with your hands. Trim the roots off, shake clean, and wash gently in a bowl of water. Store in the fridge in a bowl lined and covered with a damp cloth for one to two days. Tiny seeds are protein rich.

CULINARY TIPS

Toss chickweed in salads like alfalfa sprouts, or pulverize it into pesto for a creamy, vibrant-green pasta topping or sandwich tapenade. Whip with potatoes and cream for a frothy soup. Chickweed contains soapy saponin—a natural lather-producing chemical found in some vegetables. Saponins help the digestive system absorb minerals.

WHO EATS AND SHELTERS HERE?

Chickens eat chickweed, of course—as do quails, magpies, mourning doves, towhees, sparrows, and the American goldfinch. While ants cart the reddish-brown seeds to underground nests, ground beetles nibble delicious seeds on the spot. Even earthworm castings—those tiny, squiggly piles of soil in your lawn—harbor chickweed seeds. Cottontail rabbits and woodchucks (groundhogs) chomp chickweed whole, as do ruffed grouse, white-tailed deer, and deer mice. Bees, flies, butterflies, and parasitoid wasps lap chickweed nectar and pollen.

A host of butterflies and moths choose chickweed as a shelter for their tiny eggs.

WILD FENNEL
Foeniculum vulgare

FAMILY: Apiaceae (Carrot)
STATUS: Introduced (invasive weed) ⚠
OTHER NAMES: Common fennel, sweet anise, sweet fennel

A perennial/biennial herb growing 4 to 10 feet tall with feathery leaves up to 15 inches long, hollow stems, celery-like stalks, and an anise aroma. Feathery green leaves are similar to dill but more threadlike. The yellow flowers are in umbrella-like clusters with unequal length spokes. Tiny, oblong green seeds turn brown and ribbed with age. Unlike the vegetal cultivar known as Florence fennel, finocchio, or bulb anise (*Foeniculum vulgare* var. *azoricum*), wild fennel has no swollen, bulblike base.

Found in North America and beyond. Fennel is invasive and flourishes in vacant lots, dry fields, and grasslands and along creeks, ocean coasts, and roadsides.

POWER-PUNCH YOUR LEAFY GREENS

Leafy greens are one of the richest and cheapest sources of protein. The USDA recommends eating a minimum of three cups of dark green vegetables a week. How you cook them makes a world of difference nutritionally. Leafy greens contain fat-soluble vitamins such as A, D, K, and E. You can benefit from their maximum nutrition if you add a bit of fat.

A study in Tanzania, where people eat bushels of raw leafy green vegetables, determined that children and mothers were strangely deficient in vitamin A. After cooking five types of leafy greens in no oil, sunflower oil, or red palm oil, the accessibility of vitamin A changed. Leaves cooked without oil had a vitamin A range of 8 to 29 percent. Adding oil increased the vitamin A accessibility to 39 to 94 percent! So don't hold back—splash on olive oil, adorn with blue cheese dressing, sauté in butter or canola oil, and your body will sponge up more of the vitamins you eat.

Don't toss the water you cook greens in—add it to smoothies and soup, or drink it as a vitamin-rich tonic. Greens are rich in water-soluble vitamins including folate, which promotes healthy cell growth and red blood cell formation. Studies show 50 percent or more of the folate is destroyed when greens are heated a long time in a large pot of water. Cook these nonoxalic greens lightly and repurpose the broth for maximum benefits.

LEFT: *Wild fennel in full bloom along a disturbed waterfront*; RIGHT: *fennel sprouts*

HARVEST GUIDE

WHAT: Leaves, stems, flowers, seeds, pollen

WHEN: Stalks and tender leaves in spring; flowers, pollen, seeds summer to fall

Cut and harvest fresh green stems and feathery leaves with a knife or scissors. To gather pollen, wait until flowers have a powdery yellow pollen visible. Cut off flower clusters, or "umbles," with a knife or scissors, leaving the stems long. Put the flower stalks in a paper bag so the stems point out of the bag's top. Tie it closed and hang to dry. When the stems are brittle and dry (two to five days depending on humidity and stem moisture content), shake the bag vigorously to loosen the pollen. Open the bag and comb the remaining blooms off with your fingers. Sift the loose material through a mesh strainer. If you don't mind a grainy texture, stop there, or whir it up in a coffee grinder to make a powder. At thirty-four dollars an ounce, it is worth the effort! Gather sun-dried seed heads when seeds are brown using the same method as above.

Take care not to casually drop fennel seeds in pristine areas; fennel is aggressive and can overtake native species. ⬤ Let seed heads dry thoroughly in the bag, and the seeds will fall loose. You may need to further dry them on a sheet pan (out of direct sunlight), in a food dehydrator set to 100 degrees F on parchment paper or a silicone mat, or in an oven set to its lowest temperature on a baking sheet lined with parchment paper. Drying seeds can take several days depending on moisture content and humidity. Store bone dry in a glass jar to prevent mold.

CULINARY TIPS

Add wild fennel's young tender leaves to salads (leaves are most tender in spring). Diced seeds give bold flavor to cream-based seafood chowder. Try baking fresh-caught fish over a bed of wild fennel stalks. Rub aromatic leaves and seeds into cold-cured salmon. Drizzle fennel syrup over roasted root vegetables or fresh figs and stone fruits. Fennel leaf sorbet has a fresh licorice flavor.

Fennel pollen, surely the food of elves and angels, is another attribute of this pasture weed. The gold-green flowers produce a pollen that has a heady anise flavor. You need only a pinch for a depth charge of flavor. Lavish a ball of goat cheese in fennel pollen, sprinkle the magic dust over roasted beets and carrots, or coat scallops and sear for a flamboyant seafood dish. A paste of fennel pollen and olive oil on chicken or whitefish adds a wild anise flavor. Fennel offers a highly enriched source of vitamin C, iron, thiamine, potassium, and phosphorus.

SUPERPOWER

Thought to significantly reduce the risk of digestive disorders, fennel is packed with antioxidants that reduce inflammation and protect us from stomach ulcers. Fennel also helps control blood sugar levels, according to a 2021 review article on the anti-

Fragrant and flavorful fennel blooms (Photo by Katherine Palmer)

STORAGE TIPS FOR WILD GREENS

Many wild greens are best picked fresh and used within three days. Wash, dry, and store wild greens in the fridge in a damp cotton dish towel. Or line a bowl with a damp dish towel, place the washed and dried greens inside, and gently cover with a second damp towel. Washed and "spun" greens also store well in a salad spinner in the fridge. Blooming miner's lettuce is best eaten the day of picking.

diabetic effects of medicinal spices. As an added bonus, those little seeds reduce anxiety and lower stress.

Fennel seed has long been associated with aiding digestion in Ayurvedic medicine. Cumin seeds stimulate the secretion of bile acids, which help digestion and absorption, and dill seeds contain essential oils to soothe the digestive system and reduce inflammation. We keep digestive seeds in an airtight jar right beside the beans.

My kayaking buddy Dr. Rachelle Herdman shared this simple magic trick for reducing gas and aiding digestion after a meal of well-cooked dry beans. Mix equal parts fennel, cumin, celery, and dill seeds, and add one to two teaspoons of the blend per two cups of dry beans, with six cups of water. Simmer on the stove or bake in a low oven until soft. The seeds disintegrate into the beans and add a very mild background flavor that does not overpower other seasonings. Coriander seeds can also be included. Digestive seeds are delicious stirred into cooked rice, too.

WHO EATS AND SHELTERS HERE?

Discerning feral pigs chomp fennel roots. Rodents gnaw seeds. Grazers, including rabbits, adore small seedlings. Sparrows, finches, warblers, and towhees feast on fresh flowers and nibble seeds into winter when other foods are scarce. Bees of many stripes—honey, wild, and bumbles—collect nectar and pollen. A two-year study in Crimea of fennel-favoring insects tallied a whopping sixty species, including ants, beetles, lacewings, social wasps, hoverflies, and mud daubers.

Red-winged blackbirds build nests and raise chicks in "nettle forests"—tall monocrops of fennels in the San Francisco Bay Area's César Chávez Park in California. Mother swallowtail butterflies secure their eggs to fennel plants. Watch for swallowtail larvae in five costume changes, including a spikey black-brown caterpillar with mango blazes and a fat, smooth bud-green caterpillar coiled in black and yellow (called "parsley worms") that gorge on the stalks.

HAIRY CAT'S EAR
Hypochaeris radicata, H. glabra

FAMILY: Asteraceae (Aster)
STATUS: Introduced (weed)
OTHER NAMES: California dandelion, false dandelion, catsear, cat's ear, common cat's-ear, flatweed, frogbit, gosmore, rough cat's ear, spotted catsear

Its name may be off-putting for a food, but this dandelion look-alike perennial, with lobed, fuzzy leaves growing in a basal cluster pressed low to the ground, produces young leaves the flavor of romaine lettuce. Over time, the tiny leaf hairs become more pronounced. The wiry stems exude milky sap, grow up to 2½ feet tall, may branch at the ends, and have showy yellow dandelion-like flowers with 20 to 30 rays, each tipped with 5 teeth. The "blow balls" launch wind-borne seeds. In some locations, cat's ear is invasive and once established elbows out native plants by forming extensive colonies, shading native grasses, and preventing trees and shrubs from establishing.

LEFT: *Hairy cat's ear can have many blooms per stalk.* **RIGHT:** *Leaves press close to the ground.*

❓ CATS ON THE LOOSE

Roadways sent the cat—cat's ear, that is—running into Alaska. In Washington, after the 1980 eruption of Mount Saint Helens, the cat leapt across the blast zone. Cat's ear roots apparently form relationships with mycorrhizal fungi (as do most higher plants). A 1998 study in the blast zone found that mycorrhizal fungi helped cat's ear compete against the native plant Mertens' sedge—a beautiful, three-foot-tall clumping sedge native to our forests and meadows.

Cat's ear is displacing native species and altering the community of plants in Garry oak ecosystems and coastal terrace prairies in California. Studies have shown (and so did my yard) that mowing caused the cat to come back stronger, with more whiskery flower stalks and seeds. Best to shovel out the root if you don't want this weedy green around. Fortunately, cat's ear can't bank its seeds for long.

Native to Europe, northern Africa, and western Asia, hairy cat's ear is naturalized across much of North America and Canada from sea level to high elevations. It grows in disturbed areas such as lawns, pastures, and roadsides on every continent but Antarctica.

HARVEST GUIDE
WHAT: All parts are edible—leaves, roots, flowers.
WHEN: New leaves in spring, flowers in summer, roots in fall
Cat's ear is closely related to the common dandelion and can be gathered like it. See Common Dandelion.

CULINARY TIPS
For a tasty wild salad ingredient with a flavor like romaine lettuce, use the leaves. If you can't hack the fuzzy texture, chop them into a chimichurri or pesto. Historically, dried, roasted, and pulverized roots make a nutty, coffee-tasting beverage (see the "Roasted Dandelion Roots" sidebar in Common Dandelion above). Hortopita, a Greek pie stuffed with feta and wild greens, includes cat's ear.

SUPERPOWER
Leaves and roots contain methanolic extracts, which have antibiotic properties and are prescribed as a traditional medicine in Asia. Scientific studies confirm the chemicals are comparable to the drug ampicillin—a drug the World Health Organization

classifies as a critical medicine for bacterial infections. Research on extracts of cat's ear highlights its potential as a pain reliever, muscle relaxant, and mild sedative.

WHO EATS AND SHELTERS HERE?

Bees of many kinds seek out hairy cat's ear, as do sulfur butterflies, orange sulfur butterflies, and white butterflies; syrphid flies; and sheep. In New Zealand and Australia, where it is native, hairy cat's ear is revered as good livestock food with 10 to 15 percent protein and 1 to 2 percent calcium. Pigs uproot the plant to munch the succulent taproot. Varying hares, birds, ants, and slugs nibble the shoots.

MINER'S LETTUCE
Claytonia spp.

FAMILY: Portulacaceae (Purslane)
STATUS: Native
OTHER NAMES: Claspleaf miner's lettuce, Indian lettuce (*Claytonia perfoliata*); candy flower, pink purslane, Siberian miner's lettuce, Siberian springbeauty (*C. sibirica*)

Miner's lettuce is a mildly succulent herb that grows in dense carpets or individually. The base has a rosette of paddle-shaped leaves. Rising from the base are tall stems with distinct leaves that vary in shape with the species. *Claytonia perfoliata* has shield-shaped leaves that

LEFT: *Siberian miner's lettuce has opposite leaves.* **RIGHT:** *"Candy flower" is a nickname.* (Photos by Katherine Palmer)

LEFT: *Perfoliate miner's lettuce* (Photo by Katherine Palmer) RIGHT: *Close-up of flower and shield-shaped leaf*

clasp or fuse around the stem ("perfoliate"). White to pink 5-petaled flowers grow like a tiny bouquet in the leaf's center. *C. sibirica* can be taller than its kin—over 1 foot—and shows 2 cat's-eye-shaped leaves growing opposite one another on tall stems. Similar, but larger, flowers grow on longer multiflowered stalks.

   C. perfoliata ranges from southwestern British Columbia through the western United States. Siberian miner's lettuce grows from California to Alaska and in eastern Siberia. Look for this ground cover from the coast to middle elevations in shaded forests, stream fringes, beach uplands, and recently burned areas such as chaparral, grasslands, and drier forests.

HARVEST GUIDE

WHAT: Leaves, stems, flowers
WHEN: Winter, spring, and early summer depending on location
Leave two-thirds of the plant and take only one-third. Snip off leaves near the base with scissors. Try not to yank leaves free. Miner's lettuce is loosely rooted, and you risk breaking rootlets or pulling up the whole plant. While it can be invasive, it is also a native species that feeds birds and browsers, so don't be tempted to overharvest just because there is a lot. Store cuttings in the fridge wrapped loosely in a damp cotton napkin or in a bowl lined and covered with a moist cotton tea towel. Best to use the delicate, flowering greens within twenty-four hours.

CULINARY TIPS

Packed with vitamins A and C, miner's lettuce was harvested as a spring green by some (surprise!) Western miners. Flavor varies from juicy sweet to mildly bitter and

❓MINER'S LETTUCE LOVES A GOOD FIRE

Miner's lettuce is a prolific "seed banker." It stores up seeds in the soil and waits for a fire. Sierra Nevada researcher Robin F. Matthews discovered that, in the wake of the Foothills Chaparral Fire, miner's lettuce grew like wildfire too. The profusion of flowers quickly recharged the seed bank. Fire-generated miner's lettuce, Matthews writes, "contributes to an increased food supply for flocking birds." This is good news: some fires increase the food pantry for birds and beasts.

earthy, reminiscent of beet greens. Eaten raw, it sometimes bestows a lingering dryness. For the best flavor, gather tender young leaves and flowers in spring. Scatter the beautiful cuttings atop a salad of wild and garden greens. Munch with your trailside nibbles of hummus, cheese, and crackers. Miner's lettuce makes a lovely soup garnish or gorgeous bed for serving fish. Try lightly steamed *C. perfoliata* leaves tossed with olive oil, lemon, and salt.

WHO EATS AND SHELTERS HERE?

Pocket gophers munch miner's lettuce, as well as mourning doves, western meadowlarks, California quail, and other birds. In the blue oak savannahs of California, cattle prefer this wild green over others.

In springtime, two species of day-flying owlet moths—*Annaphila arvalis* (a graywinged beauty with yellow-orange blazes and pink fringe) and *A. diva* (zebra-striped with a brassy luster)—deposit eggs on miner's lettuce. The larvae eat the plant and shelter within it.

PURSLANE
Portulaca oleracea

FAMILY: Portulacaceae (Purslane)
STATUS: Introduced (weed)
OTHER NAMES: Garden purslane, common purslane, pigweed, little hogweed, wild water-leaf, *pourpier* (French), *verdolagas* (Spanish), duckweed, pursley, pusley, wild portulaca

Purslane is a delicious succulent and aggressive weed. Branching, round, reddish stems grow in a circular mat from a central taproot. Plump, oval, green or red-edged leaves cluster at the branch tips and along joints. Yellow, ¼-inch flowers with 5 petals bloom at branch tips. Abundant, long-lived seeds spring from lidded capsules when ripe.

Thought to be introduced from southern Eurasia, purslane grows from British Columbia to California, across much of the rest of North America, and in temperate and warm regions of the world. Look for it in garden beds, sidewalk cracks, salt marshes, and sunny, disturbed areas, such as cultivated fields, riverbanks, and wastelands, from sea level to 5,000 feet.

HARVEST GUIDE

WHAT: Leaves, stems, flowers, seeds
WHEN: Spring through fall, but summer is prime

Sprawling succulent, lemony purslane (Photo by Orest Lyzhechka, iStock)

Use your hands to uproot the whole plant or snap off the succulent stems you want to eat. If the plant is in seed, transport it in a bag so you don't act as an inadvertent Johnny-apple-WEED! Broken stem bits can sprout roots.

CULINARY TIPS

Enjoy lemony, salty purslane fresh or cooked. This mucilaginous vegetable thickens soups nicely. Try purslane stewed with pork roast, tomatillos, serrano chiles, garlic, and cumin. For salads, wash the stems and leaves and chop to bite size. A pear salad with purslane, Meyer lemon, and makrut lime leaf vinaigrette is splendid, as is purslane added to omelets. Or sauté it in olive oil with garlic and chopped tomatoes and eat with pinto beans and warm tortillas.

Purslane contains oxalic acid (a compound that is also present in spinach), which prevents the absorption of calcium into the body, so don't go hog wild on "little hogweed." (See the "Tips for Cooking Greens Rich in Oxalic Acid" sidebar later in this section.)

WHO EATS AND SHELTERS HERE?

Jackrabbits, antelope, and white-tailed deer eat it. Remarkably, seeds pass through deer and sprout near droppings in new areas. Kangaroo rats and prairie deer mice nibble the seeds, as do ground doves, four species of sparrows, and Lapland longspurs. Pollinators including small bees, flower flies, and beetles like the nectar and pollen.

Hungry larvae of the purslane sawfly "saw" into the succulent leaf's center, gorge themselves, and take up residence. Leafminer weevil larvae "mine" into and hide just below the outermost layer of purslane. You may see squiggly white feeding trails covered over by a papery sheath.

A CLIMATE CHANGE WARRIOR?

Over thirty million years, plants have evolved to use one of three pathways (C3, C4, and CAM) for photosynthesis. Yale researcher Erika Edwards and her team have discovered that purslane cells can switch between two different pathways depending on conditions. This is a hot discovery! When purslane is rooted in moist soil, it acts like a C4 plant. If drought settles in, instead of slowing or shuttering its photosynthesis factory as most plants do under drought stress, purslane keeps chugging, strategically switching its cellular machinery to CAM photosynthesis.

Purslane may help scientists develop a roadmap for developing more drought-resistant crops for a climate-changed world. Plus, you can expect to forage for this delicious climate-adaption warrior come rain or shine—far into the future.

LAMB'S QUARTERS
Chenopodium album

FAMILY: Amaranthaceae (Amaranth)
STATUS: Introduced
OTHER NAMES: Wild spinach, baconweed, fat hen, goosefoot, white goosefoot, pigweed, frost-blite, bathua in Northern India

Summer annual herb, 1 to 6 feet tall. Stems light greenish blue, sometimes streaked with purple. Leaves are diamond shaped (resembling a goose foot) lobed or unlobed, up to 5 inches long, and can be thin or succulent with a white mealy coating when young. Wind-pollinated flowers bloom midsummer to fall. Each flower has a single flat, rounded, black seed. One plant can produce from 30,000 to 176,000 seeds viable for up to four decades in soils.

Goosefoot has been cultivated worldwide for so long (as a vegetable, grain, and livestock food) that scientists are unsure about its original native range. It tends to grow where soil is disturbed, such as along beaches and in gardens, croplands, mulch piles, riverbanks, vacant lots, weedy meadows, and construction sites. It competes with soy and corn in America and Europe, where it is flagged as a pesky weed.

LEFT: *Lamb's quarters is also called goosefoot.* (Photo by Katherine Palmer); **RIGHT**: *Young leaves have a mealy coating.*

HARVEST GUIDE

WHAT: Leaves, stems, flowers, seeds

WHEN: Foliage in spring and summer, seeds in fall and winter

Use your hands to remove individual choice leaves. Or pull up the whole plant with your hands. If the plant is in seed, transport it in a bag to prevent spreading the long-lived seeds.

CULINARY TIPS

In India, lamb's quarters (known as bathua) is cultivated for use in dishes such as bathua saag (cooked leafy greens with potatoes and mustard) and bathua raita (greens and yogurt). Related to spinach and amaranth, it's a bit saltier. The small but very abundant seeds are gathered, then ground into flour. The leaves—packed with calcium, antioxidants, amino acids, and vitamins—make delicious pesto. Leaves also contain saponins and oxalic acid (some of that is broken down by cooking). Avoid eating this weedy green raw in huge amounts. It can cause stomach distress and disturbed nervous systems for some. (See the "Tips for Cooking Greens Rich in Oxalic Acid" sidebar later in this section.)

EAT HEAPS OF WEEDY GREENS

Weedy greens have no harvesting limits. Remember that a "weed" is a plant introduced from somewhere else. So pluck all the dandelion, chickweed, and purslane you can muster. Opt for recipes that use a grocery bag full of weedy greens, such as pesto, soups, salads, wine, and pasta fillings. When dinner is done, however, don't casually toss seed-bearing parts of invasive weeds such as dandelion, purslane, and chickweed into your yard or your compost unless you want a new crop in your garden.

Not all weeds are equal. Some are aggressive colonists that will invade, then quickly dominate and degrade existing plant communities, whether it is your yard, a city park, or a forest. Common fennel, while seemingly demure and feathery-soft, can grow in battalions of dense, uniform, ten-foot stands and seed prolifically. This weedy green is an invasive that deserves care while harvesting. Bag seed-bearing and vegetatively spreading plant parts of invasive weeds and throw them away. Another edible yet aggressive invasive is Japanese knotweed; see the "Don't Be a Knotty Harvester" sidebar later in this section. You can learn more about invasive weeds online from your local weed control board—yes, they exist!

WHO EATS AND SHELTERS HERE?

Substitute the word *spinach* for *lamb's quarters*, and you can begin to comprehend why sixty species seek it out. Deer, domestic pigs, sheep, crickets, sow bugs, carabid beetles, aphids, and millipedes nibble leaves. Leafminer insects tunnel into the succulent sweet spot. In winter, the protein-packed seeds are eaten by songbirds, including the Lapland longspur, horned lark, snow bunting, mourning dove, common redpoll, and many species of sparrows.

Goosefoot thickets provide hideouts for mice, caterpillars, and an A-to-W assortment of songbirds, from the American goldfinch to white-crowned sparrows.

WOOD SORREL
Oxalis oregana

FAMILY: Oxalidaceae (Wood Sorrel)
STATUS: Native
OTHER NAMES: Redwood sorrel, Oregon oxalis, shamrock plant, good luck plant, lucky clover

This 8-inch-tall perennial grows in the understory of rainforests like a cluster of shamrocks from a central base. Three green heart-shaped leaflets, sometimes with burgundy markings, fold up during rain and at night. Minute hairs fringe leaf bottoms and sides. White to pink 5-petaled flowers (sometimes with red streaks) on slender stalks rise above leaves.

Grows in damp forests from coast to mountains, California to British Columbia.

HARVEST GUIDE

WHAT: Leaves, stems
WHEN: Spring to summer (spring is prime picking)
Use scissors to snip the shamrock leaf and stems just above the ground. The stems are as delicious as the leaf. Store in a ridged container in a damp cloth and refrigerate.

CULINARY TIPS

Add wood sorrel leaves to a multitude of dishes for a delicious lemony lift. Try it with Thai coconut soups, scallops in brown butter, trout, salmon, leafy green salads with apples and candied pecans, egg or tuna salad, or as sorrel-shallot cream spooned over smokey oysters on the barbecue or campfire. On a hike, add fresh sorrel leaves to your trailside sandwich. A traditional spring tonic in Old Europe is Simple Sorrel

Wood sorrel leaves close at night. (Photos by Katherine Palmer)

Soup (see Recipes). (See also the "Tips for Cooking Greens Rich in Oxalic Acid" sidebar later in this section.)

WHO EATS AND SHELTERS HERE?

White-tailed deer and eastern cottontail rabbits live here. Juncos, ruffed grouse and sooty (blue) grouse, ground doves, mourning doves, sparrows, and the northern bob-white quail (an introduced gamebird) may nibble seeds or leaves of oxalis species.

Wedgling moth caterpillars may specialize in a diet of tart wood sorrel leaves. Watch for these bejeweled adult moths lighting on your window glass at night—flaunting fringed wings and a tiger-eye-patterned cloak. A racy, zebra-striped moth may also zero in on wood sorrel as a "host plant." In case you're out foraging for wood sorrel by flashlight and see a shy zebra-striped beauty in the shamrocks, the official name is *Trichodezia californiata*.

SHEEP SORREL
Rumex acetosella

FAMILY: Polygonaceae (Buckwheat)
STATUS: Introduced (weed)

OTHER NAMES: Field sorrel, sour grass weed, sour weed, red sorrel, common sheep sorrel

In 1891, the government of New South Wales proclaimed sheep sorrel the "worst weed ever introduced into Australia." A single tiny piece of sheep sorrel's creeping rootstock can sprout a new "sheep." The good news is this common weed's leaves have a lovely lemon bite. Look for larger arrowhead-shaped leaves, 1 to 3 inches long, in a basal cluster. Small arrowhead or elliptical leaves may be attached to the flower stem. Flowers are small (⅛ inch), mealy and dry, and yellow-green-red in clusters near the top of wiry reddish stems.

TIPS FOR COOKING GREENS RICH IN OXALIC ACID

What do sorrel, lamb's quarters, purslane, spinach, rhubarb, beet greens, Indian black tea, cocoa drinks, and some beers have in common? All contain oxalic acid, a pesky substance that can rob your body of calcium and bolster kidney stones. For healthy folks who eat a balanced diet, nibbling on raw sorrel or purslane leaves now and then doesn't pose any particular problem. However, eating foods high in oxalic acid can be a health risk for folks with a diet low in essential minerals such as calcium and iron or with intestinal malfunctions, according to S. C. Morrison of the New Zealand Institute for Crop and Food Research at Lincoln University.

Here are recommendations for preparing foods rich in oxalic acid from the wild pantry:

- **Cook sorrel or purslane.** According to a study of Indian cuisine conducted by the Lincoln University labs, cooking oxalic-rich spinach in a wok reduced the soluble oxalic acid by up to 91 percent. The percentage rose depending on how much of the oxalic acid partnered up with the available minerals (e.g., calcium, iron, magnesium) that were stored in the spinach—or in the added Indian spices.
- **Boil sorrel or purslane in soups.** Simmering sorrel or purslane dilutes the oxalic acid load simply by leaching the pesky stuff into the broth.
- **Add milk or yogurt to cooked sorrel or purslane.** When Lincoln University's foodie technicians stirred paneer (a milk-based cheese product) into their wok to make a staple Indian dish, palak paneer, the oxalic acid plummeted to almost one-tenth its usual level. A dollop of yogurt on raw purslane leaves yielded similar results. (Lactose-intolerant eaters take note: Adding coconut milk to cooked spinach dishes did not reduce oxalic acid amounts.)

Native to Europe and Asia, this common, tasty, problematic weed grows in open disturbed areas such as roadsides, gardens, lawns, pastures, clearcuts, and croplands—especially blueberry fields—and is making appearances in more pristine evergreen and hardwood forests as well as Garry oak ecosystems.

HARVEST GUIDE

WHAT: Leaves, flowers, seeds, roots
WHEN: Year-round or spring and summer (depending on location)
You can uproot this weedy plant with a gentle tug, shake the dirt from the roots, then give it a gentle rinse at home if needed. Or snap off individual leaves by hand. For gathering flowers and seeds, take the whole plant home in a bag. Try not to drop seeds and scatter the sheep.

CULINARY TIPS

Worldwide, two hundred species in the genus *Rumex* are reported to be used for food and medicine. Historically, sorrel was a curdling agent for cheese. In the Palestinian region, the lemony leaves of domesticated sorrel (*R. acetosa*) were traditionally used as savory filling for a pie called sambosek. Leaves were also sautéed in olive oil. In the Mediterranean region, young sorrel leaves are used to flavor "dolmas" when mixed with minced meat, or they are roasted.

Sorrel lemon-aid is refreshing: Pour boiling water into a canning jar with a big handful of leaves. Steep thirty minutes, strain, and stir in honey and ice. Roots plus seeds, which are mealy and dry, can be added to baked goods. (See Wood Sorrel above for more culinary uses.)

Sheep sorrel leaves have two "sheep ears" at their base.

It's best to eat small amounts of the leaves, raw or cooked, due to variable amounts of oxalic acid, which can disrupt your body's calcium balance. Interestingly, a 2017 study in *BMC Complementary Medicine and Therapies* determined a water extract of *R. crispus* actually protected against osteoporosis in mice by inhibiting osteoclastogenesis and inducing osteoblast mineralization. (See the "Tips for Cooking Greens Rich in Oxalic Acid" sidebar above.)

WHO EATS AND SHELTERS HERE?

Twelve species of sparrows can't be wrong, joined by an assortment of songbirds including redwing blackbirds, dark-eyed juncos, spotted towhees, horned larks, cowbirds, and waterfowl such as the cinnamon teal and Canada goose. The golden-mantled ground squirrel stuffs its cheeks full of seeds and leaves. Mule deer, rabbits, bobwhite quails, and ring-necked pheasants devour the whole shebang. Bees and butterflies seek flower pollen.

Blooming sheep sorrel casts a scarlet color in fields. (Photo by Katherine Palmer)

Thirty species of butterflies, including the fiery American copper butterfly, feed and harbor in sorrel, and sixteen species of aphids hide their tiny eggs in the foliage.

BITTERCRESS
Cardamine hirsuta, C. oligosperma

FAMILY: Brassicaceae (Mustard)
STATUS: Introduced and native (depending on area)
OTHER NAMES: Hairy bittercress, shotweed, lamb's cress, Idaho bittercress (*C. hirsuta*); little western bittercress (*C. oligosperma*)

Bittercress leaves add a peppery zing to salad. (Photos by Katherine Palmer)

Related to American watercress, bittercress has a similar peppery bite. Plants form a basal rosette of feather-like leaves, each with 4 to 10 opposite leaflets, but the tip is largest. Hairy bittercress grows as an annual or biennial up to 18 inches tall. Small white flowers cluster at the branch tips.

Grows in wet areas to seasonally wet forests from Alaska to California and east to the Rockies. *C. hirsuta* is largely confined to lower elevations on disturbed ground and was likely introduced from Europe. The native *C. oligosperma* is somewhat larger, taprooted, and found in moist montane environments.

HARVEST GUIDE

WHAT: Leaves, stems, flowers

WHEN: Year-round or spring and summer (depending on location)

You can easily uproot this weed with a gentle tug. Shake the dirt from the roots, then give it a gentle rinse if needed. Unless you want it to spread, harvest whole plants before seed pods appear. Ripe seedpods explode open when touched.

CULINARY TIPS

This dainty green with a peppery bite balances well with the sweetness of citrus and melon. It mellows under the velvety coolness of avocado or cream. Stuff it in a trail sandwich or spring roll for a spicy burst. Purée it for a pesto, or sauté it with garlic, olive oil, and mushrooms. For a super salad, mix fresh bittercress with fennel, radicchio, avocado, pecans, pomegranate seeds, and a balsamic vinaigrette. Or try bittercress in one of the great classic French soups, potage cressonnière, with potatoes, chicken stock, leeks, butter, and cream. Bonus: western bittercress has digestive and carminative properties that reduce farting.

SUPERPOWER

This little 'cress can pitch seeds six feet in all directions! These seeds don't nap, but sprout quickly, making it a delicious—and nutritious—nuisance in gardens and easy to introduce elsewhere accidentally.

WHO EATS AND SHELTERS HERE?

Butterflies and moths, such as the white-lined sphinx moth, gather nectar and pollen. Vital food for a tiny wild bee—*Andrena arabis*: just one-third of an inch long and built like a compact bumblebee, this little golden-haired dude is more active than other bees when the temps get cool.

COMMON FIREWEED
Chamerion augustifolium

FAMILY: Onagraceae (Evening Primrose)
STATUS: Native
OTHER NAMES: Fireweed, willow herb, great willow herb, rosebay willow herb. In Britain, "bombweed" became a moniker for fireweed during World War II for its capacity to sprout in bomb craters (and begin the healing process for war-ravaged lands).

A tall (up to 6 feet), showy wildflower with a torch of fuchsia-pink 4-petaled blooms. Leaves lance- or willow-like, 2 to 6 inches long, and alternate. Blooms from bottom to top, June to September. Bean-like pods pack up to 80,000 airborne seeds per plant that drift like a gentle snowfall. One root sends up multiple plants. Shoots are high in vitamins A and C.

Common fireweed ignites the landscape after a recent burn. (Photo by Katherine Palmer)

Fireweed is impressively adaptable: circumpolar, found across the northern hemisphere's temperate regions, including Alaska, Canada, and the Lower 48—except Texas and the hot, humid south. A pioneer of disturbed sites—clearcuts, burns, river plains, avalanche shoots, where glaciers are retreating, and railroad and road edges—as well as conifer and mixed forests, grasslands, aspen parklands, and muskegs.

HARVEST GUIDE

WHAT: Shoots, leaves, flowers
WHEN: Shoots in spring, leaves and flowers in summer
Snap new asparagus-like "shoots" off where the stem is crisp and juicy and breaks effortlessly. If it bends instead of snapping, it's too old and fibrous. Pick delicate flowers by hand and protect in a hard-sided container. Harvest leaves for tea in the beginning of July or when the plant is in full flower. Research shows this is when fireweed churns out phytochemicals—including ellagitannins (ETs) and oenothein B—associated with fighting cancer, cardiovascular disease, and neurodegenerative disorders. If plants are abundant, slide your fingers down the stalk to take off many leaves at once.

CULINARY TIPS

Cook fireweed shoots like a sort of "wild asparagus." Sauté, roast, or steam; deep-fry as tempura; add to quiche; pickle or marinate. Use fuchsia-colored fireweed petals in salad or as a garnish. Fireweed blossoms can be made into jelly or a mild-tasting syrup. Ferment and dry leaves for Ivan Chai, a flavorful herbal tea.

IVAN CHAI IS AS EASY AS PIE

Fireweed is circumpolar in the northern hemisphere and is made into tea almost universally in this region. Russian American women in Alaska taught my friend Jensy how they make "Ivan Chai" tea from fireweed leaves. After picking mature leaves, allow them to wilt and roll them vigorously between your palms. With a little practice, it forms a compact pearl with the stem in the very center. Rolling bruises the leaf so it can "ferment" as it dries. Fermenting also creates a more flavorful tea with a slightly floral, green-tea note. In the UK and Ireland—where it is called rosebay willowherb—fireweed is used in tea form to treat asthma.

Dry Ivan Chai tea pearls on a cotton cloth over a wire rack until "bone dry." Store in a glass jar in a cool, dark cupboard. Ivan Chai keeps its green-tea-like flavor for six months or more.

SUPERPOWER

Coast Salish weavers used the silky-haired seeds as soft fiber to weave with mountain-goat wool and dog hair for cozy blankets and as padding mixed with duck feathers in mattresses.

WHO EATS AND SHELTERS HERE?

Elk, mountain goat, bighorn sheep, pronghorn, and mule deer eat it as a vital spring and summer food. Black-tailed deer munch fireweed during the entire growing season, while moose in Alaska, being picky eaters, prefer the greens before they flower. In fall, pikas and chipmunks nibble pods and cache seeds. Muskrats, rabbits, song-

SKUNK CABBAGE AS SURVIVAL FOOD

The opulent skunk cabbage, *Lysichiton americanus*, has oval leaves as big as umbrellas. I clearly remember holding a skunk cabbage leaf umbrella over my head when I was four as the rain scuddered down in the Hoh Rainforest.

"Indian wax paper" is another name for this useful plant. Indigenous people used its parchment-like leaves to line earthen cooking pits, cover slats in berry-drying racks, and wrap salal berry cakes for winter use. Apparently, a natural insecticide in the leaves deters bugs. Measuring nearly five feet tall, this perennial can live sixty or so years! Another moniker, "swamp lantern," refers to the new growth that appears in late winter as a brilliant yellow torch. A Kathlamet story relayed in 1934 in *Wild Flowers of the Pacific Coast* by Leslie Loren Haskin describes skunk cabbage as a spring food eaten before the salmon returned. Before Pacific salmon inhabited coastal rivers, it kept the ancestors from starvation. As a reward for its sacrifice, the skunk cabbage received two gifts from the salmon: an elk-skin robe, the gold overarching hood or bract, and a warclub, the green-and-cream flower spike.

The aroma of skunk often precedes the sight of this bushy cabbage. That's because the new leaf growth mimics the putrid smell of composting flesh. All the better to attract early pollinators—like flies. The wise skunk cabbage has a few more tricks to ensure its success. Antifreeze chemicals coarse through the new shoot growth. The early leaves can even melt out a crust of snow! Hungry deer and bears devour it. I've seen coastal brown bears gnaw it to nubbins, and Sitka black-tailed deer have kept me up at night, crunching "swamp slaw" outside my tent.

But skunk cabbage is strictly a survival food. Don't be tempted to try it, and never raw, unless you follow vital precautions. Leaves must be boiled to remove the calcium oxalate crystals, which cause severe irritation and burning of your lips, tongue, and throat. Boiling three consecutive times works to reduce the crystals, but the water must be tossed each time. Even when prepared correctly, eating large amounts may cause vomiting and severe nausea. Do not confuse the rootstock with poisonous false hellebore! The leaves of skunk cabbage are smooth with netlike veins, while false hellebore are deeply pleated with parallel veins.

Skunk cabbage in bloom

Snap fireweed shoots off like asparagus stalks in spring.

birds, waterfowl, and upland game birds seek its tasty greens and seeds. Beekeepers transport hives to clearcuts for fireweed nectar, which is also a vital fuel for migratory hummingbirds and butterflies.

The large, stout hummingbird moth—nicknamed for its ability to hover and rapidly beat its narrow, birdlike wings as it sips flower nectar—may deposit eggs on fireweed stalks. Also called the white-lined sphinx moth, look for its caterpillar form that wields an impressive but harmless caudal thorn.

JAPANESE KNOTWEED
Polygonum cuspidatum (synonym *Fallopia japonica*)

FAMILY: Polygonaceae (Buckwheat)
STATUS: Highly invasive weed
OTHER NAMES: Fleece flower, Japanese bamboo, tiger cane, Mexican bamboo, horse-buckwheat, canne, hu zhang, kojo-kon, hadori-kon, renouée du Japon, renouée japonaise

Extremely invasive, aggressive, and fast-growing, this bamboo-like herb can bolt 4 inches a day in late spring and form dense thickets 10 feet tall that colonize native habitats. Stems are segmented and hollow with red blotches. Leaves are triangular and 3 to 6 inches long with pointed tips. Whitish flowers form spikes along zigzagging, reddish-green stems from June to September. Tall, dead stalks persist into winter. Another nonnative species from Asia, giant knotweed is taller with rounded leaf bases.

DON'T BE A KNOTTY HARVESTER

Knotweed benefits from mowing, hacking, digging, and tilling. A piece of living root or stem even a few millimeters long can sprout into an impenetrable forest of giant knotweeds. It spreads in bits and pieces in rhizome-infested fill dirt, by way of shoe soles, and by seed. Rumor has it, a scrap of Japanese knotweed sourced from an old homestead in Olympic National Park seeded miles of nearby river. So treat stem bits, roots, and seeds like potential giants.

In parts of the UK, Japanese knotweed is classified as controlled waste. It is illegal to toss scraps in household garbage. The discarded cuttings must be carted to a licensed disposal site or burned!

Safely dispose of your knotweed kitchen scraps by burning or firmly securing them in a double plastic bag before putting them in the trash. ❶ Some chefs suggest micro-waving skin peelings and such in a glass bowl until well-cooked. Don't even think of composting the litter.

Introduced to the United States from Asia in the 1870s, Japanese knotweed likely escaped from a private estate on Long Island, New York. A century and a half later, it has spread across most of the US and Canada. It is found along roadsides, forest edges, wet-lands, and especially in river corridors, where it is very hard to eradicate.

HARVEST GUIDE
WHAT: Young, rhubarb-like stalks
WHEN: Spring

Japanese knotweed stalks resemble bamboo with red and green splotches.

Harvest tender, plump pink-and-green shoots (less than 1 foot) with a knife at the base. Carry knotweed home in a bag so you don't accidently drop bits of stalk or roots ❗ (see the "Don't Be a Knotty Harvester" sidebar). Harvest only in clean areas. Knotweed is a heavy-metal hyperaccumulator. Researchers in Japan and Europe reported it had significantly higher levels of lead, cadmium, copper, and zinc when picked from contaminated soils. Avoid sites sprayed with herbicides.

CULINARY TIPS

Japanese knotweed is pernicious but delicious, with a tartness reminiscent of rhubarb. Try knotweed in anything you'd use rhubarb in: snacking cake, knotweed custard tart, pie, jam, fruit leather, chutney, simple syrup, and sorbet. Peel extrafibrous stalks before chopping; small young stalks are fine with skin left on.

While Japanese knotweed is used as a traditional medicine across Asia (it is called *itadori*, meaning "take away pain," in Japanese and is listed in the *People's Republic of China Pharmacopoeia*), some folks have GI distress if they eat more than a small portion. Go easy the first time you try it.

SUPERPOWER

Neutraceuticals have been isolated from Japanese knotweed, such as resveratrol—an anti-inflammatory compound with potential for treating chronic Lyme disease.

TOP: *Bees pollinating Japanese knotweed flowers*
BOTTOM: *Flower spikes on Japanese knotweed*

❓ "TAKING A BITE" OUT OF KNOTWEED

There's a good reason knotweed is the tenth most invasive plant in the world. It can form dense thickets that slow the flow in salmon streams and amplify water temperatures, thereby harming juvenile salmon and eggs. Tall, dead stalks and copious leaf litter decompose slowly—up to three years for stalks. The dead litter creates a thick blanket that prevents native seeds from germinating. Debris can wash downstream and create blockages, exacerbating the impacts of floods and changing the course of streams. During droughts, tall, dry thickets pose fire risks. Japanese knotweed can turn a woodland into a grassland over years. It has even been seen floating across open seas!

Japanese knotweed had no natural predators in the United States—until recently. In Ohio, the National Park Service approved a new pest management strategy to take a bite out of this pernicious (and delicious) weed. The knotweed psyllid, *Aphalara itadori*, a highly specific sap-sucking insect, may be the perfect dinner guest. It's worked in the United Kingdom as a biocontrol agent since 2010. According to the US Forest Service, "Psyllids feed on the sap of the knotweed, diminishing its energy supply and ultimately killing the plant. Researchers found that the Japanese knotweed psyllid's preference is specific to three targeted knotweeds, and it is not expected to damage any native or related knotweed family plants."

You, too, can take a *big bite* out of Japanese knotweed, but be sure to dispose of scraps appropriately (see the "Don't Be a Knotty Harvester" sidebar earlier).

WHO EATS AND SHELTERS HERE?

Young shoots are tasty greens for sheep, cattle, horses, donkeys, and goats. Bees, flies, and wasps visit nectar-rich blooms in late summer. Some beekeepers locate hives near the prolific flowering stalks for plentiful honey production. In fact, one hive's production increased almost one hundred pounds in weight in five days from a knotweed stand. No surprise the nectar produces great gobs of honey—it is 24 percent sugar (fructose, glucose, sucrose, and trisachharides).

A "shelter thief," Japanese knotweed steals habitat from amphibians, fish, and wildlife. In its native Japan, however, 186 species of arthropods (such as the Japanese beetle) and 40 species of fungus keep it in check so it can't imperialize.

TENDING WEEDS AND WILD PATCHES
LINDA QUINTANA

Linda Quintana is a northwest herbalist who lives by the four seasons, wisdom of plants, and ways of animals. She pampers her chickweed, designates a spot for dandelions in her garden, and forages from a wild raspberry patch she's tended for nearly three decades. For almost as many years, I've packed Linda's wild-harvested and garden-grown herbs on my global travels. Whether I'm drenched to my skivvies guiding in rainy Southeast Alaska or chilled from glacier-gusting winds while kayaking in the sub-Antarctic, the healing gifts of Linda's plants tip the scales in wellness's favor.

Linda flourished as a wild child in the Alaska outback in the early 1960s. She grew up without running water or a telephone, thirty miles outside Fairbanks, Alaska, where her parents homesteaded on a hundred acres of boreal forest, birch groves, and blueberry and cranberry patches. When they weren't in school, Linda and her four siblings were free to roam all summer long. One of their chores was to pick berries for jam. Linda and her siblings returned to the same sites with little wild Alaskan blueberry bushes less than a foot tall and meadows of wild cranberries—also called lingonberries—each year.

"We'd only pick where the plants were very healthy. Just learning that by instinct. And leaving them if it's not a good year." They also always left berries for the birds as well as to go to seed.

Her mother also sent the kids out to harvest yarrow and Labrador tea to dry for use in winter. If they ever felt anything coming on, they sipped the steeped herbal ambrosia. Linda and her four siblings never got sick!

Her family moved south to Washington when Linda was sixteen, and she realized the gifts she'd been given. "This may sound funny, but I had a strong sense that the Earth will take care of me, and I can take care of myself. . . . I can survive."

Decades later, entering a bell-jingling door to Linda's herb shop, Wonderland Tea and Spice, I am instantly enrobed in aromatics. Shelves of herb and spice jars stretch floor to ceiling. Chanterelles wait in brown paper bags. Elderberry-infused honey glistens darkly in pint-size canning jars. Given a hundred choices of powerful plants and six decades of herbal and fungal know-how, Linda still teaches a home-based workshop to newcomers that celebrates two simple common plants—chickweed and dandelion. She plugs the merits of tending twenty dandelion plants. She speaks to wide-eyed skeptics about growing a two-by-three-foot square of chickweed.

"People might think I have a weedy yard! But I have two sections." Linda uproots dandelions where she requires beds for other plants. However, where the dandelions grow the strongest and the greenest, she says, *"That's the dandelion patch!"* She openly confesses, "I don't care if it's my prime location in the middle of a garden! My

Linda Quintana harvesting flowers in one of her gardens (Photo by Mike Quintana)

dandelion and chickweed patches are important."

Sometimes, months or years afterward, "People secretly tell me, 'Linda, I started some dandelions! . . . I let them stay in part of the garden!' It's almost like you got to whisper this. Right? But there's nothing wrong with that. . . . That dandelion in your yard is your responsibility. Take care of it. Love it."

If you don't have land, she suggests, "you can grow chickweed and dandelion in a big clay pot or half a whiskey barrel. Chickweed grows beautifully in a mat-like circle, and oh my gosh, some of the dandelions are gorgeous." That way, at least in Washington, you can forage almost year-round.

She says, "I loved my dandelion patch from day one—taking that first spring bite of dandelion leaves . . . plucking those flowers . . . and then eating it all the way through to the bitterness of the fall—I really do love it!"

Linda laughs at herself, then says, "We went up to Banff years ago. And one of my favorite shots was a nice cinnamon bear sitting up on a little hill, his mouth filled with dandelion leaf and a flower coming out. I thought, 'Look at that majestic animal! Look at what's in that plant! There he is sitting there, just as happy as can be known . . . eating dandelions.'"

BERRIES & ROSES

When I sea kayaked alone down the Inside Passage from Alaska to Washington in the 1990s, I remember camping in a magical forest on the midcoast of present-day British Columbia. The beach was a drift of white shells. A creek whispered over mossy rocks and ledges hidden by tall trees. When I stepped into the forest, carrying my tent and sleeping bag, I was surprised (and relieved) to see a parklike landscape. Pacific crab apple trees, salmonberry, and high bush cranberry grew tall in the understory. At my feet, on the forest floor, a carpet of strawberry and medicinal plants appeared manicured. The forest was more like a pastoral orchard and herb garden than a windblown coastal beach with untamed greenery. Caretaking shined everywhere. It turns out that I may have stumbled upon a "forest garden."

Prior to European contact, cultivating forest gardens was the Pacific Coast norm, not the exception. Forest gardens—as well as estuary gardens, camas gardens, and clam gardens (also called sea gardens because they nourish crabs, sea cucumber, chitons, sea vegetables, and a host of other traditional seafoods)—were meticulously tended so more food could be produced more efficiently. Berry patches and fruit orchards were managed as copses for maximum production. Caretakers weeded out competing plants, snapped off foliage to invite more fruit, and mixed offal from salmon and game into the soil for fertilizer.

Fire management ensured that the mountain huckleberry bushes grew more prolific fruit. Fires also reduced competition from other trees and shrubs. Hot fires would kill the berry bush tops, but they sprouted from rhizomes—roots that generate new growth. Every three years or so, both lowland and alpine berry patches were carefully set afire. Timing the burn, for after the berry season and in sync with autumn rains, prevented the fire's spread. During summer months, Indigenous gardeners took advantage of natural irrigation systems too. For instance, they transplanted berry bushes from the forest's edge to misty waterfall ledges. During droughts, the waterfall's green fringe never went dry. The Mediterranean-like microclimate of waterfalls provided delicious berries over an extended season.

Before berry picking, prayers were uttered to the berry bushes who were reverently regarded as kin and approached with humility and tenderness. In "Prayer to Berries" from *The Religion of the Kwakiutl Indians*, coauthored by anthropologist Franz Boas and Indigenous ethnologist George Hunt, a woman speaks kindly to the berry bushes: "Look! I come now dressed with my large basket and my small basket that you may go into it, Healing-Woman; you, Supernatural Ones. I mean this, that you may not be evilly disposed towards me, friends. That you may only treat me well."

Long ago, people watched animals to find out when berries ripened. It was said, for instance, that when the goldfinches whistled more often, it was time for the families to begin their seasonal migration to the mountains to pick berries. Special baskets were prepared. Journey supplies were packed. Some families hiked a dozen miles from ocean villages to ridge tops. Working day after day, they filled huge baskets to the brim, packed them out on foot, then cleaned, mashed, cooked, and dried the processed berries on wood racks lined with skunk cabbage leaves. In the end, several hundred berry cakes per family made it into winter. If there wasn't enough of one berry—say, the prized salal—the other, more common berries were mixed in. Val Segrest of the Muckleshoot Tribe told me,

> I'm taught that our ancestors, as part of their food management, only har-
> vested the abundance of that year. Over three hundred different kinds of foods
> were eaten. But if there was one that just didn't look good for that year, if
> mountain huckleberry didn't have a good year, we shifted to wild strawberry
> or red huckleberry, evergreen huckleberry. We'd eat more of what was abun-
> dant and have, you know, faith in that thing returning through our honoring,
> cultivating, and doing all the things you would do in a garden.

That's a good lesson for us in times of year-round fresh and frozen cultivated berries, of increasing fires, droughts, or deluges that can affect wild berry abundance. We

❓ WILD BERRIES AMP THE ANTIOXIDANTS

Alaska's wild blueberries and huckles are high, higher, and highest in antioxidants. In a study measuring their ORAC (oxygen radical absorption capacity) levels, Alaska wild berries scored higher than wild berries from the Lower 48 and cultivated berries. What's more, dietary anthocyanins in berries—a type of flavonoid—can reduce blood pressure, improve vascular function, and improve memory, according to a review of nearly 1,200 peer-reviewed scientific articles. These benefits are especially true for older adults (both healthy and those with heart conditions). Powdered dried blueberries (which most studies used) were particularly effective.

Interestingly, while cooking berries lowers antioxidant levels and adding sugar dilutes them, berry jams and other products still contain high sources of antioxidants. But the bell ringer is dried berries. Apparently, drying berries increases antioxidant levels!

can cut a bit of wild into our domestic favorites. Wild flavors go a long way. For a beautiful example, check out my friend Vanessa Cooper's Salish Pemmican (see Recipes).

Today, with our yards full of ornamental introduced plants, it is hard to imagine that less than a century and a half ago, First Nations people were still gardening almost thirty wild fruit and nut species on the Pacific Coast. Even a partial list reads like a dream: salmonberry, Nootka rose, strawberry, serviceberry, red huckleberry, red elderberry, highbush cranberry, soapberry, black hawthorn, black raspberry, salal, Alaska blueberry, Pacific crab apple, and hazelnut.

I can't hope to cover all berries and roses in one chapter, so I've chosen ten of the most flavorful ones. Some, such as huckleberry, blueberry, and wild raspberry, are familiar as pie. Others, such as thimbleberry, native trailing blackberry, blue and red elderberry, salal, salmonberry, and Nootka rose, may be newcomers to your cupped hand. Of course, the most popularly picked berry today, the Himalayan blackberry, is included too. This cultivated chap from Europe jumped the hedgerows and turned into an invasive monster of devastating but delicious proportions.

BLUEBERRY
Vaccinium spp.

FAMILY: Ericaceae (Heath)
STATUS: Native
COMMON SPECIES AND NAMES: Dwarf blueberry, dwarf huckleberry, dwarf bilberry, dwarf whortleberry (*V. cespitosum*); oval-leaved blueberry, Alaska blueberry, highbush blueberry (*V. ovalifolium*); bog blueberry, bog bilberry, alpine bilberry, tundra bilberry (*V. uliginosum*)

All species have alternate deciduous leaves that are oval- to lance-shaped. Flowers are urn-shaped, and pink to white, but can be copper-colored. The round berries are blue black to blue, with whitish "blooms." Dwarf and bog produce smaller, sweeter berries. Oval-leaved are more mild and tart. Oval-leaved blueberries ripen earliest (usually late June). Dwarf blueberries generally ripen in late summer and early fall. Bog blueberry can hang on the bush until late summer. Each bush's ripeness depends on species, location, elevation, and weather.

Bog and dwarf blueberry are found from Alaska to California, usually in low mats 1 foot high. Oval-leaved are erect bushes more than 6 feet tall and range from Alaska to Oregon. Perennial shrubs inhabit conifer forests and open areas from low to subalpine elevations.

CLOCKWISE FROM TOP LEFT: *Dwarf blueberry blooms, dwarf blueberry fruit* (Photo by Marina Poushkina , Shutterstock), *bog blueberry* (Photo by Almondd, Shutterstock), *oval-leaved blueberry* (Photo by Katherine Palmer)

HARVEST GUIDE

WHAT: Berries, leaves
WHEN: Berries in early summer to fall
Collect individual berries and leaves from the perimeter of wild berry patches. That way, birds and other creatures can feed while under cover or at a comfortable distance. An empty water bottle with a lid is great for transporting small amounts of berries when hiking. Hard-sided containers help keep berries from getting crushed from the jostle of walking on a trail for hours, unless you plan on making jam!

While picking berries by hand takes more time and effort than using a rake, it sure pays off when it comes time to clean them at home. You will spend less time culling out twigs, leaves, unripe berries, and the occasional insect. A great trick for removing leaves and such is to roll the berries down a sloped cutting board or sheet pan covered in a bath towel. The debris sticks to the towel—for the most part.

Pick leaves for tea by hand or clip a few sprigs here and there across a wide area.

CULINARY TIPS

Who doesn't love blueberries in baked goods—pies, cobblers, crisps, muffins, fritters, scones, tarts, cheesecake, and pancakes—or plunked in yogurt? But don't forget chilled fruit soups, savory sauces for barbecued seafood and fowl, chutney, curd, vinegars, syrups, wine, cordials, lemonade, and beverages like shrubs. Try dessert pizza with shortbread crust, a "sauce" of honey-sweetened cashew cream or cream cheese, and a topping of glazed blueberries.

SUPERPOWER

Wild blueberries are high in antioxidants, with Alaska blueberry measuring the highest (see the "Wild Berries Amp the Antioxidants" sidebar above). But even cultivated berries are super health boosters.

WHO EATS AND SHELTERS HERE?

Grizzly, coastal brown, and black bears all eat buckets of blueberries mid-August to October as they transition into hyperphagia—when they pack on fat for hibernation. Ptarmigan, towhee, scarlet tanager, ring-necked pheasant, and thrushes, as well as sharp-tailed, ruffed, and blue grouse, eat blueberries. Chipmunks, foxes, skunks, squirrels, raccoon, and mice munch them too. Twigs and leaves are eaten by bear, mountain goats, elk, deer, rabbit, and varying hare. Blueberry is a vital winter browse; wildlife can reach the branches of tall, older berry stands when low-growing bushes are buried under snow. In fact, deer prefer blueberry leaves in old-growth forests over clearcuts; older stands of Alaska blueberry have leaves with a higher percentage of digestible protein and higher nutrients such as potassium and phosphorous. It's also an important food for Mariposa copper butterflies and both short-tongued bees (for example, sweat bees) and long-tongued bees (such as bumblebees).

Small animals from pica to songbirds and ptarmigan hide in the thickets. Songbirds nest in larger, older berry stands.

MOUNTAIN HUCKLEBERRY
Vaccinium membranaceum

FAMILY: Ericaceae (Heath)
STATUS: Native
OTHER NAMES: Thinleaf huckleberry, black huckleberry, black mountain huckleberry, big huckleberry, tall huckleberry, globe huckleberry, mountain bilberry

THE ALLURE OF WILD "BLUE" BERRIES

"B-b-b-bear!"

"Where?"

"Right there! In the salal bushes." I pointed with my paddle as we drifted past an island—islet really, no bigger than a two-car garage. The air smelled of honeyed fruit and sea wrack. We were on an ocean kayak trip to the Bunsby Islands in the traditional territory of the Ka:'yu:'k 't'h' and Che:k:tles7et'h' First Nation peoples, on the west coast of Vancouver Island. Our bellies bulged with buckwheat pancakes smothered in wild berries. "Storm cakes," we called them: Pinch of cinnamon, slivered orange peel, four handfuls of salal berries plucked in forty-five-knot winds. Simmer in a soot-black pot while hunkered behind a surf-slammed beach log. Pour over pancakes. Hope the tide won't rise. Don't think about bears. And we didn't—until now.

The three-hundred-pound black bear stood half hidden by salal bushes. Its rump protruded only a paddle's reach from my kayak. Every few seconds, the greenery shook violently like an earthquake. The bear's ribs were visible through its belly fur. This was not a fat Ursa ready for winter hibernation. It was a hungry Ursa, so hungry she didn't hear us approach. I put my finger to my lips to shush. No need to interrupt. Hers was a mandatory munch, not a leisurely picnic. Until the coastal rivers shimmer with salmon—which bears transform into a survival coat of winter fat—they can appear rib thin and shaggy, as if their coat is two sizes too big. I could just imagine how delicious the jam-sweet salal berries tasted as the bear wrapped her lips around a cluster and pulled back. We drifted on, leaving the berry picker alone. As we left, a flock of migrating songbirds dropped into the salal bushes and tweezed right alongside the bear. A raccoon came stumbling out, too, as if drunk with pleasure. We weren't the only ones who appreciated a good, ripe berry bursting with sweet juice.

Blueberries, huckleberries, and salal berries are three of the more commonly known wild "blue" berry producers of the Pacific Coast's heath family (Ericaceae). Another edible wild "blue" berry—Saskatoon serviceberry (*Amelanchier alnifolia*) is also worth ferreting out, but it is from the rose family (Roseaceae). Of the wild "blue" berries, only blueberries and Saskatoon serviceberry have been domesticated. Huckleberries and salal are still as wild as the day they were born. Plucked and placed on your tongue, all these varieties offer a mélange of flavors, from tart to honey sweet.

Seeing a foraging bear reminded me it was almost time for our annual pilgrimage to the Cascade mountains for a taste of wild berries. Following a September frost, we headed to the high country. At five thousand feet in elevation, the black huckleberries winked shiny as ravens' eyes from shoulder-high foliage. *Try me! Me too!* They beckoned with their juicy, tart, wine-sap flavor.

Evergreen huckleberry hangs on into late fall.

We left the huckleberry thickets in the damp forest behind, crossing two cascading creeks, and climbed the trail to a windswept ridge for dwarf blueberries. What a contrast. Appropriately named, the dwarf blueberry stretches six inches high on tiptoe. One teeny bush can freight more fruit than foliage. I swear, since they don't make much greenery, dwarf blues concentrate a lot more sweetness in their fruits. Up here on this alpine ridge, I had a lot of respect for these vulnerable little blueberries.

Each dwarf blueberry was enrobed in a smokey "bloom." Technically called an epicuticular wax, it evolved 350 million years ago and is the berry's homemade sunscreen. The wax absorbs the onslaught of UVB rays and reduces water loss. The berries across these high ridges and alpine meadows provide not only nutrient-dense food but water, too, for the bears, birds, and small animals. Their window of food gathering is mighty small compared to ours. We tasted, breathed in the distant views of Komo Kulshan and Mount Shuksan, and felt blessed to carry home a precious gift to share with our family.

Wild blue berries are antioxidant powerhouses. They've been shown to improve insulin sensitivity, prevent colon cancer, trim abdominal love handles, increase agility, improve memory, and lower cholesterol. I feel a heightened appreciation when I mix wild mountain huckleberries with cultivated berries. I understand, at last, why huckleberry feasts were held to coincide with the first mountain harvest, why girls who had participated in their first berry harvesting were honored and blessed by the Elders as the fruits of their labors were shared with the whole community, why prayers were offered.

At a recent Thanksgiving dinner, my niece churned our precious two cups of frozen huckles with port wine into a midnight-blue sorbet. She proudly passed the bowl around a long table seated with three generations of family. As we each spooned up a taste of this exquisite huckleberry sorbet, it was blue smiles of praise—all the way around.

Mountain huckleberry fruit and flowers (Photos by Abe Lloyd and Nikki Yancey, Shutterstock)

Bushes can reach 6 feet. Leaves are thin, finely toothed, ovate, and up to 2 inches long. Flowers are urn shaped, solitary, and yellow pink. Berries are shiny black, purple, or dark purple red with no pale bloom, round, and relatively large—⅜ inches long. It is the most popular huckleberry to harvest in the West thanks to the sweet, tangy flavor. It is also Idaho's honored state fruit.

Found from Alaska to California and in many western states, Minnesota, and Michigan. Grows in wet to drier locations in mid-elevation mountain forests to above timberline.

HARVEST GUIDE
WHAT: Berries, leaves
WHEN: Berries in midsummer to late summer, leaves in spring to summer
Collect individual berries and leaves with your hands. (See Red Huckleberry.)

CULINARY TIPS
See Blueberry.

WHO EATS AND SHELTERS HERE?
These berries are an important food for brown bears and black bears. Small animals including the northern flying squirrel, red squirrel, varying hare, chipmunk, and deer mouse eat them, as well as the ruffed grouse, blue grouse, and band-tailed pigeon. A host of songbirds such as pine grosbeak, black-capped chickadee, American robin, Canada jay, western tanager, and song sparrow love the berries. The foliage is an autumn food for blue grouse. Moose, elk, mule deer, and white-tailed deer eat the woody parts of mountain huckleberry.

Bumblebees and huckleberries are intertwined. Pollination by native bees is essential for berries to develop successfully (see the "Thank the Bees for Your Berries!"

❓ THANK THE BEES FOR YOUR BERRIES!

We have native bees to thank for the mountain huckleberries in our hands. Because huckleberries flower early and prolifically, they are the only food available for bumblebee queens when they emerge from hibernation. Queens must collect enough nectar and pollen to begin nesting. But some are in trouble. The western bumblebee (*Bombus occidentalis*) is being considered for listing under the US Endangered Species Act.

According to the USDA Northwest Climate Hub, "Huckleberry habitat is expected to move to higher ground and may decrease overall, due to a warmer climate, fire suppression, and extreme fire . . . [and] higher seasonal temperatures could impact pollination and fruit production of huckleberry when flowering happens before pollinators (bees) are abundant." This habitat shift could have wide-ranging impacts on the economically, culturally, and ecologically important huckleberry.

sidebar). Swarms of native bees, wasps, hornets, ants, and flies seek the pollen and nectar. In California, up to forty-three species of butterflies and moths seek mountain huckleberry as a host for eggs.

RED HUCKLEBERRY
Vaccinium parvifolium

FAMILY: Ericaceae (Heath)
STATUS: Native
OTHER NAMES: Red bilberry, red whortleberry

Long-lived understory shrub that generally grows to 12-plus feet and occasionally 25 feet in ideal conditions. Branches are green with ridges. Leaves are thin, oval, or elliptical and alternate. Waxy, singular, urn-shaped flowers range in color from yellow-pink to green-yellow or white. Round, luminously scarlet, thin-skinned berries may linger until late fall.

Alaska to California in dry-to-damp conifer forests from sea level to medium-elevation mountain areas. Loves to grow out of rotting stumps.

HARVEST GUIDE
WHAT: Berries, leaves
WHEN: Berries in summer and fall, leaves in spring to late summer

Red huckleberry bush and flowers (Photo on left by Katerine Palmer)

Pluck berries individually by hand. Collect leaves for tea by removing individual leaves with your hands, here and there from many bushes, not clipping off whole branches. As you hike out, push a few berries under the soil to help new bushes grow in suitable habitat.

CULINARY TIPS

The fruit was dried into cakes by some First Nations and Tribes and provided a delicious, vitamin C–rich winter food. (See Blueberry.)

WHO EATS AND SHELTERS HERE?

Berry-loving animals include brown bears, black bears, red fox, gray fox, skunks, chipmunks, squirrels, white-footed mice, deer mice, and pikas. Berry-loving birds range from band-tailed pigeons to bluebirds, ptarmigans to towhees, catbirds to thrushes and every species of grouse—spruce, ruffed, blue, and sharp-tailed. Blue grouse adults and chicks seek it out as a favorite food on Vancouver Island. Mountain goats and mountain beaver nibble foliage and twigs. Black-tailed deer munch shoots, leaves, fruit, and twigs.

As a winter browse, red huckleberry is especially important until it is covered by snow. The diet of Roosevelt elk, endemic to the Olympic Peninsula, may be 60 to 90 percent huckleberry browse for part of the year. In California alone, sixty-two species of butterflies and moths may deposit eggs on this special host.

Thickets serve as resting, nesting, and hiding sites for small animals and birds.

EVERGREEN HUCKLEBERRY
Vaccinium ovatum

FAMILY: Ericaceae (Heath)
STATUS: Native
OTHER NAMES: Winter huckleberry, shot huckleberry, box huckleberry, California huckleberry

Slow growing and long-lived, with a height up to 13 feet. Leathery evergreen leaves are serrate, oblong, glossy, and pale below. Pink urn-shaped flowers grow in clusters on branch sides and undersides. Berries are round, firm, and a shiny purple black. Used as greenery in the floral industry.

Grows along the coast from Central California to British Columbia.

HOW TO DRY "BLUE-BERRIES" & MORE

Food dehydrators make it easy to enjoy our summer "blue-berry gifts"—all year long. Dried blueberries, huckles, salal, and Saskatoon/serviceberries are deeper in flavor than when fresh. One handful upgrades snack mixes, powers up oatmeal, or sprinkles fun atop frosted cupcakes. Ground with nut butter or venison for pemmican, they provide nutrient-dense energy (see Salish Pemmican in Recipes). I use directions from a fave little book, *Dry It—You'll Like It* by Gen MacManiman, that I first bought to prepare meals for three months of hiking on the Pacific Crest Trail. It can take up to two days to dry berries, so be patient.

Loosely arrange berries on a screen with small holes or parchment paper in a food dehydrator. You can fasten the paper to the trays with masking tape to keep the edges from curling up. I also trim one edge to leave a paper gap of a few inches on one side. Then I stack the trays so the gap on the bottom tray is on the right, the gap on the next tray up is on the left, and so on to direct air flow back and forth for faster drying.

You need air circulation between individual berries too, so don't overload trays. To even out the drying, make sure to rotate trays, keeping the driest food on the bottom near the heat source so you don't add moisture from other trays of added, fresh berries.

You can also oven dry "blue-berries" at 140 degrees F, or a very low temperature, by spreading them out on a parchment-paper-lined sheet pan and keeping the oven door slightly ajar.

Evergreen huckleberry fruit and flowers

HARVEST GUIDE

WHAT: Berries

WHEN: From fall into early winter

Use your fingers to rake the firm, ripe berries into a container, being sure to check the undersides of the evergreen-leaf-covered branches, where they hide from sight. Berries are best after a freeze and are the last berries to mature in the seasonal round, which is late fall. A step stool can be handy for the 6-to-10 footers.

CULINARY TIPS

Indigenous families traveled long distances to pick these well-liked fruits. They were sun- or smoke-dried, mashed, and pressed into cakes. (See Blueberry.)

WHO EATS AND SHELTERS HERE?

Black bears, chipmunks, mice, bluebirds, thrushes, and scarlet tanagers eat the berries. As they ready for autumn migrations, birds home in on the black fruits rich in anthocyanins. Elk and rabbit browse leaves and twigs. Deer may crop up to 40 percent of the leaves and twigs, but all this browsing stimulates and reinvigorates the growth, much like pruning.

In Colleen Elizabeth Rossier's collaborative research with the Karuk, Yurok, and Hupa people (*Revitalizing Evergreen Huckleberries*), Indigenous practitioners monitored thirty animals in evergreen huckleberry patches, including mountain lion, elk, deer, black bear, Pacific fisher, gray fox, ring-tailed cat, dusky-footed woodrat, Douglas tree squirrel, and western ringneck snake.

Dozens of birds, including the acorn woodpecker, pileated woodpecker, quail, and a host of songbirds, shelter in huckleberry habitats. Over fifty mushroom species, including the pine mushroom (matsutake), grow in the evergreen huckle's hood. Evergreen huckleberries are mycorrhizal friendly.

SALAL
Gaultheria shallon

FAMILY: Ericaceae (Heath)
STATUS: Native
OTHER NAMES: Oregon wintergreen, lemon-leaf

A perennial evergreen shrub up to 15 feet tall. May take the form of dense understory mats. Evergreen leaves are glossy and up to 4 inches long, with a leathery texture, lemon-shaped outline, and finely toothed edges. Leaves live 3 to 4 years and grow alternately. Waxy

❓ BERRY GOOD FIRES BRING FRUIT

Huckleberries were far more common when Native people used fire to open and maintain forest clearings. But so many lives were lost after the first terrifying wave of smallpox in 1775, for which Indigenous people had no immunity, that by the 1800s prescribed fires had decreased. A century later, after huge fires such as the Yacolt Burn of 1902, which torched 238,920 acres near Indian Heaven in Washington State, the politics of the time turned to suppressing all fires. Soon forest openings with huckle patches were encroached on by trees. Since 1920, the Yakama Tribe's native berry fields in Klickitat County have "shrunk by about 100 acres per year," according to a study conducted by my botanist friends Joe Arnett and Rex Crawford. The Twin Buttes berrying spots that stretched over twelve thousand acres one hundred years ago are now one-third their original size. Picking areas that were thriving just four generations ago soon may be overgrown with forests.

Thankfully, the Indigenous Karuk, Yurok, and Hupa foresters in California manages their evergreen huckleberry picking areas with brush clearing and low-intensity fires. Low-level fires not only foster berry clearings and improve the soil but also retain the shade of dominant, unburned overstory trees.

pink flowers hang in rows of 5 to 15 like lanterns on a wire and bloom May to July. Oval reddish-blue to purple-black berries about ¾ inch long. Look for a hallmark star-shaped indent on each berry's end.

HARVEST GUIDE

WHAT: Berries, leaves
WHEN: Leaves in early summer (new, soft, and bright green), berries in midsummer (peak)

Snip or pinch off individual soft, young leaves here and there, across a broad area, leaving plenty to mature. Squeeze berries gently to test for ripeness: Hard as an olive? Underripe. Squishy? Overripe. Soft and large? Just-right ripe! Flavors and quality vary depending on location, temperatures, and rain—or lack thereof. Harvest individual berries or whole stalks of berries. At home, you can use scissors to cut multiple berries off stalks.

CULINARY TIPS

Use salal in place of all or half your blueberries in scones, jams, compote, and shrubs (see Blueberry). Leslie of Port Townsend simmers whole stems of berries in

water for hours until it becomes a thick sauce, then strains it and makes a pie filling with garam masala. Cake baker Carl of Bellingham "paints" salal leaves with melted chocolate, chills them to harden, and pulls away the original leaf for decadent garnishes! Lopez Island botanist Madrona Murphy hand crushes, ferments, and dries young leaves for a berry-flavored tea.

Traditionally, salal was a cherished trade item and winter food for Indigenous people. Berries were cooked in bentwood boxes with fire-heated rocks

Salal berries and flowers grow like hanging lanterns on a wire. (Photos by Katherine Palmer)

BERRY LOVERS OR BEAR-Y LOVERS?

Bears in the West that don't have access to salmon may be strongly dependent on summer huckleberries for essential calories to store fat for a long winter's nap. But berries have been getting scarcer. Skinny bears produce fewer cubs. Imagine having only lips and mouth and teeth to remove berries from the bush. Like us, bears can purse their lips to pull fruits free. Imagine being as big as a bear and needing to chow enough huckleberries to gain weight for the whole of winter. How much would you need to eat?

Researchers have found that the number of berries a brown bear can nosh in one minute depends on two things: First, the search time to find berries hidden in the leaves. Second, the time to lip up a berry or berries and chew. Bears and berry pickers know it's easy picking when berries are in dense clusters. But if we berry pickers high-grade and grab the most obvious, eye-poppingly-big clusters, we make it harder for foraging bears. During poor berry years, the repercussions may include the starvation of young bears.

In years when wild berry crops fail, whether from drought or unseasonal deluges that make berries drop earlier or mold, interspecies conflicts may escalate. Rangers in British Columbia's Kokanee Glacier Provincial Park invoke seasonal trail closures in oval-leaved blueberry and blue huckleberry picking areas to lower hiker and grizzly bear run-ins.

What to do? After interviewing dozens of commercial pickers, these same researchers (Christy Welch and her team from Washington, Alaska, and Montana) suggest managing and setting aside some sections of berries in specific geographic areas for human berry pickers and leaving other locations with highly visible berries to the bears. Education is likely the least controversial answer. If everyone learned how bears forage and tried to think like a bear—especially during years of poor berry production—we would be "bear-y lovers" too. Another tasty option is to plant and harvest the many delicious huckles and blueberry varieties from your backyard and community garden to enjoy predictable fruit crops.

and dried like thick jam on racks lined with skunk cabbage leaves. Salal leaves, together with seaweed and other plants, were layered with seafood in earthen pit ovens, providing flavor and moisture. Stems of fresh salal berries were dunked in fish oil at feasts.

SUPERPOWER

Like other "blue" berries, the salal berry is an antioxidant powerhouse. But it outshines them all, even lingonberry (wild cranberry), the bell ringer of antioxidants.

WHO EATS AND SHELTERS HERE?

Black bears lip up salal berries by the whole cluster. Individual berries are munched by songbirds; blue, ruffed and spruce grouse; bandtailed pigeons; and many small animals such as Townsend's chipmunk, red squirrel, and Douglas squirrel. The evergreen foliage and branches are browsed by mule deer, black-tailed deer (who also love the flowers!), elk, and beaver. A host of bumblebees, including the fuzzy-horned and black-tailed bumbles, visit the urn-shaped flowers for nectar. Hummingbirds visit the prolific blooms, too.

The brown elfin butterfly lays one egg each on a single salal flower bud so larvae will have shelter and both flowers and fruit to eat. May to July, bronze and gray butterflies take wing. Racoons, varying hares, Douglas squirrels, spotted towhee, and dark-eyed junco take cover in thickets. For years, I observed racoons on James Island Marine State Park in the San Juan Islands filching campers' toothpaste, energy bars, M&Ms, and, once, a wallet with credit card and driver's license, disappearing into salal thickets never to be seen again—until years later, when I found the entire stash of torn wrappers, complete with stolen credit card.

SASKATOON SERVICEBERRY
Amelanchier alnifolia

FAMILY: Rosaceae (Rose)
STATUS: Native
OTHER NAMES: Pacific serviceberry, western serviceberry, western shadbush, juneberry, Indian pear, shadbush, shadblow (so named because they bloom when shad fish are running)

Shrubby to treelike, up to 20 feet tall. Leaves are oval, sharply toothed on outer half. One of the first bushes to bloom. Clusters of fragrant, apple-like white flowers, about the size of a quarter. Blueberry-like fruits with a white bloom. And they aren't berries! The botanic term is *pome*—serviceberries are kin to pears and apples. Fruits vary in sweetness and size depending on weather, location, and variety. All parts of the plant contain hydrogen cyanide, but it is lowest in the fruit and higher in the buds, flowers, twigs, and leaves.

Southern Alaska to Central California and Sierra Nevada; east to Colorado, the Dakotas, and Nebraska; and British Columbia and Yukon east to Ontario. Several varieties of serviceberry have evolved in a wide range of niches including low-elevation evergreen forests, river corridors, chaparral, mountain shrub areas, and pinyon-juniper communities.

HARVEST GUIDE

WHAT: Berries, leaves

WHEN: Leaves in early spring, berries in June or July to September (depending on elevation, area, and variety)

Pick ripe purple-black berries individually or in small clusters, like you would blueberries. Gather leaves selectively—one by one, here and there—for fruity tea flavor.

CULINARY TIPS

Cultivated since 1980 for making jams, syrups, and raisins in Canada, this firm, sweet berry was traditionally dried by First Nations and Tribes into berry cakes and pemmican—a mix of fat, dried fruit, and dried pulverized meat. The whole berries were also enjoyed fresh and cooked in soups and stews or mashed with soapberries (*Shepherdia canadensis*) to sweeten them for whipping into frothy "Indian ice cream." Dried berries were a common trade item. Serviceberries can be used in place of blueberries for jams, fruit toppings, pastries, and syrups. The seeds have a pleasant almond flavor. (See Blueberry and also Salish Pemmican in Recipes.)

SUPERPOWER

The superhardy Saskatoon serviceberry can survive severe winter temps down to –60 degrees F and live for more than half a century.

WHO EATS AND SHELTERS HERE?

This early-blooming bush provides nectar for butterflies and bees. Starting in early summer, the berries are important food for a long list of songbirds and small mammals, including the robin, evening grosbeak, western tanager, sage thrasher, mantled ground squirrel, dusky-footed wood rat, and northwest chipmunk. Upland game birds,

Saskatoon serviceberry leaves resemble sporks. (Photos by Grace Meyer)

such as the sharp-tailed and blue grouse, gobble buds and fruit. During spring and deep snows, mountain goats and bighorn sheep depend on twig browse. Elk, bison, moose, and deer eat leaves and twigs. Black bear, marmots, varying hares, and beavers seek out every part—fruit, twigs, leaves, and bark.

Bison take cover in wooded draws where serviceberry grows. Butterflies and moths such as the California hairstreak, two-tailed swallowtail, and Ceanothus silkmoth lay eggs on this host. Small mammals and birds shelter in the leaves and branches.

NOOTKA ROSE
Rosa nutkana

FAMILY: Rosaceae (Rose)
STATUS: Native
OTHER NAMES: Wild rose, k'inchéiyi (Lingít for "rose hips")

Nootka rose can shoot up 10 feet and form dense thickets. Leaves are toothed, ½ inch to 2¾ inches long, compound, and odd in number (5 to 7), with rounded tips and double prickles at the leaf base. Flowers grow at branch tips and are aromatic, 3-inch-wide blooms with 5 pale-pink to flamingo-pink petals and a yellow crown of stamens. Rose fruits, called hips or haws, form at the base of the flower.

Alaska to mid-California and east to Utah and Colorado. Thrives as a solitary loner or in gregarious hedges along roadsides, coastal marshes, prairies, and streams; likes clearings in redwood and mixed evergreen forests, sea level to 2,300 feet.

Nootka rose and rose hips

HARVEST GUIDE

WHAT: Shoots, leaves, petals, fruits

WHEN: Tender shoots in spring, leaves from March to October, petals from April through July, fruits from August to late fall

Gather shoots by snapping them at their base. If they don't snap crisply, but bend, they are too advanced and woody. Leave them to grow. Peel outer skin off shoots and eat raw. Cut leaves shortly after they appear for best flavor—taking just 5 percent from many bushes. Pick two or three petals by hand, leaving three remaining petals for pollinators to zero in on. Hips are sweeter after a hard frost. Snap them off by hand.

Note that other native roses are used in the same way: prickly rose (*Rosa acicularis*), California wild rose (*R. californica*), Woods' rose (*R. woodsii*), clustered wild rose (*R. pisocarpa*), and baldhip or dwarf rose (*R. gymnocarpa*).

CULINARY TIPS

Ripe rose hips taste tangy and fruity, akin to cranberry, apricot, or a sweet cherry tomato. I freeze them whole until needed. To avoid the labor-intensive job of removing the fruit's core, simmer a few handfuls of hips in a saucepan with water, mash into a sauce, then pour the gorgeous red liquid through a fine strainer to catch the culprit rose hip hairs. Whisk in warm water, arrowroot, and honey. Stir until thickened. And abracadabra—nectar of the gods.

Use rose hips to make chilled fruit soups, harissa for fowl or pork, chutney, sorbet, sauce for ice cream sundaes, conserves, syrup, pastry filling, tarts, applesauce, pudding, fruit leather, and tea. ❗ Eating hips whole off the bush can irritate your mouth and digestive tract due to the fiberglass-like hairs in the seed capsule.

From the petals, make rose water (rose essence) or syrup to flavor lemonade, champagne vinegar, cordials, baklava, strawberry shortcake, crème brûlée, panna cotta, scones, shortbread, ice cream, and frosting. Pulverize petals for pesto, pâtés, and flavoring butter. Use whole petals for savory dishes such as rose-scented Indian rice and for garnishing fish, or freeze petals or whole roses into ice cube trays or punch bowl ice rings.

Indigenous people ate peeled tender shoots of wild rose with salmon roe or fish oil. Today they are dipped in sugar and munched like juicy candy sticks. The leaves make an aromatic tea.

WHO EATS AND SHELTERS HERE?

Nootka rose hips are called "deer candy," but elk, moose, caribou, bears, big horn sheep, and coyotes all love to nosh the hips. Juncos, grosbeaks, thrushes, bluebirds, grouse, quail, and pheasants also eat the fruits, as do a host of insects. Twigs and leaves are chomped by porcupines, squirrels, mice, chipmunks, beavers, and long-horned beetles, as well as big animals such as bear, deer, and elk. The mourning

WILD ROSE—NECTAR OF THE GODS

My first memory of quaffing roses was downing a fragrant rose petal lemonade from the Ukrainian food booth at Milwaukee's International Folk Festival. "Nectar of the gods," my father said, kneeling down to clink his pink glass with mine.

My buddy Mac spent his childhood knocking around the oak savannahs of California, where roses reach for the sun year-round. Outside his mother's door grew a behemoth twelve-foot-tall climbing rose that produced strawberry-sized rose hips. Curious, Mac ate one. It tasted both sweet and tart like crab apple. "I collected a bucketful and cut them open. The seeds were protected by tiny hairs as sharp as fiberglass," he lamented. "I tried to wash them out of the hips, but the itchy fibers caught in my fingers. Today I scrub them with a vegetable brush." Mac simmers the cleaned hips in a saucepan with water, allspice, cloves, and honey, then bottles it up.

Not all rose hips are equal. Nootka roses grow the biggest fruit of native coastal species—thumb width. Dwarf rose hips make a petite hip—pinky finger width. The introduced European species *Rosa rugosa*, also called Sitka rose, which grows "wildly" across the West, has hips the size of cherry tomatoes that can pack in 2,500 milligrams of vitamin C per 100-gram serving.

Rose hips contain a storehouse of other health benefits. Besides vitamins C, A, B, K, and E, they are rich in the minerals iron and calcium and essential fatty acids. The seeds and outer red rind contain both lutein and zeaxanthin (two antioxidant carotenoids), which protect the macula from absorbing blue light. Danish researchers studying rose hips tracked participants who consumed a daily standardized dose of rose hip powder for three to four months. Participants reduced their joint pain and stiffness enough to lower their daily pain medication.

Roses have long been used by Indigenous people to treat infections too. The *International Journal of Food Sciences and Nutrition* reported three species of wild roses in British Columbia with high antioxidants and antimicrobial powers that tackle yeast and staph infections. Western science is only beginning to understand what Indigenous science has already proven. As my friends who are traditional plant teachers love to say, "Our food is our medicine."

Some coastal First Nation communities honored the rose in dances. Women sewed the blossoms of rose, blueberry, salmonberry, and rice root into their ceremonial clothing to welcome the first spring flowers. Fishermen swabbed nets with rose branches for good luck. In steam cooking pits, aromatic rose leaves were layered around roots to give them flavor. Mixed with salmon roe, rose hips made a tasty dish.

Today, my grandson Rowan and I grind sugar and wild rose petals into flamingo-pink paste and stir it into lemonade (see Rose Petal Lemonade in Recipes). Roses are one of those rare flowers, like English lavender, that taste as intriguing as they look and smell.

Before eating rose hips, remove the fiberglass-like hairs around the seeds.

cloak butterfly loves to nibble the leaves, while the monarch butterfly, bees, and other pollinators lap up pollen.

This rose is a hardware store for native leafcutter bees, who nip off petal and leaf pieces for nesting partitions. The appropriately named carpenter bee searches for broken-off stems, digs out the pith, and makes a cozy nest! Birds and small animals, including otters, rabbits, voles, and mice, hide in the protective thickets.

SITKA ROSE
Rosa rugosa

FAMILY: Rosaceae (Rose)
STATUS: Introduced
OTHER NAMES: Rugosa rose, beach tomato, sea tomato, sand rose, saltspray rose, Japanese rose

Bristly branches grow into dense thickets up to 6 feet tall. Serrated leaves are a glossy dark green. Flowers are 5 to 10 petaled and pink or white. Sitka rose is famous for its large and luscious tomato-like hips, or haws. After the petals fall off, the hips swell into bright-orange to red globes with whiskery brown sepals. A tangy rind surrounds a core of white seeds and minute hairs.

Sitka rose is native to Asia and eastern Russia, where it grows within 100 miles of the Arctic Circle. Nearly 10,000 years ago, it was cultivated in China for perfume. It is a common cultivated rose for making preserves, jelly, wine, and pharmaceuticals and for use as a garden ornamental. Sand and salt tolerant, Sitka rose is planted along coastal beaches and sand dunes to reduce erosion. It is naturalized across the US, Canada, and Europe and is a problematic weed in Scandinavia.

HARVEST GUIDE

WHAT: Leaves, petals, fruits

WHEN: Leaves from March to October, petals from April to August, fruits (best when bright red) from August to October and sometimes into winter

See Nootka Rose. While transporting it, avoid casually dropping (and spreading) the seedy rose hips of this introduced species.

CULINARY TIPS

See Nootka Rose. Sitka rose is eaten much the same.

Eating hips whole off the bush can irritate your mouth and digestive tract due to the fiberglass-like hairs in the seed capsule. **❗**

SUPERPOWER

Recent studies suggest the phytochemicals in Sitka rose may slow or halt some cancers. Sitka rose is super tolerant of drought, frost, heat, salt, mowing, and fire; it can be problematic if you want to get rid of it.

WHO EATS AND SHELTERS HERE?

Sitka rose offers the gift of pollen for bees and other insects. White-tailed deer and cotton-tailed rabbits munch its leaves, as do leafhoppers, aphids, scarab beetles, and a host of larvae laid by moths and gall wasps. Hips are eaten like ripe tomatoes by ruffed grouse, bobwhite quail, songbirds, and mice, including the deer mouse and the white-footed mouse.

Native leafcutter bees cart petal and leaf pieces away to use for walls in their nests. The little carpenter bee may gather broken stems, remove the pith, and create a nest. Grouse, pheasants, and small animals hide in its protective thickets.

TOP: *Sitka rose blooms in magenta or white.* (Photo by Monika Becker)
BOTTOM: *Sitka rose hip*

ROSE PETAL COCOA

A romantic sip for one or two on a winter night, this cocoa is made of fairytales. Sweet, creamy, warm, and perfumed, it casts a spell over your words. In a favorite mug, stir three to four tablespoons hot cocoa mix, one teaspoon ground rose petals, and one cup hot water. Cover and let steep for ten minutes. Strain if you prefer. Inhale the bouquet of floral flavor!

SALMONBERRY
Rubus spectabilis

FAMILY: Rosaceae (Rose)
STATUS: Native
OTHER NAMES: Muck-a-muck

This raspberry-like shrub thrives in dense thickets up to 12 feet tall. During spring, succulent shoots sprout from the rootstock. By fall, the new canes can span 6 feet and don a coat of rusty-brown bark with prickles. Star-shaped magenta blooms have 5 pointed petals and yellow stamens and appear before leaves fully open. Leaves grow on alternate sides of a zigzag stalk in clusters of 3, with pointed tips, round bases, and toothed edges. The bottom 2 opposite leaves often form a "butterfly" pattern. The large, raspberry-like berries range in color from salmon-roe orange to ruby, carnelian, and plum.

    Alaska to California. Look for thickets of salmonberry in moist open forests, wetlands, and floodplains; along seashores, streams, and lakes; and on subalpine slopes.

HARVEST GUIDE

WHAT: Berries, flowers, leaves, shoots
WHEN: Fruit from May to July (later in cooler locations), flowers from late spring to summer, shoots and leaves in spring
As with thimbleberries (next entry), it is easiest to pick and eat these delicate berries right off the bush as a trailside snack. They are challenging to transport without crushing. When harvesting blossoms, keep in mind that these are future berries. Best practices are to pick individual petals, leaving half on each flower for the bees to visit. Petals guide bees like roads guide us. Use a knife or scissors to cut leaves for tea. Avoid

LEFT: *Salmonberries* (Photo by Katherine Palmer); RIGHT: *Magenta blooms appear before the bushes grow leaves.*

making tea from wilted leaves, as they contain toxins: use dry or fresh leaves only. (See the "Cuppa Berry Leaves Tea" sidebar below.)

CULINARY TIPS

Sprinkle fresh berries on salads, pancakes, ice cream, and crème brûlée. Simmer into a tangy wild berry sauce for drizzling over halibut. Make tea from fresh-picked or bone-dry leaves. Scatter a few pink salmonberry blossoms on salad greens or fresh pasta or freeze in ice cubes. Shoots, a traditional food of many Indigenous people, can be peeled and eaten raw as a vegetable or steamed like asparagus.

WHO EATS AND SHELTERS HERE?

Grizzly bears eat so many salmonberries that one pile of bear scat can have 50,000 to 100,000 salmonberry seeds, becoming a "seed bar" for rodents and birds. Pacific martens, foxes, opossums, skunks, racoons, coyote, chipmunks, squirrels, voles, mice, banana slugs, and dozens of species of songbirds nibble berries. One study found songbirds eat more red salmonberries than orange-colored ones, possibly because they are mistaken for thimbleberry—a preferred fruit. Rufous hummingbirds follow the wave of red salmonberry blooms northward during migration. Swainson's thrush love salmonberries and arrive in greater numbers along migration routes as the berries ripen. Called "salmonberry bird" by some Coast Salish people, they are said to sing the berries into ripeness.

Birds and small mammals escape into dense salmonberry brush to avoid predators. Songbirds choose them for nesting sites. Native bees also use salmonberry leaves and stems for nesting and shelter. Mountain beavers and ruffed grouse build homes in salmonberry thickets as well. Salmonberries shade salmon streams, keep waters cool, and provide leaf material for insects, which feed young salmon. In turn, salmon carcasses along stream banks feed salmonberry bushes.

THIMBLEBERRY
Rubus parviflorus

FAMILY: Rosaceae (Rose)
STATUS: Native
OTHER NAMES: Western thimbleberry, white-flowering raspberry

Thimbleberry bushes grow in 2- to 9-foot-tall thickets. The felt-soft, maple-shaped leaves are the size of a hand. Roselike blooms are the size of a silver dollar, with 5 white to pink round petals, as thin as tissue paper, growing in clusters of up to a half dozen. The raspberry-like fruits are red, soft, and squat. Both ripe and unripe fruit, as well as blossoms, can appear at the same time on a single bush.

Alaska to California. Often grows alongside salmonberry on subalpine slopes; along seashores, streams, and lakes; and in moist open forests, wetlands, and floodplains.

HARVEST GUIDE
WHAT: Berries, leaves, shoots
WHEN: Berries from July to August, shoots and leaves from late spring to summer
To harvest thimbleberries, see Salmonberry.

LEFT: *Thimbleberry bloom;* **RIGHT:** *The fruit is best right off the bush.* (Photos by Katherine Palmer)

RAMBLING WITH BRAMBLEBERRIES

The first time I kayaked alone through the Great Bear Rainforest in northern British Columbia, the fjord walls seemed to stretch for an infinite distance and height. Finally, near dark, desperate for a level campsite, I scrabbled up a barnacled rock face and tied my kayak and tent to an overhanging tree.

When I woke at first light, stomach growling, lying in my sleeping bag, I realized that I was below a ceiling of delicate, toothed leaves dappled with raspberry-sized fruit. I sat up and stuffed handfuls into my mouth.

Brambleberries are succulent, beadlike berries that hide inside a thicket of prickly canes. They are worth a few scratches and nicks. Even the sun-warmed Himalayan blackberries—with thumb-sized canes and chainsaw thorns—are worth a round of negotiating. But an even more delicious blackberry hides underfoot. The native trailing blackberry produces the Northwest's most flavorful berry by a long shot. Next time you trip over its modest, bristly canes, poke around for an exquisite treasure—an elongated

Thimbleberry and salmonberry shoots can be peeled for trail snacks.

blackberry with a wine-like complexity. But not all brambleberries arm themselves. The delicate and thornless thimbleberry has velveteen leaves soft enough for dinner napkins.

Salmonberry flavors vary from sweet to insipid, season to season, depending on rainfall and temperature. When ripe, they plump up with juice and pull free from the stem easily. Salmonberry seeds are relatively large for the *Rubus* genus and make better jellies than seedy jams.

I believe the best berries are enjoyed fresh and ripe off the bush. In Coast Salish territory, a good part of June is called "Moon of the Salmonberry." For a couple of blissful weeks each June and July, my husband and I pick our way down our forested drive to get the morning paper, all while a song from a Swainson's thrush in the tall cedars above plays on repeat. If I could, I would swim up that river of song and fall asleep in the eddy of the thrush's folded wing, my stomach full of berries.

CULINARY TIPS

Thimbleberry is often considered tastier in its eastern range than in its western range or where there is more rainfall. A perfectly ripe, juicy thimbleberry is like a velvety raspberry. Tuck these gems into crepes, or blend them with other berries into a fruit soup with almonds and cream. Reduce into a wild-garden berry syrup for grilled prawns, scallops, fish, pork loin, wild game, and fowl. Mix wild and cultivated berries in jams, tarts, pies, crisps, and salads. The shoots are a traditional food of Pacific Coast First Nations. Peel and eat the vitamin C–rich shoots raw or steamed like asparagus.

WHO EATS AND SHELTERS HERE?

Mule and white-tailed deer, moose, elk, and rabbits in logged areas, burn sites, and forests relish thimbleberries. For American black bear, thimbleberry fruits and shoots are a major food source, with the foliage being the most nutritious in midsummer. Twice, in spring, I've seen black bears eating blossoms on the Inside Passage. Squirrels, opossums, woodrats, chipmunks, American martens, coyote, foxes, skunks, raccoons, and voles eat the fruits, as do Pacific jumping mice, Townsend's chipmunk, deer mice, and dusky-footed woodrats. One researcher found a chipmunk that had about four hundred thimbleberry seeds in a single cheek pouch!

Thimbleberry shoot

Thimbleberry fruits average just two days on parent plants before being taken by birds. They are so important to North American birds that they may constitute 10 to 25 percent of diets. A study on Vancouver Island found American robins, northwestern crossbills, and Swainson's thrush are some of the birds that visit thimbleberry. The brambles are choice summer nibbles for cedar waxwings, grosbeaks, towhees, and sparrows. Pikas nibble vegetation. Dozens of bumblebee and other bee species visit blooms.

❓ HOW THIMBLEBERRY CAME TO BE A PHOENIX

Our wild raspberry-like thimbles are pretty good at recovering rapidly after a fire. High-temperature scorching fires that penetrate down into the mineral soil can be tough on these plants, but lighter fires only top-kill these hardy shrubs. Thimbleberry sprouts arrow up from surviving rhizomes, specialized roots made for just that. An example close to my home was the Whatcom Creek Fire, caused by a gas pipeline leak and explosion in beautiful, forested Whatcom Falls Park. The flames reached 148 feet tall (measured by blackened trees) but burned out in fifteen minutes due to the damp springtime forest.

The following June, as our community gathered to mourn and honor the death of two young boys and a high school senior that tragic day, thimbleberry sprouts lined the creek. They shone like bud-green candles all along the waterway. Thimbleberry seeds, however, like the seeds of our future—those three lost boys—cannot survive an intense fire. It is a lesson not lost on me today.

The multibranched bushes with large, broad leaves provide safe spots for small mammals and birds, including rabbits, squirrels, beavers and songbirds. Black bears also are reported to find cover in dense thickets. Yellow-banded sphinx moths lay their eggs on its foliage.

WILD RASPBERRY
Rubus idaeus

FAMILY: Rosaceae (Rose)
STATUS: Native
OTHER NAMES: Red raspberry, black-haired red raspberry, smoothleaf red raspberry, American red raspberry, brilliant red raspberry

The red, sweet, cap-shaped fruit has a dull sheen over a beaded surface and is generally more petite than the domestic raspberry. Plants can grow to 6 feet tall. Kelly-green leaves are oval to egg shaped, toothed, and woolly gray below; usually found in clusters of 3 but sometimes 5. Flowers bloom from May to August, depending on location. Quarter-sized white blooms with 5 oblong petals and up to 100 stamens grow in forked clusters.

Alaska to California, many western states, Minnesota, and Michigan. Wet to drier locations in mid-elevation mountain forests to subalpine zones.

HARVEST GUIDE

WHAT: Berries, leaves
WHEN: Leaves from spring to summer, berries from midsummer to late summer
To harvest, see Salmonberry.

CULINARY TIPS

See Thimbleberry and Salmonberry.

WHO EATS AND SHELTERS HERE?

Mountain beaver and bears eat wild raspberry berries and stems. Many songbirds eat the berries, including cedar waxwing, robin, Steller's jay, California jay, mockingbird, Bullock's oriole, fox sparrow, song sparrow, white-crowned sparrow, western tanager, California thrasher, sage thrasher, hermit thrush, varied thrush, brown towhee, spotted towhee, and wrentit. Small mammals including chipmunk, Douglas squirrel, and Portola wood rat nibble the berries. Black-tailed deer and elk browse stems and leaves.

Thorny, impenetrable thickets provide essential protective cover for a great variety of nesting birds, foraging birds, and small animals, including grazing rabbits, chipmunks, and squirrels.

Wild red raspberries provide cover and food for little critters. (Photos by Akchamczuk and Jennifer Seeman, iStock)

BLACKCAP RASPBERRY
Rubus leucodermis

FAMILY: Rosaceae (Rose)
STATUS: Native
OTHER NAMES: Blue raspberry, blackcap, whitebark raspberry, western black raspberry

Canes show a white to blue waxy bloom over red bark and are armored with recurved, flat spines and prickles. Up to 6 feet tall, arching to upright. Tips of first-year canes often arch down and take root. Leaves with 5 leaflets in first years, then 3 leaflets on flowering branches. White to pink flowers in clusters of 3 to 7. Fruit begins red and ripens to blue-black. Fruits summer to fall depending on location.

Southern Alaska to California, east to Utah and Montana, south to the state of New Mexico and Mexico. Blackcap raspberry thrives in open, dry, or moist woods; along stream banks; in disturbed sites; and on talus mountain slopes.

HARVEST GUIDE
WHAT: Berries, leaves
WHEN: Berries from July to September, leaves from spring to summer
Blackcaps are well armored with stout thorns. Pick carefully to avoid giving a blood sacrifice! Cut leaves off with a knife or scissors here and there. Leaves can be used for tea when dry or fresh, but not wilted.

CUPPA BERRY LEAVES TEA

I learned this beautiful tea tonic from my "Seaweed Sisters," Elise Krohn and Elizabeth Campbell, who teach traditional foods workshops for First Nations and Tribes across the Pacific Northwest. It is easy and fun to make with kids, big and little! Gather a variety of berry leaves: salmonberry, thimbleberry, huckleberry, trailing blackberry, Himalayan blackberry, blueberry, and strawberry. Add a large handful of leaves to a teapot or small saucepan and pour boiling water over all. Cover and steep overnight for a surprisingly berry-flavored tea! Always use either fresh or completely dried raspberry and blackberry leaves. Wilted leaves contain toxins.

LEFT: *Blackcap raspberry fruit;* RIGHT: *Canes feature a white to blue waxy bloom.*

CULINARY TIPS

See Thimbleberry and Salmonberry. But tip your hat to the blackcap (as well as all the other blue-colored berries) for providing a big, healthy serving of anthocyanins. They may not sound delicious, but these deep-blue, purple, and red pigments packed in blue-colored berries are part of a bigger group of plant-derived chemicals we call flavonoids. Studies show flavonoids help shield plant leaves, flowers, fruits, and seeds from stressors, including drought, ultraviolet light, and cold.

What do they do for humans? Epidemiological studies—which look at the causes and controls of diseases—suggest that eating foods rich in anthocyanins may lower the risk of cardiovascular disease, oxidative stress, and diabetes. Black and blue is good for you!

WHO EATS AND SHELTERS HERE?

Blackcaps often proliferate in clearcuts, providing a huge source of nectar for bumblebees and other pollinators. In the Oregon Coast Range, the spring flowers are a magnet for pollinators. Of the ninety-six pollinators reported, eighty were bee species, including native bumblebees. Quail, grouse, towhees, and cedar waxwings as well as opossums, foxes, and racoons, among others, eat the berries.

Heavily barbed canes serve as no-entrance bars that keep out predators and give sanctuary to birds, rabbits, and a host of small animals.

TRAILING BLACKBERRY
Rubus ursinus

FAMILY: Rosaceae (Rose)
STATUS: Native
OTHER NAMES: California blackberry, native blackberry, dewberry, Douglasberry, wild mountain blackberry, trailing Pacific blackberry, western blackberry

This vinelike bramble crawls, climbs, winds, and explores the top 6 inches of its turf for 20 feet in all directions. Canes are as slim as a phone charging cord, light green with a smoky patina when new, and brown with age. Minute thorns break off easily and can puncture but not tear your skin. Canes take root at both ends. Leaves are serrated and pointed in clusters of 3, green above, pale and prickly below, and widely spaced on the cane. Flowers are white and daisy-like with 6 narrow petals. Plants have either male or female flowers. Only the smaller female blooms beget fruit. The oblong, shiny, firm blackberries can be smaller than a pinky fingertip but pack in more flavor than the larger Himalayan blackberry.

British Columbia to Baja California, in mixed evergreen forests, chaparral, burned areas, open to dense woods, clearcuts, along riverbanks with fresh or brackish water, and entwined and under Himalayan blackberry.

HARVEST GUIDE

WHAT: Berries, leaves
WHEN: Fruit from July to August
Pick individual berries by hand. Look low under leafy mats. For tea, cut young leaves across a large area for best flavor. When making tea, use only fresh or bone-dry leaves. Wilted leaves contain toxins. (See the "Cuppa Berry Leaves Tea" sidebar earlier.)

❓ SEEDING PATIENCE

Trailing blackberry can quickly repopulate to carpet burned areas in the Pacific Northwest by sprouting and seeds. Their seed banks accumulate over many years, and even after a mature forest moves in over the top of them, they sleep below, waiting. Their gift is to germinate in huge numbers after a fire and provide succulent fruit for many animals and birds, who carry their seeds even farther as a way of thanks. This is positive news for berry pickers of all kinds as forest fires increase. That said, as to how hot of a fire the sleeping seed banks can weather, I am unsure.

LEFT: *Trailing blackberry has male and female flowers* RIGHT: *Trailing blackberry fruit* (Photos by Katherine Palmer)

CULINARY TIPS
See Himalayan Blackberry.

WHO EATS AND SHELTERS HERE?
Pileated woodpecker, Steller's jay, common raven, cedar waxwing, western tanager, black-headed grosbeak, purple finch, Swainson's thrush, pine grosbeak, California quail, ruffed grouse, and more can be found here. Mammals such as the black bear, coyote, fox, raccoon, skunk, opossum, squirrel, and chipmunk also eat these berries. Black-tailed deer feed heavily on the foliage in fall and winter until snow blankets their browse. Blackberry foliage supplies almost 50 percent of a deer's early-winter diet in Douglas-fir forests in Oregon. In spring, when other plants are still dormant, new leaves help deer prevent malnourishment. California elk munch the foliage, and it's a now-and-then nibble for mountain beaver, porcupines, and rabbits. The black-tailed bumblebee, spotless lady beetle, and a host of other insects seek the nectar and pollen.

The tangly, dense thickets are common nesting sites for wrentits, towhees, tanagers, jays, thrashers, pigeons, song sparrows, and northern mockingbirds. In California, the endangered least Bell's vireo often weaves its nest in the thickets along creeks and rivers. Even black bears take cover in trailing blackberry thickets, as do beavers, rabbits, and red squirrels.

HIMALAYAN BLACKBERRY
Rubus armeniacus (R. discolor, R. procerus)

FAMILY: Rosaceae (Rose)
STATUS: Introduced, invasive weed
OTHER NAMES: Himalayan giant blackberry, elm-leaf blackberry, Armenian blackberry

A stout-framed intruder with boldly aggressive armor and genetic wiring. Hefty canes can shoot 40 feet in 2 growing seasons. Canes can root at both ends. Alas, you can accidentally rip the humble trailing blackberries with your caught boot—not so for the Himalayans, which can rip *you!* Leaves are dark green above, white to silver and thorny below.

First-year canes bear compound leaves (oval, toothed, palmate) with 5 leaflets; second-year canes grow only 3 leaflets and berries. Flowers are prolific clusters (5 to 20 blossoms). Each flower makes a rosette with 6 white to pink petals. Robust, shiny, beaded blackberries are the size of your thumb tip and deliciously sweet and tangy.

HARVEST GUIDE
WHAT: Berries, leaves
WHEN: Berries from August to September, leaves in spring
Leaves can be harvested for tea soon after buds open. Harvest carefully to avoid thorns. Clip leaves with scissors into a paper bag. When making tea, use only fresh or bone-dry leaves; wilted leaves contain toxins. Berries are plentiful and tasty; pick them one by one or by the hundreds.

CULINARY TIPS
Blackberries are fabulous in crisps, pies, and tarts. Try a blackberry and apple pie, a galette with blueberries and blackberries, a rustic tart with blackberries and thyme,

LEFT: *Himalayan blackberry fruit;* **RIGHT:** *Himalayan blackberry flowers* (Photo by Katherine Palmer)

⬡ A TERRIBLY DELICIOUS BULLY

This voluptuous villain—the fruit of the Himalayan black-berry—is robbing us of native species by the score. One berry thicket can produce up to thirteen thousand seeds in one square meter! Seeds remain fertile for years. Saw-tooth canes sprout at both ends and grow eighteen feet in each direction. The thickets shade out native tree seedlings, including Douglas-fir, Pacific madrone, Garry oak, and ponderosa pine. Deer and other large mammals can't penetrate the brambles. Along rivers, it accelerates erosion.

Don't casually compost seeds after you strain your jelly juice or cordial. Put seeds in plastic in the garbage or burn them. ⬡

strawberry-blackberry lemon shortcake with cashew cream, pear marzipan tart topped with a dozen juicy blackberries, and blackberry-raspberry cheesecake bars. Blackberries go swimmingly with nectarines and peaches, too. For a cooling refreshment, plunk blackberries in a margarita or churn blackberry frozen yogurt or blackberry-ginger sorbet. For a savory approach, try blackberry-rosemary sauce drizzled over lamb or halibut, or ribs slathered with blackberry BBQ sauce. Go lighter with mixed salad greens crowned with blackberries, strawberries, pickled beets, red onion slivers, goat cheese, and balsamic reduction. A simple breakfast parfait of yogurt, berries, and granola is delicious. Though lovely in jellies, Himalayan blackberries make too-seedy a jam for some jam lovers.

Freeze your summer stash of berries and you can enjoy desserts like Blackberry-Peach Crisp (see Recipes) anytime. On a parchment-paper-covered sheet pan, spread berries, freeze, and then transfer them to resealable plastic bags to return to the freezer. For most recipes, you can use the frozen berries without even defrosting them!

WHO EATS AND SHELTERS HERE?

Coyotes, fox, bear, and songbirds gobble berries and disperse seeds far and wide. In urban areas, thickets of Himalayan blackberries are often a home (and snack bar) for Remy-the-rat outcasts from the film *Ratatouille*. Bunnies, opossum, and other small mammals hide out here too.

OREGON-GRAPE
Berberis spp.

FAMILY: Berberidaceae (Barberry)
STATUS: Native
OTHER NAMES: Tall Oregon-grape, wild Oregon-grape (*B. aquifolium*);
dull Oregon-grape, dwarf Oregon-grape (*B. nervosa*); barberry

Spiny, leathery evergreen leaflets arranged in 2 neat rows on opposite sides of a wiry stem lead to confusion with holly, which has spikier, waxier, often deeply lobed leaves. Oregon-grape leaflets are compound leaves and lie flat on a single plane. They can persist for years. Spring flowers are fragrant and lemon yellow, erupting from center spikes. Oval blue berries with a white bloom, ¼ to ½ inch around, grow in clusters and contain 3 to 9 large seeds. Tall Oregon-grape can rise to 8 feet and sprout multiple skinny, erect trunks. The branches have 5 to 7 leaflets. Dull Oregon-grape, the smaller of the two, has more leaflets (9 to 15) and is shaped like a 2-foot-tall bouquet on a sticklike trunk. Both root and bark are yellow and contain berberine, a powerful alkaloid.

Western North America from Southeast Alaska to Northern California (but not on Haida Gwaii). Look for tall Oregon-grape in dry, rocky, open areas, and dull Oregon-grape from sunny forests to shaded evergreen rainforests.

HARVEST GUIDE
WHAT: Berries, leaves
WHEN: Leaves in late spring to early summer, berries from summer to fall
Use your fingers to rake the berries into a container, or use garden shears to cut non-woody berry stems into a bag. Harvest just one or two new leaflets (bright green and supple) from any one branch.

CULINARY TIPS
Sorbets, ices, conserves, and wine transform into deeply flavorful treats with Oregon-grape berry juice mixed in. Try combining Oregon-grape in jelly with sweeter berries, such as dwarf huckleberry and blueberry. Mixed with a sweetener, the juice has a concentrated, robust grape flavor. The taste of new leaves as soft as rose petals reminds me of garden sorrel. Add to salads or pesto for a lemony lift. Try a splash of Oregon-Grape Infused Water (see Recipes) for a refreshing boost on a hot day!

🛑 Large doses and frequent consumption of Oregon-grape can cause diarrhea, nausea, and vomiting; kidney inflammation and irritation; liver toxicity; and allergic

LEFT: *Tall Oregon-grape*; MIDDLE AND RIGHT: *dull Oregon-grape fruit and foliage*

reactions. Pregnant women should not use any part of the plant because it is a uterine stimulant.

WHO EATS AND SHELTERS HERE?

Roosevelt elk browse the branches and leaves in winter. Black-tailed deer munch Oregon-grape into indiscriminate topiary in some areas and largely ignore it in others. Oregon-grape makes up to one-third of the winter diet of the white-footed vole, which relies on it only a little less by summer. Cedar waxwing and ruffed grouse eat the berries. Anna's hummingbirds and painted lady butterflies seek the flower nectar, and barberry loopers eat the leaves.

In the Pacific Northwest, many Douglas-fir and western hemlock forests with mixed understories of Oregon-grape and salal stay relatively snow-free and are important wintering sites for elk and deer. Small animals and birds find cover from predators in the brush.

WILD GRAPES IN THE WOODS

Oregon's state flower is Oregon-grape (*Berberis* spp., formerly *Mahonia* spp.), so it's no surprise that the home of the state governor is called Mahonia Hall. If you aren't familiar with this evergreen shrub, which bears a pleasant lemon-colored flower you can nibble in spring, it is worth introducing yourself. Oregon-grape has wonderful attributes from yellow root to yellow crown.

The evergreen leaves are commonly used in floral arrangements because they last and last, but one of the loveliest things about the leaves is that they're edible—and not just palatable but delicious. Those prickly, leathery evergreen leaves can be soft as chard if you time it right. In the western Cascades, where I live, that means late spring to early summer, when the new leaves begin to unfurl. The first cue is a yellow to light-green leaf that is cat's-eye shiny—as if shellacked. The second cue is the touch. It doesn't get more tender than this—soft, smooth, and a tad succulent. I chew one, and soon I want to chew the leaves off the whole branch because they taste like lemon drops or garden sorrel. Within a week or so, it's all over. The innocent spikes armoring the leaf edges turn sharp enough to prickle tongue and throat.

The pea-sized midnight-blue berries with a lovely white bloom, like a Concord grape, have tempted me to pop one in my craw too early. An extremely sour, almost bitter, astringency prompts my tongue to retreat. Yet, interestingly, the tartness has grown on me. After the first frosts, I find that sour juiciness just right. Traditionally, some Coastal First Nations people mashed and cooked Oregon-grape with sweet salal and huckle-berries in bentwood boxes—heated with rocks—then dried them into cakes. A gorgeous yellow dye that glows like sunshine is still made from the shredded, boiled roots.

That same brilliant yellow is the color of berberine, an alkaloid isolated from the plant itself that has long been recognized for its medicinal properties. Oregon-grape, along with its cousins, may be one of the most promising chemical factories for berberine in the world. Scientific studies show berberine has promising antitumor, anti-inflammation, and antibacterial properties—including fighting the resistant *Staphylococcus aureus*. Berberine is also a novel cholesterol-lowering drug. It is used for its glucose-lowering effects and for stimulating insulin secretion. In some traditional herbalist regimes, the saying goes "like treats like." Oregon-grape root shares the same yellow color as bile and is used to make liver tonics. This is a powerful herb. The root should be used with deference, not casually. Pregnant women should not use any part of the plant because berberine is a uterine stimulant. ❗

Tall Oregon-grape is a common landscape plant in parks, greenways, parking lots, and even the US-Canada border-crossing gardens. During the pandemic, when I was looking for inspiring ways to give back to nature with my wild-food students, we planted twenty wild berry bushes in our forest. It's been years now and the so-called

Soft new leaves of Oregon-grape have a lemony flavor. (Photo by Katherine Palmer)

tall Oregon-grapes still resemble scraggly Charlie Brown Christmas trees. Oregon-grape grows slowly. Note to self: Buy bigger bushes! Don't be a cheapskate with a wild landscape, especially if you hunger to harvest!

I gathered one cup of beautiful berries, each with a bloom (like a light dusting) enrobing their jay-blue, elongated fruit, before tucking them safely into our chest freezer beside bulging bags of garden-grown black currants, U-pick blueberries, Montmorency pie cherries from my backyard orchard, a quart of salal, and a gallon of Himalayan blackberries.

As Thanksgiving approached, I selected a one-to-two ratio of wild to cultivated berries from the frozen goods. I simmered salal, Oregon-grape, blueberries, and black currants with a bit of water. When the berries popped, I squished the juicy, steaming ambrosia with a potato masher, then nudged the sludge through a sieve. Drip, drip, drip. I didn't want to miss a drop of that tart reddish-purple elixir. At that point I could have run in twelve directions: fruit soup, compote, sorbet, shrub, sauce for wild game, pie, fruit leather, liqueur, berry applesauce, wine, syrup, or my favorite mixture—Oregon grape, salal, and garden-berry jelly.

The bubbling jelly released an aroma like luscious, fresh-stomped wine grapes. A test run on toast emitted a surprisingly complex flavor—a blend of fruit-forward sweetness with a lingering tang—reminiscent of the Montmorency pie cherries I left in the freezer. That flavorful jelly elevated a simple PB&J sandwich to haute cuisine. It was so marvelous I had to share it immediately with friends, neighbors, and the delivery driver. Next time, I'll cut the Oregon-grape and salal with buckets of invasive Himalayan blackberry and I won't have to rope and hog-tie my tongue.

BLUE ELDERBERRY
Sambucus nigra ssp. *cerulea*

FAMILY: Adoxaceae (Moschatel)
STATUS: Native
OTHER NAMES: Blue elder, blueberry elder, Mexican elder

A lanky shrub, 15 to 30 feet tall, with branches that sprout opposite each other. The wood contains a soft, pithy core that could be hollowed out for tree-tapping spigots or joining broken arrows. Floppy compound leaves, often in groups of 9, measure 6 inches long and tout sharply serrate edges. Blooms are flat-topped cream-colored sprays with multiple branches of tiny flowers. Fruits are blue ¼-inch balls with a white bloom bunched on crowded stalks.

    Western North America from British Columbia to California, and western US states to northwest Mexico. Open, dry, sunny forests, woodland edges, and roadsides.

HARVEST GUIDE
WHAT: Ripe berries, blossoms
WHEN: Blossoms from April to June, berries in midsummer
Use a knife or garden shears to clip off flower or berry clusters.

CULINARY TIPS
Blue elderberries are delicious in wine, hard cider, kombucha, sauces, syrups, and jelly. Research has confirmed the berries have antiviral actions that may help fight

Blue elderberry's flowers grow in flat clusters. (Photo by Elise Krohn)

Blue elderberry fruit (Photo by Elise Krohn)

influenza. Try the delicate blossoms in cordials and syrups and dipped in batter for fritters.

While the delicious fruits of blue and red elderberry are edible, they need to be gathered when ripe, destemmed, thoroughly cooked, and then strained of seeds. ⬤ Elderberry seeds contain hydrocyanic acid, which can cause diarrhea and nausea if the berries are eaten in large amounts.

WHO EATS AND SHELTERS HERE?

Bluebirds, magpies, western tanagers, warbling vireos, woodpeckers, grosbeaks, grouse, quail, pheasant, Townsend's solitaire, and house finch gorge on blue elderberry fruits. Hummingbirds seek the flowers for nectar. Mule deer prefer the browse in spring and summer, while elk prefer the browse in summer and fall. Spring leaves of blue elderberry have a strong aroma when bruised, but by fall, after the first frost, the leaves sweeten. Elk and other large game animals nibble the delicious buds and dried fruit in winter.

Small mammals, including ring-tailed cats, foxes, woodchucks, ground squirrels, woodrats, chipmunks, and mice, shelter in blue elderberry. The white-crowned sparrow, Lincoln sparrow, least Bell's vireo, dusky flycatcher, orange-crowned warbler, and broad-tailed hummingbird choose it for nesting. Mule deer and white-tailed deer may take protective cover here from the weather.

RED ELDERBERRY
Sambucus racemosa

FAMILY: Adoxaceae (Moschatel)
STATUS: Native
OTHER NAMES: Scarlet elderberry

A lanky shrub that may grow as a tree or thicket up to 20 feet tall with branches that sprout opposite each other. The wood contains a soft, pithy core that could be hollowed out for tree-tapping spigots or joining broken arrows. Floppy, large compound leaves are arranged opposite one another. The wide, lance-shaped leaflets are sharply toothed and grow in groups of 5 to 9. They measure about 6 inches long and have downy undersides. Creamy-white blooms are in pyramid-shaped sprays with multiple tiny flowers. Fruits are shiny scarlet ¼-inch balls bunched on crowded stalks. Leaves, flowers, and branches smell foul when crushed.

Native to both North America and Eurasia and especially common west of the Mississippi River in wet stream corridors and moist forests of fir-spruce, red alder, and Sitka willow.

HARVEST GUIDE
WHAT: Ripe berries, blossoms
WHEN: Blossoms from April to June, berries in midsummer
For harvesting tips, see Blue Elderberry.

CULINARY TIPS
For suggested uses, see Blue Elderberry. Like blue elderberry, red elderberry contains toxic hydrocyanic acid, but more of it. ⬣ Many sources list red elderberry as

Red elderberry flowers grow in clusters shaped like pyramids.

Red elderberries (Photo by Katherine Palmer)

toxic and poisonous and the blue or black elderberry as edible. Both berries need to be picked ripe, destemmed, thoroughly cooked, and strained prior to consumption.

WHO EATS AND SHELTERS HERE?

These berries are an important food for brown bears and American black bears, as they are packed with protein, carbohydrates, and magnesium. The Alaska brown bears lip it as they wait for salmon to arrive in coastal rivers. Bears eat red elderberry foliage, roots, and berries. Up to fifty-six bird species consume the fruits. They are a main course for blue grouse in Idaho during summer as well as band-tailed pigeons in Oregon. White-footed mice, racoons, and other small mammals also eat the tiny berries. In fall, Roosevelt elk in coastal Alaska and the West Coast nosh on elderberry browse; it makes up 16 percent of their diet.

Even though the leaves and branches are highly nutritious, they are bitter due to the cyanide content. After the first frost, the browse is more appealing to mountain goats, deer, elk, and bears, possibly due to lower levels of the bitter compound. In winter, porcupines, varying hares, and mice nibble red elderberry bark and buds through the falling snow. Many bees visit the flowers. Spring pollen is eaten by a flotilla of flies, but the award for tenacious pollen consumer goes to the federally threatened valley elderberry longhorn beetle, endemic to the Central Valley of California.

Shrubby forests with red elderberry are important habitat for grizzly bears. Small birds perch and find cover in the leafy branches.

THE KAYAANÍ SISTERS COUNCIL
NAOMI MICHALSEN

Grandmother Kaasei Naomi Michalsen, Wooshkeetaan, Eagle/Wolf of the Shark House, is an Indigenous food chef, teacher, and knowledge keeper of traditional foods and medicine. Her ancestral home is Berner's Bay, Daxanáak in Lingít, which means "between two points." The points protect an estuary twenty miles north of Juneau, Alaska, where for thousands of years her ancestors have harvested salmon from the glacial rivers that pour into the bay.

Like the salmon returning to those rivers, Naomi has made a full-circle journey. She worked for more than two decades helping victims of domestic violence and sexual assault (DVSA); Naomi is a survivor of abuse herself. But after years of upheaval, her recovery eventually led her on a path back to the traditional foods that nourished her in childhood.

As the oldest of five kids, she remembers being instructed to walk to Elder Irene Peratovich's smokehouse and turn the fish. "The salmon were hanging up on wooden boards, and I had to make sure the fire was still going." After so many hours of smoking, the bright-red sockeye strips had to be turned over. "I just never knew how special that was. As a kid I thought, 'Why do I have to do this?'"

In wintertime, when the low tides were at night, her family would dig clams by kerosene lantern, and as a teenager on Prince of Wales Island, Alaska—near where the Klawock River winds to the sea—Naomi gathered foods for her family from low-tide beaches: stalks of sea asparagus and sea cucumber. She remembers "getting abalone, buckets of it, and pounding abalone on the porch." Eventually, she moved to Ketchikan with her three kids and went to college—where she had an epiphany.

"My anthropology professor lectured about Native people in a positive light. She said Indigenous people were self-sufficient, strong, intelligent, we knew the land. Did you know it was the Tsimshian who first used taxol from the yew tree to treat cancer? They are the ones who learned this! Finally, my educational experience in school gave me pride. I could see where one teacher can make the biggest difference."

I asked Naomi how she became inspired to teach and share about her extensive plant knowledge.

"I grew up feeling sometimes like I didn't belong," she said. "Once I learned my history . . . then I started to want to learn the things that were taken from my family. The language, the culture, the plants and the foods . . . I felt like I had more of a purpose. . . . That is when I spent a lot of time with Elders."

With time, she said, "I began to realize that our culture is prevention. Our culture is intervention. Our cultures are healing. I started sharing my stories and presenting at conferences or keynotes at schools and community events about twenty years ago on that topic.

"When I became a grandma," she continued, "my life just kind of switched gears. I wanted to give something back And I couldn't think of a better way to be of service than with our plant relatives."

Not long ago, as Naomi and I sat in her kitchen with her husband, a Scandinavian gentle giant, we spooned up cloud-berry—reminiscent of ripe apricot—and broke open sock-eye salmon fillets fresh from

Kassei Naomi Michalsen is an Elder, grandmother, and keeper of plant knowledge. (Photo used by permission of Kassei Naomi Michalsen)

the smoker on their porch. She fed me her traditional foods: kelp salsa and pickled sea asparagus, and gave me a beautiful jar of smoked salmon to carry home. "I am so elevated," I told her. "I am about to float off the chair with happiness and pleasure from this exquisite feast."

Naomi told me that, like many Alaska Indigenous Elders, she became increasingly concerned about the future of native plants people forage for food and medicine. Competition with commercial harvesters, ATV use on muskegs, and loss of respect for plants weighed heavy on her heart. She knew education was the key, but the task seemed overwhelming.

In response, she started a business, Kaasei Indigenous Foodways, to educate and share about Indigenous foods, plants, and people. One of her projects is the Kayaaní Sisters Council. Nine Indigenous grandmothers and aunties gathered from across Alaska and created a "living document" called the "Respectful Harvesting Guidelines" for both Indigenous and non-Indigenous foragers. They are meant to be a starting point for collaborating with your own community members to protect what we love.

"The beautiful thing about the Kayaaní Sisters Council and growing this community of healers and leaders is that you don't have to do the work all by yourself," she said with a smile. "There are people like you and me everywhere who really care. I believe the ancient Indigenous prophecy that the earth will begin to heal when the grandmothers speak." (See Respectful Harvesting Guidelines in Resources.)

TREES & FERNS

Once, I slept curled inside my Christmas tree on an overnight ski trip in the North Cascades. That year, the snow forecast was bleak. But a friend and I managed to glide over a dusting of new powder to our destination—an enormous stand of ancient trees. In the grove's center, surrounded by ferns, towered a 150-foot western redcedar. Few people knew about our "Secret Tree." Outside it appeared green and alive, but inside it was perfectly hollow.

We leaned our skis against the ten-foot-wide trunk and ducked into a dark fissure between roots. Once inside, we could stand up and stretch—or hibernate like bears. We slept deeply and woke late to a darkness unimagined. Overnight, all the brilliant snow had melted. But I still recall that hour of discovery. Standing outside the Secret Tree on Christmas Day, savoring a mug of my friend's evergreen needle and licorice fern tea, I was utterly enchanted. With every sip of resinous balsam, surprising citrus, and sweet licorice, my vision grew. Suddenly I'd entered a world of forest elixirs, divine syrups, and whimsical vegetables gathered from forest trees and ferns.

Tea is only a primer to a progression of beverages made from Pacific Coast forest plants. Spruce-tip ale, concocted by boiling young Sitka spruce needles with sugar or molasses, is another arboreal drink. The tonic, rich in vitamin C, was used by early mariners to prevent scurvy on long journeys. Today, microbreweries from Alaska to Oregon dream up seasonal beers with titles like Spruce Tip Dunkel, All Spruced Up Winter Ale, and Spruce Tip IPA.

Another bold-flavored infusion concocted from evergreen needles is spruce-tip, or grand-fir-tip, syrup. Spruce syrup drizzled over grilled salmon, pit fruit, or lamb is like a splash of heady balsam liqueur. Grand-fir-tip syrup in sorbet or lemonade is a refreshing timber tonic too.

Juniper berries, which aren't berries at all, are actually the round cones of a sprawling evergreen shrub. They start out green and mature to purple black at 18 months. That's when you can crush and add them to rubs, kimchi, sauerkraut, and even chocolate truffles! They add a woodsy, resinous boost to both savory and sweet dishes.

Of course, evergreens aren't the only Pacific Northwest trees with flavorful gifts. Paper-birch syrup comes in distinct grades and flavors. It can range from dark (molasses-and-balsamic forward) to amber (fruity fig-and-apricot) to gold

These young, compact bigleaf maple blossoms will grow long and dangly as they sweeten with nectar.

FIND A LIFESPAN IN A BRANCH TIP

In the ancient rainforest archipelago of Haida Gwaii, sixty miles off the coast of British Columbia, I encountered the biggest Sitka spruce tree I have ever seen. Here in the territory of the Haida Nation, where controversial logging operations still slay the giant trees that can live more than a thousand years and grow as tall as a twenty-story building, I met a grandmother spruce with a trunk as wide as two canoes. On a three-week sea kayaking trip, five friends and I tried to form a human chain to wrap this ancient Sitka spruce's trunk. We stretched around the tree like an unshapely horseshoe.

Leaning my head back to look up the enormous trunk, I tried to imagine the layered time capsule inside this tree's vast girth. Long ago, perhaps in 1200 AD, a spruce cone fell to the forest duff. Or maybe an absent-minded squirrel cached it for a future buffet—and forgot it. Miraculously, a tiny seed sprouted—and survived. During the Little Ice Age, in the 1700s, this tree marked its five hundredth birthday. When my great-great-grandfather was hammering horse-drawn plow blades in his smithy in Denmark, the tree had been digging roots into the rich loam of Haida Gwaii for 650 years. My entire lifespan could be measured by the growth of an uppermost branch tip.

Not only had these ancient spruce trees outlived the lumber barons, but they had helped generations of animals and people survive. In emergencies, the First Nations people ate the inner bark, or cambium, for food. Vitamin-rich needles were chewed or steeped in tea. White-and-pink pitch made a pleasurable chewing gum. Spruce pitch could glue a broken canoe after lashing a crack with spruce twine. Today, the Old Ways continue to help and to heal. Indigenous women, such as Haida and Tlingit textile artist and retired professor SGang Gwaay Dolly Garza, still gather spruce roots for weaving into hats. A prized spruce root hat is rainproof! Spruce pitch is still applied to cuts and burns to stave off infection. A 2011 study showed Sitka spruce peptides have antimicrobial activities against *E. coli*, *Staphylococcus aureus*, and the fungus *Candida albicans*. I can only imagine how many medicines and meals could be served up by one grandmother tree—with her towering cathedral spire and canopy of interwoven branches—in a span of eight hundred years.

That summer in Haida Gwaii, as I unrolled my sleeping bag underneath the grandmother spruce tree, I noticed something amazing. The duff of needles and moss beneath the tree sank down as deep as my elbow. I reached up and plucked a bud-green needle cluster from a branch tip. The new growth felt as soft as daisy petals. I took a nibble. First came an acerbic dryness. Next a lemony flavor. It all made sense now. Evergreen trees are a medicine chest of phytochemicals rich in vitamin C. They keep our immune systems skookum-strong. I lay back on a pillow of fragrant spruce needles and bark chips and sent a little gratitude to the giant spruce for helping another coastal traveler compassed on the far horizon.

(caramel-and-toffee sweet). Depending on the time of year the sap is running, it's perfect for birch chai lattes and chocolate turtle brownies or drizzled atop birch-roasted vegetables. Bigleaf maple sap produces syrup as complex and sweet tasting as eastern sugar maples. Moreover, the tree's grapelike clusters of yellow-green blooms can be tossed into salads or dipped in fritter batter and drizzled with bigleaf maple syrup.

From the forest's understory, the spiral fiddleheads of lady ferns and ostrich ferns are delicious steamed and tossed with pasta, floated over the surface of soup, pickled, or battered and fried as tempura. Moreover, they're protein rich.

SITKA SPRUCE
Picea sitchensis

FAMILY: Pinaceae (Pine)
STATUS: Native
OTHER NAMES: Coast spruce, tideland spruce, western spruce, silver spruce, Menzies' spruce

The largest spruce on the Pacific Coast, Sitka spruce can tower to 215 feet; its trunk can grow to 18 feet in diameter. Mature needles arranged like a bottlebrush are sharp, stiff, and yellowish green to blue green, with 2 white bands on the top and a diamond cross-section. Cones are down hanging, finger length, and golden brown with toothed, papery scales. The bark is characterized by purple-brown scales that resemble puzzle pieces or snack chips.

Coastal forests from the Gulf of Alaska to Northern California, sea level to 2,100 feet.

HARVEST GUIDE
WHAT: New needle tips
WHEN: Spring
"Tips" refers to spring needle growth on branch tips (new buds). Harvest new, soft, and bright green needles with your fingers. Take a few side tips

Harvesting Sitka spruce: **A**, *take only the side tips;* **B**, *leave the lead tip so the tree can grow outward.*

LEFT: *Sitka spruce tree*; RIGHT: *Sitka spruce tips* (Photo by Ayesha Wise)

only. Leave the apical tip (lead tip) of a conifer branch or you will stunt the outward growth. Leave some side tips so the tree can have lateral growth too. Generally, I harvest only one of two opposite side tips, and I alternate sides.

CULINARY TIPS

Chop spruce tips and add to shortbread cookies, lemonade, ice cream, cheesecake, and veggie dips. Sprinkle finely chopped tips over smashed potatoes, roasted veggies, and gravlax. Dry and mix with artisan salt, tea, and meat rubs. Drizzle spruce syrup over lamb, wild game, roasted squash, baklava, fresh berries, and pancakes. Try seasonal spruce-tip ale and IPA available at some stores, or if you want to channel your inner brewmaster, check online recipes. Infusing beer with spruce tips adds a lovely orange color and a slight cranberry note.

WHO EATS AND SHELTERS HERE?

Blue grouse and ruffed grouse munch buds and needles. Small birds such as black-capped chickadee, pine siskin, red crossbill, and white-winged crossbill eat seeds. Beavers, porcupine, red squirrels, varying hare, cottontail rabbits, and Douglas squirrels (also called chickarees) gobble bark, wood, and seeds. White-footed deer mice and wood rats munch needles as well as seeds. Red-backed voles and red tree voles nibble needles. Mountain goats browse Sitka spruce foliage. Elk and deer eat the new shoots. Woodpeckers and sapsuckers lap up insects on bark and trapped in sap.

Deer bed down underneath the broad branches. Bald eagles build nests and roost in Sitka spruce. Small birds and mammals, including Douglas squirrels and owls, use tree cavities for nesting. Red tree voles also nest in branches. Oregon slender salamanders, chickadees, dusky shrews, wandering or vagrant shrews, coast moles, deer mice and the larvae of many butterflies and moths all rely on spruce.

GRAND FIR
Abies grandis

FAMILY: Pinaceae (Pine)
STATUS: Native
OTHER NAMES: Giant fir, great fir, Puget Sound fir, Oregon fir, Oregon white fir, California great fir, lowland balsam fir, stinking fir

A giant among true firs, it grows to 300 feet and may live to 300 years. Mature needles are shiny green, flat, up to 2 inches long, notched at the tips, usually arranged in 2 ranks opposite one another, and do not conceal the tops of twigs. They are highly aromatic when crushed, with a citrus aroma. The bark is gray when young, with resin-filled blisters, and turns furrowed brown with age. Cones stand erect and singular, like plump, 4-inch-tall plumber's candles, from midtree to crown. Like all true firs, its cones disintegrate on the branch. Mature trees have a domed (not pointed) crown.

British Columbia to Northern California and Northern Rockies. Moist conifer forests, low mountain slopes (especially north-facing or shady slopes, but also low-summer-rainfall, high-summer-temperature sites), sea level to 4,500 feet.

LEFT: *Grand fir tree;* **RIGHT:** *Grand fir branches with spring tips*

HARVEST GUIDE

See Sitka Spruce.

CULINARY TIPS

Mature tips can also be harvested, as grand fir needles retain their resinous citrus flavor when mature. For a cold-season tea rich in vitamin C, pour eight ounces of boiling water over two teaspoons of dried needles. Try fir-tip syrup lemonade and sorbet. Pulverize fresh needles and add to shortbread and homemade crackers. Use in a rub for venison and fowl. Add dried pulverized spring needle tips to flaked artisan salt. Sprinkle a dash on sautéed mushrooms for a forest flavor.

WHO EATS AND SHELTERS HERE?

Needles and twigs are winter food for deer, elk, moose, and mountain goats, and a vital part of the diet of grouse of all kinds. Fir cones provide seeds for chickadees, squirrels, Clark's nutcracker, white-footed mice, western chipmunk, yellow-bellied magpie, and pygmy nuthatch. Yellow-bellied sapsuckers drink the nourishing sap. Pika, porcupine, beaver, and varying hare gnaw seeds, bark, and wood.

Grouse, squirrels, chipmunks, and pikas find shelter and cover in young trees. Mature grand fir, near water, is a thermal blanket and cover for some big game. The thick boughs are a protective "roof" in rain or snowstorms for pygmy nuthatches, Vaux's swift, red crossbill, Williamson's sapsucker, and pileated woodpecker. Old-growth grand fir and snags provide nesting sites for owls, including northern spotted owls and flammulated owls, as well as pileated woodpeckers, sapsuckers, deer mice, bushy-tailed woodrats, American martens, fishers, spotted skunks, squirrels, weasels, and endangered marbled murrelets. Downed fir logs and hollowed-out trunks are homes to squirrels, mice, and weasels and are dens for bears.

COASTAL DOUGLAS-FIR
Pseudotsuga menziesii var. *menziesii*

FAMILY: Pinaceae (Pine)
STATUS: Native
OTHER NAMES: Giant fir, great fir, Puget Sound fir, Oregon fir, Oregon white fir, California great fir, lowland white fir, lowland balsam fir

Douglas-fir can grow over 300 feet tall and is the second-tallest conifer after Coast redwoods. Mature needles make a bottlebrush around twigs and are flat, dark green to greenish

LEFT: *Coastal Douglas-fir tree;* RIGHT: *Douglas-fir cone bracts resemble a mouse's tail and hind legs.*

yellow, ¾ to 1 inch long. Bark is dark brown, deeply furrowed, and fluted. Dangling, finger-length seed cones have oval scales and a distinct 3-forked bract that looks like a mouse tail and hind legs. Cones fall off when mature.

Central British Columbia to Central California. Sea level to mid-elevation.

HARVEST GUIDE

See Sitka Spruce.

CULINARY TIPS

See Sitka Spruce and Grand Fir. Douglas-fir needles are most flavorful as soft new growth.

SUPERPOWER

Enrobed in its cork-like, thick bark with elongated ridges and deep fissures, Douglas-fir is built to survive periodic forest fires. It can live for more than a thousand years.

WHO EATS AND SHELTERS HERE?

Seed cones are essential food for small mammals, including chipmunks, shrews, creeping voles, and white-footed deer mice. One voracious deer mouse can polish off 350 seeds in one night! Douglas squirrels cache bushels of cones for winter stores and gnaw spring's pollen cones, inner bark, tender needles, and shoots. In western Oregon,

⚠ CANARIES IN THE FORESTS?

Our beautiful evergreens and their forest homes are stressed out. According to the USDA Northwest Climate Hub, the annual average temperature has "risen nearly 2 degrees Fahrenheit since 1900 in Idaho, Oregon, and Washington. Alaska has warmed faster than any other state, with increases ranging from 2.4 degrees Fahrenheit in Southeast Alaska to 6.2 degrees Fahrenheit in northern Alaska." Our hottest years on record have spiked upward too. Trees, it seems, are serving as "northwest canaries." In southern Oregon's Klamath Mountains, Douglas-fir forests suffered a 720-square-mile die-off. *Trees on the Edge*, a report issued in 2023 by Oregon State University, cites hotter droughts, harsh conditions, and insects—primarily the flatheaded fir borer—for transforming southwest Oregon's vast evergreen forests into mosaics of umber and rust. "Firmageddon," coined by Forest Service aerial surveyor Daniel DePinte, now refers to an even more massive die-off in five species of fir trees from Northern California to Washington. Lowland western redcedars (at sites below 650 feet), west of the Cascade crest, are also increasingly suffering crown die-off and mortality.

Lower elevation forests are hit hardest, but as our climate continues to warm, forests in cooler, higher elevations will become more vulnerable. Hats off to Cal Poly Humboldt researchers who are honing forest restoration techniques to help coastal Douglas-firs become more resilient to drought, as well as a team at the Pacific Northwest Research Station that is working to identify drought-tolerant Douglas-fir populations.

small mammals harvest up to 65 percent of the total seed crop. Douglas-fir cones also provide critical energy for the winter wren, pine siskin, purple finch, dark-eyed junco, song sparrow, white-crowned sparrow, and golden-crowned sparrow. Needles are a staple spring food for blue grouse. Red tree voles gather needles and lick needles washed by rain for their water source. In winter, porcupines gnaw the inner bark of young Douglas-fir, while elk, deer, mountain beaver, pocket gophers, hares, and brush rabbits browse saplings and seedlings. Over sixty insect species munch Douglas-fir cones. Thankfully, chickadees, nuthatches, brown creepers, and woodpeckers hunt problematic insects by the beakful.

From root to crown, the long-lived Douglas-fir is a generous architect of home sites for countless forest dwellers. Cavity-nesting northern flying squirrels and pileated, hairy, and downy woodpeckers nest and roost in trunks. Red tree voles build intricate nests in ancient Douglas-fir trees where large branches join the trunk. The nests of tree voles sport separate eating areas packed with cut fir needles, a bathroom, and an escape route. Ancient Douglas-fir are also the kingdom of the endangered northern spotted owl, a predator of tree voles and flying squirrels. Several dozen species of insects take shelter in Douglas-fir, including the Cascades panthea moth and western tent caterpillar. Songbirds aplenty use Douglas-fir branches for shade, nests, and roosts. Vast underground networks of mycorrhizal fungi attach to the roots of Douglas-fir—a bond that nourishes chanterelles and other forest mushrooms.

COMMON JUNIPER
Juniperus communis

FAMILY: Cupressaceae (Cypress)
STATUS: Native
OTHER NAMES: Dwarf juniper, prostrate juniper, low juniper, ground juniper, old field common juniper, prickly juniper, common mountain juniper (also *Juniperus communis* var. *depressa*)

This prostrate, snaking, matt-forming evergreen is distinguished for being our only circumpolar conifer. It can grow upright to 5 feet tall. Its prickly needles, ¼ to ½ inch long, show dark green above and white below. Bark is reddish to silver gray, thin, and peeling. Female cones, colloquially called "berries," emerge in green coats and ripen to blue black with a whitish bloom after 2 to 3 years. Male cones are gold. Common juniper lacks the scaly leaves of its cousins—the Rocky Mountain juniper and maritime juniper.

The scientific name *communis* hints that it grows worldwide. In the Northwest, it grows from Alaska to California. It can tolerate an impressive range of conditions, from moist muskegs and bogs to high-altitude, dry alpine.

HARVEST GUIDE
WHAT: Berries and branches
WHEN: Year-round
Green, first-year berries exude potent essential oils and are used for flavoring gin. Second- and third-year berries are blue black. When cutting branches, be aware, this slow-growing shrub takes a long time to recover after overharvesting.

CULINARY TIPS
Resinous green fruits give gin and artisan beers their characteristic spicy kick. For game rubs, harvest the ripe blue berries. A little goes a long way; use just six berries

Common juniper has green berries the first year that turn blue black by its third year. (Photo by Akchamcuk, iStock)

per half pound of game, such as venison, moose, rabbit, or poultry. Add to sauerkraut. Juniper berry syrup is refreshing drizzled over roasted cauliflower or mixed into drinks. Desserts you might try: juniper-infused crème brûlée, juniper-berry chocolate ganache truffles, and refreshing juniper-lemon sorbet. Small cuttings of needle-covered branches may be added with alder to a smoker to flavor fish.

Juniper contains a highly volatile oil, terpinen-4-ol, that can amplify kidney action and cause serious kidney problems if used for too long. ⚠ Overuse can lead to convulsions. Pregnant women should be especially cautious, as the berry is a uterine stimulant.

WHO EATS AND SHELTERS HERE?

In winter and spring, mountain goats, hares, and deer browse common juniper. It's a vital food for winter mule deer and white-tailed deer. Moose nibble it sparingly and barren-ground caribou fairly often, especially if ground lichens are in short supply. American robins, black-capped chickadees, wild turkeys, Bohemian and cedar waxwings, and a variety of songbirds gobble up juniper cones. Birds are one of the most important "planters," or dispersers, of common juniper cone seeds.

Woodrats gather branches for their messy nests. Short-eared owls dream in winter roosts. Wild turkeys choose it for nesting cover. White-tailed deer, small mammals, small birds, and game birds find shade and cover in common juniper.

PAPER BIRCH
Betula papyrifera

FAMILY: Betulaceae (Birch)
STATUS: Native
OTHER NAMES: Canoe birch, white birch, káezeká (Dena'ina dialect for "birch sap")

The elegant birch can sprout single or multiple trunks that grow to 80 feet tall and 12 inches in diameter, though some reach 30 inches. Shallow rooted and relatively short-lived, birch may grow up to 100 years and can even surpass 200 years. The graceful arching trunks Robert Frost refers to in his famous poem "Birches" hint at the tree's elasticity in dealing with ice storms and trunk-climbing kids. However, once bowed, trunks don't spring up again.

Caterpillar-shaped flower clusters, called catkins, hang in groups of males and females on the same twig. Alternate teardrop-shaped leaves are dull green above, lighter below, and 1½ to 3½ inches long with doubly toothed edges and pointed tips. It would take over a million paper birch "nutlets" (the 1/16-inch fruit) to make 1 pound of seed. Tiny wings aid their dispersal into winter. Smooth, chalk-white to gray (red-brown on saplings) bark has raised horizontal streaks (lenticels) and peels like paper to reveal orange inner bark.

LEFT: *Paper birch bark;* **RIGHT:** *Edible spring leaves and male (gold) and female (green) catkins*

TAPPING BIGLEAF MAPLES AND BIRCHES

To tap bigleaf maples and birches for sap, follow the Alaska Birch Syrupmakers' Association Best Practices as well as guidelines from the University of Oregon:

- For birch: Tap only healthy trees—at least eight inches in diameter.
- For bigleaf maple: Tap healthy trees—single-stemmed maples ten inches or more in diameter and multistemmed maples at least four inches in diameter.
- Do not tap trees sprayed by pesticides (including around the roots).
- Tap holes no more than 1¾ inches deep, at a slight upward angle, using a $\frac{5}{16}$-inch to $\frac{7}{16}$-inch bit.
- Use plastic, nylon, or stainless-steel taps called spiles. (You can find tapered $\frac{5}{16}$-inch "tree-saving" spiles online if you search "maple-tapping supplies".)
- Remove spiles at the end of the season and spray hole with clean water.
- Do not plug or cork the hole.
- Tap individual trees no more than once every two to three years.

Look for the hardy transcontinental paper birch from Alaska to Newfoundland. On the Pacific Coast, it grows south to Oregon. Paper birch prefers moist forests, clearcuts, burns, and lowland open areas, but it can spring up on rugged mountain slopes or in rockslides, muskegs, and bogs. In boreal forests, this pioneering species forms vast, pure stands on burn sites, but after 150 years it is replaced by spruce.

HARVEST GUIDE

WHAT: Sap, leaves

WHEN: Sap (just as leaf buds are forming) in early spring, first leaves in spring Remove individual young leaves by hand. Snap off a twig when the sap is running for a wintergreen nibble stick. See the "Tapping Bigleaf Maples and Birches" sidebar above.

CULINARY TIPS

In Alaska, paper birch are tapped for syrup making. The ratio of sap needed is a lot steeper than from maples: 100 to 150 gallons of birch sap create 1 gallon of syrup. Reverse osmosis machines come in handy in larger sugarbush operations. They reduce water content before the sap is boiled. Birch syrup can be ordered conveniently online and comes in four grades, including a thicker, molasses-like version that is used for baking and making beer and birch candies. Birch table syrup is a delicious, sustainable, yet "barely tapped" sweetener with a rich and spicy-sweet flavor reminiscent of sorghum, horehound candy, and varieties of local honey. Blend birch syrup into marinades for meat and fish, sauces for BBQ salmon, vinaigrette drizzled over roasted root veggies or grilled peaches, or glazes for duck or goose. Crank up some birch syrup butter-pecan ice cream, or sweeten up a birch chai latte or birch pecan pie. Young birch leaves can be dried for tea or steamed. Old leaves turn bitter.

People from Scandinavia to China drink the sap as a spring tonic. "Birch water" is now bottled and shipped from Alaska. Steep a handful of young leaves for a wintergreen-flavored tea, or add young leaves to salad greens as an aromatic bitter.

WHO EATS AND SHELTERS HERE?

Birch provides an important seed supply for black-capped chickadees, pine siskins, redpolls, and fox sparrows. Moose, mule deer, elk, varying hares, porcupine, and beaver browse twigs and foliage. The sweet sap is sought by yellow-bellied sapsuckers, as well as hummingbirds and red squirrels that lap at the pecked holes. Ruffed, spruce, and sharp-tailed grouse eat birch buds, seeds, and catkins. Porcupines munch the inner bark. Small animals such as shrews and voles devour seeds.

Moose, mule deer, elk, porcupine, and varying hare find refuge in birch forests. Ruffed grouse are also called birch partridge for their love of birch forest habitats.

BIGLEAF MAPLE
Acer macrophyllum

FAMILY: Sapindaceae (Soapberry)
STATUS: Native
OTHER NAMES: Canyon maple, Oregon maple, white maple, cukáums (Cowlitz)

The largest maple in North America, this robust tree can grow 8 feet in diameter and almost 100 feet tall, with multiple trunks spreading into a 100-foot-wide crown. Long-lived, to over 300 years old, they are also the largest leaf maker of all maple trees. Dark-green 5-lobed leaves with pale undersides grow to 15 inches wide. Fragrant yellow flowers appear in hanging 4- to 7-inch clusters in April and May and are insect pollinated. The winged seeds, called a double samaras, materialize in fall and whirl downward like little helicopters.

SHADE AND SYRUP

Late winter in Bellingham usually brings mild temperatures in the forties at night. But one wild year, March roared in like a lion. By 10:00 PM the mercury had dropped to below freezing. Icy winds clacked the maples and whistled in the firs. Come morning, the sky throbbed blue. About that time, our twelve-year-old friend Wesley Finger was climbing a maple tree on his parents' organic farm and accidentally snapped off a branch. Sap dripped from the tip like soda from a straw. Thrilled with possibilities, Wesley sprinted to the farmhouse to ask his parents, "Can we make maple syrup?" Centuries earlier the Nlaka'pamux (Thompson Indians) of British Columbia had tapped maple trees and made syrup too. Wesley was onto something delicious.

Later, at a Finger family Sunday breakfast, we drizzled Wesley's bigleaf maple syrup over a stack of silver dollar cakes. We were so impressed with the maple flavor that we decided to try our hand at it. After all, we had three forested acres scattered with maple trees.

We ordered ⁵⁄₁₆-inch metal taps, or spiles (rhymes with *smiles*), called "tree-saving taps" because they are smaller in diameter and tapered. Apparently, smaller, tapered spiles allow the trees to recover faster. After sterilizing the spiles and a ⁵⁄₁₆-inch drill bit in boiling water, Chris and I used a battery-operated drill to make a hole through the bark and cambium layer of a half dozen maples ranging from eight to twenty inches in diameter. Instead of drilling straight in, we sloped the hole, so the sweetish sap ran easily. We used a rubber mallet to drive the spile into the hole and hung recycled water jugs from a fin on the spile. Every morning, as the thermometer rose above freezing, we made our rounds. One bigleaf maple tree can produce about 25 to 220 gallons in one season. Most of our tapped maple trunks bestowed us a half quart of sap each day.

A broiler pan set atop a two-burner hot plate worked as our evaporator. As the sap level lowered every half hour, we poured more fresh sap in to get enough liquid to concentrate into syrup. Of course, the evaporation time speeds up as the sap boils down. On one batch, we waited too long and discovered a crust of acrid black sugar. After days of topping off our deeper pans, we got one precious quart of amber syrup from ten gallons of bigleaf maple sap that had a robust butterscotch flavor.

Today, the Hupačasath First Nation is tapping bigleaf maples in Oregon, Washington, and on Vancouver Island in the Alberni Valley to make commercial volumes of maple syrup.

Tapping the sap of a bigleaf maple tree to make syrup

LEFT: *Bigleaf maple with moss and licorice ferns* (Photo by Katherine Palmer); **RIGHT:** *Blossoms*

Smooth, silver-brown bark becomes deeply fissured and scaled with age, often enrobed in moss and epiphytic licorice ferns.

From northwestern British Columbia to Southern California's arroyos, in forested foothills, along streams, and on steep, rocky slopes.

HARVEST GUIDE

WHAT: Sap, flower clusters, seed sprouts

WHEN: Sap from winter to early spring, flower buds and seed sprouts in spring

Sap flow is generally December to March, when buds appear, but is inconsistent and varies with regional weather. Young sprouts can be plucked from the ground one by one. To gather flowers, find low-hanging branches or use a ladder. Snip or pluck off the golden-green racemes after they open fully and smell sweet like nectar. Check for insects and tiny red samaras poking out of the flower like two red wings (a sign the sweet nectar is gone and the flowers are going to seed). A long-pole orchard clipper is handy for reaching flowers on high branches. Alternately, a windstorm will send these gifts earthward. Unopened fallen flower clusters that look like green pine cones are edible too. (See the "Tapping Bigleaf Maples and Birches" sidebar above.)

Bigleaf maple leaves can grow to be enormous, as big as a large pizza.

CULINARY TIPS

Raw sap can be drunk as a spring tonic. It contains sugar, water, vitamins, minerals, metals, amino acids, and trace proteins. Sap can be boiled down into a butterscotch-flavored forest syrup. The Hupačasath First Nation's commercial production of bigleaf maple syrup has a yield of about one cup of syrup with a 66 percent sugar content from three gallons of sap. Use the syrup for pancakes, baking, beverages, bigleaf-flavored candies, and brushing on grilled salmon or pit fruits.

Try maple blossoms in pancakes, fritters, salad, and crème brûlée, or pickled. Blossoms are best eaten the day they're picked. Fall seeds can be sprouted and boiled but are bitter. Raw spring sprouts are slightly bitter but juicy and tender.

SUPERPOWER

The profusion of dinner-plate-sized leaves creates volumes of organic material on the forest floor. Bigleaf maples are super soil builders!

WHO EATS AND SHELTERS HERE?

Elk depend on tender sprouts, twigs, leaves, and seedlings. Mule deer and mountain beaver eat leaves in summer and twigs in winter. Northern flying squirrels, Douglas squirrels, evening grosbeaks, and finches rely on protein-rich seeds in winter when other foods are scanty. Barred owls, pileated woodpecker, and mountain beaver also eat the samara fruit. Deer mice gnaw germinating bigleaf maple seeds in spring. Pacific-slope flycatchers, dusky flycatchers, Hammond's flycatchers, and brown creepers explore the crinkled bark and leafy crown for a tasty variety of insects.

Many insects eat the wood, twigs, and leaves but cause limited damage. Troublesome types, like the larvae of the carpenter worm, burrow through the maple's delicious inner bark for three to four years, weakening the tree, before transforming into moths. Female moths lay up to three hundred eggs in a bigleaf maple's bark fissures, scars, and wounds. Woodpeckers, a natural control, may eat up to 75 percent of the wood-boring insects! When chunky branches fall into streams, the decomposing wood bits feed a river of aquatic insects hunted by hungry birds and fish. Honeybees and other pollinators seek nectar.

Bald eagles dream in bigleaf maples—a popular roost overlooking a river. Pileated woodpeckers hammer out nesting cavities, and dusky-footed woodrats and harlequin ducks build nests in the big trees. Barred owls may be increasing in the Pacific Northwest in part because of logging of ancient conifer forests and the bigleaf maple forest mosaics that take their place. Roosevelt elk, mule deer, western red-backed salamanders, Pacific giant salamanders, and Townsend's chipmunks take refuge in forests with bigleaf maple. Downed branches help slow stream flow by collecting debris and creating logjams that make steelhead and salmon habitat. A one-ton cloak

❓ WHAT'S UP WITH OUR MASSIVE MAPLES?

From Washington State's northern border to the Columbia River, starting in 2011, a tree famous for its lush, massive greenery was doing something very peculiar. It was producing little leaves, shriveled leaves, red to brown scorched leaves, partial or entire crowns of dead leaves, or leaves that turned yellow prematurely in one area of the massive branches. Some bigleaf maples were dying outright. Researchers at the University of Washington collaborated with the Washington Department of Natural Resources in a multiyear study to figure out why. After ruling out specific pathogens, they determined that hotter, drier summers weakened the bigleaf maple's immune system. Fighting off pests and disease was harder under stress.

Now recognized as "bigleaf maple decline," it is happening in California, Oregon, and British Columbia too. In contrast, when researchers checked equal numbers of Douglas-fir trees at their sample sites, the firs fared better due to their higher tolerance for heat and drought. Maples growing along roadsides and in cities had the hardest time of it. Urban bigleafs cope with more pollutants, such as arsenic and chromium, and miles of hardscape surfaces that radiate heat. In the future, during hot spells, we may need to water our city tree friends. Our forest friends will benefit from keeping wild landscapes intact.

of velvet mosses, liverworts, and fluttering licorice ferns can adorn a single massive bigleaf maple. So-called canopy soil in the crotch between maple trunks provides hidey holes, moisture, and nutrients for amphibians.

VINE MAPLE
Acer circinatum

FAMILY: Aceraceae (Maple)
STATUS: Native
OTHER NAMES: Tree of the devil, wood of the devil (Scottish botanist David Douglas logged in his journals that the vine maple "is called by the voyageurs *Bois de diable* from the obstruction it gives them in passing through the woods")

This vine-like tree or large shrub sprouts multiple trunks. Up to 20 feet in length, they may sprawl across a shaded forest floor or rise in ethereal arches overhead. In sunny, open sites the vine maple appears more upright and bushier. The scientific name *circinatum* means "circular" and refers to the rounded 3- to 4½-inch-wide leaves with palmate veins and toothed edges. In spring, I've noticed the buds open like tiny cocktail umbrellas. Greenish-white flowers grow in clusters of 3 to 6. The winged seeds spread horizontally, not in a V shape, and gain a rose tinge. Autumn leaves range from yellow to orange to red.

British Columbia to Northern California in damp, shady woods, often along streams.

LEFT: *Vine maple leaf;* **RIGHT:** *Vine maple bark*

HARVEST GUIDE

WHAT: Leaves
WHEN: Autumn

The tradition in Osaka, Japan, is to collect yellow leaves after they've fallen. I like that thinking. It feels more like the tree decides when to "leave off" and share its gifts.

CULINARY TIPS

Tempura the whole, yellow autumn leaves and serve atop your favorite ice cream for a gorgeous, crispy-crunchy autumnal garnish. See Vine Maple Leaf Tempura in Recipes.

Fallen yellow vine maple leaves are a Japanese delicacy.

WHO EATS AND SHELTERS HERE?

Black-tailed deer munch the leaves. During fall migration, varied thrush overturn the fallen leaves with a deft flip of their bills and hunt for insects. Douglas squirrels slice open the tough seed capsule on the samaras (winged, helicopter-like seeds).

Songbirds such as chickadees, nuthatches, and pine siskins hunt for insects and hide in arching vine maples. Several species of squirrels and woodpeckers travel the trunks looking for insects and seeds.

LADY FERN
Athyrium filix-femina

FAMILY: Dryopteridaceae (Wood Fern)
STATUS: Native
OTHER NAMES: Northwestern lady fern, common lady fern

Lady fern fronds are shaped like lacy green feathers—narrow at the top and bottom, broad in the middle. About 3 to 9 annual fronds sprout in a funnel shape from a scaly, humped, perennial rootstock. Most specimens are 2 to 6 feet in height. Each frond's underside bears hundreds of spore patches—brown kidney-shaped to oblong bumps called sori.

Find it in shaded seeps, along stream banks, and in deep or dappled shade of moist woods. This circumboreal species crops up all across North America and Eurasia from sea level to 6,000 feet. On the Northwest coast, lady ferns range from Alaska to California.

Blanch or cook lady fern fiddleheads to deactivate the antinutrient thiaminase.

HARVEST GUIDE

WHAT: Tightly coiled crosiers (fiddleheads)
WHEN: Spring
See How to Harvest Fiddleheads later in this listing.

CULINARY TIPS

Any meal that works for garden asparagus is more delightful with fiddleheads, also called crosiers (from the word for a staff resembling a shepherd's crook). They must be blanched, not eaten raw. Try fiddleheads fried in tempura batter; dipped in fondue; blanched and added to salad with dates, orzo pasta, and lemon dressing; marinated with mushrooms and tomatoes; drizzled with truffle oil vinaigrette; grilled; pressed into crab quiche; strewn atop poached eggs or pizza; in relishes; pickled; tossed with pasta, parmesan, and lemon; roasted with goat cheese and bacon; and in cream soups.

⍰ LADY FERNS FAVOR FREQUENT RAINS

Have you noticed our lovely, feathery lady ferns may be getting shorter in the Pacific Northwest? According to Hannah Marx, a University of Puget Sound researcher and graduate student who simulated the effect on ferns of lower June rainfall through 2050, ferns may be toughing it out by reducing their size. A happy fern needs sunlight, moist soil, and nutritious dirt, among other things, to grow tall fronds. Marx's research predicts that as June rainfall decreases in the Pacific Northwest due to climate change, our ferns will grow shorter and may have a challenging time with long-term survival.

Lady fern fronds are shaped like lips. (Photo by Katherine Palmer)

The Japanese use rhizomes for pastry starch, and Russian settlers in Alaska fermented fiddleheads into home brew.

Don't eat raw fiddleheads. ⚠ They contain thiaminase—an enzyme that can reduce the body's vitamin B supply (cooking zaps the enzyme). Ironically, ferns also contain vitamin B—as well as vitamins A and C, iron, and potassium.

SUPERPOWER

Ferns are restoration experts, helping degraded soils to recover. They help filter toxins, including metals, from polluted soils. Once established, ferns support a huge family of vital soil microbes in their neighborhood.

WHO EATS AND SHELTERS HERE?

Roosevelt elk, deer, brown bears, varying hares, ruffed grouse, grasshoppers, and land snails eat fern fronds. A host of insects—white flies, red spider mites, mealybugs, and ladybugs—nibble ferns. Thrips and aphids pierce and suck the fern juice like a green smoothie.

The night-flying hummingbird moth shelters in lady ferns. Woodhouse toads, small mammals, and birds find shade and hiding spots from overhead predators in lush fern bouquets. Birds weave dry lady ferns into their nests for insulation.

FAIRY TALES

There is something utterly enchanting about eating fern fiddleheads. When you hold a handful of coin-sized green spirals, it's easy to believe in Jack and the beanstalk. I look for fiddleheads soon after the red-flowering currant and salmonberry bloom. In Alaska, I've dug through spring snow to find them hunched like praying monks in the cloister of rootstocks.

It's no surprise that the often rain-drenched Pacific Coast is home to forty species of ferns. Indigenous peoples layered ferns in cooking pits to separate fish, shellfish, or roots. They swabbed salmon and shaded berry baskets with fronds. They gathered crosiers and dug up roots. Steaming the fiddleheads is the traditional preparation method of the Tlingit, Coast Salish, and Athabascan Dena'ina. A cooked fiddlehead is tender and tastes akin to artichoke or asparagus.

But only a few ferns produce shoots or fiddleheads that are safe to eat. Ostrich fern and lady fern fiddleheads are considered safe—*if they are cooked*. However, bracken fern (*Pteridium aquilinum*)—while a celebrated delicacy in Japan and given the thumbs-up in older foraging books—is linked to stomach cancer.

Kayaking alone up an estuary river in Southeast Alaska, I was all eyes, ears, and nerves. Before I stepped on shore, I blasted the air horn twice to keep from surprising a bruin. Just upland from the stream, ferns rose in huge feathery plumes. Bear tracks, big as my boot sole, led upland. Ravens screamed. I had plans to snap off a dozen crosiers and paddle off to a bearless island to set up camp.

As I wandered among giant ferns, I called, "Hey, bear!" and asked permission: "Bears, if it's OK with you, I'm just picking my dinner. Thank you, bears." Every few feet, I knelt to select fiddleheads as high as my hand and snap them off at the base. I took only two per plant. While I picked, I kept watch.

As it happens, invisibility and ferns go hand in hand in ancient traditions. Native hunters rubbed their bodies with ferns to mask their scent. During Europe's Middle Ages, people believed carrying "fern seed" (spores) in their pockets allowed them to disappear from sight, see hidden treasures, "read the secrets of the earth," or perform the work of thirty or forty people. Shakespeare wrote of this in *Henry IV*: "We have the receipt of fern-seed, we walk invisible."

Obtaining such a powerful talisman as fern seed wasn't easy. According to myth, fern seed ripens on the eve of the summer solstice, then falls and disappears. An intruder seeking its powers might be torn to pieces by demons, or be overcome by lightning and thunder, or fall asleep under its magic spell.

I tied handfuls of crosiers into a red bandana and clipped it to my pack. Paddling out to open water, I saw storm clouds scudding over the Alaska Coast Range. It reminded me of the superstitious beliefs of my Polish ancestors: If you plucked a forest fern, then a violent thunderstorm followed. Guess I'd sling the tarp over the kitchen tonight.

LEFT: *Look for fiddleheads of lady and ostrich fern that are tightly coiled and one hand (7 inches) in height or shorter (a). Leave any fiddleheads that are too tall (b). Pick less than one-third of fiddleheads to avoid depleting rootstock. (Photo by Katherine Palmer)* RIGHT, TOP: *Gently rub off any scales (c) with your fingers until descaled and ready to be blanched (d).* RIGHT, BOTTOM: *Blanched fiddleheads*

HOW TO HARVEST FIDDLEHEADS

Use a sharp cutting tool to cut tightly curled fern fiddleheads seven inches or less in height (think "hand-span height"), or snap off by hand. Harvest from no more than a third of the plants in any given area, remove fewer than a third of the fronds from any given plant, and harvest only every other year so the ferns can recover, advises the "Alaska Non-Timber Forest Products Harvest Manual for Commercial Harvest on State-Owned Lands." A twenty-five-year study of ostrich fern showed that removing all the fiddleheads reduced the number of fronds produced for the next four years! A similar field study of ostrich ferns in Maine bears this out (see the "Forage Like

? FORAGE LIKE YOU AREN'T THE ONE AND ONLY

At the University of Maine Extension, David Fuller, an agricultural and nontimber forest products professional, researched the long-term impacts of harvesting ostrich fern fiddleheads. Over three springs, Fuller visited three natural patches growing under mature maple trees and collected 100 percent, 50 percent, and no fiddleheads. After three years, in the patch where he'd removed all the fiddleheads, half the ferns had died, and those plants that remained had suffered marked decline, producing less than two fronds per plant on average. Even in the patch where Fuller removed only half of the fiddleheads, the ferns suffered. Their fiddlehead output dropped from six to fewer than five fronds. Without enough leaves to gather sunlight and make starches and sugars for the rootstock, the plant gradually starves. Fuller's control group—where he removed zero fiddleheads—produced the same output each year.

Fuller advises ostrich fern gatherers to pass by any plant that shows visible signs of harvesting. If a fern is untouched, harvest fewer than half the fiddleheads.

You Aren't the One and Only" sidebar). When you see snapped-off fern stalks or cut stubs, scope out another fern.

After gathering fiddleheads, try to brush off as many of the brown papery scales as possible. Eating them will not harm you. You can use a toothbrush, or run cold water over the fiddleheads and use your fingers to rub them off.

OSTRICH FERN
Matteuccia struthiopteris

FAMILY: Onocleaceae (Sensitive Fern)
STATUS: Native
OTHER NAMES: Fiddlehead fern

A harbinger of spring, this perennial fern sends up fiddleheads on the heels of the last frost. Papery brown scales cover the fiddleheads, protecting the vulnerable new growth. As fronds unfurl, the scales fall free. For a proper ID, look for the distinct U-shaped groove along the inside of the frond stem.

Ostrich ferns showing vegetative (green) fronds and fertile (brown) fronds.

The ostrich fern has 2 distinct frond types. First to appear are the vegetative (sterile) fiddleheads. These stately ostrich plumes will become a crown of green ferns 2 to 6 feet tall.

In midsummer, fertile fronds can appear and grow 1 to 1½ feet tall (not all crowns display fertile fronds). In fall, the larger, vegetative ferns die to the ground. But the fertile ferns remain as dark brown spikes into the following spring. Fiddleheads emerge from a perennial crown that spreads by underground rhizomes that are easily damaged by trampling.

This fern is found in much of the northern hemisphere, including British Columbia and warmer areas of Alaska, across Canada to the eastern seaboard and down to Virginia, west to Nebraska, and north to Minnesota. It prefers alluvial floodplains and shady, moist areas beneath hardwoods such as maple and ash.

HARVEST GUIDE

WHAT: Fiddleheads
WHEN: Mid-May to mid-June
Collect only tightly coiled vegetative fiddleheads and the attached lower stalk. See How to Harvest Fiddleheads in Lady Fern.

LEFT: *Ostrich fern's brown fertile fronds*; **RIGHT**: *A vase-shaped cluster of fiddleheads* (Photo by Gingerjohns, iStock)

CULINARY TIPS
See Lady Fern.

WHO EATS AND SHELTERS HERE?
White-tailed deer, ruffed grouse, and varying hare munch fiddleheads and fronds.

Moths, including the gold-spotted ghost moth, use it as a host for their larvae. The tall, arching fronds provide cover for small animals and ground-dwelling birds.

WILDERNESS FORAGING WISDOM
JUDY BRAKEL

Today Judy Brakel lives on the ancestral lands of the Huna Tlingit in Gustavus, Alaska, north of Icy Strait at the entrance to Glacier Bay National Park. But she was born in 1939 in a fishing town 120 miles south of Juneau called Petersburg (or Séet Ká Kwáan in Lingít), and she grew up amid the hum and heyday of canneries and fish-processing plants. Judy remembers when salmon and crabs were offloaded by the gazillion at the local docks. "But vegetables at the store? You were lucky if there was iceberg lettuce and some carrots—maybe." So Judy took to foraging.

"Fish and crab," she says, laughing, "doesn't really count. But I loved to pick berries—blueberries, of course. I learned about wild greens from a Tlingit man—fiddleheads, nettles, Indian celery, violet leaves, beach greens, and beach spinach, my favorite."

Judy and her late husband, Greg Streveler, a former National Park Service scientist, grew a lot of their own food. And I mean a lot. They tended three gardens on scrabbly glacial outwash they had nurtured into rich humus. And they foraged—with a capitol F.

Before her retirement as an Alaska sea kayak naturalist-guide (and, years earlier, as an analyst for a commission to limit the number of commercial fishing permits in Alaska), Judy logged thousands of kayak miles in Southeast Alaska. Now in her eighties, Judy still launches off alone with kayak or knapsack. She goes for day trips to gather beach asparagus, sea vegetables, and berries, of course.

I asked my friend Judy—who lives in rainforest country, with glaciers, mountains, and ocean for a backyard—when foraging by foot or by kayak, besides rain gear and good

Judy Brakel checks the ripeness of highbush cranberry in Southeast Alaska.

footwear, what she never leaves home without. She shared the trio of essentials she carries in her pockets, as well as the other vital gear she stuffs in a backpack or in her seventeen-foot kayak.

Essential pocket trio:
1. **Jackknife:** "So if I went over overboard, I would have a knife."
2. **Firestarter:** "Lighter in a Ziploc with a bunch of dry lichen—*Usnea* or *Alectoria*—called 'old man's beard.' Sometimes a hunk of spruce pitch."
3. **Flashlight:** "Little metal pocket light."

Other wilderness essentials:
1. **Compass:** "Around my neck on a lanyard. Not as good as GPS, but it doesn't malfunction."
2. **An orange, plastic-bag-like tube tent and cord:** "So you can make a roofline and be inside."
3. **Sleeping pad (optional):** "It depends where I'm traveling. If the ground is cold, then it's gonna suck heat. Of course, you could use branches."
4. **Woolies:** "I'm a believer in wool. I was always telling my kids, especially my two boys, 'Don't forget your wool hat!' And that became a sort of a mom thing. You don't have to wear it, but bring it. I prize my wool camisole. Also, my wool 'wristers'— made from old wool socks with the feet cut off."
5. **Bear spray (optional):** "I use a piece of red webbing around my waist that holds a bear spray holster."
6. **Two ballast/foraging bags and a shovel:** "If I'm day kayaking, and I don't have a bunch of gear to weigh the boat down, I bring ballast sacks. Since I'm light, not big and herkie, in rough weather, ballast is going to make a lot of difference in how the kayak handles. The bags are made from an old nylon tent. I shovel in some wet beach sand or gravel. One for the bow, one for the stern. When I get to my destination, I may dump out the sand and fill them with seaweed!"
7. **Paddle leash:** "It's essential. Mine is a simple homemade affair."
8. **Flagger's vest:** "I almost got run over by a high-speed charter boat, and I real-ized I wasn't visible enough." (Author's note: During hunting season, bright vests are also recommended for mushroom foragers.)

Judy tells me how her family roved all over Southeast Alaska in a little motorboat, navigating with only a chart, compass, and pocket watch. Suddenly, her voice trails off.

"Hello, Judy? I think I lost you," I say into the phone. I think of how it would be to lose GPS power in a fog on a remote coast. After a few wordless moments, her voice returns. It feels like a public service announcement: Be prepared!

MUSHROOMS

Just how long humans have gathered mushrooms is anyone's guess. One of our earliest hints hearkens to the last Great Ice Age. The burial site of the Red Lady of El Mirón—a cave on the Iberian Peninsula—tells the story of an early mushroom forager who was seemingly was healthy, robust, rather tall, thirty-five to forty years old, and beloved—laid to rest with flowers under a hauntingly beautiful cave painting rubbed from red ochre. What researchers surmise from the shards of animal bones and botanic debris is that the Red Lady's family and band members hunted ibex and red deer, fished for salmon, and gathered herbs, seeds, and mushrooms. How do they know? Spores of agaric and bolete mushrooms were recovered from her dental calculus. Lawrence Straus, the lead archaeologist, wrote in his findings that the people of El Mirón were a lot like us: "They ate, sang, danced, told stories, reproduced, laughed, cried, slept . . . and they died"—more than eighteen thousand years ago. The Red Lady is a sister mushroom forager across time.

Some Pacific Northwest Indigenous peoples have celebrated the culinary gifts of mushrooms, while others considered them taboo. Fire-roasted chanterelles were a traditional food of the Nlaka'pamux (formerly called the Thompson Indians) of British Columbia. For untold generations, the Interior Plateau peoples of Canada have harvested the prized edible pine mushroom (*Tricholoma murrillianum*) and cottonwood mushroom (*T. populinum*), according to ethnoecologist Nancy J. Turner.

In California, Indigenous peoples understood how fire amplified the production of morels. In her wildly informative tome *Tending the Wild: Native American Knowledge and the Management of California's Natural Resources*, ethnoecologist M. Kat Anderson describes evidence that suggests they managed black morel crops with controlled burns. Today, the Southern Sierra Miwok still foster sustainable harvesting practices. Grandparents show younger generations how to gather mushrooms without disturbing the delicate mycelial threads beneath the earth so future fruits are abundant. They encourage the kids to always leave some fruits unpicked to waft spores.

Because mushrooms can't photosynthesize, they glean grub (carbon-stored energy) from something else. You could say mushrooms take three approaches to filching food. Some are laidback opportunists, happy to eat dead wood. Take, for instance, the oyster mushroom (*Pleurotus* species), whose mycelium acts like a big, thready stomach inside a tree trunk. These decomposer fungi (called a saprobe) survives by digesting dead trees.

Quite the opposite approach is employed by delicious honey mushrooms (*Armillaria* species), the thugs of the mushroom world. These parasitic fungi send out pathogens to target the roots of living trees and woody shrubs. Honey mushrooms can shape their mycelium into tough, cord-like growths called "rhizomorphs" to do their silent bidding. If you have ever eyeballed a rotting stump, up close, and seen wandering black threads about the width of a shoestring weaving through the punk wood, you were likely seeing a honey mushroom's death grip. Appropriately called shoestring root rot, this fungus can hang out in infected stumps and dead roots for decades. While honey mushrooms have a natural role in creating meadows and clearings for new trees, they also parasitize urban trees in parks and gardens, vineyards, commercial orchards, and millions of acres of healthy forests. Their success reaches epic proportions in eastern Oregon. In Malheur National Forest, one dark honey mushroom (*Armillaria ostoyae*) is known as the largest organism in the world, or the "Humongous Fungus." Its mycelium sprawls beneath a swath of forest over 1,800 football fields in size! This marauder may be up to eight thousand years old.

Not all mushrooms are tree assassins or squatters in derelict trunks. The third approach mushrooms take is to buddy up with living trees. The term for this relationship is "mycorrhiza," which translates as "fungus root." Here in the Pacific Northwest, mycorrhizal fungi include chanterelles, hedgehogs, and boletes. *Boletus edulis* buddies up with fir, spruce, pine, and hemlock, and the Pacific golden chanterelle cozies up to conifers including Douglas-fir and western hemlock.

All mycorrhizal mushrooms have specialized mycelium that can form a tiny "stocking cap" (called a mantle) over a host tree's root and between its outermost root cells. The mantle protects the tree's roots by releasing antibiotic compounds. It also provides a protective armor around the vulnerable root tissue. But the mantle's other crucial job is to grow miles of one-cell-thick filaments (called hyphae) into the soil. These wandering threads become the mycelium, or the body of the fungus. Together they work like a super-charged pump, drawing in mineral-rich water and scarce nutrients, such as potassium and phosphorus, from an area fifty or more times larger than the tree's roots. For these favors, the tree shuttles amino acids and essential sugars from photosynthesis to the mycelium for mycelium growth and to produce mushrooms. Trees can also share nutrients, water, and immunity-building chemicals with other trees through the vast, interconnected webs threading through the soil. The whole forest community benefits from mycorrhizal marriages.

In his book *Mycorrhizal Planet*, farmer and orchard master Michael Phillips writes, "Pick up a handful of old-growth forest soil and you are holding 26 *miles* of threadlike fungal mycelia, if it could be stretched out in a straight line." According to Phillips, those miles of mycelium "can sequester carbon in the soil in much more meaningful ways than any 'carbon offsets' humans could ever devise, which means focusing on

"IT'S NOT RAINING, IT'S *MUSHROOMING!*"

We were standing in a downpour in the North Cascade foothills, when I said this to my Fairhaven College students. We are studying edible and poisonous mushrooms in our Wild Food science class. For a half hour, we've seen nothing but two mushy boletes.

When we stop to gather around a downed alder trunk as long as a train car and freighted with palm-sized oyster mushrooms, everyone is giddy. Shelves of mushrooms, four, five, and seven high; white half-moons, full moons—the flush of fungi I'd been promising. Everyone is ready to dig in, especially Evan, the student who has eaten oyster mushrooms previously and is holding a tried-and-true French mushroom knife with a brush opposite the retractable blade.

"Hold on, friends," I say. "I have a new word for you! *Pleurotus* species are *saprotrophic*, meaning they eat dead trees. The Greek word *sapros* means rotten and *trophe* is nourishment. Oyster mushrooms release enzymes into dead or dying trees, like this alder, and help them return gracefully to the nutrient cycle so more forests can grow. They often appear in shelf-like clusters. Let's look a little closer."

When I lean over the log to slice a fruit, rain pours off my hood. I hold up the prized oyster fan and turn it over to show a moonrise of radiating gills—and no stem. I cut a second fruit from the log's topside.

"Note there's a short stem, and it is growing off-center. It's not smack in the middle of the cap. That's a key ID trait you can use to check against a poisonous look-alike: *Clitocybe* is a white-capped, white-stemmed mushroom that also grows on logs."

I cut fruit from the log's belly, down where leaf duff obscures the caps. "See how this oyster's stem is a panhandle, long and curved like a tobacco pipe?" Everyone is amazed at the morphological differences in one species.

Wherever an oyster mushroom fruits, it keeps its cap parallel to the ground to protect, nurture, and release spores. Mushroom mycelium is like a white-whiskered gnome that sends its cap skyward but always in relation to gravity.

"Ready to pick? Let's harvest less than two-thirds of the total. If we each cut six, we'll leave plenty of food for the birds and flies and beetles. These are called pleasing fungus beetles. Watch for their sluggish white larvae hiding in the mushroom cap flesh."

A few students give me that Mr. Yuck face. I downplay the grossness.

"Don't worry. You can avoid the tiny white larvae altogether by looking for their munching trails and entry holes. Don't cut those fruits. If you are still concerned, you can tear a cap down the center and look. They have little black eyes. If you find larvae, leave the mushroom here. Tuck it against the log. Or gift it to a classmate."

Evan gestures, nodding and pointing at his belly. Laughs of relief follow and first cuts of floppy mushrooms are held to the sky or torn in half.

"Remember, those itty-bitty larvae depend on the mushroom nursery in your hands." Realizing I had the same question twenty years ago, I add, "And what if you eat a beetle larva by mistake? They aren't poisonous. Steller's jays and robins love them and tear up the mushrooms to find them. Pick with your eyes first."

Oyster mushroom species are the third-largest group of cultivated edible mushrooms on the planet. In China, Japan, the Czech Republic, and the United States, they are grown for their nutritional, medicinal, and gastronomic qualities. Practitioners of traditional Chinese medicine grind oyster mushrooms into a powder and prescribe it as a muscle and tendon relaxant. Western scientific research links both the mushroom and its extracts to enormous health benefits. Just eating the mushroom appears to lower cholesterol, reduce precancerous lesions in the colon, and provide a dose of prebiotics. Extracts of pleuran, a beta glucan found in oyster mushrooms, also boast potent antioxidants. Recent research explored how oyster mycelium, exposed to blue light, makes shikimic acid, a precursor for making the antiviral drug Tamiflu. They can also whittle down the lignins in agricultural waste—such as mountains of corncobs and seed husks—and churn it into nutritional feed for livestock.

Oyster mushrooms are also superstars at bioremediation. They can "eat" toxic chemicals in industrial waste, contaminated soils, industrial dyes, and wastewater. In 2022, an international team of engineers and chemists studied how oyster mushrooms can break down benzopyrene (a cancer-causing chemical in engine fuel) into nontoxic minerals. More recently, an article in *Total Science of the Environment* touted the shape-shifting power of oyster mushrooms to eat plastic waste.

The truth is, we've hardly touched the tip of the oyster. But the enormous potential is growing like mycelia on a rainy day.

Flush of pale oyster mushrooms on an alder log

the health and well-being of these microscopic soil fungi is a crucial climate change solution." About 95 percent of all plants depend on mycorrhizal fungi for health and longevity! These hidden connections, working away in the darkness beneath our feet, also aid the growth of maize, legumes, wheat, squash, and even vineyard grapes. Mycorrhizal fungi have been unearthed in fossils as old as 460 million years. We are only now beginning to appreciate their gargantuan gifts.

When animals like squirrels or grizzly bears chomp mushrooms, they spread the spores like a kind of haphazard matchmaker. They help fungi meet more tree roots and help trees survive in nutrient-poor habitats. Northern red and flying squirrels also are unwitting fungal farmers. They stash prize boletes and other fungal fruits in the branches of evergreen trees to air dry. All the while, the fungus wafts spores into the forest below. These small mammals also devour belowground truffle mushrooms, which make up a bulk of their diets in late fall and early winter. Every place they visit, the flying squirrels leave fecal pellets rife with spores. Likewise, when grouse, Steller's jays, and racoons gnaw mushrooms, a dusting of spores accompanies them during their flights and walkabouts. Northern red-backed voles, another fungal connoisseur, trot across rodent runways atop fallen tree trunks between forays. The "poop and run" voles leave nitrogen-rich feces stuffed with thousands of mushroom spores.

Wild animals that consume mushrooms are more akin to pollinators, like the bees who fly about with pantaloons of pollen. Except that these "sporenators" perform a vital role for all of us. They spread genetic diversity, help mushrooms prosper, and benefit their tree associates too. These animals share wild foods into the future. How many of the wild mushrooms you've consumed were planted by our forest friends? Without this continual dance between plant, animal, and fungal kin, we would see far fewer edible wild mushrooms on our table, and, scientists say, fewer forests.

The damp fungal fiefdom between Alaska and California tops five thousand species of fungi and counting. For this chapter, I've selected five common, relatively easy to identify, and delicious mushrooms to forage: oyster mushrooms, morels, porcinis, chanterelles, and hedgehog mushrooms.

HARVESTING GUIDELINES

The most important mushroom harvesting tip is to be 110 percent sure you identify a mushroom correctly before you eat it. Many edible mushroom species have look-alikes that can cause gastric distress or worse—permanent liver damage or death. "When in doubt, throw it out." Here are tips for happy mushroom hunting.

Learn to identify mushrooms and tell edible from poisonous. Join a local mycological society or take a course in mushroom foraging from experts. Study a reputable, up-to-date field guide for your area. Learn the trees and other plants that associate with mushrooms. If you are using an older mushroom field guide, the names may no longer be current (see Mushrooms in Resources). Ask someone knowledgeable to confirm your identification. Consider using the community science app iNaturalist to help in your IDs.

Before you go, research the "personal use mushroom harvesting rules" for locations you plan to visit. This includes city, county, state, federal, and provincial parks, national forests, and Bureau of Land Management and Department of Natural Resources lands. More and more jurisdictions are placing rules online, including

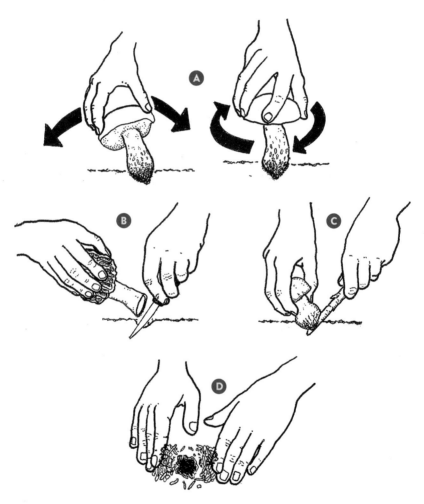

Minimize ground disturbance and compression when harvesting mushrooms: a, grasp the cap and rock it back and forth and twist; b, cut it; c, pop it out with a stick; d, always fill divot or hole.

harvest limits, species, and season. Contact a specific site manager if you have questions. If required, obtain a permit (many are free) to collect mushrooms.

Walk lightly. Compaction reduces air pockets and oxygen levels, making it challenging for mycelium to survive. If you discover and develop a secret patch, visit it infrequently.

When in doubt, leave it to sprout! Minimize "pluck and toss" by identifying mushrooms to the best of your ability in situ (in place) *before* picking. Get down on hands and knees to see the stem and cap. For example, use your phone camera to shoot a photo of the underside of the cap to see if it is gilled, toothed, or pored. Pluck up one specimen to lay on its side beside the others for study.

Pluck or cut? In 1986, the Oregon Mycological Society's Cantharellus Project began studying cutting versus plucking and, across a decade of research, found no statistical difference between either method of harvesting or not harvesting at all. Cutting doesn't disturb the mycelia or forest floor. And stumps may sprout "primordia"—tiny mushroom buttons at the base. If you pluck, fill the divot with some nearby leaf litter to help the mycelium thrive. For oyster mushrooms—which grow on dead and dying trees—either is fine.

Don't rake away duff or soil layers to expose mushrooms. An Oregon State University study of matsutake in the Umpqua National Forest found that raking away the forest floor and not replacing the litter "was strongly detrimental to matsutake production"—for nine years!

Leave behind the very young and the very old. One standard mentioned in a Puget Sound Mushroom Society harvesting rules sheet available online as of this printing is "chanterelles must have a cap diameter >1 inch." Mature golden chanterelles ("olden goldens"), for instance, are big-time spore dispersers. Some foragers cover the immature mushrooms with leaves to hide them until they can mature.

Pick no more than two-thirds of the mature mushrooms you find. Leave some behind to waft spores and to feed wild animals. Bears, deer, racoons, squirrels, mice, voles, grouse, songbirds, and a host of other small mammals and insects depend on mushrooms when other foods are scarce.

Pick mushrooms from clean environments. Mushrooms are sponges for toxic metals, such as lead, cadmium, mercury, and radioisotopes. Their mycelia are excellent "bioaccumulators."

Be a spore disperser. Carry your picked mushrooms in a net bag or basket so the spores can fall to the ground as you traipse through the woods. Tap the mushroom cap before picking to help disperse spores. Research has yet to confirm or negate these practices, but they make sense. After cleaning, return the trimmings to the woods.

Go slow: Try just a couple bites if you're eating a mushroom that is new to you. Wait and see how your tummy responds to this new fungal food. People react differently to the same mushroom species. Try only one new species at a time; avoid the "mushroom medley." Save an uncooked sample of the fruiting body, just in case. Avoid eating mushrooms raw.

Protect mushroom habitat by buying sustainably harvested, selectively cut forest timber. Forest mushrooms, such as chanterelles, boletes, and morels, live in a dynamic, often mycorrhizal, relationship with trees. Remove the forest and you eliminate the mushrooms. It may sound like a no-brainer, but US Forest Service studies show that chanterelle mushroom populations recover sooner after selective thinning than after clear-cut logging.

Support sustainable mushroom picking as a consumer. If your local store is selling, say, wild chanterelles less than one inch at the cap, mixed with adult chanterelles, or a restaurant is serving up baby chanterelles, politely ask them to please inform the foragers or suppliers they buy from to leave the babes in the woods so they can grow up and produce spores.

OYSTER MUSHROOM
Pleurotus populinus, P. pulmonarius

FAMILY: Tricholomataceae
STATUS: Native
OTHER NAMES: Northwest oyster mushroom, oyster shelf, pale oyster, tree oyster

The cap of *Pleurotus populinis* is often fan shaped, while *P. pulmonarius* may be fan shaped or lobed or lung shaped (note the word "pulmonary" in the species name). Both species of oyster mushroom sport caps with flexible, rubbery flesh and a smooth surface. The cap is domed when young, flat or flared upward when mature, and 1 to 6 inches wide. Cap color varies—whitish to buckskin beige or pinkish buff for *P. pulmonarius*. Gills are white when fresh and yellowish when dry. Stems vary from off-center to a panhandle to almost nonexistent. Aroma is pleasant, like sweetened milk. Mushrooms fruit repeatedly (seasonally) from the same dead trees or logs. *P. pulmonarius* and *P. populinus* can "fruit" both in the spring and fall.

Find oyster mushrooms on down and standing wood (snags) in forest settings. *P. populinis* grows on aspens and cottonwoods. Look for *P. pulmonarius* on hardwoods such as alder, oak, maple, and rarely on conifers.

HARVEST GUIDE
WHAT: Cap and stalk
WHEN: From spring to fall, winter in California

LEFT: *Shelves of oyster mushrooms;* **RIGHT:** *Cutting keeps your harvested mushrooms cleaner and minimizes damage.*

Cut or pluck oyster mushrooms. Cut away the adhering bark in the field. For eating, the cap is choice and stalk often tough. Wipe caps with a cotton cloth or soft mushroom brush, if needed, to remove debris. Check gills and cap meat for beetles and fly larvae and return the mushroom rejects to a forest with their host trees. The idea is to eventually inoculate more host trees with spores.

CULINARY TIPS

If you dry-sauté a handful of oyster mushrooms until the moisture is absorbed, then add butter to brown, the flavor is mild and sweet like condensed milk with a hint of almond. Try oyster mushroom tempura, pizza, ravioli stuffing, Thanksgiving dressing (a twist on traditional oyster dressing), flan, bread pudding, stroganoff, risotto, lasagna, ragout, puff pastry tarts, gravy, sesame-teriyaki stir-fry, or barley soup. Bake oysters on a sheet pan, Chef-Barry-Horton style, after brushing with olive oil and dredging in fine cornmeal, chili powder, and salt and pepper, and serve them with honey mustard sauce. Try Easy Oyster Mushroom Sloppy Joes (see Recipes). Sauté oyster mushrooms with garlic olive oil and serve on crostini with tomato, mayo, arugula, and bacon (see Recipes for Smoky Sea Bacon).

OYSTER MUSHROOM LOOK-ALIKES

Edible mushrooms you might mistake for the delicious duo of true *Pleurotus* are the shoehorn oyster (*Hohenbuehelia petaloides* group) and tough-fleshed veiled oyster (*P. dryinus*).

A smaller, thinner, all-white look-alike to oysters called angel wings grows in overlapping shelves on conifer wood. ❗ This "fringe edible" should perhaps be avoided. Although many foragers on both sides of the Pacific Rim—including myself—have relished them, angel wings (*Pleurocybella porrigens*) are responsible on two occasions for acute encephalopathy and death. In 2023, Japanese researchers published a paper linking these tragedies to three chemicals contained in *P. porrigens*. The victims were all elders with underlying kidney disease.

You can cultivate your own delectable oyster mushrooms from kits available online. One of the most delicious gifts I've received was a blue oyster growing kit. I placed the brick-sized block of myco-inoculated wood on my porch in a glass baking dish tented with a plastic bag. After a few weeks of spritzing with daily mist-baths, mushroom buds appeared, then clusters of long-necked oyster mushrooms grew. You may find cultivated oyster mushrooms in the produce section of some grocery stores and at farmer's markets too.

For long-term storage, I freeze them in "mushroom pucks" in a muffin tin. Tear oyster fans with your hands instead of cutting them up. Start at the outer edge and tear in the direction of the gills. Fry in a dry pan until copious juices are released, then mostly reabsorbed. Portion into one-half to one-cup servings in a muffin tin greased with vegetable oil. Freeze until solid. To remove, warm the underside of the muffin tin with hot tap water, whack, and stack in recycled yogurt containers or bags. Frozen, they keep beautifully for up to six months.

The winter or late oyster (*Sarcomyxa serotina*) is the pale oyster mushroom's winter cousin. It fruits in winter and as early as late fall after a hard frost. The fan-to-circular-shaped cap is as slick as an egg white, with olive green-orange colors (turning dark chocolate-orange with age). The gills are pale sherbet orange. A very short, blunt stalk with fuzzy hairs may be present. The winter oyster is edible, but pick the younger mushrooms for eating. Older winter oysters turn bitter. Some foragers blanch or boil mature caps (tossing the water). Others marinate and dry the young, sliced caps into chewy jerky.

SUPERPOWER

They may appear flimsy and passive, but when the going gets tough, these formidable fungi become carnivores, especially when starved due to a diet of nitrogen-poor deadwood. For decades, scientists have known that oyster mushrooms eat nematodes—common roundworms that make holes in the mushroom mycelium in order to slurp up mushroom soup du jour.

Until recently, scientists were puzzled by how a fungus could conjure up a chemical-zapping "nematicide." Now we know how their chemical arsenal works: When a nematode's snout nudges a tiny toxic lollipop (called a toxocyst) growing on a mycelium

Winter oyster mushroom

thread, a volatile nerve gas, 3-octanone, is released by the fungi. The gas rapidly paralyzes and kills the nematode and turns it into mushroom fertilizer. Oyster mushroom defense tactics may inspire new biocontrol agents for managing pesky parasitic nematodes in agricultural crops.

WHO EATS AND SHELTERS HERE?

Slugs, squirrels, chipmunks, and other rodents, such as deer mice, eat oyster mushrooms. Quail peck up scraps left by rodents. Grouse and black-tailed deer eat a cornucopia of mushrooms, especially in winter, when forage is limited. The pleasing fungus beetle, a small, oval, black beetle, specializes in oyster mushrooms. Larger bugs hunt for these beetles and are therefore dependent on tree oysters. Steller's jays and robins tear mushrooms apart to find insects and larvae.

MOREL
Morchella spp.

FAMILY: Morchellaceae
STATUS: Native
OTHER NAMES: Sponge mushroom, spongy, pinecone mushroom, little beehive

The best way to identify a true morel mushroom: Slice your candidate from top to bottom, and open the two halves like a book. The true morel reveals a continuous, empty chamber, like a cookie-cutter outline of a mushroom. A true morel *Morchella* has a conical to egg-shaped cap with a honeycomb or ladderlike pattern of ridges and pits, plus a hollow cap and stalk (no white fuzzy stuff) that are joined at the margins. (This is true for all but one group of species, the half-free morels: *M. populiphila* in the Pacific Northwest.) Distinguishing between species of true morels is tricky. Ongoing molecular research using the polymerase chain reaction has revealed many new morels over the years, and more keep "appearing."

There are three general groupings of true morels: black, yellow (or blond), and landscape morels. Of the black morels, most (but not all) show black-colored ridges—like the cap was rolled in black ink, with the indentations remaining lighter in color or ink free. However, a distinctive property of all black morels is that the pits tend to line up in a ladderlike way. Mushroom foragers further call black morels either burn morels, due to their propensity to emerge after a forest fire, or natural morels, because they evolved other incentives to waggle their fruit.

Two common Pacific Northwest burn morels are **sexy morel** (*M. sextelata*)—a fun name coined by ethnomycologist Daniel Winkler—and **gray fire morel** (*M. tomentosa*). The gray fire morel is also called the fuzzy-foot morel for the velvety black stem the young ones sport. The cap turns silver gray, like so many of us, as it matures. Both appear a year after a forest fire, especially in mountainous conifer forests west of the Rockies, although central British Columbia, where forest stands have been killed by mountain pine beetles, can be burn morel havens too.

Gray fire morel (Photo by Fred Rhoades)

LEFT: *East side forest morel;* RIGHT: *Mountain blond morel* (Photos by Fred Rhoades)

Two common black morels in this region that are natural morels are the **mountain black morel** or **east side forest morel** (*M. snyderi*) and **mountain blond morel** (*M. tridentina*). They don't need fire to fruit; warming spring temperatures or rain beckons the natural morel skyward. *M. snyderi* is found in the mountains near Douglas-fir, ponderosa pine, and white fir in California, Oregon, Washington, and other areas of western North America. *M. tridentina* is curiously seen on the periphery of burn sites.

Yellow morels are distinguished from black morels by their randomly arranged pits and ridges—much like a sloppy honeycomb. The egg-shaped cap's ridges don't blacken as they develop but remain yellow after the mushroom matures or is dried. The **American blond morel** (*M. americana*) pops up near cottonwoods and other hardwoods in river bottoms or near apple and ornamental ash trees in urban areas. Its cousin, the so-called **contorted blond morel** (*M. prava*), haunts the same habitat but also forests of conifers. Be cautious about harvesting morels in old apple orchards, commonly sprayed with arsenic-based chemicals that may end up in your prize morel.

A black morel that is neither a burn nor a natural morel is the **laddered landscape morel** (*M. importuna*). This urban interloper crops up in landscaped areas in wood chips or bark mulch covering garden

American blond morel (Photo by Fred Rhoades)

Laddered landscape morel (Photo by Fred Rhoades)

beds and pathways. It is found west of the Cascade Mountains in the Pacific Northwest and down into Northern California.

When it comes to eating, you don't need to fret over myco-vision details. It doesn't matter to your tongue if the morel is a black, yellow, or landscape morel. All true morels are *truly* delicious!

Mycologist and writer David Arora jokes that morels "usually grow outdoors." They can thrive in garbage dumps, sand dunes, basements, cellars, orchards, gardens, road cuts, deer trails, clearcuts, bark mulch, river bottoms, floodplains, burned forests—even bomb craters from World War II. A prolific bloom followed the Mount Saint Helens eruption, but they were too gritty to eat. In the Northwest, one prime area for black morels, according to mycologist and professor emeritus Fred Rhoades, is "east of the Cascade mountains in year-old burned forests and in the open, non-burned ponderosa pine forests." Along the West Coast, the morel season fans upward to higher altitudes and latitudes with the season.

HARVEST GUIDE

WHAT: Cap and stalk

WHEN: April or May to July or later, depending on elevation, snowmelt, and warmth of soil and air

Use a knife to cut the mushroom off at the base of the stalk. See "Harvesting Guidelines" earlier in this section.

CULINARY TIPS

All true morels are edible. If you learn how to identify "true" morels from "false" morels, then you are that much closer to the dinner table. See the "Know the Morel Imposters" section below. Clean morels carefully with a brush. They are too sponge-like and soak up water if you try to wash them. Just brush.

Never eat morels raw! ❗ Many poisonings across the country come from eating raw or poorly cooked morels. Cook them thoroughly or they can make you sick.

People generally sauté morels whole or after slicing them in half or in fanciful rings. Fold cooked mushrooms into omelets, risotto, or quiche; blend into a water-

HARBINGER OF SPRING

It was the time of white trilliums—the foaming edge of a spring heat wave. Four of us—all confessed "morel maniacs"—had driven east of the Cascade range in search of the elusive mushroom. A week before, friends had returned from Wenatchee with empty satchels. Much folk wisdom exists to help foragers judge the timing of a flush that might last only ten days. Here are three hints: look for fruiting morels when trilliums appear, apple trees bloom, or oak leaves are the size of mouse ears. A bit more reliable marker is that morels fruit after the winter snow melts, soil warms, and humidity holds.

As we stood in a grove of ponderosa pines on a balmy May day in eastern Washington, the earth under our boots had a pressed-down look. Even the air felt heavy with resinous incense, the unmistakable elixir of cottonwood sap. Where snow patches had melted, avalanche lilies carpeted the ground. Harbingers of spring, the yellow jester-hat blooms were a neon sign. The soil was heating up for black morels.

John, an elk hunter with a keen eye, spotted the first morel. It was as tall as my pinky finger, fruiting under a Douglas-fir sapling only two yards from our picnic table, but no one else among us had seen it. Pickin' was going to be easy—for John at least. Twelve hours later, after untold miles of climbing ponderosa slopes, we plucked a grand total of one dozen fruits. Humbled by the hunt, I found just one. We consoled ourselves—it was still too early. (One week hence, we learned that same ponderosa pine forest woke from its long winter nap and blazed with morels.)

Nonetheless, at $200 a pound for dried morels, we knew that we had one divine meal ahead. So how to prepare our dirt-clad dozen? Many chefs will tell you, sautéing in a lot of butter or a bit of olive oil or swimming in cream is best. Fat enunciates flavor.

We savored our cache at last, seated around a picnic table at 10:00 PM. My friend Jan had sautéed our beauties in olive oil and butter and waited until the juices were reabsorbed. We lingered over the rich but elusive flavor—nutty, earthy, sweet like cashews but with a texture like pounded steak. Morels are loaded with almost two dozen minerals, including calcium, iron, magnesium, potassium, and phosphorus. Recent studies show that eating morels can improve cardiovascular health, stimulate the immune system, lessen inflammation, and even reduce cancer risk and inhibit tumor growth.

When everyone insisted that I take the last morel, I popped it into my mouth. Darkness amplified my taste buds and helped the flavors sing. Chewing released a lasting memory of the hunt. It grew and brightened until long after we had cleaned the dishes and crawled into our sleeping bags. It hummed in my body like a song line, a stream of images and sounds, trillium-white snowfields, burnt caramel and myrrh cottonwood sap, the tremolo of loons sweeping across the still lake.

❓ HOT TIMES FOR MUSHROOMS AND BEARS

Wildlife biologists in Yellowstone National Park have observed fungal foraging by grizzly bears sixty-eight times in the field and detected mushroom spores in ninety-six feces samples. Young female grizzly bears get the grand prize for chowing the most. And we know that black bears in Cascadia eat lots of mushrooms too.

Whitebark pine seeds are a major food for bears, who sniff out protein-rich seed masses in squirrel caches. But when whitebark pine cone crops are small—and as rising drought and heat, fungus, and beetles continue to kill whitebark pines—morels and other mushrooms will likely become a more important part of the bruin diet.

Wild mushrooms provide a relatively high amount of protein and a concentration of energy comparable to that of soft and hard fruits. With only 13 to 18 percent fiber, edible mushrooms are highly digestible—good nutrition for both brown and black bears. When important foods like blueberries and huckleberries are scarce, mushrooms may make the difference between bears putting on enough fat for hibernation and successful mother-hood—and being too lean. Lean bears have lower success raising cubs. Questions to keep in mind as we forage: What animals, plants, birds, and fungi are impacted by drought, fire, insect outbreaks, disease, and tree deaths? If one foraged food is in short supply, what other critical munchies might a bear need in order to thrive? Think like a bear.

cress cream over salmon; or add to fettuccine with goat cheese and asparagus. Spoon cooked morels into ravioli or puff pastry; add to mac 'n' cheese. Simmer in stew, ragout, or stroganoff. Stuff raw morels with Dungeness crab, then bake and serve with tarragon cream. Mycologist Fred Rhoades's tip for preserving your precious morels is to dry them when fresh, then store in the freezer. To use, rehydrate in a small amount of water, strain out the grit, and add the soaking water to your morel dish.

WHO EATS AND SHELTERS HERE?

Grizzly bears frequent lodgepole pine forests to paw up black morels, false truffles, and *Russula* and *Suillus* species. Elk, mule deer, fox, raccoons, rabbits, gray squirrels, box turtles, and a variety of slugs, mushroom fly larvae, and other insects all eat the protein-rich, mineral-dense morel. Wild turkeys scratch in morel patches, but the verdict is still out if they are imbibing.

What you'll find in morels is grains of fire ash—and on rare occasions, a flat bug. Mushroom hunters Janny and Charlie—after twelve years of insect-free morels in eastern Washington—found their cache of post-fire morels crawling with "little flat bugs the size and color of black sesame seeds." They hitchhiked a ride over the Cascade Crest to Bellingham, where Charlie had them identified by an insect expert as Aradidae—or simply, "flat bugs." Go figure. There are over a thousand species! "Morel" of the story: tap and check—at least every twelve years.

KNOW THE MOREL IMPOSTERS

The imposters are early morel, false morel, and elfin saddle. Granted, not every myco-lover sidesteps the three *Morchella* look-alikes. Some experienced mushroom buffs

fancy the early morel, *Verpa bohemica*. They also know how to carefully prepare them, parboiling them first and throwing out the water before thoroughly cooking them in an open pan to remove toxins. ❗ Beginning mushroom foragers, if you are looking to bag a "true" morel (one you only need to sauté in butter and swoon over), learn these imposters and stay away!

Early morel, *V. bohemica*, also called the spring morel or wrinkled thimble cap, appears in early spring, about one to two weeks before the true

TOP: Verpa bohemica, or early morel (Photo by Fred Rhoades). BOTTOM: One way to distinguish between a false morel or brain mushroom (left) and true morel (right) is to slice it in half. If the cap and stem are one continuous cavity, it is a true morel. In false morels: a, cap hangs free from stem; b, it has cottonlike fuzz in stem; c, cap is reddish-brown; d, cap has brainlike wrinkles but no honeycomb-like pits and ridges.

LEFT: *False morel*, Gyromitra infula (Photo by Fred Rhoades); RIGHT: *Elfin saddle*, Helvella *species*

morels arrive (except in mild coastal California, where *Verpa* fruits in winter and spring). Early morels prefer riverside cottonwood stands and woods. The giveaway is their cap attachment at the tip-top of the stalk—unlike the true morels, the cap hangs like a skirt or lampshade—and the stems are "stuffed" with cottony hyphae, while true morels are absolutely hollow. Although early morels have long been eaten by foragers, they are also known to cause stomach upset. Avoid them or sample them in small doses after cooking well.

False morel, *Gyromitra esculenta*, also called brain mushroom, has a brownish cap with brainlike wrinkles or folds but lacks the pits and ridges of a true morel. There are other *Gyromitra* too: *G. infula* fruits in summer and fall, and *G. montana* pops up in snowmelt areas in late spring. Some experienced foragers eat the latter, but it is best left to the experts. Eaten raw, some false morels are deadly poisonous due to the toxin gyromitrin, which metabolizes into monomethylhydrazine—a component of rocket fuel. Even vapors inhaled when cooking are toxic.

Elfin saddles, *Helvella* species, have saddle-shaped gray to brown caps. The stems are sometimes pitted. They are more or less toxic and shouldn't be eaten.

PORCINI
Boletus edulis complex

FAMILY: Boletaceae
STATUS: Native
OTHER NAMES: King bolete, American bolete

Porcinis are large, robust mushrooms with tubes under the cap instead of gills. The porous tube layer is firm and white on young porcinis and becomes spongy and olive with age. At all ages, it peels easily away from the cap's fleshy underside. The off-white, tan, brown, or red-brown bunlike cap has a leathery surface that turns tacky when wet. The stalk is firm, club shaped, up to 10 inches tall, and white or brownish in color, with a coarse fishnet pattern (reticulation) on the upper portion. The cut flesh is white and stays white; it doesn't bruise blue.

The porcini complex includes *B. edulis* var. *edulis*, the California king; *B. edulis* var. *grandedulis*; and the white king, *B. barrowsii*. The related spring king (*Boletus rex-veris*) is found on the east side of the Cascade Mountains; it fruits from late spring through summer. All are delicious, edible boletes related to the king bolete, porcini. The inedible look-alikes are easy to learn with a little practice by referring to a good regional mushroom guide.

All of the boletes are mycorrhizal and live in close harmony with trees. In the Northwest, porcinis grow in association with conifers, such as Sitka spruce, shore pine, Douglas-fir, and oaks (California), in lowland to subalpine mountain forests. Sometimes found in association with birch and aspen too.

HARVEST GUIDE

WHAT: Cap and stalk

WHEN: Late spring to fall and into early winter (California)

See "Harvesting Guidelines" earlier in this section. Porcinis are often infested with fungus-gnat larvae, who love porcinis as much as the rest of us. You can clean your finds by cutting off the bottom of the stem to check the number of fungus-gnat

LEFT: *A trio of "kings"* (Photo by Fred Rhoades); RIGHT: *Note the netlike reticulation on the bulbous king stem.*

CASCADE KINGS

"Great day for mushroom views," I said, laughing. My husband, Chris, and I were hiking through the inside of a cloud on a mountain trail famous for spectacular panoramas. Mist swept past us. Ferns and huckleberry bushes dripped. At 4,800 feet in elevation, the loamy path traversed a subalpine fir and hemlock forest. We both knew from the elevation, tree species, and recent stormy weather that my comment wasn't far from the truth. Surely, we were entering porcini paradise.

Like black huckleberries and blue gentian, some porcinis are wild mountain dwellers. True, they like lowlands too. But after a fall rainstorm, go high. Fortunately, these delectable mushrooms often aren't far off trail, since they appreciate disturbed soils. The bad news is the young and most delectable porcinis—called buttons (or "number ones" in the industry)—camouflage themselves like rocks. Mature porcinis, on the other hand, tend toward gargantuan—standing up to one foot tall, with an equally broad cap. There's a reason they're also called king bolete.

The *Boletus edulis* complex is circumpolar, and when Europeans settled in the New World, they brought their Old Country names for this prized edible with them, including "little pig," or porcini in Italian. Whatever you call this prized edible, it is worth going out of your way to enjoy.

Fifteen minutes down the trail, I spotted the first candidate in a steep gorge. The enormous cap looked like a well-risen baker's bun. The robust stalk, flared at the base and tapered at the apex, had a sturdy quality.

All too often, a full-grown porcini, called a "flag" by commercial harvesters, is wormy with fungus fly larvae. Nonetheless, its size "flags" your attention. It says, "PSST, more of me may be hiding nearby." As I climbed down the ravine, bushwhacking through wet brush, I looked for humps and rocklike hillocks in the forest duff. Groping around the soil not far from the flag, I found two "babies" poking up from the moss.

Four key features distinguish the king. First, the cap's underside must have white tubes—not gills—packed so dense as to look like a cut raw potato with tiny pinpricks. (Sometimes I shoot

These four "little piggies" went home with Chris and me.

the underside of the cap by putting my phone on the ground. That way, I don't uproot unnecessarily.) Second, a smooth, creamy to red-brown leather cap. Third, a stout, bulbous stalk, off-white and embossed with a netted (reticulate) design. Fourth, no bruised blue flesh anywhere. But I didn't get past one. The photo shouted, "Gilled mushroom! Fooled you!"

Still on my knees, looking across the ravine at the gargantuan king, I glimpsed a new perspective. The lining of the king's broad crown revealed olive-gold sponge. It was overripe. Days earlier, this would have been worth picking. Its flesh would have been firm and the cap only partly open. Even if the "number twos" (in quality, as the commercial harvesters call them) house a few resident larvae, or "worms," you can pare out the wormy bits onto the forest floor.

A low whistle like a red-tailed hawk pierced the air. Chris was signaling. Twenty feet behind a giant spruce, he'd found a button trail—three egg-sized hills in the duff. Given a few scrapes with his knife, they transformed into porcinis. Unearthed, resting in his dirty palms, the chubby porcini buttons resembled their Italian translation, "little pig." Two of these little pigs went into my pack and wee, wee, wee all the way home.

larval (maggot) tracks. They seem to work their way up from the bottoms of the stems. Sometimes, if you cut off enough of the stem, you can get a larva-free upper part to bring home. In any case, you can decide how many larvae you can tolerate. If you decide not to remove larvae, be forewarned, you may not get your bolete home before the happy nibblers have eaten their fill!

CULINARY TIPS

Porcinis are rich in glutamines and have extravagant flavor. (Think MSG, but in healthy form.) Grind dried porcini bits into a powder and you will have a secret in your spice rack: porcini dust. Dry one-eighth-inch-thick slices of fresh porcini in a food dehydrator. Cut the dried steaks into half-inch pieces with scissors and grind pieces in

Lovely little king porcini (Photo by Hannah Moench and Cub Finney)

FIRE-ROASTED MUSHROOMS ON A STICK

Myco-chef Patrick Hamilton says his favorite way to prepare wild mushrooms when he's foraging in the Sierra Nevada is to roast them on a stick over a campfire. "So simple and delicious!" Don't forget to add a bottle of good vino, some butter or olive oil, and a starry night sky. Maple or any local hardwood branches make great roasting sticks.

Spear morels or bolete slices (or if your hunt was fruitless, use shitake or cremini mushrooms), and then smoke them on a stick over the coals of a fire. Sauté in butter until well cooked. Serve on pasta tossed in olive oil and generous shavings of parmesan. The nutty complexity is worth every dollar! Your taste buds will sing.

a nut or coffee grinder. Store the porcini dust in a glass jar with a tight-fitting lid. Sprinkle porcini dust on hashbrowns, lamb brushed with olive oil, scallops, fish, pork loin, or steak, then sear for an unbelievably flavorful crust. Stir the magic dust into gravy and soup. Try fresh-shaved raw porcini in salad, or fold smoked porcini into an omelet, risotto, mushroom tarts, or savory bread pudding.

Some people peel off the tubes on mature specimens, eating only the white flesh. Porcinis are a treat grilled, pickled, marinated with duck and ginger, ground into pâté, or simply seared in an oiled pan over a campfire! Before cooking porcinis, clean them by gently wiping the cap and stems with a damp cloth. Use a vegetable peeler to rid them of any dark spots. To preserve porcinis, slice, dry in a food dehydrator, then store in the freezer in an airtight container to preserve flavor. Like morels, rehydrate in a small amount of water (just enough to cover the pieces) and then use the flavorful rehydration water for preparing your dish.

WHO EATS AND SHELTERS HERE?

Northern red squirrels and flying squirrels harvest mushrooms and hang them amid tree branches to dry, then cache the food for winter in hollowed-out witches'-brooms—ball-like thickets of branches made by rust fungus. Red-backed voles—like linebacker mice in furry coats—stash porcini bits in the earth, where they sprout. Our largest North American land mollusk, the banana slug, eats cap, gills, and robust stalk right to the ground. (I wonder, are their mucosal trails speckled with spores?) Fox sparrows and a host of other birds enjoy boletes too.

Larvae of beetles, moths, and butterflies begin life tunneling through caps and stems, before gaining wings. Wild fungus flies love many mushrooms, but their larvae especially find a feast in king boletes.

PACIFIC GOLDEN CHANTERELLE
Cantharellus formosus

FAMILY: Cantharellaceae
STATUS: Native

Easy to identify, these goblet-shaped mushrooms have a cheery gold to dull yellow-orange color and decurrent folds or ridges that run under the cap and down the stem. The folds may branch or fork near the cap's edge. Caps run 1 to 4 inches wide and have a suede-like texture. Young golden chanty caps may be lightly domed with an in-rolled edge. Mature caps often flare upward, turn wavy on the edge, and show a slight dip, sometimes a perfect resting spot for needles and forest duff. Caps and stems bruise yellow brown. The flesh is firm but rubbery and flexible, not brittle.

Second-growth and, less commonly, old-growth evergreen forests, from Southeast Alaska to Northern California, plus the oak woodlands of Northern California. Mycorrhizal with Douglas-fir, western hemlock, and other conifers such as spruce and pine.

HARVEST GUIDE
WHAT: Fruiting body
WHEN: Midsummer to late fall (until freezing temperatures set in), fall to winter (in milder areas and microclimates of California)
See "Harvesting Guidelines" earlier in this section.

A gold rush of chanties (Photo by Chris Moench)

SINGING MUSHROOMS

The word *chanterelle* derives from the Greek *kantharos*, meaning "goblet" or "cup." In French, *chanter* means "to sing." I like to think of Chanticleer, the ignoble rooster in Chaucer's *Canterbury Tales*, singing clear as the daylight from his barnyard perch.

Guess what? Chanterelles sing. My husband swears by it. One August, we were bumping up a washboard Forest Service road, climbing through second-growth Douglas-fir and western hemlock. Suddenly, Chris hit the brakes, pulled over into the weeds, and ran into the woods.

I thought he'd drunk too much green tea. Minutes later, he reappeared holding a bouquet of golden chanterelles. They were as beautiful as flowers, with an aroma of apricots. The underside of the fluted cap and stem had vertical ribs like corduroy.

"How did you know to pull over here?" I asked, feeling both amazed and incredulous. Chris is infamous for trickery. Yet he swore he hadn't seen the chanterelles glinting from the road. Nor had he previously visited this particular patch.

"I just knew. They were singing," he told me.

A year later, following a late summer rain, we returned to the same spot with net bags in hand. At the drip line of a stove-sized Douglas-fir trunk, under a crisscross of sword ferns and Oregon-grape, we found a haul of trumpeting golden chanterelles.

They looked like still-life blossoms waiting for Georgia O'Keeffe. Nearby, youngsters winked under needles and duff. We plucked a few adults, brushed off the dirt, placed them in our bag, and walked deeper into the forest.

Chanterelles defy cultivation (they need tree roots to buddy with). Rising from dead leaves, these cheery yellow fruits evoke sunshine on dark winter days. Next to cod liver oil, chanterelles are one of the most concentrated natural dietary sources of vitamin D. Dried chanterelles retain their potency for up to six years.

A brush or a bandana wipes dirt free.

CULINARY TIPS

Chanterelle flesh is firm and fibrous like chicken breast, with a fruity odor akin to apricots or pumpkin. The mild, earthy forest flavor pairs splendidly with anything buttery or cream based, such as a cream soup or custard tart, as well as grain and egg dishes, fowl, wild game, steak, and seafood. Chanterelles are fabulous roasted, baked on pizzas, or pickled. Avoid masking the chanterelle's delicate flavor with too many competing ones.

Clean chanterelles ready to be cooked

Choose chanterelles that are firm and have no soft or mushy spots. Clean them by brushing off dirt and debris, or wash them quickly under running water just before using. Tear or cut for cooking. Fresh sautéed chanterelles release moisture, so allow the flavorful juices to reabsorb. A word of caution: Some people experience gastric distress from chanterelles, especially if they're undercooked, so cook them for at least fifteen minutes, and go easy the first time you partake. You can freeze chanterelles to enjoy out of season. Sauté them in a little butter or olive oil. Pack them in their juice and freeze.

WHO EATS AND SHELTERS HERE?

Golden chanterelles can persist a month and a half to as long as ninety days! I once tested this by taking a photo of a two-inch-tall chanterelle beside a Douglas-fir and then hiding it under bigleaf maple leaves. A month later, it was three inches tall and still picture-perfect. Almost three months later, it was still standing, but half the cap was edged with rot like old pumpkin. Squirrels, deer, elk, moose, bears, and even wild boar have all been observed in the vicinity of chomped chanterelles. Yet, here in the Northwest, only in exceptionally dry years have folks seen signs of partly eaten chanterelles. Insects don't seem to touch them, and neither do land mollusks like the otherwise funga-voracious banana slugs.

Research now suggests high levels of the pigment beta-carotene, which gives the chanterelle its egg-yolk-yellow color and packs it with antioxidants, may act like an insecticide to deter insects and grazing animals like deer and voles. Perhaps this explains the chanterelles' long lives.

ENCHANTINGLY EDIBLE CHANTERELLES

Here are other scrumptious chantys in our region. Research is expanding the *Cantharellus* group, so check a recent regional mushroom guide for updates.

Cascade chanterelle (*C. cascadensis*) occurs in arcs and groups in Douglas-fir forests from coastal British Columbia to the Oregon Cascades and California Sierra Nevada. It has a stocky, golden stem and thick, forked ridges that include cross veins more often than other *Cantharellus* species.

White chanterelle (*C. subalbidus*) favors mature and old-growth Douglas-fir conifer forests, and sometimes second-growth forests too. This choice edible is white to cream with a stout, robust body.

Rainbow chanterelle (*C. roseocanus*) lives with Sitka spruce, lodgepole pine, jack pine, and Engelmann spruce west of the Rockies. This large, stocky chanterelle has a pinkish cap and apricot gills that pale with age.

Winter chanterelle (*Craterellus tubaeformis*), also called yellowfoot chanterelle, is a tasty edible with fragile flesh. It grows in Sitka spruce, Douglas-fir, and western hemlock forests from Alaska to Northern California. Often fruits in clusters, in moss or bogs, or by wet woody debris, late fall to winter. Cap top is dull orange to light brown with a dip or hole. Under cap shows pale decurrent, forked ridges. Hollow stem with yellow base or "foot."

CLOCKWISE FROM TOP LEFT: *Cascade chanterelle, white chanterelle, winter chanterelle, rainbow chanterelle* (Photos by Fred Rhoades)

KNOW THE GOLDEN CHANTERELLE IMPOSTERS

Friends and students have brought me bags of woolly pinespike and false chanterelles to "eyeball, just in case," before cooking them up. These look-alikes share colors, decurrent gills, habitats, and seasons with our prize. However, "true" chanterelles in the genus *Cantharellus* have shallow, ridgelike, decurrent gills, often with cross veins. Chanties don't grow on wood; false chanterelles do. A good way to tell if you have a golden chanterelle in hand is to tear it in half longways, from stem to cap. They have sturdy, flexible, rubbery flesh that is stringy when torn like string cheese or cooked chicken breast! The imposters are more brittle and crumbly.

Woolly pinespike (*Chroogomphus tomentosus*) has a cap shaped like a red-orange vase or funnel lined with medium-sized scales that look woolly. Edible but unremarkable.

False chanterelle (*Hygrophoropsis aurantiaca*) when mature has a funnel-shaped orange caps (sometimes browning in the center); sharp, forked orange-yellow gills; and thin flesh. They grow on logs, woodchips, and humus. May give you a bellyache. ❗

Jack-o'-lantern (*Omphalotus olivascens*) grows on wood and has bladelike gills. This somewhat regionally uncommon but fantastic-looking mushroom glows ghoulish green at night and shouts *poisonous*! ❗

TOP TO BOTTOM: *Woolly pinespike, false chanterelle, scaly vase chanterelle* (Photos by Fred Rhoades)

Scaly vase, scaly chanterelle, or wooly false chanterelle (*Turbinellus floccosus*) has an orange, stout, vase-like cap with a deep depression and orange to rust-orange concentric scales. Decurrent pale ridges are irregular and crinkly. Avoid all scaly chanterelles in the Northwest. ❗ People report nausea, vomiting, and diarrhea after eating it. A similar species, *T. kauffmanii*, has a cap shaped like a tannish-brown vase or funnel-lined with large, abundant, coarse scales, and it has wrinkly gills and folds. ❗ Like the scaly chanterelle, leave it in the forest.

HEDGEHOG
Hydnum spp.

FAMILY: Hydnaceae
STATUS: Native
OTHER NAMES: Hedgehog, sweet tooth (*Hydnum repandum* group); wood urchins, wood hedgehog, Oregon bellybutton hedgehog (*H. oregonense*); western wood hedgehog (*H. washingtonianum*); Olympic hedgehog (*H. olympicum*); honey hedgehog (*H. melitosarx*)

Hedge your bets on this delicious and easy mushroom to ID! If you see small spines or "teeth" under the cap (imagine a ceiling of miniature stalactites), you have found a "toothed" mushroom! The teeth are actually tubes for dispersing spores and easily break loose with the push of your finger. Hedgehog caps are dry and smooth like apricot skin. Cap color ranges from buff to apricot orange. Both the stem's exterior and flesh are white. Mycologists are still sorting out new species. Taking note of the tree species where you find your hedgehogs bristling will help with identification. Meanwhile, any hedgehog makes a great edible; they have no worrisome, poisonous look-alikes. Note that other toothed mushrooms are tough fleshed, not brittle.

Pacific Northwest from Alaska to California. Find them in deep mosses under conifers, including Sitka spruce and black spruce. They also partner with evergreen huckleberry.

HARVEST GUIDE
WHAT: Cap and stem
WHEN: Late summer, fall, or early winter depending on location
See "Harvesting Guidelines" earlier in this section

CULINARY TIPS
Closely related to chanterelles, hedgehogs have a similar taste and texture; use them like chanterelles. Toothed mushrooms can be a soil magnet; trim off dirty stem butts while in the forest, unless you want to comb the fragile teeth for bits of debris later. Hedgehog flesh is brittle and crumbles, so be careful transporting them. When I don't have a basket or hard-sided container, I wrap the hedgehogs in a bandana or tuck them into my wool hat for a careful carry in the top of my pack.

SUPERPOWER
Recent research shows an Asian *Hydnum* with antioxidant and antimicrobial umph. Like apples, green tea, red wine, and onions, it also packs in quercetin, an antioxidant

LEFT: *Hedgehog heaven*; **RIGHT**: *Look for tiny teeth, or tubes, under the cap.* (Photo by Chris Moench)

and anti-inflammatory, as well as ferulic acid, a free-radical scavenger. Some studies suggest *Hydnum* also has anticancer properties and may help build resistance to the bacterium staphylococcus.

WHO EATS AND SHELTERS HERE?

Insects and their larvae seem to leave hedgehog mushrooms alone. The red squirrel is rumored to eat them—along with at least forty-five other mushroom species.

TREES POINT THE WAY TO MUSHROOMS
PATRICK HAMILTON

After finding Patrick listed online as a mushroom foraging teacher in the Bay Area and admiring his impressive bio, I cold-called him. We talked for two and a half hours.

Patrick, also known as the myco-chef, has been mushroom foraging and cooking for over forty years. He confessed to me, an hour in, that his girlfriend jokes, "Hiking with you is like hiking with a dog. You stop and sniff things, taste them, you go all over the forest, stop at this tree, then that bush."

Funny, because that is also how our conversation unfolded. It was more like a continuous burst of interrelated topics. We'd immerse ourselves in a story, then find a tangential mycelial thread that took us wandering in an entirely different direction. The topics jumped from magic mushrooms, to seaweed, to "exploding things with dynamite," to kayaking in Alaska, to fire-roasting chanterelles on a stick in the High Sierra under a field of stars.

"I love campfire-roasted mushrooms." Patrick sighed. "So simple and delicious! Jennifer, what's your favorite way to prepare chanterelles?"

"Hmm . . ." I tried to think of something unusual—after all, he was *the* myco-chef. After a moment, I blurted out, "Pickled or—"

"*Pickled?* Nah! You obliterate the forest flavor! Agh! But tell me, what do you add to the brine?"

"Apple cider vinegar, garlic, and bay."

"Of course. What else?"

"Fresh thyme."

Typical.

"Um . . . and wild Sonoran oregano."

"Ah . . ."

Myco-chef Patrick Hamilton (Photo used by permission of Patrick Hamilton)

To avoid lingering under the myco-chef's displeasure, I fast-forwarded to my second chanterelle prep technique: "Or chanterelles dry-sautéed in their own juices!"

"Now you're talking. Have you heard of the mushroom called Canadian bacon?"

"No, but I know of a bacon-flavored seaweed called dulse." I was being a smart aleck now.

"Oh really? Well, I'll have to try that dulse of yours! These mushrooms are famous for growing in Gustavus, where you guide kayak trips."

"Hmm. What do they look like?"

"Blue . . . blue chanterelles."

"Can they look purple, and do they grow with Sitka spruce and western hemlock?"

"Yes, that's it!"

Wow. I guessed right. I didn't know the mushroom by name. But I knew the trees, even though I was a thousand miles away in a Douglas-fir forest. Knowing the trees led me to the right mushroom.

Patrick says his students aren't as interested in chanterelles as they are in finding black morels.

"Those are the hardest mushrooms to find." He sighed again. "Sometimes we don't see a one. Folks get disappointed, because they paid a lot of money for my class. I tell them, 'Hey, you learned a lot of geology and botany, how to tell a noble fir from a white pine tree. That's how you find a lot of mushrooms: you need to know where they like to grow.'"

SEAWEEDS & BEACH VEGETABLES

OK, let's face the music. Seaweed from the seashore can be slippery, rubbery, drippy, even mucosal. Yet more and more foragers are turning into seaweed slickers. "Kale's ocean cousin"—kelp—is debuting on menus, market shelves, and in the offerings of online wild food purveyors. Without looking too hard, you can find kelp chips, kelp pasta, sea lettuce popcorn in three flavors, and vegan "sea bacon" (smoked, fried dulse). Brewers and distillers are beckoning buyers with winged-kelp-infused gin and bull kelp beer. Still, most folks on Planet Ocean remain timid about inviting seaweed to the dinner table or happy hour.

I sympathize with "skelptics." I remember my bewilderment at age eleven when a cafeteria server in a Tokyo youth hostel ladled me up a breakfast bowl: kelp swirled into a miso broth and a cellophane-wrapped seaweed sheet. Where were the scrambled eggs? The buttered toast?

Over time and tides, I have learned to love seaweed. A month-long sailing trip on the Inside Passage in my roaring twenties convinced me of seaweed's extraordinary gifts. There were five of us. We had all agreed to carry only limited food stores (oatmeal, olive oil, homemade survival biscuits). We'd rely on handlines for catching fish, a spinnaker of good luck, and guidance from our most valuable crew member, "Ethnobotanist Alan," who taught Northwest Indigenous and edible plant use at a community college. I'll never forget feeling so alert and alive with hunger. And how, somewhere in drizzly Johnstone Strait, while I shivered cold and hungry in a leaky raincoat, a single handful of plucked-fresh nori seaweed amped my energy three-fold. I was sold on seaweed.

Now, each New Year's Day, I mark my calendar six moons ahead for the low tides of spring and summer. I call my "Seaweed Sisters"—a half dozen dear friends from the Coast Salish tribal communities. We go out in our rubber boots, with grateful hearts, holding our net bags and scissors as the tide draws away from the shore to reveal an undersea garden: sea lettuce, rockweed, rainbow leaf, sea cabbage, feather boa, bull kelp, and most cherished of all—"black seaweed," akin to nori.

Sea veggies are some of the prettiest vegetables in the world. They grow in hues of scarlet, burgundy, tarnished copper, gold, and brilliant green. Some are shaped as intricately as Italian lace. Others grow as delicate as feathers or as tall as trees. A few are crinkled like seersucker. Many are as soft and supple as silk scarves. Hold a leaf to sunlight, and it turns as translucent as cathedral glass or as filamentous as frost on a windowpane. Some people even mount these delicacies on art paper and frame them.

And only sea vegetables dance! They jump and jerk to the bass thunder of waves. They shimmy and shake to the ebb and flood tide. Consequently, sea vegetables are the most nutritious vegetables on Earth. Transforming minerals into delicious, easily digestible food is the sea vegetable's raison d'être. Instead of rooting around in dirt all day, drawing in whatever minerals are present (or lacking) in cultivated soil, sea vegetables dance in a nutritious broth that holds every mineral known to humankind.

Why not try some vitamin Sea? Bull kelp, weight for weight, offers up to six times the calcium of cow's milk. Sea lettuce packs in almost twice the protein of eggs. Nori (the sheet that wraps your sushi roll) and sugar kelp get far higher marks than beef on their amino acid scorecard. Nori has almost twice the vitamin C of oranges. Sea veggies are a good source of vitamin K and B vitamins, including B12. That's great news for vegetarians and vegans, whose diet may be lacking in B12 and some amino acids. But keep in mind that nutrient loads in sea vegetables swing like the tide during the growth season. A Danish study found sugar kelp contained a high of about 10 percent protein in November and a low of just 1 percent in May. Nonetheless, sea vegetables mostly still surpass land vegetables and grains when it comes to vitamins and minerals.

Most of us have been noshing on seaweed our whole lives; we just didn't know it. Seaweed extracts such as algin, agar, and carrageenan are common ingredients in prepared foods, used as gelling, thickening, and stabilizing agents stirred into ice cream, salad dressing, pudding, yogurt, boxed soups, and nut milks. A sparkling, clear beer or a fruity, translucent wine has carrageenan to thank as a clarifying agent. And if you love wild-caught seafood, then you've probably eaten seaweed. Did you know wild salmon get their omega-3 and omega-6 essential fatty acids from the seaweed, phytoplankton, and land plants they gulp directly or consume secondhand?

Eating seaweed hasn't hurt you. More than likely, it has helped. Seaweeds are high in fiber and low in saturated fat and sugar. They contain a pharmacopeia of good-for-you phytochemicals too. Brown seaweeds, such as bull kelp and rockweed, are rich in fucoidan and phlorotannin. Those are big words with even bigger potential to reduce risk factors for type II diabetes, heart disease, and obesity. They also fight inflammation, cancer, aging, and Alzheimer's. They are antimicrobial and effective anticoagulants (to help avoid stroke). Stores of sodium alginate are also packed in brown seaweed cells, which bind with radioactive compounds (such as strontium 90), then whisk them out of the body in stool form.

FORESTS OF THE SEA

Jacques Cousteau famously called the Pacific Coast's kelp forests "sequoias of the sea." It's an apt comparison. These swaying algae live in towering undersea groves as tall as a ten-story building. Anchored to the ocean floor by rootlike fingers, crowned by fluttering blades, they look more like trees than seaweed.

Like terrestrial forests, kelp forests support a rich, layered ecosystem from floor to canopy. Sea otters spool lithely in the uppermost leaves for anchorages, then dive for abalone, urchin, and crab. Jeweled top snails and China-hat limpets slide up and down the kelp's sturdy elastic stalks, lapping up dinner. Shimmering herring, rockfish, and throngs of kelp perch take cover in the leafy shadows, while toothy lingcod and sea lions patrol the edges. Even the kelp's rootlike anchor—a holdfast—is a condo for thousands of crabs, brittle sea stars, sponges, and blue mussels that cling to its nooks and crannies. In short, kelp forests are a hub of activity and key to ecosystem diversity and health.

Once, on a full-moon night in Southeast Alaska, I paddled in my sea kayak toward a giant bed of bull whip kelp. The kayak's hull bumped over unseen kelp leaves and stalks, then stopped. A comet trail of green sparks slashed the jet depths as a harbor seal spiraled underneath the hull. An explosion of luminous darts scattered as herring zoomed for cover. Microscopic plankton—called *Noctiluca* (meaning "night light")—were lit up from the merest agitation of every moving creature in this undersea forest. The swishing tail fin of a kelp perch radiated fans of light. Jellyfish pulsing through the black universe flashed brilliantly, then dimmed, as they opened and closed in search of food.

Historically, bull kelp was one of the most versatile marine materials used by Northwest coast Indigenous peoples. Cells evolved to grow at a sixty-degree angle to the stipe, which allows the bull kelp to "whip dance" in the storm waves without breaking. Indigenous fishers processed the elastic stipes for stretchy fishing line, harpoon lines, and rope. They meticulously split and cured the cut stipes by soaking them in salt and fresh water, drying them, rubbing them with dogfish oil and other animal fats, and repeating the process for up to a year. The hollow stipe and bulb were used as a container to carry water, Hudson's Bay Company molasses, and eulachon fish oil. The fish-oil-laden kelp stipes were shouldered inland over coastal mountains on the so-called grease trails. The Nuu-chah-nulth people made skin salve by filling kelp bulbs with heated deer fat and resinous cottonwood buds. Once the fat solidified, the mold was peeled away, leaving a hand-sized block of salve. Kelp was traded to inland First Nations and Tribes for a source of iodine and to treat goiter. Kelp blades served as flavoring and moisture for pit-cooked foods. Blades were layered over fire-heated rocks, clams, and other seafood. One hollow bull kelp stipe, cut like a long-necked funnel, was inserted into the firepit and used for adding water, creating a steam bath for seafood.

I had come in search of some succulent kelp blades to wrap a fresh-caught salmon to be barbecued. I lifted a bull kelp stipe and bulb as large as my forearm onto the kayak deck, and sliced two blades with my sheath knife, making sure to cut each blade at least two feet up from the large, bulbous float. By cutting in the "meristem," or continually growing part of the blade, you don't stop the kelp's natural growth.

A kelp harvest impact study by the Department of Natural Resources (DNR) of Washington tested winged kelp and sugar kelp, clipping some approximately one foot above the holdfast (Washington law) and others right at the stipe (illegal because you leave no fluttering blade). Only the kelp cut a foot above the holdfast recovered and grew. But a DNR survey of kelp harvesters' buckets found that well over half the people snipped their sea veggies either close to or at the bare-bone stipe. (See "Harvesting Guidelines" for additional recommendations.)

En route to shore, I passed a recently exposed boulder as big as a Volkswagen Beetle, draped with puckery sugar kelp and golden feathers of winged kelp. Sugar kelp has a natural sweetener, mannitol, commonly used as a sugar substitute in diabetic-supportive foods because it doesn't change the glycemic index. I cut two ruffled egg-shaped blades, the length of my arm, a foot above the holdfast and rolled them up like a scroll.

Of all the culinary kelps, winged kelp is by far one of the most mild and versatile. It cooks up quickly into a buttery-tasting leaf with a hint of steamed asparagus. The Japanese call this delectable, mild-tasting kelp wakame. Our Pacific wakame is a close cousin to the Japanese wakame (*Undaria pinatifida*) found in dried flakes in miso soup packs. Added to soups, it imparts a pleasing umami flavor to the broth. Sweet and nutty, fresh winged kelp is fabulous when lightly sautéed in olive oil. Every leaf has two different textures—a crunchy midrib reminiscent of cucumber, and a supple outer leaf.

To collect winged kelp, I lifted one golden feather at a time and trimmed off the upper one-third with my knife. The family jewels of winged kelp hide in two dozen or more bladelets growing opposite each other in bunches at the base. All three kelps I harvested that evening in the wild are also commonly grown on kelp farms from Alaska south to the Salish Sea—the transboundary waterway between Washington and British Columbia.

Once on shore, I laid the yard-long, ribbonlike leaves of bull kelp and frillier sugar kelp out on our camp's picnic table. My husband rubbed the salmon with olive oil and garlic, rolled it up in the leaves, and placed it on a rack above the fire coals. After twenty minutes, he flipped the whole shebang and roasted the other side. The outer layers were burned black, but when he cut it open with a sharp knife, the inner leaves glowed kelly green.

We served our lovely salmon with a vibrant tangle of wakame sunomono—delicate snips of lime-colored ribbons of winged kelp, blanched for fifteen seconds, sliced thin as fettuccine, then marinated with rice vinegar, sesame oil, ginger, and a pinch of sugar. Snippets of winged kelp's midvein rib gave the salad a cucumber crispness. We ate our fresh feast by candle lantern and toasted the kelp gardens for their role in it all.

A bull kelp bed

For thousands of years, people of the Pacific Rim and beyond have gathered edible seaweeds. Giant kelp and other seaweeds were identified in hearth remains in Chile's fourteen-thousand-year-old Monte Verde archeological site. Today, our Pacific Coast offers a delicious underwater forest of golden-brown, crimson, and green sea vegetables. It's high tide we invite them to our tables!

In this chapter, you will learn about eight notables grouped by color—brown, red, and green. The edible brown seaweeds described are bull whip kelp, giant kelp, winged kelp, sugar kelp, and rockweed. The red edible seaweeds are nori (called "black seaweed" by First Nations and Tribes), dulse, rainbow leaf, Turkish towel, and Turkish washcloth. And the green seaweeds are sea lettuce, string lettuce, and sea hair. Don't be bummed if you can't easily harvest wild seaweed at a beach; you may have easier pickin's online. Five of the seaweeds featured here are currently being farmed on the West Coast. We'll also explore two briny beach vegetables that skinny-dip during the highest tides: beach asparagus (also called sea bean or pickleweed) and goosetongue (seaside plantain).

HARVESTING GUIDELINES

Obtain a recreational seaweed harvesting license, if one is required where you plan to gather seaweed. At the time of publication, to harvest in Washington, you need to buy a shellfish and seaweed harvesting license, which is available at sportfishing

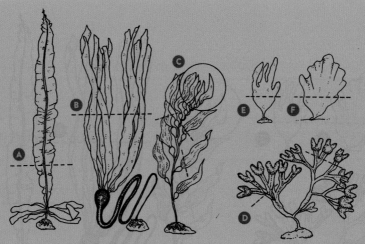

To sustainably harvest seaweed, always leave the anchor point in place: a, cut winged kelp and sugar kelp **at least one foot** above the holdfast; b, cut bull kelp blades **at least two feet** above the bulb; c, cut giant kelp's uppermost perennial blades and lower blades as directed by state regulations, which may vary; d, cut fucus here and there; e, and f, cut **only half to two-thirds** of a blade for dulse, sea lettuce, nori, rainbow leaf, Turkish towel and washcloth.

ERRATA: An error was made in the seaweed harvesting information on p. 179. Refer to these corrected guidelines: ". . . cut bull whip kelp blades (*Nereocystis*) **at least** twenty-four inches above the bulb. Cut short-stemmed kelps (e.g., winged and sugar kelp) **at least** twelve inches above the holdfast . . ."

stores and online. Neither Oregon nor British Columbia require licenses. If you are an Alaska resident, you can harvest for personal or subsistence use and do not need a permit. If you are not an Alaska resident, then you need to buy a valid sportfishing license. For updates, check with your local agency:

- Alaska Department of Fish and Game
- British Columbia Ministry of Agriculture and Lands
- California Department of Fish and Game, Marine Resources Division
- Oregon Parks and Recreation Department
- Washington Department of Fish and Wildlife

Read up on your local regulations. Know where and how to harvest each species and how much you can take. Daily limits, equipment, and techniques differ up and down the coast. In Washington and California, you can pick ten pounds (wet weight) each day.

Know which tidelands and ocean areas are off-limits for harvesting. For instance, harvesting seaweed is prohibited in ecological reserves, marine reserves or refuges, provincial parks, and most national or state parks, including underwater state parks. More than 60 percent of Washington's intertidal areas are privately owned. In Alaska, the state owns all intertidal and subtidal lands from the mean high tide out to three miles. In Oregon, all coastal lands between the vegetation line and mean low tide are part of the state's Ocean Shore State Recreation Area and are held in public trust.

Use a knife or scissors to cut blades. Using rakes or forks damages habitat and holdfasts. SGang Gwaay Dolly Garza, a seaweed educator on Haida Gwaii, recommends blunt-tipped children's scissors.

Cut kelp blades outside the plant's growing region and leave

Seaweed harvesting tools: cooler with ice packs, cutting tool, bags, license, boots, guide, and scale. Washington regulations required a scale at time of publication. (Photo by Katherine Palmer)

part of the blade to photosynthesize. For example, Washington law says to cut bull whip kelp blades (*Nereocystis*) twenty-four inches above the bulb. Cut short-stemmed kelps (e.g., wing and sugar kelp) twelve inches above the holdfast to ensure that the species can continue to grow. In Alaska, you can harvest attached bull kelp stipes for food. In Washington, however, only beached and unattached bull kelp stipes can be harvested.

Cut seaweed here and there over as large an area as possible. Clear-cutting patches impacts marine habitats and creatures—from crabs to fish to plankton to shorebirds. Also consider gathering from several sites instead of all in one spot.

Leave holdfasts attached to the seafloor or rocks. In most areas it is illegal to remove holdfasts. They serve as condos for undersea creatures. It may look like a curious rootlike ornament to you, but it's a kingdom to a baby octopus. Dulse regenerates blades from the holdfast's nubbin. Pluck it and you erase a future generation.

Harvest only what you can ID and only as much as you can process. Seaweed can spoil easily after it is cut or if it warms up in a sun-exposed plastic bag. Take a cooler with ice packs and cloth, net, or plastic bags for storage. Pick cleanly. Use a different container for each species to make them easier to sort later. Remove all seawater. Leave seaweed bags open to breathe. You have hours or days (depending on the species) to dry, freeze, cook, or pickle your veggies. Plan ahead about how you will process, store, and preserve your precious sea veggies.

Move with awareness, and watch where you step! You can crush a lot of life trying to get to your prized sea veggies. At low tide, seaweed is a blanket that hides crabs, snails, sea stars, anemones, and more. Rainbow leaf and fucus do not regrow branches when damaged underfoot.

Leave seaweed with eggs on the beach. Before you cut, take time to look at each blade and meticulously remove critters so they have a chance to survive. In early spring, herring leave massive amounts of eggs, a half inch thick or more, on kelp blades. It is illegal in most states to harvest this without a special permit.

Rinse blades oceanside before bagging. Wave cut seaweed underwater to dislodge tiny animals, such as snails, crabs, isopods, and beach hoppers.

Consume safely by harvesting at clean sites. Seaweed can absorb PCBs, DDT, flame retardants, and chemicals in fuel. Avoid sewage outfalls due to potential for contamination by bacteria, norovirus, and hepatitis. Know the history of your beach regarding hazardous waste sites, logging facilities, manufacturing areas, and industrial sites. Seaweeds are a magnet for radioactive isotopes and arsenic, as well as metals such as mercury, lead, and cadmium. If areas are closed to shellfish harvesting due to fecal contamination, the seaweeds may be tainted too. However, seaweeds are not affected by PSP (paralytic shellfish poisoning) or domoic acid. Whenever possible, harvest on open, wild coasts or in clean, well-circulating waters.

Support First Nation and Pacific Islander/Asian families who may be picking where you harvest too. They may use the resource for renewing culturally and spiritually significant foodways, sharing knowledge from Elders to youngers, strengthening food sovereignty, and harvesting for individual and community use in their traditional territories and usual and accustomed harvest areas, which is a legal treaty right.

Be aware that state and provincial laws allow "recreational harvesting" of seaweed for personal consumption only. It is illegal to sell or barter the seaweed you gather with a recreational harvest license. You would need a commercial license to sell your seaweed.

There are traditional ways of harvesting *Porphyra abbotae,* used by Indigenous knowledge holders in northern British Columbia and Southeast Alaska, that follow different techniques. I respect these time-honored ways of Indigenous traditional harvesting based on millennia of stewarding seaweed beds for food. During the approximately three-week window when "black gold" is at its prime, Indigenous harvesters wind long blades around a hand or forearm, then pull the bunch to break off the seaweed. If you are Indigenous and learning this special harvest technique from Elders at, say, the annual spring seaweed camps, follow their best practices.

HOW TO STORE SEA VEGGIES

When you're in the field, storing perishable sea veggies can be tricky. Exposed to too much heat, they can faint into a limp, goopy pile. That's a bit surprising, since many seaweeds (sea lettuce and nori, for instance) can dry to parchment paper at low tide and rehydrate into a silken scarf at high. Wet-harvested, however, the sea vegetable's clock of decomposition starts ticking.

When I'm out on a beach, I carry a cooler with ice packs. When I'm sea kayaking, I tuck them right behind my seat. Stored in net bags, they can keep cool for hours. On land or a boat deck, a plastic bag left in the sun warms up quickly. I usually rinse seaweed only when it's on the beach and gritty with sand. At home, I avoid rinsing kelp in fresh water until I'm ready to use it. Rinsing can degrade the blade and cause blistering. Use within a day or two—or store it for later use by freezing or drying. Freeze your preferred portions in plastic bags. Rinse in fresh water just before you use it to remove ice crystals or any unpleasant briny aroma. Sea veggies keep six months in the freezer.

To dry blades, hang on a line with clothespins like kelp stockings, or lay on a screen or tablecloth in the sun outdoors until crisp. Alternatively, dry seaweed in an oven: on parchment-paper-lined baking sheets and dry at 200 degrees F or the lowest possible temperature until crisp. Or use a food dehydrator set at 110 degrees F.

If you store bone-dry seaweed in airtight jars with desiccant packets, it keeps for years. Snip into bite-size pieces before hydrating. For winged kelp blades, I scissor out the chewy midrib and reserve it for salsa and grains.

Hang large blades on a clothesline.

BULL WHIP KELP
Nereocystis luetkeana

FAMILY: Laminariaceae (grouping: brown algae and kelp)
STATUS: Native
OTHER NAMES: Bull kelp, bullwhip kelp, ribbon kelp, sea otter's cabbage, bulb kelp, golden bulb kelp, horsetail kelp

Bull kelp is one of the fastest-growing sea vegetables in the world. It can grow to be more than 100 feet tall! The long, hollow, whiplike stalk (stipe) terminates in a grapefruit-sized bulb (nematocyst) crowned with 2 clusters of ribbon-shaped blades reaching about 30 feet long, though sometimes they grow as long as 120 feet. Both bulb and stipe are hollow and filled with a mix of gases—carbon monoxide, oxygen, and nitrogen—that buoy the blades to the surface.

Fertile blades show dark-chocolate-brown reproductive patches (sori) the size of your foot sole. I like to say these are the "kelp children." Leave them on the beach or in the water. When they are ripe and ready, the "spore patch" will detach, leaving a hole in the blade. The patch sinks down to the seafloor and releases thousands of microscopic spores. Spores sprout into female plants (egg factories) or male plants (sperm centers). Fertile eggs release an odiferous calling card by wafting out pheromones. Alerted sperm zero in—and shazam!—a baby bull kelp plant is born. A mere 5 adult kelp plants produce enough spore material to seed a 100-acre seaweed farm and grow up to a million pounds of delicious kelp!

Alaska's Aleutian Islands to Central California wherever the sea is in motion: surf-pounded coasts, headlands, and channels, and sheltered bays with currents. Anchored sub-tidally, bull kelp grows into canopy-forming undersea forests in water up to 56 feet deep.

LEFT: *Bull kelp bed in Alaska;* **RIGHT:** *Bull kelp grows up to 1 foot a day.*

❓ HELP THE KELP

In some areas of Washington's Puget Sound, scientists have tracked a disturbing 96 percent loss of bull kelp. Helen Berry of the Washington State Department of Natural Resources and her team have recorded a 63 percent loss since nautical charts first marked kelp beds as navigation hazards starting in 1878. Elevated sea temperatures, low concentrations of nutrients, and pollution seem to be the culprits. Thankfully, kelp beds flagging shorelines with strong currents and deep-water mixing zones are likely serving as refugia for sheltered areas of Puget Sound.

The bull kelp in south Puget Sound is too precious and rare to harvest. If you do harvest bull kelp between Alaska and California, go to more open shorelines with wave action or channels with strong currents.

HARVEST GUIDE

WHAT: Leaves (called blades), stalk (called stipe), bulbs
WHEN: Blades (in peak form) late spring to summer, stipes summer to winter
At the time of publication, **it is legal only in Alaska to harvest live, attached bull kelp stipes**. Check your local regulations. Look for beached stipes with a uniform brown color that lacks white mushy spots. See "Harvesting Guidelines" earlier in this section.

Bull kelp has declined severely in Washington over the past century and a half. ❗ See the "Help the Kelp" sidebar to learn more.

CULINARY TIPS

See the "Culinary Uses of Kelp" sidebar below.

SUPERPOWER

Bull whip kelp can grow a whopping one to two feet a day. One record-breaker measured 118 feet from holdfast to wavy fronds! That's longer than a double semitrailer truck! As kelp blades grow and mature, the tips degrade and shed. In the process, called senescence, bits get carried off by ocean currents. Those kelp snack packs serve as a coastal foodbank for thousands of animals, including us. They feed legions of hungry bacteria. Zillions of zooplankton—think seafood in microscopic forms (baby Dungeness crab, wiggly prawn larvae). Rivers of tiny fish. Acres of oysters. Countless clams. Untold urchins.

IS IT OK TO GATHER KELP WASHED UP ON A BEACH?

Have you ever toed over a drift of seaweed wrack? And then a flurry of beach hoppers started *boing boing-ing* everywhere? These frisky, shrimplike critters graze on the composting confetti of the red-green-brown seaweed you just schmeared on your shoe. Brian Ulasky, a University of Alaska Fairbanks researcher, counted over forty-seven-thousand hopping, crawling, squirming invertebrates—including coastal centipedes and pseudoscorpions—dining on Homer-area wrack across a six-month period. I call them "kelp composters," and they are also survival food for migrating shorebirds. Waves and rain eventually wash the last gooey bits of kelp out to sea.

Herein is the final stage of the kelp compost cycle: kelp fertilizer. Gardeners swear by the stuff. Field trials show yields increase by as much as 24 percent. Don't get too excited and dash to the beach with buckets and garbage bags, though. Check seaweed harvesting rules and guidelines first. And remember, beached wrack isn't seaweed gone to waste. It's kelp before it grows springs, wings, fins, and feathers.

Cut bull kelp blades at least 2 feet above the bulb so that they can continue to grow.

These seafoods in turn feed rafts of sea otters and scores of bigger fish, like herring and anchovies, that feed even bigger fish—like sheepshead, black rockfish, and salmon. An oyster's diet is up to 70 percent kelp. A rockfish's hovers at 40 percent. How do we know this? Seaweeds carry distinct signatures of fatty acids and carbon. Scientists can trace these signatures across the coastal food web. In the Aleutian archipelago, David Duggins and his team of marine ecologists discovered kelp-derived carbon in clams, oysters, crabs, and cormorants. At Friday Harbor Lab in Washington's San Juan Islands, Duggins's team traced the fatty-acid signature of bull kelp to salmon, black rockfish, and kelp greenling.

That's not all kelp offers. It can reduce ocean acidity in the neighborhood. Oysters raised in aquaculture near kelp grew plumper meat and thicker shells. Kelp provided both food and a mild halo effect that reduced ocean acidification in its vicinity.

WHO EATS AND SHELTERS HERE?

Under the sea, swaying beds of kelp are salad bars for northern kelp crabs, graceful kelp crabs, lacuna snails, chitons, limpets, and sea urchins. Pacific blue mussels, oysters, forage fish, and clams eat decaying kelp bits. Beach hoppers munch beached kelp, as do deer. Stable isotopes of kelp and kelp carbon are found in most seafoods, which means cormorants eat kelp indirectly, as do whales, sea lions, and coastal brown bears. If you eat seafood, so do you!

Over a thousand animals and plants—too many to list here—inhabit the "Kelp Belt" of the Pacific Northwest. Here are a few: sea otter, spotted harbor seal, pelagic cormorant, red octopus, kelp bass, Pacific herring, rockfish, pinto abalone, California spiny lobster, California sheepshead, and gumboot chiton. And don't forget the other understory seaweeds that find shelter beneath kelp canopies.

GIANT KELP
Macrocysistis pyrifera

FAMILY: Laminariaceae (grouping: brown algae and kelp)
STATUS: Native
OTHER NAMES: Macro kelp (*M. integrifolia* and *M. pyrifera* are now considered one species)

One of the fastest-growing kelps in the world, giant kelp can shoot up 14 inches a day and reach 180 feet long. Imagine a sea vegetable 18 stories high! Fingerlike holdfasts as big as dinner plates live up to 7 years and can sprout several stipes 4 inches thick. The gold cord-like stipe may have 100 or more individual blades flagging from top to bottom, moving like little windsocks in the ocean current. Shaped like overgrown lasagna noodles, these wavy, tooth-edged blades amplify water turbulence, helping the kelp feed better on carbon dioxide and minerals from the sea.

Giant kelp has 2 distinct kinds of blades: Fertile blades (sporophylls, spore-producing blades) are nearest the holdfast. Higher up, the vegetative blades have a pear-shaped, gas-filled float to buoy the 16-inch-by-3-inch blades. At the tip-top, new blades sprout to eventually split off from their siblings. In California, giant kelp is commercially harvested using a boat mower, then processed for its gooey alginate for the food industry or dried for nutrient- and mineral-dense kelp supplements.

❓THE FUTURE OF KELP FORESTS

Yes, it's true, our iconic, wild, propeller-clogging, cold-water kelp forests are losing ground. Over the last fifty years, more than one-third of the world's kelp ecosystems have declined. Losses are linked to marine heat waves and ocean warming, pollution, competition from invasive kelps, and hungry leagues of sea urchins. Heat waves starve kelp by limiting nutrient flow as warm water sprawls atop cool, nutrient-rich water. A stratified ocean means nutrients can't mix about in the vast soup.

Then there's the unintended imbalance of predators and their prey. In Central California, recreational overfishing of adult sheepshead (a fish that targets purple sea urchin) plus sea star wasting disease (a vanishing act that turned the purple-sea-urchin-eating, twenty-something-armed sunflower stars into ghostly piles of bones) led to a sea urchin population explosion. In some places, the urchin numbers grew by 164 percent. Consequently, up to 90 percent of the kelp forests between Central California and northern Oregon were chewed to nubbins by purple urchin.

But there's a holdfast of hope in the ancient strategies of coastal kelp. Microscopic stages (gametophytes) can delay their development on the seafloor and create a "bank" of microscopic forms until they can literally "grow up" in more favorable ocean conditions. And researchers and community scientists are taking stock of mature coastal kelp by boat, airplane, drone, satellite, dive, paddleboard, sea kayak, and even comparative nautical charts (circa 1870). The "help kelp!" rally cry is building a wave of momentum. In 2020, "The Kelp Plan" was launched in support of the conservation and recovery of Puget Sound's kelp forests. Dozens of commercial seaweed farms are being licensed in Alaska, British Columbia, and Washington. Partnerships with First Nations, Tribes, and nonNatives are cautiously and collaboratively building kelp aquaculture into a coastal industry—as they should. Meanwhile, divers in California are "weeding out" voracious kelpivores—the purple urchins munching kelp to nubbins—by the truckbed full. The urchins are then fattened in tanks, like high-end tilapia, and sold to restaurants and seafood entrepreneurs. I hear it takes a bunch of uni scooped from many palm-sized purple urchins to stuff a sizable sushi roll. It's worth repeating: If you can't beat 'em, eat 'em!

What can you do to help the kelp forests? Order up uni-crowned sushi rolls with California purple urchin and a side salad of farmed sea veggies! Support kelp restoration and responsible seaweed farming in your region. Harvest wild kelp only in areas where populations are robust and healthy.

LEFT: *Giant kelp washed up by the tide;* RIGHT: *Kelp undulates underwater* (Photo by Natalie Ruffing, iStock)

Grows in extreme low intertidal (perhaps as little as 10 feet above seafloor in parts of Alaska) to subtidal rocky reefs on open coasts. In the eastern Pacific, it ranges from Kodiak Island, Alaska, to Baja California, Peru, Chile, and Argentina, and in the southern hemisphere, from New Zealand to the sub-Antarctic and around the Falkland Islands.

HARVEST GUIDE

WHAT: Float, leaves (called blades), stalk (called stipe)

WHEN: Blades from spring to fall, beached kelp from fall to winter

Giant kelp grows from a meristem area at the top. According to Alaska Department of Fish and Game regulations, you must not cut or dislodge giant kelp from its anchor point. Only the uppermost blades, the part that grows perennially, may be harvested. Do not cut it more than one foot below the water surface. Giant kelp cannot be harvested where herring are spawning. Check the regulations for your state or province, and see "Harvesting Guidelines," earlier in this section.

CULINARY TIPS

Raw giant kelp blades can be slippery due to alginic acid. To reduce the slippery factor, blanch fresh or frozen blades (dip quickly in boiling water). Layer blanched blades in lasagna for a gluten-free noodle. Brush melted butter on dry blades in place of phyllo dough for "kelp-kopita." Swap in blanched kelp blades for grape leaves in Greek dolmades. Giant kelp is used as edible parchment for baked fish. Dry and pulverize for salty seasoning (sea-soning!). Blanch and then cut the stipe into thin disks for salsa or chutney or grain dishes. Pickle the pear-shaped float! Giant kelp is a vital part of

⚠ AVOID ACID KELP

As you are harvesting, learn to see and avoid "acid kelp," the color-changer known as *Desmarestia*. This brown seaweed has two forms: a furry foxtail and a flat ribbon with side blades showing a toothed edge and vein pattern. If in doubt, take a nibble. It won't kill you. It will taste lemony or slightly bitter due to sulfuric acid. Avoid tossing acid kelp into a bag with other seaweed. It will bleach them all white and turn them gloppy, spoiling your catch. My light keeper friends, the Roses, made a pickling vinegar with acid kelp.

TOP: *Witch's hair;* BOTTOM: *Flattened acid kelp*

the late-winter herring-roe-on-kelp fishery in Southeast Alaska and British Columbia. For thousands of years, First Nations have gathered this prized roe on seaweed.

WHO EATS AND SHELTERS HERE?

Bat stars eat youngsters. Purple urchins and giant red urchins nibble holdfasts and may cut the kelp loose. Pinto abalone, dusky tegula snail, northern kelp crab, and concave isopod munch stipes and blades.

In Southern California and northern Baja California, researchers found almost eight hundred animals linked to giant kelp and three hundred other seaweeds! About one hundred fish species depend on giant kelp forests, say researchers Rita O'Clair and Sandra Lindstrom in their book *North Pacific Seaweeds*. Sea otters sleep amid giant kelp fronds. Bryozoans, a frosty crust of colonial animals, inhabit the blades. These crusty hitchhikers reduce the kelp's ability to sip nitrate and ammonium from the sea's soup, but they also ooze ammonium, which the kelp uses. The grape-sized dusky tegula retreats upstalk to flee the many-armed predatory (and giant) sunflower sea star. Floating rafts of storm-torn kelp may shelter hundreds of tiny invertebrates, fish, and hitchhiker seabirds. Kelp rafts ferry tiny animals and kelp spores to new coastlines and seed genetic diversity.

WINGED KELP
Alaria marginata

FAMILY: Alariaceae (grouping: brown algae and kelp)
STATUS: Native
OTHER NAMES: Wing kelp, broad-winged kelp, honey ware, edible kelp, American wakame, Pacific wakame

This seaweed is an annual with a golden-brown feathery shape and a prominent, flat mid-vein. Blades are up to 10 feet long and 8 inches wide. Look on the lower stipe for 8 to 40 "wings" (sporophylls) up to 12 inches long. Don't cut off these reproductive wings! Leave future generations behind.

Look for winged kelp on low-intertidal to mid-intertidal rocky beaches, exposed boulders, and coastal cliffs along the open coast and in more protected waters with active currents from Alaska to Central California. It may grow on the holdfasts of other kelps.

HARVEST GUIDE
WHAT: Leaves (called blades)
WHEN: Spring to early summer (optimal)
By summer, blades are often shredded and torn by wave action. See "Harvesting Guidelines" earlier in this section.

Winged kelp (Photo by Hannah Black, courtesy of North Cascades Institute)

CULINARY USES OF KELP

There are many creative ways to use your foraged kelp.

Blanch it. Sugar kelp, giant kelp, bull kelp, and winged kelp blades are like pasta of the sea—big, waving noodles. Blanched, they transform into a bud-green sheet of pasta with a medium tooth. Use them whole as seafood lasagna noodles, or carefully roll and slice the (slippery!) blades matchstick thin for fettuccini.

Candy it. Candied stipe can be used in ice cream mixes and cakes and as a chewy surprise in a chocolate truffle. Fold crispy sugar kelp or dulse into melted chocolate.

Dice it. During the last minutes of cooking (to maintain the lovely green color), slice fresh kelp into half- or one-inch pieces with a knife or scissors and stir into hot bouillabaisse, chowder, grain dishes, soups, sautéed vegetables, or shakshuka.

Dry it. Dried bull whip kelp blades surprise the tongue with an intensely salty zing, and winged kelp's mild and delicate flavor profile makes it a versatile ingredient. Crumble "sea prosciutto" on pizza, Caesar salad, egg dishes, and soup; sprinkle dried kelp flakes on ice cream, fresh melon, sliced nectarines, or chocolate sauce; or add pulverized dried kelp to banana bread, brownies, pie crust, cookies, sourdough bread, and rustic artisan bread (see the "How to Store Sea Veggies" sidebar, earlier, for drying instructions).

Fry it. For an even crispier, flakier, and more delicate condiment, fry pieces of fresh or dry kelp (the size of playing cards) in canola or grapeseed oil for a few seconds on each side. Flake over pizza (it tastes like anchovies) or watermelon-and-avocado salad with a squeeze of lime (reminiscent of prosciutto; see Watermelon Kelp Salad in Recipes). Fry large pieces of fresh kelp blade in beer-batter tempura.

Pickle it. Kelp bread-and-butter or dill pickles are a nutritious swap for a cucumber pickle. Add blades to pickled cauliflower, asparagus, dilly beans, beets, and kimchi.

Stuff it. Hollow bull kelp bulbs welcome grain, meat, mushroom, or nut stuffing. Bake and slice them into rings.

Cut seaweed into pieces "no longer than the tines of a fork," as chef Vincent Nattress taught me.

LEFT: *Winged kelp is named for the dozens of winglike sporophylls on the lower stipe.* RIGHT: *Blades drying in the sun*

CULINARY TIPS
See Giant Kelp.

WHO EATS AND SHELTERS HERE?
Sitka black-tailed deer munch winged kelp when thick snow covers browse. A host of herbivores graze winged kelp, including black turban snails; purple, red, and green sea urchins; and the slow-moving pill bug of the intertidal zone, the kelp isopod.

Many creatures who shelter in bull whip kelp and giant kelp also shelter here.

SUGAR KELP
Saccharina latissima (formerly *Laminaria saccharina*)

FAMILY: Laminaria (grouping: brown algae and kelp)
STATUS: Native
OTHER NAMES: Sugar wrack, sweet wrack, sugar tang, sea belt, devil's apron, poor man's weather glass

This perennial lives 3 to 4 years. The golden-brown, egg-shaped blade lacks a midrib. Blades in sheltered sites are thinner, tear easily, and have two undulating rows (bullations) at the base; blades growing on exposed coasts are thicker, leather-like, and closely wrinkled. Grows to 10 feet (3.5 meters) long and 8 inches wide, with stipes 20 inches long. Grows fastest from winter to early spring. Holdfast is fingerlike, with a firm grip.

Sugar kelp evolves into wavy or strap-like blades, depending on wave patterns and water velocity.

Commonly farmed from Washington to Alaska and across the northern hemisphere. Widespread in the Arctic and on both sides of the Pacific. Low intertidal to subtidal (around 60 feet, or 30 meters), usually in areas lower than winged kelp. Sugar kelp prefers sheltered waters with a medium force of sloshing waves.

HARVEST GUIDE

WHAT: Leaves (called blades)
WHEN: Optimal from early spring to early summer
Leaves become shredded by wave action in late summer. See "Harvesting Guidelines" earlier in this section.

CULINARY TIPS

See Giant Kelp. Brown seaweed, such as rockweed, winged kelp, and sugar kelp, pack in iodine. For instance, a 5-gram serving of *Fucus* ranges from 650 to 3,650 micrograms of iodine. The tolerable upper intake level of iodine per day is 1,200 micrograms. Check with a knowledgeable health practitioner if you want to eat brown seaweeds daily.

WHO EATS AND SHELTERS HERE?

Kelp crabs, bristle worms, prawns, ribbon snailfish, and dusky turban snails feast on sugar kelp. Roving sheep in

Note the two undulating rows (bullations) on sheltered blades.

Scotland's Orkney Islands munch their way over fields of seaweed, much of it sugar kelp.

Creatures who shelter in giant kelp and winged kelp also shelter here.

FUCUS
Fucus distichus, F. spiralis

FAMILY: Fucaceae (grouping: brown algae and kelp)
STATUS: Native
OTHER NAMES: Rockweed, popweed, popping wrack, bladderwrack, paddy tang, black tang, old man's firecrackers, sea wrack, lady wrack (*F. distichus*); spiral bladderwrack, spiral wrack, flat wrack (*F. spiralis*)

Look for this robust olive-brown to gold seaweed growing in dense dreadlock mats on rocky beaches. Fronds (blades) are strap-like with an upraised midrib and repeatedly split into Y shapes. In early spring to summer, fertile tips sport pudgy, rabbit-ear-shaped bladders filled with a clear gelatin of millions of microscopic eggs and sperm. At low tide, the shrinking bladder forces eggs and sperm through the bumps on the surface. Empty bladders act as air balloons

LEFT: *Spiral wrack grows higher in the intertidal zone than rockweed does.* **RIGHT:** *Rockweed is also known as bladderwrack or popweed.*

OOZING INTO THE MAINSTREAM

While solo kayaking the Inside Passage, the first thing I do when setting up camp, after staking a rain tarp, is to cut fucus seaweed fronds from the beach rocks—for tea. I pour one cup of hot water over a handful of chopped fronds and brew the tea for ten minutes so the subtle flavors seep out.

The warm, oceany broth reminds me of chicken bouillon. Not only is fucus rich in dietary fiber, it harbors the hunger suppressant polyphenol. Scientists discovered that sea vegetables containing polyphenol deactivate the digestive enzymes of grazing periwinkle snails. It's no surprise that fucus is a common ingredient in fasting teas.

The same ocean flavors that seep into my tea add a delicious note to steamed seafood. For thousands of years, First Nations coastal cooks gathered heaps of fucus and other seaweeds for wrapping, steaming, and roasting pit-fired foods. Over time, with climate change, the vegetation has changed. For instance, Elders from Tsartlip Nation told me that seaweed no longer washes up on their beaches in huge drifts. Today they use bigleaf maple leaves instead, but they lack the flavorful moisture of fucus.

You may already be familiar with this common edible seaweed by the sound it makes underfoot: *POP!* Popweed and old man's firecrackers are monikers that suit this olive-gold sea veggie with a shaggy, dreadlock appearance. Fucus is easy to spot, especially in spring or summer, when it sports its signature look: leagues of tip-growing, pudgy, rabbit-ear-shaped bladders. Those Bugs Bunny balloons are loaded with a wonder goo I call fucus mucus. I rub it on sunburned skin; the gelatinous stuff works like aloe vera to relieve irritation and swelling. Studies show that calcium alginate, a substance in fucus, helps heal wounds.

Health benefits aside, fucus is delicious and fun to eat. France, a world-class leader in cuisine, recently became the first European country to regulate and encourage the consumption of twenty-one species of awesome algae as vegetables and condiments. France's list of sumptuous sea vegetables includes not one but two species of fucus.

I take a bow here to Mac Smith and his unbridled imagination. One sizzling August day, he lay on a beach watching the ocean breathe. A zephyr wind sent a sun-dried fucus float tumbling by. He grabbed the golden-green puff and broke it open. He popped the curious morsel in his mouth. It was so satisfyingly good that he combed the high-tide beach wrack for more. At dinner, he tore open a foil packet of powdered cheddar cheese from a boxed mac 'n' cheese mix. In one of those aha moments, Mac sprinkled a bit of powdered cheddar on a sun-dried fucus puff. The cheese didn't stick too well, but the taste was splendid. Mac experimented at home until he could replicate the crispy health-food snack by baking nickel-sized fresh fucus tips (with a half inch of the blade attached at the neck so the goo doesn't seep out) until crisp and puffy, then adding organic cheddar cheese powder. The goo dries into a light, meringue-like fiber.

to lift fronds toward the sun at high tide. *F. spiralis* has a telltale flange around the edge of the swollen tip—like a crimped pie crust—and wavy to spiraling (not flat) strap-like blades. Fucus is relatively long-lived and can flourish up to 5 years on its round holdfast.

Fucus distichus quilts rocks and cliff walls in the high to mid-intertidal (the upper to middle part of rocky beaches) from Alaska to Southern California. *F. spiralis* lives higher on the beach and has an overlapping range with *F. distichus*. *F. spiralis* also thrives in Iceland and on Atlantic shores from Europe to North Africa and eastern North America.

HARVEST GUIDE

WHAT: Upper fronds and tips
WHEN: Petite tips and fronds in spring; bulbous, fertile tips and fronds in summer
Use a cutting tool to harvest bulbous, fertile tips that are nickel-sized or smaller.

Larger tips can be off-putting to many eaters. Cut off the tips, retaining some of the strap-like blade below. Or snip a few whole fronds, here and there, from each plant. Spread your harvesting over a large area.

CULINARY TIPS

You don't need much to bring out the ocean in a grain of fucus. Pour boiling water over a handful of fresh fucus fronds or one teaspoon of dried, chopped tips for a cup of "ocean-flavored" tea to stave off an appetite. Plop a handful of fresh tips in a pot of steaming clams or add a few pinches of dried, pulverized fucus to paella or seafood chowder. Steam fish on a bed of fucus. Or try my pal Mac Smith's fave—dry tips into "sea puffs" in a food dehydrator. Set at 100 degrees F until the gooey center turns to crispy sea foam.

When sautéed or blanched, fucus tips turn vibrant green and have a nutty flavor. They will revert to gold

TOP: *Dried fucus "sea cheetos"*; BOTTOM: *Note the piecrust-like edge on the tips of spiral wrack.*

brown if you continue heating them, so serve sautéed tips immediately or shock blanched tips in ice water.

SUPERPOWER

Fucus, like all the brown sea vegetables, contains fucoidan (few-COY-din) and phlorotannin (FLER-o-tan-in)—chemicals with antiviral, anticancer, anti-inflammatory, anti-Alzheimer's, and anticoagulant properties. A stellar blood thinner, the phytochemicals in fucus have been compared to heparin, an anticlotting drug widely used in hospitals. Early in the COVID-19 pandemic, a scientific article reported that fucus polysaccharides were considered a safe and effective alternative agent for preventing or treating pulmonary fibrosis and for reducing inflammation in COVID-19 patients.

WHO EATS AND SHELTERS HERE?

Deer, northern kelp crabs, beach hoppers, and isopods eat fucus. Both black bears and coastal brown bears lip it up inadvertently as a kind of side dish when they forage

SOOTHING FUCUS

You can now find this soothing ocean potion in skincare products from British Columbia to New Zealand: sumptuous bladderwrack face serums to increase skin hydration; foot- and bath-soak flakes to tamp down inflammation; antiaging cream to lighten those age spots. Sound like hype? Not really. Fucus mucus is oozing into mainstream markets inspired by a plethora of scientific research.

Fucus boasts impressive properties that go beyond skin deep. Traditionally, iodine-rich brown seaweeds, such as fucus and laminaria, were eaten to treat thyroid deficiencies. Pulverized and packed into gel caps, this versatile alga is prescribed by contemporary Chinese, naturopathic, and Coast Salish health practitioners for a myriad of maladies from underactive thyroid to enlarged prostate.

The larger, gelatin-filled floats of fucus work well for squeezing on seaweed foragers' sunburned skin, cuts, and bruises. Once, I slipped while jumping out of a skiff onto seaweed-slick boulders, hitting my right glute so hard I yelped in pain. So I grabbed two big handfuls of rockweed with pudgy floats and stuffed that wad of gooey seaweed between my injury and long underwear. A few hours later, I swapped the poultice out for a fresh wad. By bedtime, my injury was only a palm-sized pink circle—no bruise, no pain.

for shore crabs and gunnel fish or rake barnacles loose with their claws. Periwinkle snails devour fucus in summer, inducing the algae to make antigrazing chemicals.

Black katy chitons, ribbon snailfish, Pacific false limpets, acorn barnacles, beach hoppers, shore crabs, isopods, and periwinkle snails of all kinds (Sitka, checkered, rough, and small "winkles") live under that floppy "fucus-thatch roof." When the tide drops, these creatures are vulnerable to sun and wind (overheating and desiccation), as well as a host of predators from shorebirds to ducks, not to mention a crushing blow by a Goliathan human forager traversing an ankle-tall fucus forest.

NORI
Porphyra and *Pyropia* spp.

FAMILY: Bangiaceae (grouping: red algae)
STATUS: Native
OTHER NAMES: Purple laver, red nori, black seaweed, mei bil (Kashaya Pomo for "sea leaf"), laak´usk (Lingít), sgíw (Haida), hla'ashg (Tsimshian), chishi-ma-kuro-nori (Japanese)

Nori's reddish-brown to olive-gray blades vary in shape, from ruffled circles attached by a tiny but stout pinpoint holdfast to rosettes of multiple blades. One species grows like long, silky burgundy scarves from overwintering bull whip kelp. Nori is only 1 cell thick, and you can see your fingers through it. It is more slippery feeling than dulse and rainbow

Nori, also known as black seaweed, is a treasured traditional food in many First Nation communities.

BOOST YOUR HEALTH AND FLAVORS

The first time I tasted wild nori, it was served up in crispy handfuls from a recycled cereal box in the remote First Nations village of Gwayasdums on Gilford Island, British Columbia. The dark, crumpled wads had a vaguely pearlescent, purple-black surface. They tasted of smoked salmon and crunched like popcorn. I didn't know it then, but the Elders who had picked and processed this seaweed by hand weeks earlier were sharing one of their most cherished traditional foods and trade items.

Nori is the Japanese name for two genera of red seaweed—*Pyropia* and *Porphyra*. Of the nearly two dozen species that flag the Pacific shores, *P. abbottiae* is said to be the tastiest and has a relatively brief season compared to its nori cousins. It is called "black seaweed" and "black gold" by First Nations because it dries to a lustrous black and is highly valued. During high tide, the blades appear like blooming roses on underwater cliffs and boulders. Come low tide, they droop like spent party balloons. Black seaweed peaks in late May. Soon after, it degenerates into something resembling a wave-beaten white tissue—or nothing at all. But before that, pound for pound, nori costs as much as steak! Thank goodness so many other species of tasty nori bloom into late summer, since nori, no matter the species you pick, is a nutritional powerhouse.

Nori is one of the healthiest foods on Planet Ocean. Dried nori is almost 30 percent complete protein. Exceptionally digestible, it is loaded with minerals such as iron, potassium, calcium, iodine, and zinc and vitamins A, B1, B2, B3, B6, B12, C, and E. And it apparently lowers blood cholesterol. I was sold on its vivacious benefits long before I looked at a nutritional chart. During monthlong coastal kayak expeditions, whenever I felt my energy lag, I paddled up to a rocky shoreline, cut off a few blades of nori, and popped them in my mouth. Or I'd reach into my jacket pocket for sun-dried nori nuggets. Within fifteen minutes, I could feel an energy surge. It was nature's version of an energy drink.

Apparently, it is even more nutritious (*bioavailable* is the word) when prepared using First Nations culinary traditions. This painstaking and time-intensive process hearkens back hundreds if not thousands of years. It is no less impressive than the European traditions of curing prize olives or aging artisan cheese. Traditional foodways involved gathering and partially drying black seaweed on intertidal rocks by arranging them in square patterns while waiting for family members fishing by canoe to return. First Nations women fermented the squares of slippery blades in a spritz of clam or chiton juice. The partially fermented leaves were pressed into redcedar boxes between layers of cedar branches. Women packed the boxes so tightly that the lids had to be tied with cord and weighted with rocks. After several days, the seaweed blades were aired, re-spritzed, then returned to the boxes. The process was repeated, after which the nori was cut, dried, and smoked beside the fire. The result was a highly prized possession served at potlatches; traded for mountain goat meat, wool, and eulachon oil (rendered from small smelt); and given as gifts. It was even more valuable nutritionally because the fermentation apparently makes it a cinch to digest.

It's no secret that nori is delicious. The Japanese have been rolling sushi rice in dried leaves (called nori maki) since the early 1700s. Hawked from food stalls as one of the first fast foods, nori was so valuable it could be used as currency to pay tribute taxes as early as the eighth century. Japanese farmers grow the luscious blades on nets suspended by poles in quiet, shallow bays or on rafts in deep water. In 1963, these pelagic farmers even built a shrine overlooking the Ariake Sea to honor the British phycologist (seaweed scientist) Dr. Kathleen Drew-Baker, who cracked the code on nori's complex life cycle by discovering it had two life cycle stages: one as a filamentous hair on the inside of seashells and one as a silky blade. And eureka! Drew-Baker's attentive eye enabled Japanese nori mariculture to become a billion-dollar industry. Today, a Shinto priest prays over the nori-goddess shrine daily.

On this side of the Pacific Rim, I pay homage to another red seaweed too. I've discovered wild dulse, *Palmaria mollis*. Catching sight of its scarlet, palm-shaped blade waving in the shallow water turns my anticipating tongue into a tide pool. "Sea bacon" is the name sensationalized in the media recently. Dulse is now grown in bubbling terrestrial tanks for year-round eats. As it grows and rolls about, it maintains a bushy form like an ocean-going tumbleweed. In the kitchen, when I toss a blade of dulse seaweed in a sizzling-hot pan with oil, it crisps up like sea bacon. Anything bettered by bacon—potato salad, sandwiches, scalloped potatoes, maple-syrup-drizzled pancakes—is fair game for sea bacon.

leaf. It dries into a deep purple brown to black with a sheen, hence the Indigenous name "black seaweed."

Found in Japan and across the Pacific Rim to Mexico. A treasured and culturally significant seaweed from California to Alaska and Japan, nori was traded widely among First Nations and Tribes. Look for nori growing amid barnacled rocks high up on a beach and down to the lowest tide mark, from the upper intertidal to low intertidal, as well as on cliffs and as an epiphyte on bull whip kelp. In the Aleutian chain, it is a traditional food harvested in late winter through spring by crawling beneath shore ice at low tide.

HARVEST GUIDE
WHAT: Leaves (called blades)
WHEN: From late spring through summer (into late winter in some regions)

Cut here and there with scissors or knife. Take half the blade. Leave the pinpoint holdfast and the rest of the blade to regenerate. *P. abbottiae* (black seaweed) peaks in British Columbia and Alaska during May. Other species, such as *P. perforata* (purple laver), peak later.

CULINARY TIPS

Nori has a mineral-rich umami flavor thanks to high levels of glutamate. Drying, fermenting, and roasting the blades—as coastal First Nations have traditionally done—imbues the seaweed with sweet, smokey seafood notes. Pulse dried blades in a food processor for nori "flour" or seasoning. Toss with popcorn for a superfood snack. Dust on grilled scallops, potatoes, corn on the cob, or seafood chowder. Blend nori "flour" into savory pie crusts for a nutty flavoring and nutritional wallop. Ounce for ounce, nori costs more than steak, so learn to dry your own! (See Smoky Sea Bacon in Recipes.) Stuff fresh nori blades with rice filling and sear in hot oil. Fry fresh, bunched blades for oyster-flavored tempura.

Nearly two dozen species of Porphyra and Pyropia live along the Northwest coast.

❓ THREATENED BY TINY HITCHHIKERS

Some black seaweed (*Pyropia abbottiae*) in Alaska and British Columbia is being fouled by a green-gray diatom (a single-cell alga) called *Licomophora*. The hitchhiking alga competes for nutrients and light and its telltale grayish layer can cause an unsavory metallic flavor and odor. The diatoms seem to be increasing in spread and frequency. Seaweed researcher Dr. Jennifer Clark partnered with Wuikinuxv and Heiltsuk First Nations to figure out why black seaweed was disappearing on the central British Columbia coast. During a double-whammy heat scenario, when a massive stretch of warm seawater in the North Pacific in 2014–15 was followed by an El Niño in 2015–16, the black seaweed died back. In 2017–19, Clark learned that when temperatures cooled, the seaweed recovered, but not to its former glory. You can help by serving as a community scientist and reporting *Licomophora* on black seaweed on the app iNaturalist.

WHO EATS AND SHELTERS HERE?

Limpets, conic snails about the size of a quarter, scooch along rocks grazing on nori and other seaweeds. Three prickleback fish—the ribbon, rock, and black prickleback—graze on nori gardens.

All the grazers above hide in nori's soft scarves, along with crabs, worms, barnacles, and a plethora of periwinkles, also called *Littorina* snails.

DULSE
Palmaria mollis, P. hecatensis

FAMILY: Palmariaceae (grouping: red algae)
STATUS: Native
OTHER NAMES: Pacific dulse, thin dulse, red ribbon, red kale (*P. mollis*); stiff red ribbon (*P. hecatensis*)

Palmaria's scientific name means "like the palm of a hand." *P. mollis* is flat, glove-like, dull, reddish pink, and thin. *P. hecatensis* is thicker, leathery, mitten- or strap-like with one or two lobes, burgundy to rich red, shiny, and annual. *P. mollis* is biennial, meaning it has blades that sprout from the prior year's stumpy holdfast. Both Pacific dulse species have large male blades (the blades people harvest) and microscopic female plants you simply don't see.

Both species grow on rocks and have overlapping ranges, but *P. mollis* extends north to the Bering Sea and south to Southern California. The delicate blades of *P. mollis* grow lower on the beach—subtidal to mid-intertidal in semi-protected coasts, while the leathery, more durable *P. hecatensis* blades are found in the low to mid-intertidal, often on more wave-exposed coasts. Atlantic dulse (*P. palmata*) doesn't grow on our coast, but it is a traditional food that has been harvested for centuries across eastern Canada, Iceland, Ireland, and France, where it is still celebrated today.

HARVEST GUIDE
WHAT: Blades
WHEN: Spring to fall
See "Harvesting Guidelines" earlier in this section.

CULINARY TIPS
Dried dulse blades are nutty and salty. Deep-frying dried, lightly smoked dulse fronds until crispy creates a texture and flavor like bacon. Snip whole, dried dulse into ½-inch pieces, and add to stir-fries, rice, grain dishes, and soup—but toward

Stiff red ribbon dulse

the end of cooking time. Try dulse flakes in melted butter for topping baked spuds or root vegetables and a dulse-chili-scallion-butter rub for roasted corn on the cob. Applewood- or alderwood-smoked dulse is delicious atop ice cream. Mediterranean cuisine uses dulse to flavor ragout and give it a lovely blush.

SUPERPOWER

When Ireland's potato crop failed during the potato famine of the mid-1800s, devoured by a fungus called late blight, seaweed may have spared desperate coastal communities from malnutrition. Dulse boasts up to 20 percent protein (higher than almonds) and a significant amount of minerals (calcium, magnesium, potassium, iron) and vitamins (B1, B2, B12, K). It was historically boiled and eaten in Wales and Ireland as a deworming medicine. Recent studies reveal *Palmaria* contains "seaweed sunscreen," or mycosporine-like amino acids (MAAs), which shield the seaweed from harmful sun rays by absorbing ultraviolet radiation (UVR). Nature's sunscreen is attracting the attention of biotech industries.

WHO EATS AND SHELTERS HERE?

Abalone, sea urchins, sea hares, limpets, and pea-sized periwinkles eat dulse.

I've seen blood stars, gunnel fish, and red rock crabs hunkering under dulse blades on a low-tide rocky beach, as well as other critters. See Nori.

RAINBOW LEAF
Mazzaella spp.

FAMILY: Gigartinaceae (grouping: red algae)
STATUS: Native
OTHER NAMES: Iridescent seaweed (*M. splendens, M. linearis, M. dewreedei*)

Underwater, they shine with rainbow colors. Above water, the smooth, rubbery blades may have a reddish-purple, burgundy, or golden-brown hue. A shielding cuticle on the seaweed's surface reflects white light (all the colors), much like oil on water. The cuticle doubles as armor against nibbling grazers. Blade shapes vary from oval to flame-like tapers, usually longer than 8 inches. The fleshy perennial holdfast resprouts blades. Pull a blade of rubbery rainbow leaf between your hands and it stretches. Its look-alike, dulse, snaps off crisply and a nibble yields a cucumber crunch.

Rocky beaches, mid- to low-intertidal zones from Alaska to Baja California, Mexico. (The new species *M. dewreedei* is found—so far—only in Central California, on Haida Gwaii, and on Vancouver Island, British Columbia.)

HARVEST GUIDE
WHAT: Blades
WHEN: Peak season from late spring to summer, washed up as storm wrack in winter
To harvest, leave perennial holdfasts and see "Harvesting Guidelines" earlier in this section.

CULINARY TIPS
See Turkish Towel & Washcloth.

Rainbow leaf looks iridescent underwater.

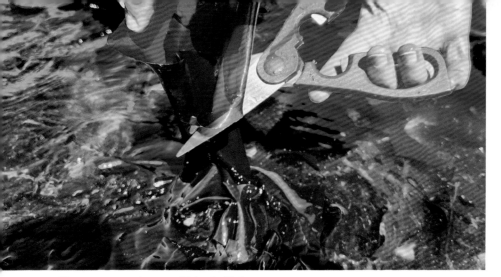

Harvest no more than two-thirds of a blade.

WHO EATS AND SHELTERS HERE?

The shy rock prickleback—a hardy, eel-like fish that can live for eleven years—relishes this seaweed, as do isopods, urchins, and the black turban snail, an ultra-thick-shelled mollusk the size of a black olive. Urchins, however, are mildly deterred from eating rainbow leaf by an "unknown chemical defense," says marine scientist Kathy Van Alstyne and her team.

Who shelters here? The Pacific false limpet and, on the base of the blades, a doily-like encrusting bryozoan. Bryozoans are colonies of tiny animals that sieve plankton from the sea.

TURKISH TOWEL & WASHCLOTH
Chondracanthus spp., Mastocarpus papillatus

FAMILIES: Gigartinaceae, Phyllophoraceae (groupings: red algae)
OTHER NAMES: Turkish towel (*Chondracanthus* spp.); tar spot, sea tar, grape-stone, Turkish washcloth (*Mastocarpus papillatus*)

Nubby on both sides like a bath towel, the reddish-purple to yellow blades of Turkish towel can reach 30 inches long but are commonly 12 inches. Smaller bladelets may grow from the base or edges, and the anchor point is a small, short disk. Turkish washcloth, one of the Pacific Northwest's most common seaweeds, has a female blade that is nubby on both sides, like a terry washcloth with upraised bumps (papillae). The burgundy to brownish-red blades grow up to 6 inches long and are often Y shaped and curled at the edges. Annual blades

sprout from a thick, rubbery, blackish crust, resembling a spill of tar, that can live almost 90 years. This durable seaweed withstands both desiccation and high temperatures.

Turkish towel lives on exposed headlands and sheltered sites from Southeast Alaska to Baja California, Mexico, in the low to mid-intertidal and down to 60 feet. The thickest blades grow on wave-washed, exposed open coasts. Turkish washcloth grows on rocks in the mid- to high-intertidal zones from Alaska to Mexico, as well as in Russia and Japan. In California, it also grows on California mussel shells.

HARVEST GUIDE

WHAT: Blades

WHEN: Peak season is late spring to fall, washed up on beaches (after storms) in winter

Snip portions of blades that are a uniformly deep brown-burgundy color with no snail-chewed holes. Remove only one-third to one-half of the blade with a knife or scissors. For washed-up specimens of Turkish towel, collect only thick burgundy-red blades without pink or white degradation patches.

CULINARY TIPS

The blades of Turkish towel, Turkish washcloth, and rainbow leaf have a natural, gelatin-like goo packed into their cell walls. This carrageenan-rich thickener is extracted commercially and used

TOP: *Note bladelets on side of Turkish towel.*
MIDDLE AND BOTTOM: *Turkish washcloth sprouts from a tarlike crust.*

as a gelling agent in pudding and ice cream (in Recipes, see Chocolate Ocean Pudding in a Nutty Shell).

WHO EATS AND SHELTERS HERE?

The black turban snail, brown turban snail, Pacific purple sea urchin, and white abalone eat Turkish towel. When there is limited shore real estate, some seaweeds will plunk down a holdfast on a seaweed like Turkish towel. The poor things may lack chemical defenses to resist other algal tenants. Snails serve as meticulous mowers, clipping the epiphytic hitchhikers by munching them off young blades, allowing sunlight to reach the blades as they mature. The snails switch to gorging on the dinner-plate-sized blades once they've grown big and luscious. The shy rock prickleback grazes on Turkish washcloth along rocky shores. One study found that the diet of plate limpets (a sea snail with a conical "top hat") included up to 60 percent sea tar (the crust phase of Turkish washcloth).

The blades of Turkish washcloth trap bits of sediment and moisture, creating a refuge for tiny snails, crabs, beach fly larvae, sea worms, and other tiny creatures. The crust is a garden sheltering vulnerable green seaweeds just beginning life. One study found more than half the crusts of Turkish washcloth provide a home for one-celled *Codiolum*, the precursors to larger blades of green seaweed species such as sea lettuce.

SEA LETTUCE
Ulva spp.

FAMILY: Ulvaceae (grouping: green seaweed)
STATUS: Native
OTHER NAMES: Sea lettuce, water lettuce, green laver, aosa (Japanese) (*Ulva fenestrata*); sea hair, gut weed, green string lettuce (*U. intestinalis*); slender sea lettuce, green string lettuce, link confetti (*U. linza*)

Photosynthetic green and thin as cellophane, sea lettuce is so transparent you can almost read a newspaper through the blade. Blades vary greatly in shape. *U. fenestrata* blades are fan shaped to long and slender and can be full of holes like a colander. Though typically smaller than notebook paper, blades can grow to 3 feet, varying from ruffled to flat. If the edges are white, the species has released its reproductive parts, leaving a wake of tattered cellulose. The holdfast is a minuscule disk.

Look for sea lettuce on high-tide rocks, in tide pools, and hitchhiking on rockweed. It can also grow free-floating on the surface of still bays and lagoons.

SEA LETTUCE: THE PARSLEY OF THE SEA

I was sailing up the Inside Passage of British Columbia with four guys on a homemade trimaran sailboat in the spring of 1983. We meandered into a mud-bottomed bay where towering mare's tails of seaweed grew under the still surface. We had just caught a greenling cod with translucent-blue flesh. We swabbed the fillets in beer batter and tossed the scraps into a chowder pot. Alan, an ethnobotanist, decided we needed fresh veggies too. I paddled out to a floating emerald mat of sea lettuce as thick as a Persian rug. I thrust my paddle underneath like a giant spatula to lift the edge. It pulled loose in dripping sheets of photosynthetic-green—*kersplat*—onto the boat's deck. Back on shore, we snipped it into pieces with a Swiss Army knife and added it to the chowder. It became our parsley of the sea.

Fresh sea lettuce tastes mildly of zucchini or cucumber with a mineral aftertaste. No wonder: it's jammed with iron—eighty-seven milligrams per cup (one hundred grams). That's thirteen times the iron content of spinach. Sea lettuce is also 12 to 20 percent protein and rich in vitamin A, calcium, and fiber. A sea lettuce in the *Ulvaria* (dark sea lettuce) genus even contains dopamine—a forerunner of adrenaline.

Sea lettuce thrives in almost every ocean. The skinny cousins of the flouncy sea lettuce are string lettuce (*Ulva linza*) and sea hair (*U. intestinalis*). All are abundant and underutilized foods in the Americas. Yet in Europe, green, brown, and red seaweeds have been elevated and are now novel ingredients in a food frontier whose tide has come.

I spread sea lettuce on beach rocks to sun-dry to a potato-chip crispness and then munch it for snacks that taste like mineral-rich nori. Long ago, many coastal First Nations harvesters dried both nori and sea lettuce into cakes, stored them in airtight wood boxes, and then chopped them apart and reconstituted them in nourishing winter soups, much like we might a dehydrated soup mix. Historically, the Quileute of Washington State applied fresh sea lettuce to sunburned lips as a salve. And nursing mothers applied soothing sea lettuce to their breasts to relieve pain. Let's face it, what worked for thousands of years as ocean food and medicine is still a darn good idea.

Sea hair and string lettuce are the skinny sea lettuce cousins. They are elongated and cylindrical (versus wide like a leaf of lettuce). Sea hair is only 0.2 inches wide and 8 to 20 inches long—a kinky tube with a pinprick-sized holdfast at its top (hence the scientific name *intestinalis*). It signals fresh water. (That's a gift for a stranded sailor or sea kayaker!) String lettuce has blades wider and longer (up to 18 inches) than sea hair. It is only tubular at the very base, near the holdfast. Most of the blade is a long green ribbon with a ruffly edge.

Sea lettuce (*U. fenestrata*) is found worldwide and far-ranging in the Pacific and Atlantic Oceans and sub-Antarctic islands. Sea hair (*U. intestinalis*) grows luxuriantly where fresh water seeps out from intertidal cliffs or beaches, as well as in tide pools along the Pacific, Atlantic, and Antarctic Oceans. *U. linza* grows in protected bays on rocks and small cobbles in the mid- and low intertidal and on bull kelp; it is found almost worldwide.

HARVEST GUIDE

WHAT: Blades

WHEN: Most tender in spring, less tender in late summer

Gather when entirely green—not white edged—for best taste. Cut one-third to half of the blade. Harvest here and there across a large area; don't clearcut.

As you harvest, check for tiny periwinkle snails, isopods, and beach hoppers, and move them into the uncut sea lettuce. Rinse sandy blades in seawater before bagging, and keep them cool on ice. Cut sea lettuce spoils easily—up to two days in the fridge is all you get; it is best used fresh within eight to twelve hours of picking. Dry for best flavor, or freeze as soon as possible. Green string lettuce grows epiphytically on bull kelp stipes, so you can easily trim the waving green fringe off floating kelp—which reduces the potential for grit. Squeeze out excess water from the tubular, fresh sea hair by scrunching a wad in your hand before bagging it.

CULINARY TIPS

Use fresh or dry in sunomono seaweed salad, or in ceviche, miso soup, seafood chowder, omelets, quiche, tabouli, and in rice and quinoa dishes.

TOP TO BOTTOM: *Sea lettuce, sea hair, and string lettuce*

❓ GREEN TIDES GROWING WORLDWIDE

When sea lettuce (*Ulva*) tears loose from its tiny anchor and floats away, it doesn't die as it drifts off to new horizons; it grows and grows. In the right conditions (sunshine, warm temperature, calm weather, a shallow bay, scant seaweed grazers, or an infusion of nutrients from sewage or overfertilized lawns, gardens, and farms), this seaweed can bloom into a lethal, living blanket.

These "green tides" wreak havoc worldwide. To give you an idea of the scale of the problem, imagine a tarp an acre or more in size tossed over a bay, shading the undersea garden of swaying kelp and eelgrass. As the algae and vegetation deteriorate, zillions of bacteria deplete the bay of oxygen, creating dead zones for fish and prawns.

If a vast green tide of sea lettuce washes up on a beach, it smothers the critters underneath, like clams and brittle stars. Even crabs can "cook" under a heat-trapping lid. If thick and expansive enough, the mat may release hydrogen sulfide, a toxic gas that smells of rotten eggs and at high levels messes with animals' ability to process oxygen. *That's* a problem.

The solution is to stop feeding green tides: fix leaky septic systems, reduce lawn fertilizer, and swap in organic gardens or native plants for manicured lawn.

In Italy's busy Venetian Lagoon, where ten species of sea lettuce thrive in the nutrient-enhanced waters, there's a bright solution to the problem. Renewable sea algae will soon fuel a forty-megawatt power plant. When given too much ulva, make electricity!

Dried blades flake nicely. Grind dry blades in a spice grinder to make a colorful dusting for goat cheese, seared scallops, sushi, taters, or a seaweed-macadamia-nut crust on fish. Mix with salt for green seasoning. Shake onto buttered popcorn. Make the Japanese condiment furikaki: sea lettuce flakes, toasted sesame seeds, salt, sugar, bonito flakes, and chili peppers. Think of sea lettuces as the "parsleys of the sea."

WHO EATS AND SHELTERS HERE?

The brant or barnacle goose, circumpolar saltwater cousins of the Canada goose, works the shallows in tidal estuaries, tipping tail up to nibble on sea lettuce blades and eelgrass. Sea urchins and a host of other invertebrates—abalone, sea hares, periwinkle snails, chitons, amphipods, emerald crabs, and, of course, the "sea lettuce isopod" (a brilliant-green, ocean-going "pill bug")—find sea lettuce irresistible. Indirectly, mallards, buffleheads, and wigeons all benefit from sea lettuce meadows, where they hunt and gulp wiggly invertebrates hiding in the sway.

Harvesting sea lettuce with a knife

Brant geese build seaweed into their nests. Beach hoppers, Sitka periwinkles, checkered periwinkles, and sea lettuce isopods hide in the blades' folds. Barnacles, chitons, amphipods, and shore crabs keep moist during low tide amid the anchored curtains of ulva. Sea slaters (marine relatives of sow bugs) choose sea hair as their favorite food.

In the San Juan Islands in Washington State, I have observed butterflies and yellow jackets visiting fresh water-seep tide pools where sea hair is abundant. Perhaps one of sea hair's gifts is being a guardian of vital freshwater holes!

❓ LETTUCE EAT COOKIES!

Sea lettuce (*Ulva* species) thrives worldwide. And you don't need a minus tide to gather a cup or two. You can find this lettuce look-alike high on the beach. It grows prolifically both in nature (see the "Green Tides Growing Worldwide" sidebar above) and in mariculture operations from Baja to Bangladesh. It amplifies health benefits when added to recipes for common foods we already celebrate sans seaweed.

Consequently, commercial research kitchens worldwide are simmering, boiling, roasting, and baking with a pinch of sea greens. For instance, scientists hired by the food industry are concocting fish burgers with 0.5 percent sea lettuce to amp protein, fiber, and nutrition. In Southeast Asia on the Bay of Bengal—where over 250 species of seaweeds grow and seaweed farming has a long history—bakers are experimenting with ulva in cookies. Panelists scrutinize the baker's fresh-from-the-industrial-oven seaweed cookies for color (too many green flecks?), moisture (soggy? crispy?), spread factor (pancake-ish or waferlike?), texture (chewy? flakey? slippery, ewww?), pH (too acidic?), and density (mouth feel). And then there's nutritional analysis. Discriminating panelist "tasters" tolerated up to 5 percent seaweed in ulva cookies. The fat content reveals high amounts of healthy lipids—omega-3 and omega-6 fatty acids. The results? Sea lettuce cookies could be marketed as a health food! Want to have some fun fooling your friends into trying seaweed cookies? Try making Sea and Sunshine Cookies (see Recipes).

BEACH ASPARAGUS
Sarcocornia pacifica (also *Salicornia pacifica*)

FAMILY: Amaranth (previously Chenopodiaceae, or Goosefoot)
STATUS: Native
OTHER NAMES: Sea bean, pickleweed, salt marsh pickleweed, pickleplant, saltwort, chicken claws, pigeonfoot, Pacific samphire (morphed from Saint-Pierre, patron saint of fishers); slender glasswort (*Salicornia depressa*)

Although some chefs call it sea bean, beach asparagus isn't really a bean at all but a salty and salt-loving succulent. Sage-green cylindrical stems, less than a pencil's width, sprout freely on sprawling branches. Instead of leaves, sea bean has scales and jointed stems, giving it the folksy name "pigeonfoot." Spring to early fall, this perennial grows as a luxuriant mat.

A nibble of this delightfully crispy veggie exudes a juicy burst of ocean salt and minerals. How does that zingy flavor persist? Hail the hearty halophyte—which literally means "salt plant"—for the trade secrets buried in its cells. Sea beans have tiny pumps that move the salt into a pantry of sorts, or "vacuole." When the vacuole is packed full of salt, that plant cell expires. That's right. Job done. New cells take over and continue the 24/7 saltery. In late summer, minute trios of wind-pollinated flowers dot fertile joints. Autumn season burnishes the upper branches red. Patches of *Salicornia rubra*—also called Pacific swampfire, a ruby-colored cousin—resemble red lakes splashed across inland alkaline flats.

Come winter, the once-succulent *Sarcocornia pacifica* stalks dry to a crisp. The vegetation blows away. Seeds even smaller than chia, 1 to 1.5 millimeters wide, boast spiky life jackets to float and bump along the marsh edges. If they hook into mud before a pintail duck

To harvest beach asparagus, either carefully snap them, or use a knife or pair of scissors to cut them off.

❓HAIL THE HEARTY HALOPHYTE

Long ago, the Native peoples of the Pacific Coast knew the superfood benefits of beach asparagus, which also goes by "sea bean." Coastal messengers and Indigenous traders, traveling by foot or small boat from oceanfront villages, up rivers, and over mountain passes, carried pouches of precious sea bean to sustain them on their arduous journeys. Kwäd~y Dän Tsâinchí ("Long Ago Person Found") may have been such a traveler. He lived 550 years ago but suffered a mishap on a glacier in remote northern British Columbia, near traditional trade routes. Scientists, working respectfully with the guidance of Indigenous advisers, recovered pollen from coastal sea bean on his robe and in his stomach after his body was found in Tatshenshini-Alsek Park in the late 1990s.

I've lost count of the times I've kayaked into a serene bay at high tide and discovered a welcome mat of beach asparagus, a satisfying snack on a hot day. Nibbling a few segments restores the minerals I've sweated out paddling. A sizable handful (100 grams) packs in 1,922 IU of vitamin A, 45 milligrams of calcium, and almost 2 grams of protein, plus traces of iron, riboflavin, niacin, fat, and—you guessed it—a burst of sodium.

In old-world Europe, the versatile beach asparagus served as more than table fare. Sodium-rich branches were once used for making primitive glass. Dried in towering stacks, burned to ash, and fused with sand, the species gained the name glasswort—or literally, "glass plant." The same ash, leached with lime, makes caustic soda. Mixed with animal fat such as goat's milk, it transforms into a sudsy bar of soap.

Today, in an era of dwindling freshwater supplies and increased soil salinity, beach asparagus is being heralded as a potentially lucrative and sustainable crop for coastal desert habitats. Cultivating beach asparagus with somewhat saline water may help coastal desert communities produce a marketable food that lowers job scarcity.

gulps them, they may sprout. New sea bean shoots also sprout from the perennial rhizomes, specialized roots that generate new plants from broken bits. I like to tell my students, "A bit of broken rhizome can *rize* up into a brand-new plant."

Look for beach asparagus on protected coastal beaches and salt marsh borders in the high-intertidal zone, where it gets highest-tide dunkings. *Sarcocornia/Salicornia pacifica*'s coastal casa is the state of Alaska to Baja, Mexico. But a host of pickleweed relatives thrive worldwide on the seaboard of the Atlantic, Europe, Africa, and New Zealand.

HARVEST GUIDE
WHAT: Succulent green stem tops
WHEN: Spring to summer

Harvest from unpolluted sandy beaches and salt marshes—away from present and historic industry, marinas, or sewage outfalls. Collect from the patch's edges, not the center. Remember, you are Gulliver the Giant among knee-high trees. Walking atop this "forest" breaks off umpteen branches. Snap off or cut pieces from the green top stems. Succulent segments break cleanly at pickleweed's joints. (Lower, older vegetation often has a "woody

Beach asparagus with red tips in bloom

toothpick" core, and after flowering, even top joints can turn woody.) For flavoring, you don't need much, just one or two handfuls.

CULINARY TIPS

Beach asparagus tastes like superconcentrated salt with a hint of bitter. A popular vinegar pickle in seventeenth-century France led to its alternate name, pickleweed. Like garden beans, beach asparagus can be blanched, steamed, sautéed, pickled, or used raw. Tips can also be dried, powdered, and used as a salt substitute.

After blanching or boiling for thirty to forty-five seconds, douse beans in ice water for up to thirty minutes to reduce saltiness, dry and then plate over seafood such as whitefish, shrimp, or scallops for a tangy, mineral-rich condiment. Toss blanched or raw sea bean in Greek salad. Purée blanched sea beans in cream soups. Toss blanched or steamed with lemon juice and toasted almonds. Blanched beach asparagus freezes well and retains color for months. Or sauté segments with olive or sesame oil and add to rice, quinoa, or scrambled eggs. Add pickled beach asparagus to mustard sauce to give it a briny finish. Quick pickling keeps the vegetables crisp, but cooking softens the pickles and fades them to olive gold.

Wilted beach asparagus (found during August droughts) can have a pungent ocean flavor. To reduce the saltiness, soak stems for eight hours in fresh water, rinse, and use as if fresh.

SUPERPOWER

Besides providing a cool condo and green grocery for scads of critters, sea bean mortars the mudlicious sand and gravel to shore. Think of it as a living net that prevents high-tide waves from washing away beaches in bays and salt marshes. (Another reason to avoid harvesting from the patch's center, which will break up this protective barrier.) Beach asparagus's powers don't end there. Some salt marshes in California have high selenium sluicing in from coastal mountain streams. Too much selenium can be toxic to both plants and animals. Beach asparagus volatizes selenium, transforming it into a gas that blows away and disperses across a broader area. *Shazam!* Safer selenium levels for all.

WHO EATS AND SHELTERS HERE?

Snow geese, Canada geese, gadwall, and greater scaup munch the stems of beach asparagus during migration. Pintail ducks eat the tiny seeds.

In San Francisco Bay, the salt marsh harvest mouse burrows into the luxuriant mat (its only habitat) and dines on segments like corn on the cob. California Ridgway's rail—endangered by wetland loss and degradation—nests in stands of pickleweed, leaving only when the highest tide flushes them out. Take care not to trample their nests! Shore crabs, barnacles, and snails live under and amid sea bean stalks. Beach hoppers—shrimplike critters with spring-loaded tails—hunker in the greenery to avoid hungry song sparrows. They retreat into burrows amid pickleweed roots at low tide. In San Francisco's Elkhorn Slough, researchers are studying if burrowing beach hoppers not only provide oxygen to sea bean roots, but also possibly provide a significant flush of nitrogen-rich fecal fertilizer. Salt marshes can be nitrogen-poor habitats. Healthy "hoppers" could mean more robust "bean" growth!

GOOSETONGUE
Plantago maritima

FAMILY: Plantaginaceae (Plantain)
STATUS: Native
OTHER NAMES: Sea plantain

This succulent, grasslike herb grows to about 12 inches tall. Leathery, green, lance-shaped leaves with an irregular, mildly toothed edge rise from a singular base like rays of the sun. Each leaf has ribs on the back, and in cross section is a half-moon with 3 to 5 celery-like threads. Goosetongue's green flowers grow on a dense spike that overtops the leaves. Don't confuse sea plantain with poisonous arrowgrass ❗, a perennial that grows in similar places, which smells of cilantro when crushed and has a base of overlapping leaves in one plane—much like an iris.

TOP: *Goosetongue* (Photo by Gerald Corsi, iStock);
RIGHT: *Arrowgrass, a poisonous look-alike*

Estuaries, rocky shores, and sandy soils along the coast in the wave-splash zone to high intertidal, where it gets a dunking from the highest tides.

HARVEST GUIDE

WHAT: Leaves
WHEN: Spring to summer
Use your fingers to snap off succulent, crisp leaves from the basal rosette. Remove leaves here and there from many plants across an area. Taste for bitterness first: plants vary with rain exposure and across the beach gradient, depending on how often they are doused in salt water.

CULINARY TIPS

Some fondly nickname this beach veggie the Alaskan green bean. You can treat them just like salty green beans and sauté briskly in olive oil

Lagoon lined with goosetongue in Glacier Bay, Alaska

and garlic to keep the crunch, blanch, and serve with butter and toasted almond; pickle in a vinegar brine (minus the salt); or slice the long, thin spears on the diagonal and toss with salad greens for a briny crunch. During long coastal trips, I pluck fresh leaves—reminiscent of salty romaine lettuce—and nibble them raw with cheese and crackers. Loaded with vitamins A, C, and K, they are a coastal traveler's multivitamin.

WHO EATS AND SHELTERS HERE?

Bears mow it. Deer trim it. Geese nibble the leaves to nubbins. At the highest tides, when the grasslike blades are underwater, crabs, snails, isopods, and fish such as herring move into the shallows to feed while hidden under deep cover. Goosetongue, like beach asparagus and eelgrass, not only provides cover for animals but also releases free oxygen and sequesters carbon. The dense canopy and roots protect shores from storm-wave erosion: you could say that sand and mud shelters in goosetongue too!

FINDING HER WAY BACK HOME
VAL SEGREST

Valerie Segrest, an enrolled member of the Muckleshoot Tribe, is a knowledge keeper of traditional food and medicine wisdom, a nutritionist, and a leader in the movement to revitalize Coast Salish food culture and improve Indigenous health.

Val was in her senior year at Bastyr University studying nutrition in 2010 when we first met. A short while later, Val attended a seaweed workshop I was teaching. As we walked a low-tide beach carrying bags of fresh-cut winged kelp, nori, and fucus, we both blurted out, "Hey, can I hang out more with you?"

We've been "seaweed sisters" ever since.

I asked Val how she came to fall in love with traditional foods. Her story is one of being lost, being found—and a miracle.

"My mother was given up for adoption—well, taken by the Catholic Family Services at three months old. And then her documents were made confidential. We knew that we were Native people but didn't know where we were from or what tribe we belonged to."

Growing up, Val was exposed to wilding, permaculture, and farming and growing food. Her adoptive grandfather was a farmer in Lynden, Washington.

"He spent most of his days out tending his beautiful, straight rows of potatoes and corn and radishes. My grandma would bake fresh bread every Sunday. As a young child, I spent almost every day with them and my mom, a single parent. They were all fantastic cooks."

Her adoptive aunts were all plant people. At Christmas, Val would get plants or bulbs wrapped in paper and was told not to rip them open. "Treat them like tiny children."

"My Auntie Marge lived up on Sumas Mountain on forty acres. She was a permaculturist and woman of the woods. I would spend spring break and summer vacation at her house. I would just be on this hill, me and my auntie, and she'd take me out foraging and harvesting in her backyard. She'd say, 'Go to my garden and harvest as many different leaves as you can for a crazy salad.'"

When Val was six years old, her mom took a job working for the military, managing a store that provided goods and services for the troops. They traveled to Guam, Japan, and Crete, experiences that shaped Val's values and perspectives when it came to food traditions.

"Greece was such a game changer for me because I really learned how important it is to savor food and to commune over food at the table. Families in Crete accepted us and welcomed us wholeheartedly to join them at their table and cultural feasts. They would slaughter a goat, roast it, pour big cups of wine and gorgeous plates of olive oil with

Val Segrest (Photo by Gea Ungaro)

vegetables and fresh feta. We would sit and eat and talk for an entire day. Eating for eight hours was completely normal. . . . I learned really quickly that this type of knowledge and family values were the wealth of the Greek culture. I understood the power of carrying food knowledge in a family and family tradition. And this [sharing] had been going on for thousands of years."

One autumn, when Val's mom was visiting Washington, she attended a tribal center's Halloween party. There, a woman in a witch costume saw a family resemblance in Val's mother. They pieced the history together. The witch told Val's mom, "You are Muckleshoot! I was the last to hold you before they took you away."

"We found our way back home!" recalled Val. "It felt like a miracle."

Val came back to work with her tribe and her Elders and to learn about her family history.

People in the Muckleshoot community told her, "Your Ancestor Ollie Wilbur lived to be 108 years old. Her claim to longevity was eating her traditional foods." Ollie believed that if people had access to traditional foods and ate more of them, they could heal themselves, and it was common for her to give people who visited her a healing dose of cod liver oil. This was a sentiment she shared with several Coast Salish Elders.

"I changed my whole life after that. Because this, to me, felt like a calling. I needed to figure out how to help people consume more of their traditional foods. I went to school to earn a degree in nutrition and food systems strategies. I have held my practice in community nutrition that focuses on Native food sovereignty initiatives ever since." Today Val is cofounder of Tahoma Peak Solutions, a Native woman–owned firm focused on Indigenous problem-solving and storytelling. Val works on culturally appropriate storytelling, food sovereignty, and cultural-educational resources, as well as trainings and community classes.

"To me, you know, all these things sort of come full circle. I often tell people I got carried away on the wild foods parade at that time because it was just like, 'This is it. This is what I was put here to do.'"

SHELLFISH

Besides fishing for salmon, there is nothing more quintessentially Pacific Coast than clam digging and crabbing. For a good part of the calendar year, if you visit the coastal beaches from California to Alaska—in rain or wind, by sun or lantern glow—you see the signs. A family launches an aluminum skiff, layered up like a cake with Dungeness crab pots. A mom shoulders clam shovels as her kids trot beside her swinging buckets toward the surf. A retiree in hip waders hoists a giant "clam gun" (a metal tube), aligns it over a clam hole by the light of a headlamp, pushes it into the sand, and then pulls the gun upward by the handles. And *abracadabra!* He suctions up a razor clam. An Elder shows a grandchild how to shuck a butter clam. These scenes are as true as tides.

One crack of my dog-eared *Shells and Shellfish of the Pacific Northwest* field guide by Canadian marine biologist Rick Harbo reveals 225 species of shellfish. And that's just a shovelful of what's out there. From native littlenecks to Olympianlike-jumping heart cockles (they can pogo-stick on their muscular foot away from predators) to ten-pound geoducks with elephant-trunk siphons, we are heaped with diversity—and delight. Labyrinthine coastlines and maritime weather create clam heaven with surf-hammered outer beaches, mile-long sand spits, sheltered bays, islands, sounds, gravel bars, mud-rimmed estuaries, a temperate climate, plankton-soup currents, and nourishing coastal upwelling. It's no wonder that more than 109 million geoducks are buried happily in the mudflats of Puget Sound. It's the largest congregation of marine animals in the world.

Amazingly, the tools for excavating clams have changed little over the centuries. For thousands of years, carved hardwood digging sticks were the tools of choice for First Nations clam harvesters. One museum piece I saw doesn't look that different from the narrow metal clam shovel I purchased at my local sporting goods store. Historically, clams were a treasured food for trade, feasts, and survival and were tended in engineered clam gardens (see "The Rising Tide of Ancient Aquaculture" sidebar, later). The hip-deep swaths of crushed shells—called a "midden" or kitchen refuse heap—blanketing the waterfronts of coastal First Nation villages, from the Salish Sea to Alaska, are glowing proof of an ancient love affair with shellfish.

Cooking up acres of clams took weeks. After digging clams, women steamed, shucked, roasted, and dried the sweet, chewy morsels for winter use. One delicacy—yarrow-skewered clams—imparted a sage-like flavor to the smoked meat. Clams were also dried with crushed thimbleberries for a raspberry tang. While back-weary clam digging was generally women's work, men gathered shellfish too. On calm days, Haida fishermen speared sea urchins and crabs from their canoe bows. Eaten raw from the shell, fresh sea urchin was an ancient mariner's boxed lunch.

Today, I always look forward to a coastal kayak trip planned around a minus tide. There is nothing quite like scooping up a "sea egg" by net or kayak paddle, returning to shore, cutting the spiny creature in half, and scooping out the urchin roe with a knife. The blunt-tipped spines have no venomous sting, a harmless-to-humans armor for protecting the golden treasure trove inside. Spread on crackers, the harvest-moon-gold roe tastes creamy, rich, bright, and sweet—like a good, fresh oyster. After eating it, I feel 110 percent *awake*, like I could paddle untold miles—it's that energizing.

In this chapter, you'll find a special sampler of delicious Pacific Coast shellfish from both deep-water and low-tide beaches: razor clams, hard-shell clams, the invasive savory clam, mussels, Dungeness crab, and sea urchins. Just so you know, I didn't cover oysters in this book due to limited space.

HARVESTING GUIDELINES

Get a recreational shellfish harvesting license or permit if required. There are specific regulations, such as catch limits and sizes, for most species in this book, including clams and crabs. At the time of publication, Alaska, British Columbia, Washington, Oregon, and California require shellfish harvesting licenses. For updates, check with your local agency (see "Harvesting Guidelines" in the Seaweed & Beach Vegetables section for a list of agencies.)

Get a copy of your state or provincial fishing regulations. Learn to identify all species you might catch, trap, net, or dig. Daily limits, equipment, and techniques differ up and down the coast.

Know which tidelands and ocean areas are off-limits. It's illegal to gather shellfish or sink a line in state underwater parks, research reserves, ecological reserves, shellfish preserves, and marine reserves or refuges. Some provincial parks, national and federal parks, and state parks may restrict shellfish harvesting. Just because a beach isn't posted, it doesn't mean it's public.

Call your area's nearest "Shellfish Safety Hotline" or "Marine Toxin Hotline" before harvesting. Not all beaches are monitored or signed with closure warnings. Get updated reports on shellfish exposure to paralytic shellfish toxin (PST), and domoic acid poisoning (DOP), which is also called amnesic shellfish poisoning (ASP). PST affects any filter-feeding shellfish (clams, oysters, barnacles, etc.) and their predators, such as moon snails. DOP/ASP occurs in sardines, anchovies, Dungeness crabs, mussels, and razor clams. Eating shellfish containing these toxins can be fatal, and you can't see, taste, or smell the toxins when present. ❗ Cooking or freezing doesn't deactivate either biotoxin. Some of the highest levels of toxin were found in British Columbia mussels—sixteen lethal human doses per quarter pound. Fortunately, mussels can clear toxins in weeks and be safe to eat. Butter clams and savory clams, however, harbor toxins for up to two years. "Red tides," caused by species of phytoplankton in the *Alexandrium* genus, may not look red at all. Blooms typically occur in warmer months, between April and October.

Collect only what you can process, and keep goodies cool after harvesting. Warm fish, crabs, and shellfish can become bacterial minefields, making them unsafe to eat. Take a cooler and frozen ice packs for transport.

In Washington, you are legally required to refill the holes you dug to hunt shellfish. Piled shovelfuls may suffocate nearby clams in their burrows. Other creatures, such as sand worms and sea stars, die from exposure to sun, rain, and wind. Exposed shellfish risk predation from birds and other predators. Tuck discarded shellfish back where you found them so they can fill your plate next year.

Avoid polluted areas. Don't harvest shellfish or drop crab traps near industrial sites, sewage outflow (including highly populated shores with older homes and potentially leaky septic systems), stormwater outflows, or marinas—which can be collection grounds for toxic levels of chemicals. Hepatitis C and bacteria lurk in water contaminated by farm and human sewage. When waters warm in summer, vibrio, a type of bacteria, can contaminate fish and shellfish. Cooking is only your second-best option. Avoidance is always best.

TOP: *Clam digging tools: a clam gun and small-bladed shovels;* BOTTOM: *Crabbing tools: a wire crab trap, bait box, rope, marker buoy, bucket, and cooler.* (Photo by Katherine Palmer)

Handle your bycatch with care. Whether it's undersized or soft-shelled Dungeness crabs or an unintended sea star, gently place sea creatures back into the water. Throwing crabs off a dock or boat injures them.

WINTER DIGGERS

All up and down Copalis Beach, on the west coast of Washington State, people are stooped in rain slickers, shovels working the sand. It's 4:39 PM on January 10—a small window during the winter low tides when the beaches are open to razor clamming. Winter low tides occur at night, so we're dressed with lots of layers under our raincoats and pants. The sun set minutes earlier, and darkness hovers in the forested dunes as we walk two hundred yards toward the roaring surf, carrying headlamps, shovels, and plastic bags.

We're on a mission. Three friends and I drove four hours from Bellingham to try our luck. Four hours may seem like a long drive for a sack of clams. But during the 1963 Seattle World's Fair, my family drove two thousand miles from the cornfields of Wisconsin to the shores of Washington to hug big trees, visit the fair, and do as the natives do—dig clams. While camping on the Olympic Peninsula's coast, we baptized our World War I camp shovel in Pacific surf and chased our first razor clams deep to China. We ate the tender ivory meat in chowder cooked on a Coleman stove.

For years afterward, my father savored that adventure by displaying one highly lacquered razor clam shell, splayed like butterfly wings, in our china cabinet. He'd bring it out when company visited as a talisman of our travels. "You ever see a clam like this?" he'd say. "Look how thin the shell is." He'd hold it to the sunlit window. "As translucent as porcelain. You can see the shadow of your finger behind it." The guests would pass it around, taking turns at the window. "Mmm! Were they delicious! What fast diggers, huh, Punkin'?" he'd say.

On Copalis Beach, the agile sanderlings are fast diggers too. They have surf foraging down to a comic art. Whole flocks sprint over the wet sand in fast-legged rivers. Without pausing, they tweeze up morsels from the equally fast-moving scalloped wave lines. I am digging as fast as I can, stabbing at the beach like a sanderling, but the clams keep digging faster. A siphon appears for an instant, like a submarine scope, and then sinks into the gloppy punch bowl my shovel carved out.

Digging for razor clams at low tide in winter at Mokrock's Beach, Washington

Russ, a sympathetic neighboring clam digger from Tumwater, tells me, "You should have been here yesterday. No rain. Low surf. Clam holes showing everywhere. It was easy. We all got our limit. This is pretty challenging."

My wet, sandy fingers are whitening on the shovel. Razor clams thrive on sand beaches thrashed by winter waves. In such a tough neighborhood, young razor clams grow up quickly or die. At two years old and four and a half inches, a mature female razor clam can dig one foot a minute and pump out ten million eggs. But only 5 percent of the baby clams will survive to adulthood. Hungry sanderlings, water temperatures, disease, and coastal currents scour down those numbers quickly.

To make sure enough clams are available for Native diggers and others, states set some game rules. In Washington and Oregon, as of this writing, a full day's limit is fifteen clams. And you must count—and keep—what you dig: big, small, whole, or busted in two. The number of intentionally or accidentally discarded clams runs about two million per year in Washington State alone. The old adage "Haste makes waste" holds true for razor clam digging. It's all too easy to get carried away in the excitement of the chase and bust a gorgeous clam in half or cut its neck with the shovel blade.

"What's the secret?" I ask Russ, hoping he'll tell me how to unearth some dinner.

"Tap the sand with your shovel handle. Wait. Look for a clam hole to open up. They'll squirt water if they are trying to escape and go down."

Tap, tap, tap. Suddenly—whoosh—a little fountain of gray magma appears in the wet sand where once there was nothing! But in seconds, a wave rushes in and obliterates everything, including my excitement.

Tap, tap, tap. Look, look, look. The waves sluicing back and forth over my boot toes are hypnotic. I wait for the bare sand to reappear. Suddenly a hole opens like magic.

I rush in, push the shovel blade in ocean-side of the hole, unearth the sand, toss it, and look for a clam. Nothing. On the second dig, I hear the surf rushing closer. In seconds, the sea will slosh around my boots, pour into the hole, and erase all the progress.

I quickly toss the second shovel of sand over the dry beach. Just as the wave wraps around my boots, a miniature snorkel appears. The razor clam's siphon!

Gray seawater gushes in and buries it.

Dig! Quickly! My hungry belly is shouting orders now. I lift a great shovelful of gray sloppy water. Suddenly the clam plunges into a retreating wave—*kersplash!*—and logrolls down the beach. Soon I am running as fast as a sanderling, arm outstretched.

A second before the wave fills my boots, I grab the gold. What a shiner! Glossy and amber as if freshly shellacked. It reminds me of that admirable clam we kept in our china cabinet—only this beautiful swimmer's shell has risotto written on it. Now I understand the Quinault phrase ta'a Wshi xa'iits'os—"clam hungry."

PACIFIC RAZOR CLAM
Siliqua patula

FAMILY: Pharidae
STATUS: Native
OTHER NAMES: Northern razor clam

The prettiest clam on the coast, the razor's shell is shiny amber gold to olive. It's surprising this delicate, thin-shelled clam loves beaches with crashing surf. But paired with a muscular foot, the streamlined, razor-sharp shells make for the perfect drilling device. These can disappear into the soupy beach sand all too easily. The rectangular shells with rounded edges are about the size and shape of an eyeglass case. Razor clams are either male or female and simultaneously expel eggs and sperm into the surf. The largest clams reach 7 inches. In Alaska, they can live 18 years due to slower growth rates and colder water temperatures. In Washington, their lifespan is 5 years.

Found on surf-pounded sand beaches in the intertidal area from California to Alaska. They also can be found in a few sheltered bays along the coast and at depths up to 180 feet. The most abundant populations live on the coastal beaches of Haida Gwaii, Vancouver Island, Oregon, and Washington. Most of these areas support Native fisheries as well as sport and commercial razor clamming. Average depth in the sand is 2 to 3 feet.

HARVEST GUIDE
WHAT: White meat
WHEN: Year-round (Alaska), check regulations (British Columbia, Washington, Oregon, California)
Clams are generally harvested by digging with a shovel or using a "clam gun." See "Harvesting Guidelines," earlier in this section.

CULINARY TIPS
Try the sweet, tender razor clam's meat in risottos, ceviche, fritters, chowders, soups, and dips—or the ever-popular way: dredged in batter and fried to a golden brown. Beware of overcooking—they quickly turn from tender to rubber-band chewy.

HOW TO CLEAN LARGE CLAMS
It can seem daunting, but with a little practice, a sharp knife, and a pair of scissors, you can clean any large clam, such as the razor clam or horse clam, in a few minutes. Soon you'll have a mound of mildly flavored white-and-pink meat ready for risotto, chowder, fritters, or pasta sauce.

Blanch the clams in boiling water for ten seconds, or place them in a colander and pour boiling water on them until they open. Plunge in ice-cold water to stop the cooking, or the clam will be tough when fully cooked.

Run a knife along the inside of each shell to cut the meat free. Cut both adductor muscles (located at each end) and remove the clam. You should see a siphon (neck) attached to a creamy mantle (breast—a strip of muscle that runs from top to bottom), stomach (bulging and dark brown) and digestive tract, and gills. Razor clams show a white, sock-shaped digging foot at the bottom.

If it's not white or pink, don't eat it. With a knife or scissors, cut away the digestive tract and gills (the darkest parts). Save the siphon, mantle, and foot. Cut open the foot and squeeze to remove the crystalline style—a small rod that helps dissolve the silicon shells of plant plankton.

Slice off the siphon's top half inch. Insert a knife or scissors into the siphon hole and cut open from top to bottom. Rinse. Insert the knife or scissors into the second, inner siphon and cut open. Rinse meat well. For horse clams, pull the brown outer skin off the blanched siphon in sheets and scrape the remnants with a knife.

WHO EATS AND SHELTERS HERE?

When urchins are scarce, sea otters dig for razor clams. Young clams are food for shorebirds such as the sandpiper. Dungeness crab, starry flounder, green sturgeon, white sturgeon, and glaucous-winged gull all eat razor clams.

Commensal pea crab and commensal nemertean worms live inside the clam's mantle—the soft outer flaps of skin inside the shell that surround the clam's soft body. You can remove them when you clean the clams and return the little fellows to shallow water where you first dug the clams.

Pacific razor clams

HORSE CLAM
Tresus nuttallii, T. capax

FAMILY: Hiatellidae
STATUS: Native
OTHER NAMES: Pacific gaper, fat gaper, horseneck clam

Many people mistake the horse clam for a geoduck clam. A cousin of the geoduck but with a less flagrant neck (siphon), the horse clam is not as big but is still a hefty mollusk at 2 to 4 pounds. Like a geoduck, the horse clam's shell is about 8 inches long, chalk white to yellow, and flared where the siphon pokes out, and the siphons cannot retract completely (hence the name "gaper"). However, the horse clam is more round than square and has patches of brown leathery skin (periostracum) on the shell; the siphon has a brownish skin. *T. nuttallii* is longer than *T. capax*, with horny plates on the siphon tip, and often has a wreath of barnacles and seaweed. In shallow water, the visible siphon tip (called a "show") is lined with tentacles. At low tide, look for a telltale round dimple the size of a fifty-cent piece in the sand or mud. It's easier to dig horse clams than geoducks, which live in much deeper water and dwell deeper too.

Buried 1 to 2 feet in sand, gravel, or mud in low-intertidal bays from Alaska to California. Shares the same areas as butter clams. Accessible during minus tides and by diving. Two species thrive on the Pacific Coast: *T. nuttallii* is more common in the south; *T. capax* is a northerner.

LEFT: *Horse clam (Photo by Björn Jacobs-Frithiof);* **RIGHT:** *Horse clam siphon membrane peels off like a sock after blanching.*

CLAM GOSSIP

It was early June when I landed my kayak on a low-tide beach on the central coast of British Columbia. As I slogged up the incline, sulfurous mud stuck to my sandals. A geyser spurted from the beach, then another. The Coast Salish stories, my Suquamish friend Jules told me, have a juicy explanation for these phenomena: clams—especially big clams—were banished to the ocean floor because they wouldn't quit gossiping.

I wondered what those hidden tongues were saying. But as I tied my bowline around a driftwood anchor, the only words that came to mind were those of a Heiltsuk fisherman I'd passed earlier that morning. He'd asked where I was heading with such a heavily loaded kayak and fishing gear, and when I told him Rivers Inlet, he said, "You'll find a lot to eat as you paddle south. Our people like to say, 'When the tide is out, the table is set.'"

I liked that kind of gossip. As the beach expanded in size, so did my appetite for clams. But I had no shovel. Paddle-shaped digging sticks, carved of yew wood, were the powerful excavation tools of choice for many Coast Salish clam diggers. My kayak paddle was too delicate to use for prying, so I rummaged the driftwood line for a stick or busted boat plank. But there were only logs and kindling. Then I spotted a giant clamshell. Broad and sharp as a garden trowel, it turned out to be the perfect scoop—and strong, as long as I didn't hit a rock.

After four deep scrapes, my clam scoop removed the top two inches of muddy sand and exposed the squirters. Five clams, tiny as walnuts, retracted their short fused siphon tips. The cross-hatching on their shells told me they were littlenecks, named for their slender two-inch necks, or feeding siphons.

Littlenecks have delicately sweet, slightly chewy meat. In the next eight inches, my scoop scraped a rock—chalk white and large as a baseball. I reached into the hole and lifted out a five-inch clam! The hefty black hinge and concentric grooves—like water rings from a tossed stone—said butter clam.

Butter clams are aptly named. The mild, buttery meat makes them the king chowder clam. Commercial harvesting has been done by hand (and later dredging) since the 1900s. For over a half century, British Columbia's biggest clam export was butter clams. Many of those clams exited the province in tin cans. This enabled the coast's salmon canneries to run year-round, canning butter clams in winter and salmon in summer. It's rumored that butter clam nectar was the original secret ingredient in Mott's Clamato juice. In the mid-1980s, the market dropped out when fast-growing Manila "steamers" became vogue. But the most ingenious processing method was by First Nations women, who fashioned necklaces of dried butter clams as travel food for expeditions.

For many coastal First Nations, clams, it turns out, were a staple second only to salmon. Shell middens nine thousand years old are piled nine feet tall from generations of tossed kitchen scraps—a testament to the people's love of clams. The middens record human appetite down through the centuries, chock-full of butter clams, cockles, blue mussels, barnacles, and bones. Where I was digging, a white drift of shells glowed above the driftwood and rose like a snowbank under the lowest cedar branches.

As the tide slipped farther down the beach, I noticed a long wall of rocks emerging parallel to the beach where a half dozen new geysers shot up. Years later it dawned on me that this beach was very likely a "clam garden." Called a wuwuthim in the Tla'amin language, such rock walls were built to extend the "soil" area for growing clams. I looked at my small pot of clams—six littlenecks, one butter clam. Why bother digging for so many small ones when I could have one Goliathan clam down the beach?

I filled my shallow excavation and ran out onto the newly exposed mudflat and started digging around a fifty-cent-sized dimple in the sand. The deeper the hole got, the heavier the wet sand in the scoop. Soon the hole turned into an elbow-deep sink of gray water. But if I lay on my belly across the sun-warmed sand and plunged my bare arm into the forty-five-degree water, I could tickle a hard bump with my fingertips.

I dug my sandals into the mud, held my breath, and plunged both arms in. The clam filled my fingers like a small football. I tugged and wriggled until I sat upright with a dripping clam in a leather jacket. "Thank you," I said, as I wiped wet sand away with my sleeve. A dead giveaway that you have a horse clam is the chocolate-brown skin (periostracum) coating the shell and a thick brown turtleneck that can't retreat. Horse clams are so abundant these days, shellfish regulators wish we'd eat more of them.

For lunch that afternoon, I steamed up littlenecks in a broth of rockweed and wild onions and sliced the horse clam neck as thin as mica for sushi. It tasted sweet and crisp, like fresh abalone. I marveled at how this clam beach had sustained so many before me. It's no surprise that according to a beautiful origin story of the Indigenous people in Haida Gwaii, sixty miles west across Hecate Strait, the first people emerged from a giant clamshell.

Northwest hard-shell clams, which include littlenecks, cockles, butter clams, horse clams, and geoducks, sport a relatively tough armor of calcium carbonate. Unlike the delicate razor clam that burrows into sandy beaches, hard-shell clams can root into substrates made of mixed gravel, mud, and sand.

A boiling-hot saucepan with a splash of water or wine will pop open small- to medium-sized shells. A quick blanch or filet knife can open a large clam. Use the tender meat for chowders, fritters, risottos, or breaded and sautéed clam strips. Then slide your chair up to a sustainable and delicious feast.

A pea crab sticking out of a horse clam (Photo by Björn Jacobs-Frithiof)

HARVEST GUIDE

WHAT: Siphon, mantle meat with tiny foot called the belly. Toss the gutball.

WHEN: Refer to your local shellfish harvesting regulations. Check a local biotoxin hotline for shellfish closures for your specific beach.

See the "A Bucket of Tips for Enjoying Horse Clams and Geoducks" sidebar below and "Harvesting Guidelines" earlier in this section.

CULINARY TIPS

See the "A Bucket of Tips for Enjoying Horse Clams and Geoducks" sidebar below and cleaning tips in Pacific razor clams.

WHO EATS AND SHELTERS HERE?

The moon snail drills into the horse clam and sips it up. Dungeness and cancer crabs, short-spined sea stars, sunflower sea stars, and the hairy triton all eat horse clams. According to marine biologist Rick Harbo, "The lightly-sculptured Odostome snail feeds on the siphons and . . . more than thirty snails were seen nibbling on a single siphon." Poor dear!

Three species of commensal pea crab may live in the mantle cavity inside the shell and dine on diatoms the clam siphons in or eat plankton off the fluttery skirt of the mantle. Sargassum seaweed, an invasive species, may grow on the siphon tip.

Digging for horse clams

This niche gives the seaweed a head start to inhabit mudflat beaches it otherwise couldn't attach its holdfast to. Sometimes a nemertean worm can be found peacefully coexisting in the clam's shell.

PACIFIC GEODUCK
Panopea generosa

FAMILY: Hiatellidae
STATUS: Native
OTHER NAMES: Mud duck, king clam, gʷídəq (Lushootseed, the Indigenous language of Puget Sound)

One of the largest and longest-lived burrowing clams on the West Coast. In 2000, a geoduck tipped the scales at over 8 pounds, according to Washington Department of Fish and Wildlife biologists who weighed and verified the hefty clam at Adelma Beach, Discovery Bay. That's the weight of a gallon of milk. Average size for a single geoduck dug (not dived for) by a Puget Sound recreational harvester is 2.5 pounds. These deep dwellers can stretch their trunk-like siphon 3 feet from their hiding spot in the seafloor. The siphon cannot be fully retracted. An 8-inch, rectangular, gaping white shell envelops the body like a vest. Geoducks inhabit water depths over 300 feet and once buried, cannot move. They may live up to roughly 170 years.

Geoducks are found from Alaska to northwest Baja California. Depth: 2 to 3 feet in substrate.

HARVEST GUIDE
WHAT: Siphon, mantle meat with tiny foot, "belly"—toss the gut ball

❓ CLAM-PING DOWN ON POACHERS

Climate change is heating things up for geoduck clams, and poaching is making things even harder. In Asia, where most of the commercially harvested geoduck in the US and Canada is sold, one clam can fetch up to $300. Clam poaching is already a problem. In the San Juans, I have heard reports of clandestine divers leaving bags of geoduck on the seafloor and returning at night to retrieve them.

Back in the late 1980s, the "Clam Scam" occurred after one poacher was suspected of selling one million pounds of unreported geoduck harvested outside of legal picking areas. The court case became one of the greatest fraud suits in Washington State history. The convicted poacher was fined near $350,000 and spent two years in prison.

But even as poaching heats up, geoduck adults can survive longer in warmer seas than larvae can, but as sea temperatures increase, the Pacific geoduck may shift to the north or into deeper water to find cooler temperatures. Warmer waters also may increase disease.

WHEN: Refer to your state or province's shellfish harvesting regulations. Check a local biotoxin hotline for shellfish closures for your specific beach.
See the "A Bucket of Tips for Enjoying Horse Clams and Geoducks" sidebar below and "Harvesting Guidelines" earlier in this section.

CULINARY TIPS

One ingenious use for geoduck meat is clam cakes—simply pulverize meat in a food processor and substitute in a crab cake recipe for a delicious treat. An easy rule to

Geoduck clam (Photo by Chris Moench)

A BUCKET OF TIPS FOR ENJOYING HORSE CLAMS AND GEODUCKS

These tips are courtesy of fisherman Ficus Chan, an environmental educator from sea to shore, tide to table.

Look for a low-tide event at your local beach, at least minus 1.5 feet for horse clams and minus 2.0 feet for geoducks. In summer, lows are usually during the day, a pleasant time for clamming. But summertime is also more often affected by potential shellfish-related illnesses due to marine biotoxins and vibrio (see "Harvesting Guidelines" earlier in this section).

Always harvest as the tide goes out. Helpful tools are a sturdy cylinder made from a five-gallon bucket with the bottom cut out, a bucket to hold your catch, and a kneeling pad or tarp. Wear waders if you have them, and prepare to get muddy!

Walk out at low tide until you start seeing squirts of water coming out of circular dimple holes in the mud about the size of fifty-cent pieces or Canadian dollar loonies. Center your rigid plastic clam cylinder over the breathing hole, shimmying it down as far as you can, before digging out as much mud and sand as you can. The bottomless tube will keep sand from collapsing into your hole as you dig. You should find your horse clam about 12 to 18 inches down and your geoduck, 24 to 36 inches. Avoid grabbing and pulling the clam out by the siphon. You will most likely tear the siphon off, leaving the rest of the clam to die in the mud.

To prepare the large clams for a meal, you will need a pot of boiling water, an ice water bath or really cold running water, a cutting board, and a sharp knife. Separate the clam meat from its shell by running a sharp knife along the inside of the shell. Follow the directions in the How to Clean Large Clams section in Razor Clams earlier.

Belly meat can be cut into one-inch chunks, dredged in flour or starch, and deep fried

The bottomless bucket method prevents sand from collapsing into the digging area or a surprise wave from flooding it.

in oil. These belly nuggets go well with any seafood sauce.

Many foragers and chefs consider the siphon meat akin to abalone. To prepare the siphon to eat, remove the outer skin first. This is easy to do by blanching the siphon in boiling water for about five seconds. Peel the loosened skin off with a knife. The geoduck's skin peels off easier than the horse clam's—almost like one long sock. The siphon meat can be sliced extra thin for ceviche, sashimi, poke, or stir-fry. It is sweet, succulent, and mildly crisp.

Push the bottomless bucket into the sand over the dimple that indicates a clam breathing hole.

follow as you prepare large clam meat for the pot: if it's not white or pink, don't eat it. (See the "A Bucket of Tips for Enjoying Horse Clams and Geoducks" sidebar.)

WHO EATS AND SHELTERS HERE?

Reports from Monterey Bay and Southeast Alaska say otters and dogfish can dig out a geoduck buried in the mud. Moon snails, pink sea stars, red rock crabs, and Dungeness crabs all eat geoduck. The siphon tips are nibbled by bat rays, starry flounder, spiny dogfish, and cabezon.

Small white to transparent pea crabs live in the siphon and mantle of the geoduck. Flatworms find a symbiotic home in the geoduck's shell.

Geoduck

LITTLENECK CLAMS

At first glance, the Manila littleneck and native Pacific littleneck look confusingly similar—oblong or roundish shells, 3 inches wide, with a latticework of upraised concentric rings and radiating ridges. Their black-tipped siphons disappear completely inside shells that close tight, leaving no gap where the siphons exit.

MANILA LITTLENECK CLAM
Venerupis philippinarum

FAMILY: Veneridae (Venus Clam)
STATUS: Introduced
OTHER NAMES: Manila steamer, Japanese littleneck clam

Compared to Pacific littlenecks, Manila clams have more elongated shells, split siphons, a smooth inner shell rim, and often a purple or yellow marking on the shell's inside. The outer shell may be brown, cream, or gray, or show brown rays or chevrons. Quick-growing, they mature in 2 years, which makes them popular for mariculture.

Native from China to Siberia, the Manila littleneck clam stowed away with oyster seed shipments from Japan in the 1920s and has since spread from California to British Columbia. Find them in mud, gravel, and sand beaches. Because they live higher on the beach (high- to mid-intertidal zone) than the native Pacific littlenecks, and don't bury themselves beyond 2 to 4 inches, they can freeze in winter.

PACIFIC LITTLENECK CLAM
Protothaca staminea

FAMILY: Veneridae (Venus Clam)
STATUS: Native
OTHER NAMES: Steamer, Tomales Bay cockle, common littleneck, rock cockle, hardshell, rock clam, native littleneck

Pacific littlenecks have a lattice sculpture of concentric rings and radiating lines, but a more rounded shell than the Manila. Up to 3.5 inches long and gray, cream, or brown, often with brown mottling in mountain-range patterns, rays, or a checkerboard. Key traits are a fused

LEFT: *Manila littleneck clam*; RIGHT: *Pacific littleneck clam*

siphon, a white inner shell, and a file-like inner shell lip. Pacific littlenecks reach full size in 4 to 6 years and can live 10 to 15 years.

Littlenecks prefer to live in the mid- to low-intertidal zone (lower on the beach than Manilas), 6 to 10 inches under clay or gravel mixed with mud or sand, in protected bays and estuaries and subtidal zones up to 60 feet, from northern Mexico to Alaska, Siberia, and Japan.

HARVEST GUIDE

WHAT: Meat (all of it)

WHEN: Littleneck clams can easily be found at 0 to minus 1.0 tides. Refer to your state or province's shellfish harvesting regulations. Check a local biotoxin hotline for shellfish closures for your specific beach.

Use a shovel, rake, pick, or fork to sort through gravel. See "Harvesting Guidelines," earlier in this section.

CULINARY TIPS

Littleneck clams are choice and flavorful. The beautiful shells and bite-size meat makes them lovely for bouillabaisse. Drop whole into a simmering broth and wait seven minutes before serving. Steam with wine and savory or sweet herbs, such as fennel and orange zest. After steaming, toss with pasta or rice. Steamed clams can be skewered on stems of yarrow or rosemary, then smoked on the barbecue.

HOW TO CLEAN SMALL CLAMS

Littleneck clams and savory clams are petite morsels you can simmer in broth (whole in the shell) and serve after they open. Butter clams, while larger, are usually not gutted. They can be steamed open and chopped whole—after cutting off the black tip of the siphon, which can concentrate toxins. That said, a few sandy clams can taint a tasty dish. Follow these easy steps to remove grit inside and out.

Scrub clams with a firm brush under cold running water to remove outside grit or oceanic growths.

Discard chipped, crushed, or broken shells. Partially open shells should be tapped or pinched shut a few times and run under cold water. Throw out clams that don't clamp tightly.

Soak clams in a large pot with four quarts of cold water mixed with a half cup of salt and a handful of cornmeal for a minimum of thirty minutes (and as long as three hours) for "internal scrub power." As the clams filter water to breathe, they work out the sand.

Your littleneck clams, butter clams, and savory clams are now restaurant-ready for grilling, steaming in wine, or adding to a simmering bouillabaisse or pasta sauce. For tips on how to shuck your small clams, see Rosie's Butter Clam Fritters in Recipes.

WHO EATS AND SHELTERS HERE?

Crabs of all kinds, including Dungeness, cancer, and red rock, eat littleneck clams. Octopus and drill snails, such as the leafy hornmouth snail and moon snail, sip them like smoothies. Pacific staghorn sculpins nip off their siphons. Diving ducks eat them whole. Gulls drop them—*splat!*—until they open, then snack on them.

❓ HAVE A HEART FOR HEART COCKLES

Historically, the heart cockle was one of the most important shellfish harvested by some Coast Salish tribes. Today, almost one hundred years later, ocean heat waves are causing die-offs of this clam, which lives only a few inches below the surface of the beach. Low oxygen levels (hypoxia) and pollution have also resulted in the widespread death of cockles in the Salish Sea. In the summer of 2018, I observed a massive die-off of heart cockles at Ships Bay, beside the San Juan Ferry Terminal, during a heat wave. Julie Barber, shellfish biologist with the Swinomish Indian Tribal Community, wrote in a 2019 paper, "Climate change may be slowly bringing conditions on some beaches above survival thresholds for cockles, which are not well buffered from air temperature extremes during low tides due to their relatively shallow sediment burial depths."

The Suquamish Tribe is culturing heart cockles until they reach an age they can survive better in the wild. There are plans to place them in PVC geoduck tubes that are pressed into the sand and have a screen top. Water can enter but predators cannot dig out the clams.

HEART COCKLE
Clinocardium nuttallii

FAMILY: Cardiidae
STATUS: Native
OTHER NAMES: Basket clam, Nuttall's cockle

The largest cockle on the West Coast, it can grow to a half foot long. Viewed from the side, this clam is heart shaped, hence the name *Clinocardium* ("sloped heart)." Ribs (34 to 38 of them) radiate from the umbo, or pointed end. Shell color is beige to mottled with brown blotches.

From the Bering Sea to San Diego, California. They prefer sheltered sandy beaches and eelgrass-covered mudflats, at the low intertidal to 100 feet.

HARVEST GUIDE
WHAT: Meat (all of it)
WHEN: Refer to your state or province's shellfish harvesting regulations. Check a local biotoxin hotline for shellfish closures for your specific beach.
Use a shovel, pick, or fork. Dig one to two inches. See "Harvesting Guidelines," earlier in this section.

CULINARY TIPS
Heart cockles make excellent chowder or fritters.

WHO EATS AND SHELTERS HERE?
Dungeness crabs trap cockles and then chip away the cockle's shell using their strong claws. Sunflower sea stars hunt and dig them up, but now they are nearly absent from Alaska to California. Gulls and river otters crack cockles exposed

Heart cockle shells have deep ridges and a zipperlike closure. They appear heart shaped when viewed from the side.

near the surface. I have seen husks of broken cockles littering the sand in a bay at very low tide outside a Pacific octopus den.

BUTTER CLAM
Saxidomus giganteus

FAMILY: Veneridae (Venus Clam)
STATUS: Native
OTHER NAMES: Smooth Washington clam, Washington clam, Washingtons, Martha Washingtons, quahog, beefsteak, money shell, Koo'tah (Olamentko)

Butter clams have oval, chalk-white shells inside and out (although some stain black or brick red in anaerobic mudflats), a minuscule opening for the siphon, and uniformly thick shell halves (rounded at both ends and etched with fine concentric ridges, with no radiating lines). Look for the telltale large black hinge ligament. The black-tipped siphons are about 1½ inches long. These clams live up to 20 years. Learn how to differentiate butter clams (at any size) from other clams, since they are especially vulnerable to carrying and keeping

❓ OCEAN ACIDITY AND SHELLFISH

Shopping for basic needs, heating our homes, enjoying our burgers and coffee beans, banking air miles—we all contribute carbon dioxide into thin air. Thankfully, our oceans suck up about a third of the carbon dioxide from the atmosphere. But too much carbon dioxide in the ocean of life upsets the recipe for healthy shellfish. Oceans run more acidic. Carbonate ions—the vital building blocks of calcium carbonate, which hardens the shells of clams and crabs—become more scarce. Our shellfish buddies have a harder time making and keeping their shells thick. The shells of butter clams began to dissolve after just two weeks when tested in a tank of water with levels of ocean acidity predicted by the year 2100.

Today, the oyster industry in Washington State has a sophisticated machine that injects sodium carbonate into hatchery water to reduce the problem so we can have delicious oysters on our plates. It's a short-term solution as carbonate levels continue to drop. Don't clam up! Buy local, and eat local. Plant a garden of wild and cultivated deliciousness you can walk to. It might just be a clam garden!

Butter clam shells are chalky white (often stained), with concentric rings and a large brown hinge.

toxins that cause paralytic shellfish poisoning (PSP), which they pick up from ingesting the dinoflaellate *Alexandrium catanella*. Butter clams can keep the toxin for up to 2 years. It's a good reason to harvest from beaches monitored by the state or province and cut off the black siphon tips, which concentrate the toxin.

The low intertidal is where you'll find this clam nestled, 10 to 18 inches down in sand, gravel, or shell beaches in protected bays and estuaries from Alaska to Northern California. The butter clam can also live in waters up to 120 feet deep.

HARVEST GUIDE

WHAT: Meat

WHEN: Refer to your state or province's shellfish harvesting regulations. Always check a local biotoxin hotline for shellfish closures for your specific beach. ❗ Butter clams are especially susceptible to harboring marine biotoxins.

Use a shovel, rake, pick, or fork. A tide of minus 2.0 or greater is best for butter clams. See "Harvesting Guidelines," earlier in this section, and the "Be Biotoxin Aware" sidebar below.

CULINARY TIPS

Butter clams are blue-ribbon chowder clams. They are also delicious dipped in whisked egg and panko breadcrumbs, then fried. ❗ **Important note:** Always remove the dark siphon tips of butter clams, where the toxin that causes PSP may concentrate.

THE RISING TIDE OF
ANCIENT AQUACULTURE

Looking west from the forested bluff at Kiket Island, on the Kukutali Preserve in the Salish Sea, I could see two long lines on the low-tide beach. One was a lively assembly line of sixty people passing stones hand to hand from a gargantuan rock pile. The other line was a curved necklace of rocks at the throat of the bay. It mirrored the shore but was manifesting, rock by rock, near the low-tide mark.

Happy chatter and laughter punctuated the salt air. Courtney Greiner, project manager for the Swinomish clam garden, wrestled a barnacled boulder into the wall's landward side. Alana Quintasket, Swinomish Senate Vice Chair, tipped a boulder into the ocean side. Julie Barber, Swinomish lead shellfish biologist, carefully snugged another rock from the assembly line, into the two-foot-tall ridge.

This June afternoon, as part of the Salish Summit—a gathering of community members from the Cross-Pacific Indigenous Aquaculture Collaborative Network—almost thirty tribes were gathered to learn about restoring traditional aquaculture practices. Tribal members and other volunteers came from Palau, Guam, Hawaii, Alaska, British Columbia, and Washington. Before the day's end, they would relocate twenty thousand pounds of rock and extend the wall almost two hundred feet. They would help bolster tribal food sovereignty, increase clam production, provide a place for multigenerational learning and healing, and reduce the impacts of climate change on an important traditional food. This is the first modern-day clam garden wall built in the United States.

Swinomish leaders and scientists learned about building ancient clam gardens firsthand in 2017, when they traveled to Russell Island, near Fulford Harbor, British Columbia. First Nations have partnered with BC Parks for over a decade to restore traditional aquaculture sites. Joe Williams, Swinomish community shellfish liaison, was blown away by his experience on Russell Island. "We went up for this nighttime tide. Some Elders were sitting by a fire on a beautiful white sand beach. But it wasn't sand. It was shells, thousands of years of shell hash. I walked onto this beautiful little garden they're restoring. A man told me, 'You're probably going to be moving some rock. So be ready.' Well, I picked up that first rock and I swear to God, it just hit me like a ton of bricks. One of my ancestors handled this rock thousands of years ago! I was restoring some of the work that they did. It was just super powerful for me because my family comes from that area."

How does a clam garden work? Quintasket explained it this way: "Once the wall is put in place, it begins to trap sediment. It's a long process. Like it'll go beyond my lifetime, but gradually, it decreases the slope of the beach to the optimal habitat for clams, the lower intertidal zone. Clams thrive in that area."

A 2016 study on the central coast of British Columbia found that butter clams were 2.4 times higher in density in clam gardens than in unmodified beaches. Amazingly, those gardens had been tended for less than 150 years. Clams aren't the only species to thrive behind the walls. They are truly "sea gardens." The rock walls will one day sprout a kelp forest. Kelp attracts Dungeness crabs, red rock crabs, sea cucumbers, chitons, red turban snails, and octopus—all culturally important foods for Northwest coast Indigenous communities. I asked Williams and Quintasket, "What do you feel when you're working in the clam garden?"

"I don't feel so pessimistic," Williams said. "When you show up on the beach and everything is peaceful, and you're there to be a good steward, it just feels like all of our relatives come out to visit. It always seems like the eagles come out and the clams are just squirting away like they're just happy to see you. Right? All of their relatives are all together again."

Williams continued, "When I'm in that place, in that space where my ancestors lived and thrived through some of the hardest times imaginable for the human species—like through ice ages and through unimaginable climate change, and I'm looking, trying to be quiet and pay attention to these teachings—what I realize is that my ancestors left us a playbook for how to survive through all these hard times that are coming. It is like a perfect gift, right?"

Quintasket said, "Oh, man, those days that we get to go out to the clam garden to work on it, or even those nights where we just get to go out and be with it, and see it, and see the changes, and know that it's still just the beginning—it's incredible. And I love that the rock walls come from Alaska, down here to Coast Salish territory. They go all the way down into the South Pacific. These types of teachings go across the entire Pacific Ocean. I was always taught that a lot of people think that it's the water that divides us. But the water is what connects us. It keeps us together. It allows us to share space and to share knowledge."

Building a rock wall at the Swinomish Indian Tribal Community Clam Garden

WHO EATS AND SHELTERS HERE?

Staghorn sculpins bite off the siphons, but they can sense the PSP toxin and will spit it out. Sea otters, Dungeness crabs, and moon snails love butter clams. The sunflower sea star was a former predator, until sea star wasting disease nearly wiped them out.

The quarter-sized pea crab lives inside its mantle. The clear, matchstick-sized crystalline style in the clam has a bunch of large spirochaete bacteria living in it as well.

SAVORY CLAM
Nuttallia obscurata

FAMILY: Psammobiidae
STATUS: Introduced
OTHER NAMES: Varnish clam, savoury clam, chocolate clam

Palm sized—3 to 3½ inches wide—savory clams have a shiny, oval, dark brown, thin shell with a purple interior. Find them 1 to 2 inches below the sand or gravel.

Native to Japan, Korea, and the Yellow and Bohai Seas of China. Introduced to southern British Columbia, Washington, and all estuaries in Oregon. Prefers sand, gravel, and mud in the mid- to upper-tintertidal zone.

ABOVE: *A small sea star and anemone at home in a butter clam shell* (Photo by Chris Moench)
BELOW: *Savory, varnish, or chocolate clam all describe this invasive.*

VARNISHING THE REPUTATION OF AN INVASIVE

Cupped in my palm, the clam with a shiny chestnut-brown jacket and royal-purple interior was as baffling as it was beautiful. In the early 1990s, I found it splayed open like a stranded butterfly on a white shell beach. Even though I'd surfed my kayak up this beach on Chuckanut Island in Bellingham Bay for seven years, I'd never seen this strange bivalve before. At home, it defied every black-and-white clam photo in my field guide *Sound and the Sea*, coauthored by my marine biology professor Dr. Jerry Flora. I was stumped.

Now I understand why. The varnish clam, also called dark mahogany, purple mahogany, or savory clam, hails from far away, across the Pacific Rim. Apparently, in around 1988, it hitchhiked undetected in ballast water. It took only a few tenacious microscopic larvae to reach the Port of Vancouver in British Columbia and ride a waterslide to freedom to seed the West Coast. Ten years later, the newly varnished generations had moved west out the Strait of Juan de Fuca, around the Olympic Peninsula, and into practically every estuary in Oregon. The territorial expansion continues up the west coast of British Columbia.

Why are they so successful? In part because the wee plankton can spend a long time—up to two months—bobbing along in ocean currents. They tolerate a wide range of salinities and temperatures. Larvae bubbling in laboratory tanks grew fastest at 68 degrees Fahrenheit. That's a plus in warming seas. Once the clam larvae settle on a beach, they push their way in, shoulder to shoulder, or umbo to umbo, with our commercially important littleneck clams. (I imagine them trying to shove the other clams aside with that elbow-like point nearest the hinge, called an "umbo.") Apparently, Manilas do manage to keep many of them at bay in the mid-intertidal. Varnish clams have no choice but to settle in oceanward or beachward of the Manila clam nation's turf. So, clam-hungry diggers, take note, you can find the greatest densities by digging up beach and down from the Manila clams.

A recent survey counted seven hundred varnish clams in one square meter of beach sand. When I told my husband that this clam, *Nuttallia obscurata*, is classified as an "aquatic nuisance," he snorted. "Hah, that clam sounds far from obscure! They should name it *Nuttallia abundata* or *Nuttallia prolificata*."

British Columbia is a kingdom for clam aquaculture. They farm varnish clams—along with geoduck, Manila, and littleneck. To increase market interest in the US and Canada, a couple of savvy seafood sellers from Vancouver, British Columbia, registered the market name "Savoury Clam" for the varnish clam with the Canadian Food Inspection Agency. To promote the clam for the restaurant market, a food trade show in Vancouver featured "Savoury Clams" in an *Iron Chef* demo.

HARVEST GUIDE

WHAT: Meat

WHEN: Refer to your state or province's shellfish harvesting regulations. Always check a local biotoxin hotline for shellfish closures for your specific beach. ❗ Varnish clams have a propensity for taking up more biotoxins and keeping them longer. Use a shovel, rake, pick, or fork. See "Harvesting Guidelines," earlier in this section, and the "Be Biotoxin Aware" sidebar below.

CULINARY TIPS

The succulent, sweet meat is reminiscent of mussels and perfect for bouillabaisse and chowder. They are exceptionally tender compared to farmed Manila clams. Note that with a thinner shell, they cook faster than Manilas. If you are cooking a dish with both Manilas and savory clams, begin with the Manilas and plop in the savories two to three minutes later.

WHO EATS AND SHELTERS HERE?

Dungeness crabs, red rock crabs, and racoons prefer the thin-shelled savory clam to the thicker-shelled littleneck clam. More bang for the shuck. A shellfish researcher calculated that a racoon can forage over 8 percent of its daily needs in ten minutes of dining on savory clams. Lewis moon snails, oyster catchers, northwestern crows, and glaucous-winged gulls all seek out the clams. Migratory surf scoters and white-wing scoters—stout sea ducks with skookum-strong bills—dive for thousands of Manila

❗ BE BIOTOXIN AWARE

It may be the savory clam's unusual feeding technique that gives it more potential to take up shellfish biotoxins. At the beach, it collects food in two ways—filtering out plankton particles from the water and tickling the sand with its foot to release detritus from the mud. Consequently, like its cousin the butter clam, the savory clam has the capacity to store paralytic shellfish toxin (PST) at greater levels and for longer—more than a year after a toxic bloom subsides.

Always check shellfish hotlines the day you dig. Some beaches can be closed for butter and varnish clam digging but not for other shellfish. According to the Department of Fisheries and Oceans of British Columbia, savory clams actually take up and get rid of PST in about the same amount of time as Pacific oysters and Manilla clams. In short, the verdict is still out.

and savory clams between their fall arrival in the Strait of Georgia and their departure in spring. Juvenile flatfish nip the clam's siphons off, but they regrow and become a kind of renewable snack bar for flatfish.

Savory clams run a guest house for the juvenile pea crab (*Pinnixia faba*).

MUSSELS

PACIFIC BLUE MUSSEL
Mytilus trossulus

FAMILY: Mytilidae
STATUS: Native
OTHER NAMES: Edible mussel, bay mussel, black mussel, foolish mussel

Shells are purple blue to black, sometimes root-beer brown, and up to 3 inches long. Both shell halves are mirror images of one another and have a teardrop outline. The outside surface is smooth, with concentric lines. The interior is pearled blue. Flesh is creamy white. Amber elastic threads (byssi) anchor the shell in place. A long "foot" has a special gland that produces the amazing elastic that stretches into byssal threads (called "beards").

Pacific blue mussels can form large beds along quiet, sheltered bays and fjords. They are also abundant on exposed rocky points. Look for them during minus tides. This adaptable species ranges from the Arctic Ocean to Northern California, eastern Russia, and the north Atlantic Ocean.

Pacific blue mussels (Photo by Katherine Palmer)

THE ANCIENT TASTE OF SEA AND TIDES

In the territory of the Ka:ˈyuːˈk ʼtʼhʼ and Che:k:tles7etʼhʼ First Nations, on the northwest rim of Vancouver Island, ancient time collides with the present on an island in Kyuquot Sound. While snorkeling over a rocky point on an unusually calm autumn afternoon, I looked down and saw a carpet of petrified mussels covering the seafloor in overlapping puppy piles. Sleeping en masse for 150 million years or more, one is bound to get cozy with one's neighbors. Each shell was crescent shaped, with deeply grooved concentric rings. I swam a yard farther up toward the surface, and suddenly I was in the present again. California mussels, *Mytilus californianus*, covered the underwater rocks. A king-sized bed of them grinned orange underneath blue hard hats.

On our coast, we have the distinction of having the largest mussel species in the world—the California mussel. In cold waters they grow slowly. Not so in California's temperate seas. These massive shellfish can expand to a half foot long in just three years. The mussel shells in this island's chilly shallows looked twice the length of my frigid fingers. They wore leather coats with radiating bumpy ribs.

I took another stilted breath and dove down into the bone-chilling sea to look again. This time, I realized that living blue mussels were attached by leagues of byssal threads to the backs of the ancient mussel-like fossils. Somehow, without knowing, these creatures had become neighbors on a 150-million-year-old bridge across time.

Earlier that day, I'd picked up another remarkable old shell from the beach drift. A gargantuan California mussel—or half of one. Faded as old denim, the once-pearlescent center shown dull as a cataract. The curved outside looked battered and pocked with drill marks from predatory snails. The walls were so thick, the hungry drill snails had given up! First Nations hunters sharpened California mussel shells into harpoon heads for spearing whales, sharks, and porpoises, and fishers crafted large, sturdy specimens into artful knives. By patiently sharpening the long, curved outer lip and grasping the hinged, upraised edge, it morphed into a perfect tool for filleting salmon. These ulu-style knives were often used by women who expertly filleted hundreds, if not thousands, of salmon each year in preparation for drying and smoking. Even after steel knives became commonplace, the Ka:ˈyuːˈkʼtʼhʼ fishers chose a mussel-shell knife for a First Salmon Ceremony, because steel blades might offend the salmon. Just two hundred years ago, the shell in my hand would have been a fisherwoman's treasured friend.

Above the water, in the giant kelp bed fifty feet away, a sea otter surfaced with a cluster of mussel shells. Its translucent whiskers dripped with seawater. Otters have a metabolism like a pubescent teen: they eat often and in large quantities. With no blubber layer, their heat comes from fuel—like shellfish—and their plush fur, which packs in a million hairs per square inch (more than all the fur on your average house cat). Clicking two mussels together, the ingenious otter cracked them open and wolfed them up.

Both Pacific blue mussels and California mussels were gathered by coastal Indigenous people. Shell middens with discarded mussel shell fragments bear this out. Traditionally, the Tlingit and Kwakwaka'wakw dried mussels for winter use. If food supplies were low or stormy seas halted fishing and marine mammal hunting, fresh mussels served as emergency food. The tough shells, roped in place by byssal threads, could be pried loose with yew-wood digging sticks, wedges, and scrapers made of stone or bone. Eaten raw, steamed, boiled, roasted, dried, or smoked, they were revered by some and considered poor man's food by others. Accessible year-round but approached with caution, mussels were not collected by the Manhouset when herring was spawning or in summer, when shellfish toxins can be more prevalent. This wisdom is born out in a tragic historical account of 135 Koniag men from Kodiak Island who died in Tlingit territory after eating contaminated mussels.

But otters—and glaucous-winged gulls—may share a life-saving trait we humans lack. These sensitive shellfish harvesters can sense paralytic shellfish poisoning (PSP) toxins and upchuck the tainted shellfish.

Much as I would have liked to have a seafood dinner for two that evening after snorkeling, I restrained. Caution, I reasoned, is best when harvesting mussels from the wild. Filter-feeding mussels strain water at about two and a half quarts per hour. Their high metabolic rates allow them to flush potentially fatal toxins like PSP faster than other shellfish. But I had no access to a health department shellfish toxins hotline or hospital if I became sick.

A week later, my kayak buddy and I were on the east side of Vancouver Island and had a chance to gather wild mussels again. This time, the beach was monitored, and our bellies responded. We happily steamed them in ale and a splash of seawater, then sopped up the juice with bannock bread baked in our folding skillet.

Every time I eat mussels, I feel like I wake up. They taste of the sea and tides, of honey and salt. It's amazing that something that tastes like dessert can be so good for you. Packed with protein, vitamin B12, selenium, zinc, and folate, mussels are low in fat too. It's no wonder mussels are now one of the most popular farmed shellfish on Planet Ocean.

California or ribbed mussel bed in Haida Gwaii (Photo by Chris Moench)

CALIFORNIA MUSSEL
Mytilus californianus

FAMILY: Mytilidae
STATUS: Native
OTHER NAMES: Big mussel, sea mussel, rock mussel, ribbed mussel

Shells may be as long as your hand and show a dozen or so ridges radiating across the blue-black surface. The interior hides a pearled sunset in hues of purple and blue. The meat is orange. The large, thick half shells make a perfect spoon for campers or scoop at home.

Found near wave action from the Aleutian Islands and Alaska south to Baja, Mexico. Large beds cover surf-pounded rocks, pilings, and seamounts—some over 300 feet deep.

HARVEST GUIDE

WHAT: Meat
WHEN: Usually fall through spring. Summer can be iffy, due to marine biotoxins. Refer to your state or province's shellfish harvesting regulations and a local biotoxin hotline for shellfish closures for your specific beach.
Use a knife to cut byssal threads and make removing the shell easier. Pull the mussel free using a rocking and twisting motion. See "Harvesting Guidelines," earlier in this section.

California mussels have a ridged blue-black surface, with a pearlescent interior.

CULINARY TIPS

Simple favorites include mussels steamed in ale or white wine and mussels smoked over an open campfire grill. At home, try mussels and chorizo in marinara, steamed mussels in vermouth with herbs and shallots, mussels and wood sorrel sauce, curried mussels, grilled black pepper and garlic mussels, risotto with mussels and saffron, or cioppino-style seafood stew. Substitute mussels for clams or oysters in almost any recipe.

WHO EATS AND SHELTERS HERE?

A host of seabirds—harlequin ducks, Barrow's goldeneyes, surf scoters, and black oystercatchers (which can gulp their body weight in shellfish each day)—eat mussels. Mew gulls, glaucous-winged gulls, and crows crack them open like walnuts by dropping them from on high, then gobble the sweet meat. Shiner perch, pile perch, anemones, crabs, and mink all nosh mussels. Larval California mussels are eaten by shiner surfperch. Young mussels are a favorite food of crabs and shorebirds. Sea otters slurp up mussels. Drill snails, such as the frilled dogwinkle, have their own little dentist drills in the form of a file-like tongue and use them to cut into the California mussel's calcium roof and sip out the contents. Many sea stars—the six-armed star, mottled star, purple star, and sunflower star—wrestle them open and then insert their stomachs. Purple sea stars, all arms for mussels, are such major predators that their constant nibbling from below keeps the mussels from growing deeper.

The beds are a fortress that protects snails, ribbon worms, polychaete worms, isopods, amphipods, and hundreds of tiny larvae from pounding waves and predators. The little hidey-holes between mussel shells pack and retain sediment, much like a tree's roots anchor soil in rainstorms, so little life-forms can flourish too. In one California mussel bed, researchers identified three hundred species, from oysters to octopus to ocean worms to tiny black sea cucumbers!

DUNGENESS CRAB
Cancer magister

FAMILY: Cancridae (Rock Crabs)
STATUS: Native
OTHER NAMES: Dungee, market crab, commercial crab, Pacific crab, edible crab, common edible crab, Pacific edible crab

Compared to king, snow, and tanner crabs, Dungeness crabs are the compact cars of the large Northwest crab world. Eight flat walking legs and an impressive set of white-tipped

CRACKING GOOD CRABBING

Sumdum Glacier and Mount Sumdum, rising above Holkham Bay in Southeast Alaska, share the same quirky name. Although it sounds like the banter of a bored tourist on a passing cruise ship, the name predates Captain Cook and George Vancouver. The Tlingit natives who canoed these iceberg-plagued passages to spear crabs and hunt seals named the area Sumdum to mimic the sound of thundering glacier ice. Sum Dum has a double meaning in Lingít, as well. It's a phrase that makes my mouth gush like a glacier-melt stream—"good crabbing."

In my late thirties, when I worked as a naturalist and kayak guide aboard the MV *Pacific Catalyst* (a 1932 classic wood ecotour boat), I knew Holkham Bay by taste. At that time, it was a prolific place for crabs. One afternoon, as I lowered three crab traps as big as semitruck tires over the *Pacific Catalyst*'s rail to my friend Carl in the waiting dinghy, I could hear the ice repeating its name in the distance—sooom dum!

Each crab trap was made of two metal hoops covered with netting. A crab "escape hatch" in the side was tied with thin cotton string, in case the contraption was accidentally dragged off by a flotilla of icebergs to deeper water. Three days from summer solstice, our crabbing that day was still an ongoing experiment. Carl kept meticulous notes on successful baits, locations, and depths. We packed different "smellies" in each trap: fresh halibut skin from last night's catch, a turkey leg, and the surefire crab magnet—a punctured tin of cat food.

At one favorite secret spot and two new locations, we heaved the traps overboard. A day later, pulling pots was heavy business. We took turns grasping and pulling up the wet rope, hand over hand, bracing knees against the tipping dinghy's side. But what a place to pull for your dinner. A humpback whale the size of a school bus churned up the seas for forage fish and krill a hundred yards away. Two bald eagles hitched a ride on a translucent blue iceberg. A sea lion somersaulted past the dinghy, tossing a flat fish as it bit off mouth-sized bits.

When the crab pot surfaced, the crowded "dungees" clicked and clacked. All in all, we counted eighteen crabs, with thirteen keepers—males that surpassed the legal minimum size limit. To measure, we used a plastic crab ruler held against the back shell just inside the horned tips. Regardless of size, females, recognized by their broad U-shaped abdomen apron, are protected. We gently slipped them overboard.

Killing a live crab for your dinner with one blow is an art. Carl preferred to use his mercifully quick crab guillotine. Seated on the boat's back deck, he held the crab's pincers and legs against its body with gloved hands, raised the crab overhead with pointy nose down, and slammed the crab's nose against the far edge of a hardwood block. It killed the crab instantly and sheared the back shell off, revealing the meat.

Dungeness crab (Photo by Katherine Palmer)

When kayak camping, I use a slightly different method taught to me by a Lummi Nation crabber. Like Carl, I grasp the pincers against the two sides of the shell and raise the crab above my head, but then I break it in two over a sharp rock edge—right down the back shell's imaginary midline. Rinsed in the ocean, cleaned of gills and viscera, it's ready to fit in my camp cook pot, where it's boiled in water for twelve minutes. It becomes the sweetest meat in the sea.

Why settle for packaged, precooked crab that is often oversalted when you can have fresh, honey-sweet flakes of crabmeat right from Mother Nature's biodegradable container? A loaf of crusty bread, a bottle of wine, an ocean view, and fresh-cracked crab on a beach log—it's hard to top that.

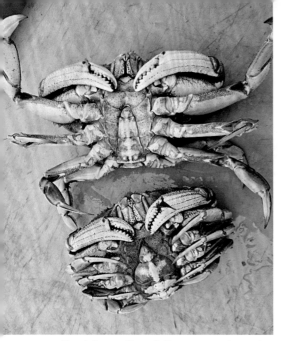

The abdomen of a male Dungeness crab, top, is narrower than that of a female, bottom. (Photo by Tom Tran)

pincers fold neatly under their broad, ivory-grooved and burgundy-purple shell (carapace). Full-grown males span about 10 inches and females just over 7 inches. Ten "teeth" rim the front of the carapace on each side of the eye stalks. Dungees eat such a broad range of food that it's too many to list here (116 prey species have been identified in their stomachs). Contrary to popular opinion, they aren't just scavengers. They hunt, and they like fresh seafood, including razor clams, mussels, oysters, octopus, and fish.

Pribilof Islands, Alaska, to Southern California. Sandy or muddy-bottom bays and eelgrass beds—and in Southeast Alaska on bay bottoms of cobble, shell, pebble, and silt.

HARVEST GUIDE

WHAT: Meat in claws, legs, and leg attachment areas

WHEN: Refer to state or provincial harvesting regulations for seasonal openings. See "Harvesting Guidelines," earlier in this section.

CULINARY TIPS

Dungeness crab meat, is sinfully delicious cracked from the shell and eaten boiled, baked, grilled, steamed, or pit-roasted. Try it rolled in enchiladas or sushi, or fold it into risotto, fritters, paella, omelets, and quiche. Stir it into chowder, cioppino, bouillabaisse, mac 'n' cheese, or slaw. Stuff it into avocados, fish filets, or jalapeño peppers. And of course, don't forget Consummate Crab Cakes (see Recipes).

WHO EATS AND SHELTERS HERE?

In every stage of life, Dungeness crabs are preyed upon. Marine worms, including the Dungeness egg-worm, may eat 55 percent of the eggs (females carry up to 2.5 million eggs tucked under a broad, skirt-like flap on their undersides). Free-swimming larvae are eaten by coho and chinook salmon, herring, copper rockfish, sardines, seabirds, and whales. Staghorn sculpins and pink sea stars eat the newly settled pea-sized crabs, called megalops. Juvenile crabs fall prey to larger Dungeness crabs, skates, birds, stur-

⚠ BUTTER EAT CLEAN CRABS!

Crab "butter" is a delicacy, famous for the seafood-intense flavor it lends to rice, fish dishes, and other specialties in Asian, Filipino, and Northwest cuisine. While fat-rich, crab butter isn't the drizzle you apply to crab legs. It's the fatty, briny yellow-green mush inside the crab shell's cavity—a kind of liver and pancreas combo.

Be sure to harvest crabs from clean areas—the less urban the better—to reduce your exposure to metals or PCBs, which can accumulate more in fat so than crab meat. Consumption guidelines for crab butter in Washington State range from four servings a month for the San Juan Islands or eastern Juan de Fuca Strait to zero in Seattle's Elliott Bay. If you are concerned about exposure, you can always steam or boil just the crab legs—but for a wildly un-urban dungee dinner—see Butter-of-the-Sea Crab Bowl in Recipes.

geon, halibut, English sole, starry flounder, and marine mammals. Smaller crabs are torn apart by the invasive green crab too. Adult crabs are grabbed by octopus, halibut, wolf eels, crows, bald eagles, harbor seals, sea lions, and both sea and river otters.

SEA URCHINS

GIANT RED SEA URCHIN
Mesocentrotus franciscanus

FAMILY: Stronglyocentrotidae
STATUS: Native
OTHER NAMES: Sea eggs, uni (Japanese, in sushi), big red sea egg, táutsáup (Haida)

The giant red sea urchin tips the scales at 1 pound and can live for 150 years! King of the coastal urchins, its 6-inch oval exoskeleton and nearly 3-inch-long spines guard a booty of 5 delicate golden packets of roe. Giant red urchins blush scarlet to dark burgundy.

Found across the Pacific Rim, from northern Japan to Baja, Mexico, down to 400 feet. Like the green and purple urchins, giant red urchins savor near-shore kelp forests. Find

LEFT: *Giant red urchin*; RIGHT: *Green urchin* (Photo by Katherine Palmer)

giant red urchins during the lowest tides along surf-pounded coasts, channels with strong tidal currents, and protected rocky shores.

GREEN SEA URCHIN
Stronglyocentrotus droebachiensis

FAMILY: Stronglyocentrotidae
STATUS: Native
OTHER NAMES: Little green urchin, green sea egg

The smaller, sage-colored green sea urchin grows to 3.5 inches across and resembles a bristly chestnut. It has more delicate spines than the purple or red sea urchins.

Green sea urchins live in both the Pacific and the Atlantic and range circumpolar across the northern hemisphere in areas protected from surging waves. The densest populations live in 30 feet of water, but they can inhabit the abyss of Davy Jones's locker—grazing on a snow of kelp bits and detritus to 3,800 feet deep.

PURPLE SEA URCHIN
Stronglyocentrotus purpuratus

FAMILY: Stronglyocentrotidae
STATUS: Native
OTHER NAMES: Purple spined urchin, purple urchin

Royal purple in color, these urchins grow up to 6 inches in diameter, spine tip to spine tip. The sturdy, 1-inch spines act like pickaxes to excavate a cave from soft stone. This allows the urchin to take shelter on surf-slammed coasts, but it may become trapped in its hiding hole when it grows. It often has shell bits and algae flecks stuck to its tube feet like camouflage. Like the red and green urchin, the purple is a seaweed connoisseur. On the underside of its body, an urchin's jawbone and 5 spade-shaped teeth are arranged into a fascinating structure called Aristotle's lantern. Purple urchins can replace their teeth in 75 days.

Purple sea urchins range from Alaska to Baja California in the lower intertidal to 215 feet deep.

HARVEST GUIDE
WHAT: Gonads (roe)
WHEN: Best roe from October to February. Winter storms make harvesting treacherous, so try in early fall before the storms. Keep in mind that urchins from degraded habitats are not likely to yield high-quality roe due to a lack of food (kelp).

LEFT: *Purple sea urchin;* RIGHT: *Green sea urchin*

"SEA EGGS": FUEL, FAT, AND FLAVOR

On the islands of Haida Gwaii, sixty miles west of British Columbia's central coast, fishermen of the Haida Nation once leaned out from canoes, agile as herons, and speared "sea eggs" off cliffs and rocks. One of the favorite places to harvest sea urchins was called Styuu taa gaayingaats or "eating sea urchins while you are floating," according to Haida Elder Solomon Wilson in "The Knowledge and Usage of Marine Invertebrates by the Skidegate Haida People of the Queen Charlotte Islands." Elder Luke Swan of the village of Manhouset on Vancouver Island described how a sea urchin spear worked. A long cedar pole lashed with three yew-wood spikes was used to spear the giant urchin off a cliff. A quick twist of the spear prevented the animal from falling off the spear as it was lifted out of the water into a canoe. The fishers used an elongated stone or a yew-wood wedge to crack open the urchin's spine-armored shell, revealing the five golden roe packets the size and shape of grapefruit segments. Sea eggs were often devoured on the spot, scooped out with fingers and rinsed in seawater. The briny delicacy is reminiscent of sweet cream and oysters.

Not everyone agrees on the merits of urchin roe. Even my wild taste buds found urchin to be an acquired taste. Today, however, I'm a convert. Urchin is my shellfish of choice on kayak trips. It's chock-full of fuel, fat, and flavor—perfect for expedition paddling or an elegant beachside dinner. Catching an urchin, however, is another matter.

Giant red sea urchins lurk below the water line—usually just out of reach. But they can live as deep as three hundred feet or more. At low tide, I paddle along a cliff looking for a pie-sized red glow. Most of the time it's a giant red sea urchin, but it could be a plump strawberry anemone or an orange encrusting sponge. The right red, the splash of scarlet color, is key. You could paddle all day in a yawning, steep fjord and not see a one. It also has to be the right cliff—one exposed to surf or a strong tidal current. A narrow passage with a small window of slack tidal water works fabulously. Slack tide, when the water is barely rippling along, is the pause between the ocean's ebb tide and flood tide. That's the moment a kayaker has access to the urchin's kingdom. (See the "Harvest Guide" for urchins and How to Clean a Sea Urchin section below.)

Traditionally, people all around the Pacific Rim, from Japan to Mexico, slurped up urchin. On the Northwest coast, the Kwakwaka'wakw First Nations of British Columbia traditionally prepared sea eggs three ways, according to early 1900s writings in a favorite tome, *Ethnology of the Kwakiutl: Based on Data Collected by George Hunt*, compiled by Franz Boas. Sea urchin roe was roasted beside a fire until blackened, slow boiled in a kettle, or left overnight in a dish submerged in a river to "firm up."

Today, along the same coast, scuba-clad commercial divers swim along the kelp beds, handpicking urchins and tossing them into net bags. Hand-collecting means little bycatch of other species.

Northwest coast sea urchins come in three types and colors: green, purple, and red. While all those spines can be intimidating, they don't contain venom like their cousins in the tropics. Just follow the step-by-step instructions in How to Clean a Sea Urchin section (below), and you'll soon find a gold mine inside that armor. World-class urchin roe—the color of pirate gold—sells for upward of thirty-five dollars a pound, but you can net or pluck your own at a very low tide and discover the fresh, fruity flavor. The delicious red and green sea urchins are the varieties people most commonly fish for. Purples offer more petite uni bites.

LEFT TO RIGHT: *Purple, giant red, and green sea urchins*

A thick slab of toasted home-made bread is the perfect platform for a smear of sea eggs. Just drizzle the toast (or pilot biscuit) with olive oil, smear with a jam-like coating of urchin roe, and bite in! The roe of one giant red urchin slathers two pieces of toast; it takes four or more green or purple sea urchins for a jammy spread.

Before harvesting urchins, refer to your state or province's harvesting regulations for open seasons and locations, and size and catch limits. Harvest urchins at a minus tide—preferably one of the lowest of the year. Go out on foot or in a small boat on a calm, flat-water day. As you move along the rocky cliff or shore, look carefully through the water for the red blush of a giant red urchin, the purple smear of a purple urchin, or the sage-green burred chestnut of a green urchin, which also hide in kelp.

You can scoop up an urchin with a metal-rimmed fishing net. I've also had success using my hat as a net or reaching for the urchin with both bare hands, fingers spread. But my favorite method is to use the kayak paddle like a hockey stick and tap the urchin off the wall with one quick, accurate, up-scooping stroke. But be forewarned: an urchin feeling the slightest tap will forcibly grip the rock with

Sea urchins use their mobile spines and tube feet to catch food and move.

leagues of sure-stick tube feet. Don't count on a second try. Just one fluid sweep and you will have your meal.

CULINARY TIPS

Fold roe into scrambled eggs, whisk into cream soups and vinaigrettes, or stir with warm cream cheese and roasted garlic for a cracker spread. Purée roe in gazpacho, serve atop sushi or pizza, smoke over an alderwood fire, chill in custard, or toss with pasta. Or try the roe fresh, scooped naked from the half shell—my favorite. See the "Sea Eggs: Fuel, Fat, and Flavor" sidebar above.

WHO EATS AND SHELTERS HERE?

Sea otters, octopus, wolf eels, horn sharks, bat stars, rock crabs, and spiny lobsters prey on delicious giant red sea urchins. Adult California sheepshead, a large species of wrasse, love red urchins and crunch them with powerful jaws. When sheepshead were experimentally removed from an isolated California reef, the population of urchins shot up 26 percent in a year.

Oregon triton snails drill into the shell and sip green-sea-urchin smoothie. Common ravens, American crows, and gulls nip them off rocks and fly fifteen to thirty feet up, then drop them—*crack!*—onto the beach rocks. Sea otters swim on their backs and—using their chest as a dinner table—mash two urchins together to break them open. Eider ducks and river otters dive for urchins. Red king crabs find them tasty too.

Sea otters love to munch purple sea urchins so much that eating them stains their teeth and bones purple. Leather and purple sea stars eat urchins. Giant green anemones chow on unwary urchins that stilt across their fleshy, green, disk-like mouth. Spiny lobsters tear them up for food.

❓ SEA URCHINS, SEA STARS, AND KELP, OH MY!

The giant sunflower sea star (*Pycnopodia helianthoides*)—up to a meter across and sporting up to twenty-four arms—was a voracious predator of purple and green urchins, until a disease that came to be known as sea star wasting syndrome (SSWS) decimated these lions of the northeast Pacific. It ramped up in 2013 and affected twenty-two other species of sea stars. Scientists estimated a loss of five billion giant sunflower sea stars in just three years, driven by wasting disease and warming seas—hard to fathom! The settling in of a multiyear heat wave on the coast made things worse. Historically stable kelp forests, the rich nurseries of the sea, became "urchin barrens" as exploding populations of urchins gobbled up seaweed and more. (See the "The Future of Kelp Forests" sidebar in Seaweeds & Beach Vegetables.)

An abrupt shift from a species-rich to a species-poor coastline dominated by urchins is now the norm in parts of Northern California. New efforts are underway to restore the marine ecology. Culling and killing sea urchins reduces their prolific grazing, giving kelp beds a chance to recover, while culling and "ranching" urchins in tanks allows for a longer time to build up roe so that they are commercially valuable.

Another tactic is to bring back the keystone species that eats urchins. At the University of Washington, the giant sunflower sea star is successfully being raised in captivity, and the Scripps Institution of Oceanography has successfully spawned a trio of sunflower sea stars and are collaborating with others to reintroduce these vital urchin predators. The question that haunts the kelp forest, sea urchins, and their harvesters is how future climate change will further affect the reproduction of sea urchins, as well as the health of their predators and kelp forests.

HOW TO CLEAN A SEA URCHIN

North Pacific red, green, and purple urchins can be cracked open fresh just before serving. They are worth the effort since each one contains a treasure trove of deeply flavorful golden roe within the intimidating armor. But that's part of the urchin quest. Follow these steps to clean your urchin.

Opening a sea urchin, even a giant sea urchin, is easier and less messy than you think. You'll need a sharp knife, spoon, pot or cutting board, and a bowl of cold, salted water. A cutting board works fine for small green or purple urchins. For the large red urchin, place it in a small bowl or pot to keep it from rolling around as you cut it. Place the sea urchin in the vessel (or on the cutting board) with the underside facing

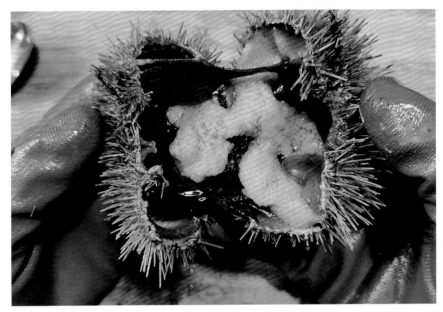

When you cut a green sea urchin in half, you can see the viscera (the part that appears burgundy) and edible golden-orange roe.

you. Look in the center for the mouth—five spade-shaped teeth arranged like flower petals and encircled by shiny skin. The mouth is your target. Say your thanks, then be quick about your business.

Push the knife tip into the center of the five teeth and press down firmly. When the knife hits the bottom, rock it forward and back until the urchin breaks into two equal halves. Work quickly. The spines may fold in to block the cutting. Keep your resolve and the knife rocking.

Lift the two urchin halves and pour any liquid or bits of seaweed out. You will see five golden-orange pieces of roe, soft as custard, clinging to the interior walls. Gently remove each tongue-shaped piece of roe by running the spoon from bottom to top.

Gently rinse in a bowl of salted water. Remove any brownish membranes. Drain or pat dry. Reserve on a plate with wax paper. Cover and refrigerate until ready to use. Fresh urchin smells fruity, not fishy! But it perishes in two to three days.

QUW'UTSUN CHEF SHARES FOODWAYS
JARED QWUSTENUXUN WILLIAMS

Jared Qwustenuxun Williams is a Cowichan chef and Indigenous foods educator on a mission to revitalize traditional Salish foodways. He spent his youth learning traditional harvesting and food preparation skills, including smoking salmon. His first teacher was his beloved Salish grandmother, who would ask him to harvest a leaf by finding its shape. She'd say, "This is the leaf I need. . . . You must go outside and harvest. . . . You are my hands and feet." Today, Jared works with Elders and knowledge holders to keep the practices alive.

Jared and I were introduced by our mutual friend Fiona when I was researching seaweed in the Salish Sea. I learned Jared's passion for traditional food was matched only by his devotion to his two young boys and wife. I asked him if his kids were as keen on traditional foods, given the unhealthy yummies and bubbly drinks that surround us with their perfect storm of low fiber and high sugar, salt, and fat.

"The Elders say, 'What you eat when you're young, you eat when you're old.' When my eldest was very young, a year old, one of his first foods was smoked salmon. He would chew on it all the time when he was teething. Then we had our other child. When you have two very young children, life is overwhelming. . . . So the second child didn't get that opportunity. He went right into eating Western food when it was available."

Ten years later, Jared's older son still loves traditional foods. But the younger one says, "'Yuck, that isn't really what I want, Dad.' And I appreciate that. I don't ever encourage him to eat anything he doesn't actually want to eat."

I could relate! My four grandboys all love their mac 'n' cheese and energy drinks. So I asked Jared what we can do to help our children connect with traditional and wild foods and take care of the animals and plants we eat.

"Really, I think it's about walking the walk, laying a road ahead of them so they have options. When I was young, nobody highlighted the value of what they were trying to share with me. They just shared it the way they knew how. The more we lean on children to do one action, the more they resist us. I know that's how I was."

When Jared was eight, his grandmother went out of her way to make him a special traditional food—oyster. "There was white rice and dried fish and this fried oyster on my plate. I easily ate all the rice and the dried fish, and then I was like, 'Oh, I'm not actually hungry anymore.' And so she put my plate with the dishes by the sink and left it there."

"And she says, 'Oh, it's OK, son.' Well, you know how children are. I'd be running around the house and about an hour later, 'Oh, I'm so hungry, Grandma. I'm so hungry.' And she walks me into the kitchen, walks me over to the dishes by the sink, and grabs that

Jared Qwustenuxun Williams (Photo courtesy of Qwustenuxun)

oyster. And she says, 'Here you go, son. This is all we have.' And yeah, that was all we had."

Jared ate the oyster. "And it was amazing."

Not wasting food and only harvesting what you need were lessons Jared was reminded of constantly as a child. His Elders explained the connection between all things; they taught him that almost every creature in our world was once a human. And those humans were then changed into these other things. The Clam People. The Salmon People. When you're harvesting, you're removing an ancestor, your relation.

Jared left home in his twenties to learn to be a chef. His journey included culinary arts school, working as a line cook and then sous chef in Victoria, and managing the Elders Kitchen at Cowichan Tribes. Today, at 40, Jared cherishes fatherhood and time outside with his boys. They hike the mountains, explore the Cowichan River valley, and sail around Salt Spring Island. They are learning the Hul'q'umi'num' (Cowichan language) names for the islands, mountains, harbors, animals, and plants.

Jared says there are twenty vegetables and fruits that "we just eat while we're out there walking around. From young shoots to flowers and berries, whatever we can— we eat. They can remember it if they can eat it. Oh, my goodness, can they ever! Nowadays, they know what's ready and what will be ready after that." Crab apples, salmon, chanterelles, nettles.

During salmon season, Jared's family fishes together. "My dad is there, I'm there, and the boys are there. They witness the harvest. They witness me cutting it all up. . . . That can be thirty at once. They witness me hanging and drying the fish in our smokehouse . . . a weeklong job. You check on it every hour to ensure it's being looked after the right way. And that's twenty-four hours a day. . . . I hand out all of that dried fish to Elders and to all the adults. . . . I don't ask for money. I don't ask for trades.

"There is a value in working hard to look after what we have, and then to share that out. Because in that action, the Elders that receive, reshare their wisdom with us. Because we are generous, those who we are generous with are generous with us. And it just goes around and around and so [I am] just walking them on that road."

OPPOSITE, CLOCKWISE FROM TOP LEFT: *Winged kelp, Nootka rose hip, Dungeness crab* (Photo by Katherine Palmer), *bigleaf maple blossoms, black morel mushrooms*

RECIPES
FOR
FORAGED
FOODS

Blanched, chopped nettle sprouts ready for soup, grains, and more!

These featured recipes are organized by the book's six major sections. You'll learn that foraged foods can be very flexible! One wild morsel can often replace another—sorrel for purslane, blueberries for huckleberries, nori for dulse, clams for mussels, or chanterelles for hedgehog mushrooms—you get the idea. Using these recipes as guides, have fun mixing and matching foods for a truly wild Pacific feast!

WILD & WEEDY GREENS

SPRING NETTLE CURRY SOUP

I made this soup one April Fool's Day after foraging in the Chuckanut Mountains. Hand-high nettles stood like green pagodas in a sunlit clearing behind our house. As I clipped off the tops, a varied thrush sang its two-note love song from a maple tree. Through my old, torn gloves, I got walloped with nettle stings. Perhaps I was an April fool for not buying a new pair, but I was so enchanted, I didn't care. Every prickle said, "Wake up! It's spring, you fool. Take this medicine!"

This soup has become a rite of spring for our family. I look forward to making it every year. We recently experimented by adding a garnish of sautéed spring oyster mushrooms and morels—yum!

MAKES 12 SERVINGS

2 tablespoons olive oil

1 large yellow onion, chopped

3 cloves garlic, minced

4 to 5 teaspoons curry powder, or to taste

10 medium red potatoes, cut into ½-inch cubes

3 large carrots, sliced into ¼-inch-wide half circles

¼ cup chicken bouillon paste

8 cups fresh-picked nettle tops (2 cups blanched/steamed, chopped)

1 (13.5-ounce) can full-fat coconut milk

Salt, to taste

In a large soup pot, on medium heat, sauté onion, garlic, and curry powder in olive oil. Stir until onion is well-coated and slightly clear on the edges, about three minutes.

Add potatoes, carrots, chicken bouillon paste, and enough water to barely cover vegetables. Cover with a tight-fitting lid. Turn heat to medium high. Cook until potatoes and carrots are fork-tender, fifteen to twenty minutes.

To blanch nettles, use tongs to transfer 8 cups of fresh nettle tops into a pot with 4 cups of boiling water for ten seconds. (Save the broth!) Blanching removes the sting but retains the bright mineral flavor. Use tongs to transfer the blanched nettles to a chopping board. Chop and add to soup.

Stir in nettle broth and coconut milk. Adjust spice by adding more curry. Salt to taste. Serve with crusty bread.

CLOCKWISE FROM TOP: *Spring Nettle Curry Soup (p. 265); Multigrain Nettle Pancakes; Cocoa Truffles with Roasted Dandelion Root (p. 268, Photo by Lisa Harper)*

MULTIGRAIN NETTLE PANCAKES

This recipe has been handed down and modified from father to son in my husband's family for more than three generations. Each new generation is cautioned never to disclose it to their spouse, lest the spouse find no other value in keeping their husband around. After two and half decades of happy marriage, Chris was willing to take a risk and divulge it here—as long as you guard it from your spouse! He says, "You'll need about four cups loosely packed fresh nettle tops to make one cup of blanched greens. After steaming or blanching the nettles, squeeze dry and collect and drink the juice!"

Leftover batter stores well in the fridge for three days, or you can cook the extra batter into four-inch cakes, freeze, and toss them in the toaster for a quick breakfast cake smothered with nut butter and homemade jam.

MAKES ABOUT 18 (6-INCH) PANCAKES

½ cup oat flour

½ cup barley flour

½ cup all-purpose or whole wheat flour

½ cup cornmeal

½ tablespoon baking powder

½ teaspoon baking soda

½ teaspoon cinnamon

½ teaspoon cardamom

¼ teaspoon salt

2 cups buttermilk, plus more as needed

2 eggs

2 tablespoons unsalted butter, melted

1 tablespoon honey

½ tablespoon grated ginger root (optional)

1 cup steamed or blanched nettles, very finely chopped

Vegetable oil, for cooking

Bigleaf maple syrup (see Syrup Note), for topping

Fresh berries, for topping (optional)

In a large mixing bowl, sift together the three flours, cornmeal, baking powder, baking soda, cinnamon, cardamom, and salt.

In a separate mixing bowl, mix the buttermilk, eggs, melted butter, honey, and ginger.

Mix the dry and wet ingredients together with a few quick strokes. Add the finely chopped nettles to the batter, and mix gently but thoroughly.

Cook on a lightly oiled, hot cast-iron griddle or skillet turned to low heat for about two to three minutes per side or until golden brown.

Cook's Note: When the grandkids visit, they love to eat Grandpa Chris's made-to-order "creature cakes." All you have to do is add a bit more buttermilk to make the batter fluid enough to pour artfully onto the hot griddle. Play around to achieve the right consistency.

Use a ladle or big spoon with a narrow tip to stream the batter so you can make finer lines. To start, try simpler creatures like sea stars, slugs, and salmon, and then graduate to flying birds with outstretched wings. Creature cakes are approximations and may require creative insight to interpret!

Syrup Note: See the "Shade and Syrup" sidebar in the main Trees & Ferns identification section. In place of bigleaf maple syrup, you can use birch syrup, or your favorite store-bought maple syrup.

COCOA TRUFFLES WITH ROASTED DANDELION ROOT

Rumor has it that the first hand-rolled ganache truffles were thought by the French to resemble a woodsy underground mushroom. I've made these melt-in-your-mouth chocolate truffles for holiday gifts. I highlight roasted dandelion root, which lends a malty, nutty, butterscotch flavor. (See Common Dandelion in Guide to Wild Morsels for roasting instructions.) I've also successfully used rose petals ground with sugar, ground juniper berries with a shot of gin, and wild raspberry liqueur.

The ganache (a preparation of chocolate and cream) thickens as it cools. After hand-rolling a truffle, you can dust it in a bath of cocoa powder, roasted or raw chopped nuts, or coconut flakes or dip it in tempered chocolate for a hard shell. The secret to making decadent truffles is high-quality dark chocolate.

MAKES 3 DOZEN WALNUT-SIZED TRUFFLES

½ cup heavy whipping cream

¼ cup sugar

⅛ cup finely ground dried and roasted dandelion root

¼ teaspoon vanilla extract

9 ounces bittersweet chocolate, roughly chopped

3 tablespoons unsalted butter, at room temperature

½ cup sifted unsweetened cocoa powder

In a medium saucepan, bring the cream, sugar, dandelion root, and vanilla to a boil. Immediately turn off the heat and add the chopped chocolate. Whisk until smooth. Set aside to cool slightly.

Stir in the butter when the mixture is still warm (but not hot, to keep the oils from separating). Pour into a wide glass baking dish. Cover with aluminum foil and chill in the fridge until solid, one to two hours.

Set out two baking sheets lined with parchment or wax paper. Prepare a small bowl with the unsweetened cocoa powder.

Run a chilled melon-ball scoop or a small spoon across the top of the solidified ganache. Roll it between your palms to form a smooth, round ball—a sticky job if you have warm hands that melt the chocolate. Wash your hands every so often, or coat them in cocoa to keep the ganache from sticking. If the ganache becomes too soft to handle, return it to the fridge or put it in the freezer for a few minutes. Roll each truffle in unsweetened cocoa until thoroughly coated.

Store truffles in a sealed container in the fridge. If you stack them, separate the layers with parchment or wax paper. Truffles will keep for two weeks in the fridge or a month in the freezer. Allow truffles to warm to room temperature before serving.

DANDELION-DAIKON KIMCHI

Kimchi is a fork-sized feast that gives a big boost to your digestive system's health. At its best, kimchi is a seasonal expression of what is regionally available. This particular recipe offers a tsunami of flavor, starting with a rush of saucy heat, crisp daikon, bitter dandelion, sweet apple, and detonations of ginger. It was perfected by my Kimchi-Whiz club. Four students and I tested five kimchi variations based on a mother recipe. The winner was perfected by community farmer Kate Teele (aka Kimchi Kate), who tended both farm-fresh cabbage and jars of kimchi.

Feel free to swap out the dandelions for other wild greens or sea vegetables such as kelp. Four thumbs-up to the Kimchi-Whiz wizards—Grace, Betsy, Reed, and Kimchi Kate!

MAKES 2 QUARTS

9 cups chopped Napa cabbage (cut lengthwise, then chop crosswise)

2 cups chopped dandelion leaves

½ cup sliced daikon radish (cut into matchsticks)

½ cup shredded carrots

½ cup sliced apple (cut into matchsticks)

1½ tablespoons salt

2 tablespoons minced garlic

1 tablespoon minced ginger root

½ teaspoon red miso paste (optional)

¼ cup gochujang (Korean chili pepper paste)

1 tablespoon fish sauce

1 cup water

In a large bowl, combine the cabbage, daikon, carrots, apple, and dandelion with the salt. Mix by massaging with your hands (gloved or bare) and working the salt into the veggies and apple until you see juices being released. Let sit uncovered for one to two hours. At this point, you should see juices in the bottom of the bowl. In a small bowl, mix the garlic, ginger, red miso, gochujang, fish sauce, and water. The additional liquid makes a saucy porridge that can evenly coat all the vegetables.

Pack the kimchi into two sterilized quart glass jars. Use a wooden spoon to press firmly against the mixture to let the air escape. Cover the jars with a clean cloth.

Check in after roughly eight hours to ensure the kimchi is under a layer of juices. If not, pour in enough filtered water to cover everything in ¼ to ½ inch of liquid. You may need to add a weight of some kind to keep the mix under the liquid so it doesn't mold. You can buy glass pickle weights, use a round sterilized stone, or even set a clean plastic bag on top of the kimchi and fill it with water.

Keep the kimchi for two days at room temperature to charge up the fermentation process. After two days, it's ready to eat. Stores well in the fridge for up to three months or even longer.

WILD PILE SALAD

Wild Pile Salad (Photo by Katherine Palmer)

A wild pile of greens enlivens our taste buds. The twang is twangier, the heat, hotter. Bittercress is a miniature of arugula but with more fire. The lemony zing in wood sorrel, sheep sorrel, and purslane rivals lemon concentrate. The pungency and vigor of wild greens, call it "yang" if you wish, can balance the reservedness, or "yin," of garden greens. For instance, earthy bitters in dandelion leaf and Siberian miner's lettuce can offset the airy lightness of leaf lettuce. Lamb's quarters, called "wild spinach," is crisper and more mineral-forward than farmed spinach.

Wild greens can kick up the fiber a notch too. Hairy cat's ear is somewhat fuzzy in texture but surprisingly romaine-like in taste. Chickweed, on the other hand, is as light as fresh alfalfa sprouts (remember those?) and tastes mildly of sweet corn. Featherlight dandelion petals taste of hay and mild honey. Don't be shy about tossing a wild pile of foraged finds in with your farmed greens. That said, pick a dressing that balances the more assertive flavors of wild greens. Lemony vinaigrettes can be too acidic. A good match is a dressing with a bolder flavor but slight sweetness like Rose Hip Balsamic Vinaigrette (see recipe in Berries & Roses). Note that Japanese knotweed is an invasive species; see the "Don't Be a Knotty Harvester" sidebar in the main entry for that species.

- **Chickweed**: succulent; mild, fresh corn flavor
- **Dandelion flower petals** (minus green base): delicate; hay and honey
- **Dandelion leaf**: mildly bitter; robustly bitter after blooming
- **Goosefoot**: like salty spinach but mildly succulent
- **Hairy cat's ear**: romaine-like, fuzzy; older leaves are mildly bitter
- **Japanese knotweed** (young leaves and stalks): tart rhubarb
- **Lamb's quarters**: minerally spinach flavor
- **Miner's lettuce**: crisp, succulent, mild
- **Purslane**: lemony crisp, succulent, mildly mucilaginous
- **Sheep sorrel**: lemony, chewy; fibrous stem
- **Siberian miner's lettuce**: astringent; succulent stem and leaves
- **Western bittercress**: peppery; delicate lobed leaves

- **Wild fennel**: feathery leaf; crisp stalk; anise-flavored flowers, seeds, and vegetation
- **Wood sorrel**: lemony leaf and stem; delicate texture

Accompaniments: Try adding beach greens—pickleweed, goosetongue, and lamb's quarters—for a briny crunch. They launch a frigate of ocean flavor across your tongue (also see Wild Beach Greens Stir-Fry). To complement the greens, add roasted yams or delicata squash rings, roasted chickpeas or curried lentils, goat cheese or creamy avocado, and pickled fireweed shoots (see Fermented Dilly Fireweed Shoots) or juicy garden tomatoes. Garnish with toasted pumpkin seeds or hazelnuts, sliced or whole rose petals, fireweed blooms, and bigleaf maple blossoms or sprouts—and swoon!

Salad ingredients: a, lady fern fiddlehead; b, wood sorrel; c, Nootka rose petals; d, lamb's quarters; e, young Japanese knotweed leaves; f, hairy cat's ears; g, new soft leaves of Oregon-grape; h, salmonberry bloom; i, chickweed; j, common fennel; k, sheep sorrel flower stalk; l, sheep sorrel leaves; m, Siberian miner's lettuce; n, dandelion leaves and blossom; o, bigleaf maple sprout; p, common fireweed shoots (Photo by Katherine Palmer)

SORREL AND LEEK BAKE

This recipe is used with enormous gratitude from (and a green thumbs-up to) Lane Morgan's *Winter Harvest Cookbook*. Growing up near Puyallup, Washington, Lane Morgan used to roam the woods behind her house with a copy of *Ethnobotany of Western Washington*. Now she lives in Bellingham and grows camas and huckleberries in her backyard. Lane says, "The first spring sorrel comes up while overwintered leeks are still in their prime. This Swiss-Italian dish was no doubt a gardener's creation!"

Sheep sorrel and French sorrel have oxalates that reduce calcium absorption, but a nutty swiss cheese and parmesan restores the balance (see the "Tips for Cooking Greens Rich in Oxalic Acid" sidebar in Guide to Wild Morsels). A study published in the *American Journal of Clinical Nutrition* bears this out: when milk calcium and calcium oxalate were eaten together, the calcium provided by the milk was fully absorbed! Feel free to use either French sorrel, sheep sorrel, or wild wood sorrel—or a combo.

SERVES 3 AS A MAIN DISH OR 4 AS A SIDE

4 eggs

½ teaspoon salt

¼ teaspoon pepper

1 cup yellow cornmeal

1½ cups cold water

1 pound French sorrel, coarsely chopped

1 pound leeks (about 4 medium), white part only, sliced thin

¾ cup grated swiss cheese

3 to 5 tablespoons extra-virgin olive oil, divided

2 tablespoons grated parmesan cheese

Preheat the oven to 375 degrees F.

Beat the eggs in a small bowl until light. Add the salt and pepper. Put the cornmeal in a medium bowl and gradually add the cold water, stirring constantly until it is well mixed. Stir in the eggs, and then fold in the sorrel, leeks, and swiss cheese.

Grease a large, shallow casserole or baking dish with 2 tablespoons of the oil. Pour in the vegetable mixture, level the top, and sprinkle with the parmesan cheese. Drizzle the remaining 1 to 3 tablespoons of oil on top (use the larger portion for a more country-style polenta, which is often served with oil poured over the top like salad dressing).

Bake until set and lightly golden, up to an hour. Let cool slightly and serve warm.

GINGER RICE WITH FORAGED GREENS

I rely on this savory dish in foraging workshops; it fills up the hollows when we are all so hungry after harvesting! It comes together quickly when the rice is cooked ahead of time. All you need is an oversize pot and a large bowl with cooked brown rice (about ½ cup per person). Toss everything together and enjoy your foraged gifts! For the greens, use dandelion leaf, nettles, hairy cat's ear leaves, lamb's quarters, thinly sliced fennel stalks and fronds, fireweed sprouts, goosefoot, whatever is poppin'. If you're at the coast, consider adding goosetongue and beach asparagus, kelp sliced into one-inch squares, minced nori or sea lettuce, or rockweed tips no bigger than nickels. No fresh kelp? Just soak ½ cup dry winged kelp in 1 cup boiling water and drain.

MAKES 8 SERVINGS

2 tablespoons olive oil

1½ tablespoon toasted sesame oil

1 large yellow onion, chopped

1 cup chopped wild or weedy greens

2 cloves garlic, minced

1 cup fresh seaweed (optional)

1½ tablespoon grated ginger root

1 tablespoon tamari

2 tablespoons dried dulse or winged kelp (wakame) flakes

4 cups cooked brown rice

Toasted sesame seeds, for garnish (optional)

Sriracha

Heat a large, heavy-bottomed pot with olive and sesame oil over medium-high heat until the oil shimmers.

Sauté the onion until clear, then add greens, garlic, fresh seaweed (if using), ginger, tamari, and seaweed flakes, sautéing for another two to three minutes until tender but slightly crunchy.

Toss in the rice and mix well to heat. Garnish with sesame seeds and serve with sriracha.

Photo by Frieda Hatten-Beck

FERMENTED DILLY FIREWEED SHOOTS

This is a super adaptable recipe for preserving both wild and garden veggies. You can swap in seasonal gifts from garden and forest—raw green beans, carrots, asparagus, cauliflower, beets, blanched fern fiddleheads, or a colorful combo! It is inspired by a dilly bean recipe from my botanist buddy Katy Beck. One November, Katy gifted me a quart of her famous dilly beans for my birthday. After one bite of the zippy, briny beans—dripping with dill-iciousness—I was tempted to snarf the whole jar! In the fireweed patch in our yard, new shoots arrow up between the old, silvered stalks around April. I thought, why not try asparagus-like fireweed shoots?

The best fireweed shoots are about one pencil thick, snap crisply at the base, and are less than one foot tall. If they bend, but don't snap, the stalk is too fibrous to eat. Strip leaves off stalk sides. Trim top leaves to an inch long. Cut longer stalks in half (no longer than four inches) to fit in the jar. If you are lucky enough to have a year-round garden, swap a few sprigs of fresh dill for dried. These fermented shoots make unusual gifts and contain a world of healthy flora for your tummy.

MAKES 1 QUART

Early fireweed stalks (enough to fit snugly in a quart-sized jar)

1 tablespoon dry dill seed

1 tablespoon dry dill leaves

½ teaspoon coriander

1 clove garlic, crushed, or more to taste

2½ cups of filtered or spring water

2 tablespoons noniodized salt

¼ cup sugar

½ cup apple cider vinegar

Wash and trim fireweed stalks.

Place the dill seed, dill leaves, coriander, and garlic in the bottom of a clean quart-sized jar. Pack fireweed stalks vertically into the jar so there is as little empty air space as possible. The stalks should be packed tightly enough that they don't float when the brine is poured in. The tops of the stems should be at least 1½ inches below the top of the jar.

In a medium saucepan, heat the water, salt, sugar, and vinegar over high heat. Bring to a boil, stirring until the salt and sugar are dissolved. Remove from heat and allow the saltwater brine to cool to room temperature.

Pour the brine into the quart jar until the fireweed stalks are submerged and there is 1 inch of headspace at the top of the jar. Gently jostle and tap the jar until all the trapped air bubbles are released.

If needed, use fermentation weights or a sterilized stone to weigh down and submerge the fireweed stalks. Cover the jar with a loose lid, coffee filter, clean cloth secured with a rubber band, or a fermentation airlock

device. As the fermenting process begins, the fireweed will bubble. Place the jar on a tray to catch any overflowing brine.

Let the jar of fireweed stalks ferment at room temperature for seven to ten days in a cool, dark place, like a cupboard or pantry.

Check the liquid level occasionally and refill with brine solution as necessary to the 1-inch headspace level. To make more brine, mix 1 teaspoon of salt with a half cup of water.

After seven days, remove the weights and test the flavor. Pickled fireweed shoots should have a pleasant, zippy, dilly, briny, mildly sweet flavor. When they are ready, put a standard canning lid on the jar, and move the jar to the refrigerator.

The refrigerated fermented fireweed stalks may be enjoyed for several months.

SIMPLE SORREL SOUP

In many European countries, sorrel soup, with its natural lemony flavor, is a rite of spring. Traditional soup recipes simmer the leaves into a dark green mush, which some folks find less appealing. If you pulverize the sorrel leaves with butter into a pesto-like paste, the butter fat will preserve the bud-green color that shouts, "It's spring!" Sorrel is a perfect match for a cream base.

You can use sheep or wood sorrel equally well. If the sheep sorrel's midvein is tough, stack the leaves and cut across the veins to minimize threads; scissors work well. Avoid using cast iron or you'll risk blackening the greens.

MAKES 2 SERVINGS

2 tablespoons salted butter, softened

1 cup chopped fresh sorrel leaves (stems removed prior to chopping)

2 teaspoons olive oil

1 small shallot, minced

2 cups half-and-half

1 teaspoon chicken or vegetable bouillon

Salt and pepper

2 whole sorrel leaves, for garnish

Pulverize the butter and leaves in a food processor or electric grinder until they form a green pesto-like paste. Set aside.

Heat a stainless-steel or nonstick skillet over medium-low heat and add the olive oil. When the oil shimmers, add the shallot and sauté until clear, about two minutes.

In a medium bowl, whisk the bouillon into the half-and-half and stir into the skillet with the shallot. Stir well. When the mix almost reaches a boil, remove from heat.

Stir in the butter-and-sorrel paste. Mix until the soup is a smooth green broth. Season with salt and pepper. Divide the soup between two bowls and garnish each with a sorrel leaf.

FOOL'S RHUBARB PIE

A student of mine, Emma Gelino, researched pernicious but delicious Japanese knot-weed—also called fool's rhubarb—for a wild food course I teach at Fairhaven College. The assignment included cooking with the wild or weedy food. Emma's knotweed pie is a state-fair blue-ribbon winner, if you ask me. Use spring-tender, fat, juicy shoots less than one foot tall. If filling is too fibrous, strain through a sieve, then spoon into crust.

Follow careful protocols when harvesting and handling knotweed and disposing of its scraps to avoid inadvertently planting more of this invasive plant, one of the top 10 worst in the world. ❗ See Japanese Knotweed and the "Don't Be a Knotty Harvester" sidebar to learn how to correctly harvest and dispose of any plant material. For this pie, remember the adage "If you can't beat 'em, eat 'em!"

MAKES 1 PIE

FILLING

5 cups peeled and chopped Japanese knotweed shoots (¼-inch pieces)

1½ cups water

1 cup sugar

3 tablespoons cornstarch

1 teaspoon ground cinnamon

Pinch of nutmeg

PIE CRUST

1 cup all-purpose flour

1 teaspoon salt

8 tablespoons unsalted butter, cubed

1 to 2 tablespoons ice water or vodka

Add the filling ingredients to a medium saucepan. Stir until mixed and bring to a boil. Immediately lower the heat and simmer for thirty minutes, or until thick and not watery. Allow to cool.

While the filling is cooking, make the crust. In a large mixing bowl, combine the flour and salt and then add the butter. Use a pastry cutter, fork, or your hands to incorporate the butter until pea-sized chunks remain. Add as little ice water as possible to help everything stick together. Mix slightly, then form a ball of dough. Chill for fifteen minutes in the fridge, then roll out into a round piece of dough. Fit the pie crust to the pie pan.

Preheat the oven to 425 degrees F. Pour the cooled filling into the pie shell and bake for about an hour, or until mostly set (it will set more once cooled). Serve cold, and add vanilla ice cream if desired.

BERRIES & ROSES

BLUEBERRY SEA ASPARAGUS SALAD

Executive Chef Amy Foote's job is to nourish and heal people back to health through traditional foods. On any given day at the Alaska Native Tribal Health Consortium (ANTHC) medical campus, in Anchorage, Amy might prepare moose, reindeer, caribou, deer, seal, hooligan, halibut, duck, salmon, fiddlehead ferns, beach asparagus, and a variety of Alaskan berries.

"Providing a taste of home is critical in the healing process. We see our patients relax and share stories of a time when they were well, out harvesting and spending time with loved ones," says Amy. "Traditional foods heal our patients, they are comfort, they are healing, they are home."

Amy's trademarks are fusing healthy "town food" with nutrient-rich traditional foods and a big ladle of love. Her "chagamisu," based on Italian tiramisu, uses chaga, an antioxidant-rich edible shelf fungus that grows on birch trees. But healing food doesn't have to take hours to prepare. Take, for instance, this crisp, bright summer salad. Simple and nutrient dense, it features wild Alaskan blueberries, sea asparagus, and kamut, with a tangy citrus-honey dressing and peppery zip. Substitute farro or quinoa for kamut, as you like.

MAKES 4 SERVINGS

SALAD
1 cup whole kamut grains
2 cups chopped bite-size beach asparagus, cleaned of rocks and debris
2 cups fresh blueberries

DRESSING
Juice and zest of 1 orange
½ cup balsamic vinegar
3 tablespoons soy sauce
2 tablespoons honey
1 tablespoon sesame oil
1 tablespoon black pepper
1 teaspoon red pepper flakes

In a medium saucepan, simmer the kamut in 3 cups salted water until tender, about thirty minutes. Drain and then chill until cool.

In a large bowl, mix the beach asparagus, blueberries, and cooked kamut.

Combine the dressing ingredients in a small bowl and whisk to blend. Add the dressing to the salad and toss to combine.

Chill and serve.

SALISH PEMMICAN

Pemmican is a high-energy blend of foods used to sustain a traveler on a long journey. Recipes vary by region. In the Pacific Northwest, traditional recipes might include pounded dried venison and deer tallow kneaded with dried saskatoon berries. A coastal pemmican might include ground salmon, and an interior recipe might use bitterroot, sunflower seed meal, berries, and fat.

This recipe from Vanessa Cooper is inspired by her Lummi tribal heritage and rooted in her teachings of the use of traditional plants for food and medicine. As Vanessa explains, "I take pride in who I am and where I come from and am so grateful to be able to pass on the teachings to my precious grandchildren, JoVanna, Marciano, and Alo. I give thanks to the Creator for providing all that is needed to live a healthy, sustainable lifestyle."

Substitute ingredients as you wish. For dried meat, use venison, elk, or beef. For berries, choose from salal berries, blueberries, huckleberries, cranberries, or other dried berries. For nuts and/or seeds, use any combination of hazelnuts, cashews, sunflower seeds, or almonds. Finally, nut butter options include almond, cashew, and peanut butter.

MAKES ABOUT 50 BALLS

1 cup dried meat
1 cup dried berries
1 cup raw nuts or seeds
⅓ cup nut butter
Sesame seeds, for garnish (optional)
Coconut flakes, for garnish (optional)

Chop the meat into very small pieces.

Place the dried berries, nuts, and nut butter in a food processor and finely chop. Add the dried meat and pulse again. The pemmican should stick together like dough.

Roll the dough into balls and coat with sesame seeds or coconut flakes if desired.

Store pemmican in a sealed container in the refrigerator or in a cool, dark place. It will keep for several months.

SALAL BERRY SCONES

These stovetop scones from Victoria-based food writer Emillie Parrish are perfect for camping! Using self-rising flour means you don't have to pack baking powder. In her *Life in the Northwest* blog, *Berries and Barnacles*, Emillie says, "Salal berry scones are my favorite way to serve salal berries! They really let the berries take centerstage and shine. . . . Though the recipe may seem like you're making pancakes, they're more similar to Welsh cakes or griddle cakes. I serve them like scones, fresh and hot with a smear of butter." Emillie's teen, Max, suggests adding lemon zest to enhance the flavor of the salal berries.

MAKES 4–6 SCONES

½ cup salal berries

1 cup self-rising flour

2 tablespoons sugar

¼ cup cold salted butter, cubed, plus more for serving

1 large egg, lightly beaten

Milk or water, if needed to thin batter

Lemon zest (optional)

Rinse the salal berries, rubbing them to remove any leaves and fluff that may be stuck to them. Set aside.

In a medium bowl, mix the flour and sugar. Use your hands, a fork, or a pastry blender to rub the cubed butter into the flour mixture until you have a nice, even crumb.

Stir the berries into the flour mixture, then mix in the egg. Be careful not to overmix.

Heat a cast-iron skillet or camping pot over medium-low heat. Once hot, drop two tablespoon-sized balls of dough onto the skillet, then flatten them out with the back of a spoon. You may need to add a bit of water or milk to get the scones to the right consistency for dropping. Alternatively, you can form the scones into small cakes with your hands; you'll need to wash your hands before and after you're done.

Dry-fry the scones, flipping them over halfway through, about three minutes on each side. Check the first few to make sure they're cooked through before serving. Serve immediately with butter.

ROSE HIP BALSAMIC VINAIGRETTE

Here's a twist on a classic vinaigrette recipe. It follows the 3:1 ratio of oil to vinegar but adds rose hips—the fruit of the rose plant. This is a great dressing for a wild green salad, as the olive oil tames the assertive bitters in dandelion, hairy cat's ear, western bittercress, and Siberian miner's lettuce. The balsamic vinegar and maple syrup add sweet notes. Rose hip sauce tastes a little like tomato and apricot, with a bit of acidic tartness.

MAKES ABOUT 1½ CUPS

¼ cup crushed dried rose hips, seeds and brown ends removed (or ¾ cup fresh rose hips, seeds removed)

¼ cup balsamic vinegar

2 tablespoons minced shallot

2 teaspoons Dijon mustard

2 teaspoons maple syrup (optional)

¼ teaspoon salt (optional)

¾ cup olive oil

Make rose hip sauce from rose hips: Simmer dried hips with ¾ cup water in a small saucepan, covered, for twelve to fifteen minutes, or until the rinds are soft. (For fresh rose hips, simmer in ½ cup water.) Give the rose hip sauce a stir now and then to break up the hips. After ten minutes, add a splash of water if the sauce is so thick it is sticking to the pan bottom. Set up a fine-mesh strainer atop a small bowl. Using a rubber spatula, push the rose hip mash through the strainer. Scrape any rose sauce off the strainer's underside. You should have about ¼ cup of sauce.

To make the vinaigrette, whisk together the rose hip sauce, vinegar, shallot, mustard, maple syrup, and salt in a medium bowl. Drizzle in the olive oil as you continue whisking until emulsified. Rose hips are full of pectin, so add a dash of water if the dressing is too thick for your liking. Store in a covered glass jar in the fridge for up to two weeks.

ROSE PETAL LEMONADE

While camping in the eastern Cascades, my grandson Rowan and I came across a dozen Nootka rose bushes brimming with five-petaled blossoms in fuschia pink. "Have you ever tasted rose petal lemonade?" I asked Rowan. I predicted his answer. After all, it was a baited question. And Rowan bit the bait. Soon we were gathering one or two quarter-sized petals from each flower within reach. "Be sure to leave petals for the bees. They need a signpost to help them find the pollen." Rowan was eight years old and so careful to do exactly what I instructed. "We just need a tiny handful."

Back at camp, we used our large vegetable knife to mince the rose petals into a paste. We swirled it into a water bottle with the lemon juice, sugar, and water. "Let's shake it good, then let it sit and soak up the flavors." A long half hour later, everyone got a sip—Grandpa, Rowan's little brother, his parents, and Nana Jenny. We were like bees to nectar—buzzing with desire for more!

MAKES 3 CUPS

3 tablespoons sugar, plus more as needed

1 tablespoon fresh Nootka or Sitka rose petals

2 to 3 lemons, juiced

2 cups water

In a spice grinder or food processor, whir the sugar and rose petals into a paste. Alternatively, use a mortar and pestle or chop the petals into a paste and mash them into the sugar.

In a quart-sized glass jar, mix the rose petal paste, lemon juice, and water. Cover the jar and shake well.

Let sit for a half hour. Adjust the sweetness with more sugar, as desired, and serve.

282

BLACKBERRY-PEACH CRISP

Just as Pacific Northwest trails waft a heady aroma of ripening Himalayan blackberries, peaches arrive at the farmer's markets and stores! This crisp, with a scoop of ice cream, may be our berry favorite summertime dessert. This ultra-flexible recipe is fantastic with just about any seasonal fresh or frozen fruit. Toss in plums, pears, apricots, raspberries, blueberries, cherries, apples, or a combo of whatever is around. This recipe produces a fairly juicy filling; if you like a stand-up-the-fork pie filling, double the cornstarch.

MAKES 6–8 SERVINGS

FILLING

4 cups blackberries

4 cups peeled and sliced peaches

2 tablespoons lemon juice

2 tablespoons granulated sugar

2 tablespoons cornstarch

1 teaspoon grated ginger

Pinch of cayenne

TOPPING

½ cup unsalted butter

¼ cup canola or vegetable oil

1 cup oats

1 cup all-purpose flour

1 cup packed brown sugar

½ cup chopped walnuts

1 teaspoon vanilla extract

½ teaspoon ground cardamom

¼ teaspoon almond extract (optional)

¼ teaspoon salt

Preheat the oven to 375 degrees F.

Combine the berries and peaches in a large bowl. In a small bowl, whisk together the lemon juice, sugar, cornstarch, ginger, and cayenne. Toss sugar mix with the fruit to coat. Transfer to a 9-by-9-by-2-inch pan (or similar size).

To make the topping, melt the butter with the oil in a small saucepan or in a bowl in the microwave. In a large bowl, mix the butter and oil with the oats, flour, brown sugar, walnuts, vanilla extract, cardamom, almond extract, and salt. Leave some clumps visible.

Spread the mixture atop the pan of fruit filling. Again, keep some good-sized clumps visible.

Bake for forty minutes, or until the fruit is bubbling and the top is beautifully brown. Cool twenty minutes. Serve warm with a scoop of ice cream, or let cool to room temperature and enjoy.

Photo by Travis Williams

HUCKLEBERRY-APPLE DUTCH BABY

A Dutch baby is "the perfect pancake," according to my friend Elise Krohn, herbalist and native plants educator. As a child, she would beg her grandmother Betty to make Dutch babies for breakfast. Now her daughter carries on the tradition, and they developed this recipe with huckleberries and apples, making them even more delicious. They are excellent for breakfast or for dessert!

MAKES 4 SERVINGS

2 tablespoons unsalted butter

2 tablespoons packed brown sugar

1 teaspoon cinnamon

1 apple (such as Fuji or Pink Lady), sliced

½ cup huckleberries or blueberries

3 large eggs

½ cup flour

½ cup milk

¼ teaspoon salt

1 tablespoon powdered sugar (optional)

1 tablespoon fresh lemon juice (optional)

Preheat the oven to 425 degrees F.

Melt the butter in a 12-inch cast-iron or ovenproof frying pan over medium-high heat, and stir in the brown sugar and cinnamon. Add the apple slices and cook until they soften (about three minutes) before sprinkling the huckleberries or blueberries over the top. Remove from heat.

In a blender, whir together the eggs, flour, milk, and salt. Pour the egg mixture into the pan (do not stir). Transfer to the oven and bake until puffed and brown, about fifteen minutes.

Sprinkle with powdered sugar and drizzle with lemon juice. Slice and serve warm.

BLACKBERRY LEMONGRASS SHRUB

Both sweet and zippy, shrubs elevate any cocktail or mocktail. Plus, the fermented syrup is good for your belly. Add a splash of club soda or kombucha and drink as is, or mix in your favorite spirit for a refreshing, fizzy drink. Or simply jazz up your water bottle with 2 table-spoons of this delicious elixir. This recipe comes from my Jane-of-all-trades book-research assistant, Grace Meyer.

Every naturalist food writer could use some Grace. She has a knack for deciphering complex scientific papers and mining them for "Who eats this?" and "Who shelters here?" There, she finds treasures: for example, 50 percent of the early-winter deer forage in the Douglas-fir forests of the Oregon Coast Range is trailing blackberry. Grace can field sketch a blackberry so lifelike that I want to pluck it off the page and pop it into my craw. Plus, she's a kick-ass cook and rip-roaringly funny.

MAKES 2 CUPS

2 cups blackberries
½ cup honey
¾ cup sugar
1 cup apple cider vinegar
½ teaspoon orange zest
½ teaspoon lemon zest
1 stalk lemongrass, minced

Place the blackberries in a clean, quart-sized canning jar and smash them with a wooden spoon. Mix in the sugar and honey. Set aside.

In another quart-sized jar, mix together the apple cider vinegar, orange zest, lemon zest, and lemongrass.

Seal the jars and refrigerate for twenty-four hours.

Combine the contents into one jar and refrigerate for ten days.

Strain and enjoy. Store any remaining shrub in a clean jar in the refrigerator for up to six months. But I bet my favorite berry pail that it won't last that long!

OREGON-GRAPE INFUSED WATER

Myk Heidt, a wild plants and medicine educator, is steeped in traditional plant wisdom. For years, she tended and managed the 13 Moons Community Garden for the Swinomish Indian Tribal Community, where prickly Oregon-grape stands guard over the bog garden. Myk developed the recipe after reading that the pioneers made jelly out of Oregon-grape, as the deep-purple berry clusters reminded them of tiny grapes. That got her to thinking about Oregon-grape juice, and the experimenting began. She doesn't use any sugar in the recipe because, as she says, "the bright, tart flavor profile stands alone well with the small addition of bright-yellow lemon slices."

MAKES 1 QUART

A handful of ripe Oregon-grape berries, plus more for serving

Fresh lemon slices

A few stems of soft, new Oregon-grape leaves

Put the berries in a quart-sized jar and gently crush them with a wooden spoon. Add a few slices of lemon. Fill the jar with cold water, cap the jar, and shake well.

Allow the contents to settle, then strain into glasses.

Plop a few ripe, uncrushed berries into each serving glass along with a stem of tender new Oregon-grape leaves. Serve and enjoy!

BLUE ELDERBERRY OXYMEL

This super tonic is an immunity builder and offers cold support as well as a soothing pre-scription for coughs. You can sip it straight from a teaspoon, dilute it in sparkling or warm water, or stir it into herbal tea or a smoothie. Myk Heidt, who served as the community environmental health coordinator for the Swinomish Indian Tribal Community, says she was introduced to Blue Elderberry Oxymel when she was a new mom and had first moved to the Pacific Northwest. She recalls, "Our naturopath recommended it for our young brood during the fall and winter months. It became a 'traditional medicinal' in our household."

Oxymel refers to the mixture of honey and vinegar. You can also use dried blue elderber-ries, which can be purchased online, at herb stores, and at some community food co-ops in the bulk section. Blue Elderberry Oxymel is potent for at least six months if kept in a dark cabinet—but some references put its shelf life as much longer. While oyxmel is delicious for adults and kids, please be sure to substitute maple syrup for honey for children one year or younger.

MAKES 1 PINT OR MORE (DEPENDING ON JAR SIZE)

Ripe, fresh blue elderberries
Raw wildflower honey
Unfiltered apple cider vinegar

Fill a glass jar one-third full with ripe blue elderber-ries (or reconstituted dry berries that were covered in warm water and soaked overnight).

Add honey and apple cider vinegar in equal amounts until there is only a half inch of headspace at the top of the jar. Cover and shake the jar vigorously. Let the jar of oxymel sit in a sunny window for four to six weeks. Shake several times per week.

Strain through a fine-mesh strainer lined with cheese-cloth to catch the seeds. Then use a funnel to pour the oxymel into dark-glass dropper bottles. Label and date, and store in a cool, dark place.

I freeze oxymel in pint-sized glass jars and eat one tablespoon daily during cold and flu season.

RED ELDERBERRY SAUCE

This tart and tangy sauce is excellent served over cheesecake, roasted salmon, or baked brie. Be sure to remove all stems from the berries before you begin and carefully strain out the seeds after cooking. It is tedious work, but the stems, seeds, and leaves have toxic compounds that will give you a bellyache and nausea. ❗ See the cautionary note in Red Elderberry.

MAKES ABOUT 2 CUPS

2 cups red elderberries, destemmed

About 1 cup water

½ cup honey (or more to taste)

1 teaspoon cornstarch, mixed with 1 tablespoon water

Put the berries in a medium saucepan and cover with water. Bring to a boil. Turn heat to medium and simmer until soft, about fifteen minutes.

Line a fine-mesh sieve with two layers of cheesecloth and strain the berry mixture to remove the toxic seeds. Push the berry pulp through the cloth and mesh with a rubber spatula. Gather the cheesecloth corners together and twist the bundle of mash to get the last pulp to ooze out.

Add honey and whisk in the cornstarch slurry to thicken. Transfer the mixture back to the saucepan and simmer for five more minutes.

Use immediately, or let cool and store in an airtight container in the refrigerator, where it will keep for two weeks. Freezing will preserve the sauce for six months.

TREES & FERNS

SPRUCE-TIP SALT

Gather fresh, soft spruce tips (the new needles expanded from an end bud) from tree branches in the spring or early summer, depending on elevation. Be sure to never collect the lead tip (the tip at the farthest end of a branch). Doing so stunts the tree's growth—take tips only from the side of a branch. I take only one of the two side-growth tree tips. That way, my tree friend has plenty of new branch growth going both outward and to the side. Think like a nesting bird and imagine the future hiding places, perches, and shade you are leaving for forest animals. Grand fir or Douglas-fir tips also work well in this recipe.

This salt makes a lovely finishing salt for roasted vegetables, eggs, and fresh corn on the cob. Use it on seafood, including butter-fried spot prawns, scallops, and your favorite fish. Don't forget the fries!

MAKES ABOUT ½ CUP

¼ cup chopped spruce tips

¼ cup kosher salt

In a small bowl, mix the tips and salt together. Grind the blend in a spice grinder in batches, or all at once in a food processor.

To dry in an oven or beside a woodstove, spread the mix in a thin layer in a glass baking dish or oven-proof plate. Dry on low heat (approximately 100 degrees F) for two to three hours, stirring once per hour. To dry in a food dehydrator, spread the spruce salt on parchment paper (you may need to weight the edges if you have a fan in your dehydrator). Stir once per hour. Depending on how moist the tips were and the ambient humidity, the salt usually dries in two to three hours.

Store in a sealed glass jar for up to three years in a cool, dark cupboard or pantry. The spruce essence will fade slightly and may become caked (stuck together) with time. Just shake the jar before using.

Photo by Mac Smith

EVERGREEN-TIP TEA

Each spring, when the newly sprouted needles of the four most common conifers of the Northwest coast emerge, Mac Smith, my lifelong foraging friend, makes this vitamin C–rich forest beverage. Mac picks enough of the bright green, tender branch tips to dry for a whole year's worth of tea. Although you can make the tea with fresh needles, Mac suggests drying them for a more intense flavor (see the Spruce-Tip Salt recipe for drying instructions). You can make tea from each individual species, or mix and match with what is available.

MAKES 4 CUPS

4 cups water

1 tablespoon dried Douglas-fir needles

1 tablespoon dried grand fir needles

1 tablespoon dried western hemlock needles

1 tablespoon dried Sitka spruce needles

Juice of 1 lemon

1 tablespoon honey

In a large pot, boil the water. Remove from heat, add the needles, and let steep for five minutes.

Add the lemon and honey, strain, and serve.

GRAND FIR SORBET

This is one of my family's favorite sorbets. I make it year-round. In spring, I harvest the soft, bud-green needle tips. The rest of the year, I harvest the mature needles, usually after a good fall or winter storm gifts me some windfall–grand fir branches. Look for glossy green needles that smell of citrus when broken in two. I think it just might be one of the cheeriest aromas in the world! If you can't find grand fir, you can substitute the spring-soft needles of Douglas-fir or Sitka spruce. Keep in mind, the older needles of these two trees do not have the flavorful and aromatic notes that grand fir maintains from youth to maturity.

A "tip" for the future: tree tips freeze well in a sealed container for up to a year, so you can use them year-round to flavor sorbet, syrup, seasonings, baked goodies, and spirits.

MAKES 8 SERVINGS

4 cups grand fir needles, trimmed from a windfall branch

4 cups boiling water

3 cups sugar, plus more as needed

Zest of 1 lemon

2 tablespoons fresh lemon juice

Sprig of grand fir, for garnish

Make a grand fir tea by placing the fir needles in a medium saucepan and pouring in the boiling water. Cover and simmer for twenty to thirty minutes. For the most robust flavor, set aside overnight to absorb the needle essence.

Strain the tea, measure, and pour it back into the pot. Add as much sugar as you have tea; for example, if you have 3 cups of tea, add 3 cups of sugar. Heat over medium heat, stirring to dissolve the sugar, and whisk in the lemon zest and juice to distribute the flavors.

Cool the sorbet mixture to room temperature in a large bowl or glass baking dish to increase the cooling surface, then chill uncovered in the freezer to almost freezing. Add the mix to an ice cream maker and follow the manufacturer's directions. If you don't have an ice cream maker, here's an option from my chef friend Lynn Berman: Freeze the sorbet mix overnight in a shallow glass baking pan. You should be able to cut the frozen sorbet into chunks with a sharp knife. Puree the frozen chunks in a food processor until smooth to break up the crystals and make a smoother sorbet. Refreeze for approximately three to four hours.

Serve in chilled dishes with a sprig of grand fir.

TOP: *Maple blossoms knocked down by the wind make for easy picking.* **BOTTOM:** *Artful manda-la-inspired salad made with maple blossoms*

MAPLE BLOSSOM FRUIT SALAD

Celebrate the blooming of the bigleaf maple tree—called the paddle tree by Coast Salish people, who prized the wood for strong canoe paddles. The flowers and sprouts are both edible. Here's a spring salad featuring the whimsical and delicate flower clusters, tossed with lime-ginger maple-syrup marinade, tart currants, apples, raspberries, and sweet and spicy pecans. The first time we made this salad for a friend's Passover dinner, we used our cherished bigleaf maple syrup. You can also sweeten the dish with syrup from East Coast or Midwest sugar maple trees—it's delicious no matter the tree.

Salmonberry blossom petals add a bright garnish. The star-shaped fuchsia-colored blossoms appear around the same time as maple blossoms. I don't pick whole salmonberry blossoms—just two of the five petals so they continue to make fruit.

MAKES 6 SERVINGS

¼ cup rice vinegar

¼ cup extra-virgin olive oil

Juice of ½ lime

1 tablespoon grated fresh ginger root

3 tablespoons maple syrup, divided

2 cups fresh bigleaf maple blossoms

1 apple, sliced into crescents

¼ cup black currants or blueberries

¼ cup whole frozen raspberries

Scant 1 tablespoon salted butter

½ teaspoon cinnamon

Pinch of cayenne

Pinch of salt

½ cup whole pecans

Salmonberry blossom petals, for garnish (optional)

Preheat the oven to 350 degrees F.

Make the marinade: in a small bowl, whisk the rice vinegar, olive oil, lime juice, ginger root, and 1½ tablespoons of the maple syrup until well blended.

In a large bowl, toss the maple blossoms, apple, currants, and raspberries with the marinade until well coated. Set aside.

Heat a small sauté pan over medium-low heat. Add the remaining 1½ tablespoons maple syrup, butter, cinnamon, cayenne, and salt. Heat until bubbly. Add the pecans and stir to coat. Continue stirring until the syrup has evaporated, about five minutes. Spread the nuts on a baking sheet lined with parchment paper. Transfer to the oven and bake for ten minutes. Remove and cool, about twenty minutes.

Add the candied nuts to the salad just before serving, and garnish with a tiny handful of torn salmonberry blossom petals if desired.

EVERGREEN TREE COOKIES

This recipe is provided by my friend Elizabeth Campbell, an ethnobotanist, herbalist, organic farmer, native and traditional plants educator, and member of the Spokane Tribe. Elizabeth explains that evergreen trees are both food and medicine that have been used by Indigenous people for thousands of years. They are mineral rich, immune stimulating, and high in vitamin C, with a light citrusy flavor. Evergreen trees are also well-known for their bright, cheery aromatics and uplifting, resilient properties. We bring evergreens into our homes during the darkest months of the year to keep our spirits bright.

Evergreen boughs can be gathered year-round. Take care to gather boughs from clean environments. Spruce, hemlock, and grand fir needles can be substituted for Douglas-fir. Note, however, that for spruce, while newly emerged spring tips are tender, the mature needles are sharp! Take care gathering the mature needles. In this recipe, using more needles leads to a stronger flavor.

MAKES 18–24 COOKIES

- 4 to 6 tablespoons fresh Douglas-fir needles
- ½ cup sugar, divided
- 1 cup salted butter, lightly softened
- 1 to 2 tablespoons fresh orange or lemon zest (optional)
- 2 cups all-purpose flour

Preheat the oven to 350 degrees F.

Grind the Douglas-fir needles and about half of the sugar in an herb grinder, clean coffee grinder, or food processor until finely ground.

Add the ground needles to a large mixing bowl with the remaining sugar, butter, and citrus zest. Mix well with a spoon.

Slowly add the flour, ¼ cup at a time, mixing between each addition until all the flour is incorporated.

Separate the dough into two balls and place on a large piece of parchment paper. Form 2-inch-thick disks and place them in an airtight container or resealable plastic bag, or wrap them in plastic. Put the disks in the refrigerator for an hour or in the freezer for fifteen to twenty minutes.

Line a baking sheet with parchment paper. Roll out one disk between two pieces of parchment paper until about ¼ inch thick. Cut into trees or other shapes, rolling extra dough cuttings out again until all the dough has been used. Keep the second disk in the refrigerator until ready to use. Repeat the process.

Bake for eight to ten minutes, until the edges are lightly toasted. Transfer to a cooling rack for five to ten minutes before serving. Store cookies in an airtight container at room temperature. They can also be frozen in a sealed container and will retain their aromatics and flavor for a month or more.

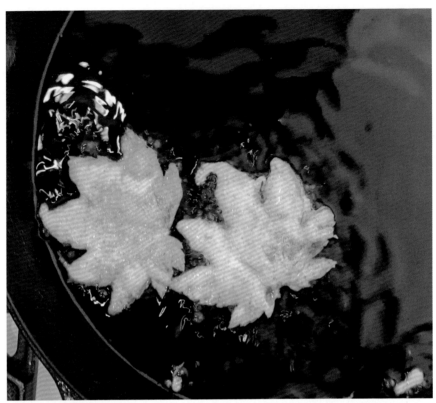

VINE MAPLE LEAF TEMPURA

While writing a portion of this book in the San Juan Islands, I noticed a young black-tailed deer standing on its rear legs to nibble branches of vine maple leaves, but it only pulled down gold leaves to eat, not green leaves. When I shared the story with my husband, he told me that our dog was eating gold maple leaves too. Turns out the golden leaves are edible! In fact, yellow maple leaf tempura—known as momiji tempura—is a tradition in Osaka, Japan. Only yellow maple leaves are gathered, and always from the ground.

After being preserved in salt water or dry salt for one year, the leaves are ready for tempura. Not wanting to wait, I soaked our delicate leaves in a saltwater bath for one week. My friend Lisa Harper dreamed up this recipe and then battered, fried, and photographed these beauties. Golden and crisp as the autumn air, they were almost too pretty to eat!

MAKES 6–10 SERVINGS

PRESERVED LEAVES
12 to 20 yellow vine maple leaves
2 tablespoons salt

TEMPURA
1 cup all-purpose flour
1 cup cold carbonated water
2 tablespoons sugar
2 tablespoons sesame seeds
1 egg, lightly beaten
Pinch of salt
Canola oil, for frying
Maple syrup, cinnamon, or ice cream, to serve

Gently rinse the leaves in a bowl of cold fresh water. Drain, stack, and set aside.

In a medium bowl, mix the salt with ⅓ cup fresh water. Stir to dissolve the salt. Put the leaves in the bowl, and push them around in the solution to be sure salt water is bathing each leaf on both sides.

Cover and leave at room temperature for one day (or as long as one week if you need to wait for an opportune time to make tempura).

Pat the leaves dry before coating with batter. To make the batter, add the flour, water, sugar, sesame seeds, egg, and salt to a mixing bowl and whisk until just combined. Set aside.

To a cast-iron skillet or other heavy pan, add oil to about ¾ inches deep. Heat to 375 degrees F.

Dip leaves into the batter one at a time, coating both sides. Drop into the hot oil. Fry for approximately twenty to thirty seconds on each side, or until nice and golden. Set on paper towels to cool before serving.

Drizzle with maple syrup and sprinkle with cinnamon or serve atop ice cream.

SQUASH WITH BIRCH SYRUP AND PECANS

In 1990, Michael and Dulce East, of Talkeetna, Alaska, made their first batch of birch syrup in a small wood-fired pan at their Kahiltna River homestead. "Though it was strong and dark—and probably slightly burnt—we decided it was unusual and good," says Dulce. The couple grew their love of birch syrup into an art and business, Alaska Birch Syrup and Wild Harvest. They raised a family, treasured their life in the birch forest, and in 2023, passed the torch to a robust trio of youthful birch syrup aficionados.

In Dulce's recipe, savory delicata squash is stuffed with tart-and-sweet apple, pecans, spices, and a few spoonfuls of tangy birch syrup. It's a serving of sunshine on a winter day. Alaska residents may be able to find birch syrup in local shops; otherwise, order online—or tap your own! See the "Tapping Bigleaf Maples and Birches" and "Shade and Syrup" sidebars in Trees & Ferns in Guide to Wild Morsels.

MAKES 4 SERVINGS

2 delicata or acorn squashes
2 tablespoons salted butter
1 medium apple, diced
⅓ cup chopped pecans
2 tablespoons birch syrup or birch honey
¼ teaspoon cinnamon
¼ teaspoon ground ginger

Preheat the oven to 375 degrees F.

Cut the squashes in half and scoop out the seeds. Bake for thirty minutes, cut side down, on a greased pan.

In a medium saucepan over medium heat, melt the butter and add the apple, pecans, birch syrup, cinnamon, and ginger. Bring to a simmer for five minutes.

Spoon the mixture into the squash halves and bake for about twenty minutes, or until golden brown.

Serve immediately.

FIDDLEHEAD FERN QUICHE

Fiddlehead ferns are little bundles of delight. Some say they taste like asparagus. This recipe comes from Ayesha Wise, a wilderness guide, boat chef, naturalist, and forager in Alaska. Ayesha says, "One of my favorite things to make for a breakfast crowd is a smoked salmon quiche. When you combine fiddleheads and salmon, you get the finest from the land and the sea."

The quiche can be baked a day in advance, cooled completely, and stored in the refrigerator, covered. Reheat it at 350 degrees F for thirty minutes. For more about gathering fiddleheads, see How to Harvest Fiddleheads in Lady Fern in Guide to Wild Morsels.

MAKES 8 SERVINGS

1 cup fiddleheads, papery scales removed

4 eggs

2 cups heavy cream

1 teaspoon smoked paprika

Salt and pepper, to taste

⅓ pound of smoked salmon, broken into bite-size flakes

A 9-inch prebaked pie crust

2 cups grated gruyere cheese

Boil a pot of water and submerge the fiddleheads for fifteen minutes. Strain in a colander and run cold water over them to stop the cooking process.

Preheat the oven to 375 degrees F.

In a medium bowl, whisk together the eggs, cream, paprika, salt, and pepper until well mixed.

Neatly arrange and evenly spread the fiddleheads and smoked salmon in the prepared crust. Top with the cheese and then pour the egg mixture over all the ingredients.

Put the quiche on a baking sheet and bake on the top rack for twenty minutes, then turn the heat down to 350 degrees F and bake on the middle rack for thirty to forty-five minutes. The quiche should puff up a bit and jiggle when finished.

Remove from the oven, let cool for ten minutes, and serve warm.

MUSHROOMS

SMOKED PORCINI RISOTTO WITH PORCINI STEAKS

Foraging for wild mushrooms and cooking Italian-inspired dishes is spun into Tom Debari's DNA like mycelium is woven through tree roots. Tom is founder and former chef-owner of Milano's restaurant in Glacier, Washington. In Italy, Tom's ancestral homeland, where mushroom hunting is as popular an obsession as pasta, fresh porcini (a.k.a. *Boletus*) mushrooms are a celebrated part of the cuisine. These stately fungi also grow prolifically on the western slope of the North Cascades—in the forests near Tom's home. This recipe goes back to his father-in-law, Serifino Cerasa, a native of northern Italy, and incorporates Tom's passion for smoking foods, which complements the large, meaty king boletes.

You'll need to have access to a smoker to prepare the fresh mushrooms and also have some dried boletes on hand, which you can dry yourself or purchase. Drying mushrooms concentrates the flavors, and reconstituting gives you a nice broth for cooking the risotto. If you don't have a smoker, Tom suggests grilling the prepared mushrooms on high heat for one to two minutes per side before arranging them on top of the finished risotto.

MAKES 4 SERVINGS

6 to 10 (⅜-inch-thick) slices fresh porcini

6 tablespoons extra-virgin olive oil, divided

4 cups slightly salted water or chicken stock

1½ cups dried porcini mushroom pieces

1 medium white onion, diced

1 cup arborio rice

1 cup dry white wine

¼ cup unsalted butter, divided

½ cup finely grated parmesan reggiano or pecorino romano

Chopped fresh sage, for garnish

Preheat a smoker to 160 to 180 degrees F. Brush the sliced porcini with 2 tablespoons of the olive oil and place in the smoker.

Smoke the mushrooms for about an hour. There should still be plenty of moisture in the mushrooms; do not let them get too dry or you will lose that beautiful texture. Tasting is really the best way to know when to pull them off the smoker. Set the smoked mushrooms aside.

In a large saucepan, warm the salted water or chicken stock to 200 degrees F. Remove from heat and soak the dried porcini mushrooms in the liquid for thirty minutes. Remove the mushrooms, set aside the soaking stock, and chop the reconstituted mushrooms into ½-inch pieces.

In a straight-sided, stainless-steel sauté pan over medium-low heat, sauté the onion in the remaining olive oil until translucent, about ten minutes.

Raise the heat to medium high and add the arborio rice, stirring for a couple minutes to coat the rice in oil.

Add the white wine to start the rice-cooking process, stirring regularly. When most of the wine is gone, add about ½ cup of the reserved mushroom-soaking stock and stir. Allow most of the stock to absorb before adding more, stirring all the while. Add the reconstituted mushrooms when the rice is just starting to soften, about ten minutes in.

Continue this process until the rice is tender but not mushy. The whole process from when the rice is added to when it's done, should take twenty to twenty-five minutes. Add 3 tablespoons of the butter and the cheese, and stir in well. Transfer to a platter.

In a separate pan, warm the smoked porcini slices and sage in the remaining 1 tablespoon butter, and then arrange them on top of the risotto.

Note: It is OK to substitute dried shitake mushrooms for dried porcinis.

Photo by Katherine Palmer

EASY OYSTER MUSHROOM SLOPPY JOES

Here's an easy fix for a mushroom camping trip—or tired foragers. Just sauté oyster mushrooms and add your favorite barbecue sauce, buns, and a spicy slaw mix. For harvest tips, see Oyster Mushroom in Guide to Wild Morsels.

MAKES 4 SERVINGS

¼ medium purple cabbage, thinly sliced

Juice of 1 small lime

¼ cup chipotle mayo

4 cups oyster mushrooms, tough stems removed

Vegetable oil, for sautéing

½ cup barbecue sauce, or more to taste

2 teaspoons olive oil or butter

4 hamburger buns

In a medium bowl, mix the cabbage with the lime juice and chipotle mayo. Set aside.

Tear the mushrooms along the gills from the outer edge of the fan to the center (where the stem grew). You want to imitate pulled pork and build up a good pile of stringy, thin pieces—about three to four gills in one tear.

In a large sauté pan over medium heat, cook the mushrooms in a bit of oil until the juices are reabsorbed and they are beginning to brown and turn crisp on the edges, about fifteen minutes. Remove from the heat, add BBQ sauce, and mix well.

Pile the barbecued mushrooms on campfire-toasted buns drizzled with olive oil or butter, and distribute the chipotle-lime slaw onto each.

WILD MUSHROOM STROGANOFF

Earthy and hearty, this stroganoff can be made with or without the venison, says Elder and Indigenous chef Kaasei Naomi Michalsen of Alaska (see Note). In autumn, whenever Naomi is given the gift of deer from her Tlingit huntress friend, she makes this special dish for friends and family. Naomi, a traditional foods consultant for Kaseii Consulting, told me, "What I really love, more than taking people out on plant walks—because I love being outdoors—I really love, even more, now, cooking up the food! So not only learning how to identify things, but how do we learn to eat these foods and to try and preserve them and share them?"

For the wild mushrooms, Naomi uses a mix, such as morels, chanterelles, boletes, and hedgehogs, as well as button and cremini mushrooms. Any meaty mushroom works well, she says. For the venison, roast, steak, or backstrap will work well. And for the broth, choose your favorite from beef, chicken, and vegetable.

MAKES 4 SERVINGS

1 to 2 pounds venison, sliced thin (optional)

Flour or cornstarch, to coat the meat (if using)

2 tablespoons vegetable oil

¼ cup dry white wine

1 cup wild mushrooms

¼ cup melted butter

2 tablespoons roughly chopped onion

2 cloves garlic, minced

1 cup broth

½ cup sour cream

1 to 2 tablespoons chopped fresh parsley or dill

Salt and pepper, to taste

Egg noodles or brown rice, for serving

If using meat, put the venison in a bowl, sprinkle in flour or cornstarch, and stir to coat. Add the oil to a large sauté pan over medium-high heat. Sauté the venison for two to three minutes, or until browned on all sides. Remove the venison from the pan and set aside—but keep the drippings in the pan.

Add the wine to the pan and stir for one minute to loosen up the drippings. (If not using meat, skip this step, or add the wine and deglaze the pan before adding broth.)

Add the mushrooms (or cook the mushrooms first as you would the venison, remove, and deglaze as well), butter, onion, and garlic. Sauté for a few minutes, or until the onions are softened.

Add the broth, bring to a simmer, and cook for another few minutes.

Turn the heat to low. Add the sour cream, fresh parsley, salt, and pepper. Simmer on low for two minutes.

Serve over egg noodles or brown rice.

Note: Make this vegetarian by replacing the venison with another cup of mushrooms and using vegetable broth. You can also substitute cremini or another favorite mushroom.

PORCINI CAMP SCRAMBLE

Charlie and Janny Cunningham are mushroom foragers who live in the North Cascades. They developed this recipe on a camping and foraging trip for porcini (king bolete). "When we are out mushrooming, we don't do hotdog-and-bean camping. Every morning at camp, before we go out, we must have a hearty breakfast," Charlie says. Janny sizzles diced bacon over the campfire in a cast-iron skillet. She stirs in chunks of pre-boiled red potato, fresh porcini slices, and four eggs cracked right on the edge of the pan. "We serve it up with fire-toasted slabs of homemade bread," says Charlie. "With lots of butter, of course!" adds Janny. "We do all the things when we are camping that we don't do at home."

This fortifying meal will sustain four hungry foragers for a morning of climbing up and down the mountainsides, ducking under logs, stepping over roots, and bushwhacking—all while looking for "shrumps," mushroom humps pushing up through the forest floor.

MAKES 4 SERVINGS

6 strips center-cut bacon, diced

6 red potatoes, parboiled (see Note) and cut into ½-inch chunks

1 to 2 cups of porcini mushroom, sliced

4 eggs

Pepper, to taste

4 thick slices homemade bread

Salted butter

Heat a cast-iron skillet on a metal grate over a campfire (or on a camp stove).

Add the bacon. When the bacon fat liquifies, add the potatoes and mushrooms. Cook until the potatoes are golden brown and the porcini is flexible and soft.

Crack the eggs into the pan and stir them to perfection. Season with black pepper.

Keep the scramble warm in the pan while you prepare the toast.

Place a layer of heavy aluminum foil over the fire grate. Arrange the bread slices atop the foil. Toast one side until golden crisp, then flip to toast the top side. Slather with butter and serve alongside the scramble.

Note: Before departing home, parboil the whole, unpeeled potatoes (Janny uses potatoes about the size of a tennis ball) for about fifteen minutes, or until a fork can pass through the center but the potato is firm. Let cool, and pack in bags in the cooler.

CASCADIA MUSHROOM CREAM SAUCE

This delicious and simple mushroom cream sauce works great with a variety of cultivated and wild mushrooms, according to Isabel Machuca-Kelley and Alex Winstead, coconspirators of Cascadia Mushrooms in Bellingham, Washington. The secret to an ultra flavorful, umami-rich mushroom sauce is dry-sautéing the mushrooms first. For a successful dry-sauté, quarter or chop the mushrooms into chunks (thinly sliced mushrooms burn easily). Alex also adds two handfuls of smoked salmon after the cream for a smokey flavor.

MAKES 2 SERVINGS

⅓ cup dry white wine

⅓ cup chicken or vegetable broth

1 tablespoon tomato paste

1 pound fresh mushrooms, chopped into bite-size pieces

2 tablespoons olive oil

3 cloves garlic, minced

½ teaspoon kosher salt

Black pepper, to taste

¾ cup heavy cream

¼ cup half-and-half

1 tablespoon chopped fresh parsley

In a small bowl, whisk together the wine, broth, and tomato paste until well blended. Set aside.

Heat a large skillet over medium until hot, and dry-sauté the mushrooms. As they heat, the mushrooms will release moisture. Stir occasionally. They are done when slightly golden brown and dry. It takes up to ten minutes, depending on variety and moisture content.

Add the olive oil and garlic and cook for a couple minutes until aromatic, or when the garlic barely begins to brown. Pour in the wine mixture all at once. Add salt and pepper. Bring the sauce to a steady simmer and cook until reduced by almost half, about five minutes.

In a small bowl, combine the cream and half-and-half. Turn the heat to low and gradually whisk the cream mixture into the sauce until combined. If you prefer a thicker sauce, simmer to perfection. Stir in the parsley and serve immediately.

Photo by Frieda Hatten-Beck

BAY FOREST CREPES

What better way to spend a golden-leaf day in the Pacific Northwest than mushroom hunting? Lynn and Fred Berman, retired owners of two former Northwest eateries—Innisfree and Pastazza—enjoy making Bay Forest Crepes in the evening with fresh foraged chanterelles. Crepes are versatile and easy to make but demand your undivided attention. You can do yourself a favor by doing a bit of prep before you head into the woods—make the crepes, prepare the vegetables, and peel and devein the prawns—then this dish can be table-ready in twenty minutes. This recipe calls for about one pound of prawns; to stretch the amount, you can cut them lengthwise.

MAKES 4 SERVINGS

CREPES

4 eggs
2 cups milk
1¼ cups all-purpose flour
½ cup unsalted butter, melted and cooled
Pinch of salt

FILLING

2 tablespoons butter
4 tablespoons shallots, sliced
2 cups sliced chanterelle mushrooms
½ teaspoon Spike seasoning, or your own spice blend
Pinch of white pepper
16 to 20 spot prawns, peeled and deveined
½ bunch kale, washed, rib removed, and coarsely chopped (about 1 cup)
½ cup heavy cream
3 tablespoons dry sherry

In a deep medium bowl, beat the eggs. Add the milk, flour, melted butter, and salt. Beat until smooth and no lumps of flour remain.

Heat a 9-inch stainless-steel skillet with sloping sides over medium heat. Using a small ladle, pour in just enough batter to leave a thin coating in the pan when tilted in all directions. The crepe is ready to turn when just slightly brown and beginning to pull away from the pan at the edges, thirty to sixty seconds. It's easiest to turn the crepe with your fingers, using a heatproof rubber spatula to gently lift an edge. Cook for another thirty to sixty seconds on the other side.

Think of the first few as test crepes, and adjust the thickness of the batter with another tablespoon of flour or a splash of milk. Lay crepes on a rack to cool. If you're not going to use the crepes right away, store them flat on a covered plate in the fridge. Remove crepes from the refrigerator at least an hour before using to bring to room temperature.

To make the filling, in a large stainless-steel skillet over medium heat, melt the butter and sauté the shallots till clear, about three minutes. Add the chanterelles, Spike, and pepper, and cook for about five minutes.

When the mushrooms are just beginning to soften, add the prawns and cook until they curl and are opaque. *Do not overcook* or they will become tough and rubbery.

Add the kale and quickly stir all the ingredients together. Immediately remove the vegetables and prawns with a slotted spoon to a bowl, leaving the liquid in the pan.

Add the cream and sherry to the pan and reduce the mixture to a thick, custard-like consistency over medium heat, up to three minutes. Remove from heat and return the vegetables and prawns to the pan to warm and coat with sauce.

Fold each crepe in half and then in half again, forming a wedge shape, then stuff with the filling. Pour a bit of sauce over the top of the crepes and serve immediately.

SEAWEEDS & BEACH VEGETABLES

KELP PICO DE GALLO

A refreshing salsa—perfect for grilled halibut, omelets, or chips! At my seaweed workshops, every time we serve a big bowl of kelp pico de gallo, it disappears quickly. This is a great entrée dish for friends and family trying fresh seaweed for the first time. Kelp stipes or mid-vein ribs of wing kelp—blanched or raw—provide a cucumber-like firmness. You can substitute canned tomatoes for fresh.

MAKES 7 CUPS

6 tablespoons fresh lemon juice

1 cup chopped sweet white onion

2 cups blanched and chopped kelp (¼-inch pieces)

4 cups chopped tomatoes

1 bunch cilantro leaves, chopped

2 to 3 jalapeño peppers, seeds removed and minced

4 cloves garlic, minced

2 tablespoons chili powder

Hot sauce, to taste

Corn chips, for serving

In a medium bowl, pour the lemon juice over the chopped onion and kelp. Let marinate and soften for one hour.

In a separate medium bowl, combine the tomatoes, cilantro, jalapeño, garlic, chili powder, and hot sauce. Mix in the lemon juice, onion, and kelp, and serve with chips.

PICKLEWEED SALT

Pickleweed is a petite sage-green succulent with segmented branches that sprawls in the estuaries of the Pacific Northwest. Also known fondly as beach asparagus, it makes a beautiful mineral-rich salt with a briny finish! To achieve a lovely forest-green salt, blanch the pickleweed before drying in a food dehydrator overnight.

This recipe comes from my friend Kimber Owen, of Gustavus, Alaska. Kimber wears more hats than anyone I know, including encyclopedic naturalist, forager, cook, and devoted owner of a ninety-seven-foot World War II US Navy harbor minesweeper, the M. V. *Sea Wolf*. With Kimber's background in equestrian therapy, the ship was redesigned for accessibility adventures in Alaska and the Inside Passage. As a naturalist on the ship, I remember grazing beach asparagus from a sea kayak with a guest who had difficulty walking. Foraging can be so healing! Kimber, a repurposing queen, suggests placing desiccant packs from vitamin jars in the sea salt jar to reduce moisture absorption and caking.

MAKES 4 OUNCES

1 pound pickleweed, rinsed

Fill a medium bowl with an ice water bath. Set aside.

Bring a medium pot of water to boil.

Use a strainer small enough to dunk into the pot to blanch pickleweed in batches for forty-five seconds each, then shock in ice water. Drain and let cool.

When cool, pat dry between two towels. Set a food dehydrator to 90 to 105 degrees F and dry the pickleweed overnight until crisp, about nine hours.

Grind in batches in a food grinder and store in a spice jar with a desiccant packet. This is a great finishing salt to sprinkle over rice, pasta, vegetables, fish, tofu, or salad—and as a delightful dash on soup.

TOP: *Kelp blades make edible parchment wrap for steamed salmon (Photo by David Bialik);.*
BOTTOM: *Cucumber-Seaweed-Sesame Salad garnished with raw (brown) and blanched winged kelp (p. 312)*

KELP-WRAPPED STEAMED SALMON

My Seaweed Sisters and I baked these lovely kelp-wrapped salmon portions at a seaweed cooking workshop I taught at the Lower Elwha Tribe Community Center kitchen. On sea kayak trips, I've prepared a variation using a makeshift steamer—a large pot with a half-inch of water and beach stones to hold the seaweed-wrapped salmon above the water. This recipe describes both techniques. The kelp wrap turns a beautiful deep green when steamed.

Eat these delicious morsels like finger food, including the wrap itself—with no sticky, oily fingers. Double the marinade to prepare a dipping sauce if desired.

MAKES 4 SERVINGS

¼ cup olive oil
1 clove garlic, minced
Sea salt
1 (2-pound) salmon fillet, deboned
16 pieces of kelp blades (about 4 by 5 inches)

Mix the olive oil, garlic, and salt in a small bowl and set aside.

To bake the kelp-wrapped salmon, preheat the oven to 400 degrees F. Cut the salmon fillet into sixteen 1-inch-wide strips from back to belly. Spoon or brush the marinade on both sides of the strips.

Wrap each strip in one layer of kelp and place them seam side down on a greased baking sheet. Bake twelve to fifteen minutes, until you see white fat congealing on the open end.

To steam the kelp-wrapped salmon while camping, prepare a pot with a half inch of water and a steamer basket or clean beach cobbles on the bottom. Cut the salmon fillet into eight 2-inch-wide strips from back to belly. Spoon or brush the marinade on both sides of the strips. Wrap each strip in two pieces of kelp—sealing all ends.

Steam the packets in two batches over a campfire or cook stove. The cooking time will vary depending on your heat source, but it should take fifteen minutes or more once the steam forms. The salmon is done when white fat is congealed at either end; you may need to open one packet to check.

Cool briefly and serve warm, with extra marinade as a dipping sauce alongside if desired.

CUCUMBER-SEAWEED-SESAME SALAD

This refreshing, crisp, umami-rich salad is a bell ringer at every seaweed workshop. It is inspired by a Japanese salad called sunomono. And it is so easy! Even kelp-hesitant eaters crack a smile. It is also so adaptable. Fresh or dried seaweed works equally well. Beachside, I use fresh kelp blades from winged kelp, giant kelp, or sugar kelp blanched in boiling water for ten seconds (till they change from brown to green). For dulse, I use fresh unblanched blades. A handful of minced fresh sea lettuce, stirred in at the tail end, adds bright color. I call it parsley of the sea!

At home, you can swap seaweed flakes for the fresh sea veggies: winged kelp (also called Pacific wakame), sugar kelp, and dulse are a few of my favorites. Or make your own; see the "Culinary Uses of Kelp" sidebar in the Winged Kelp identification section for grinding instructions. To compensate for the dried seaweed flakes, shake in a bit more rice vinegar and sesame oil and allow the flakes time to soften in the vinaigrette dressing. Serve as a side to complement crab cakes, fish, sushi, or stir-fry, or all by itself garnished with toasted sesame seeds. For a vegetarian option, add marinated cubes of tofu.

MAKES 6 SERVINGS

- 2 tablespoons seasoned rice vinegar, plus more as needed
- 2 teaspoons toasted sesame oil, plus more as needed
- 2 teaspoons tamari or soy sauce
- 2 teaspoons grated fresh ginger root
- Pinch of cayenne
- ½ cup chopped blanched fresh winged kelp, or 1 tablespoon dried seaweed flakes
- 1 large English cucumber, very thinly sliced into half moons
- 1 scallion, very thinly sliced
- Salt, to taste
- Pinch of sugar (optional)
- 2 teaspoons toasted sesame seeds

In a medium bowl, whisk the vinegar, oil, tamari, ginger, and cayenne. Mix in the seaweed, cucumber, and scallions. Taste and adjust with salt, sesame oil, or vinegar to your liking. Add a pinch of sugar or more cayenne—for more sweet or heat. Toss well.

Garnish with the toasted sesame seeds. Serve chilled, or immediately if beachside.

WATERMELON KELP SALAD

We make this salad at our seaweed workshops all the time. It is amazingly easy and flavorful! This makes enough to serve plated salads for a big summer picnic with friends and family, but it's easy to halve with a smaller melon.

MAKES 12 SERVINGS

- 1 foot-long or basketball-sized watermelon
- 6 avocados, sliced
- 2 cups crumbled feta cheese
- 2 scallions, very thinly sliced
- 6 limes, quartered
- 1 cup dried kelp pieces

Cut the watermelon into 1-inch-thick rounds, halve the rounds, then cut into triangles and remove the rind. For each serving, arrange one triangle of watermelon on a plate and top with the avocado slices, crumbled feta, and a scattering of scallions. Lay two lime quarters on the side of each plate.

Place the dried kelp blades (see the "How to Store Sea Veggies" sidebar in the main Seaweed & Beach Vegetables identification guide for drying instructions) in a small bowl for easy reach so that guests can scatter the kelp atop the salad and squeeze fresh lime juice over it all. Eat immediately!

BRUSSELS SPROUTS AND WINGED KELP

Fall and winter brussels sprouts are a bit like zucchinis in the Pacific Northwest. They proliferate. You can find them in stacked net bags at groceries and arranged on platters with an artsy balsamic drizzle at haute eateries. They pair beautifully with sea veggies too. In fact, a plate of these delectable nuggets should come with a warning: addictive! They harbor the perfect trio of tang, sweet, and flame. Oh, and did I mention a subtle umami too?

MAKES 4–6 SERVINGS

2 pounds brussels sprouts, halved

1 cup thinly sliced carrot

¼ cup slivered yellow or red onion

¼ cup olive oil, plus more for oiling pan

½ teaspoon salt

1½ tablespoons aged balsamic vinegar

1 tablespoon maple syrup

½ to 1 teaspoon sriracha

2 tablespoons winged kelp (wakame) flakes

Preheat the oven to 400 degrees F.

On an oiled sheet pan, distribute the brussels sprouts, carrot, and onion. Don't forget the leaves that have fallen off the sprouts. They become deliciously crispy.

Drizzle the olive oil atop the veggies, sprinkle with the salt, and mix with your hands to coat.

Roast twenty to twenty-five minutes until beautifully browned and tender. Give it a good stir after ten minutes and again after fifteen minutes. Remove from the oven and toss with the balsamic vinegar, maple syrup, and sriracha to taste.

Sprinkle in the seaweed flakes and stir well. Taste to check for a balance of sweet, salt, and acid. Adjust as you wish and serve warm or chilled.

SALMON CEVICHE WITH SUGAR KELP

Make use of all those unctuous salmon scraps with this recipe from chef Sven Hooson. Sven and I met on the good ship *Sea Wolf*, where he cooks for adventurers. It's perfect for the "spoon meat" or scrapings of a filleted carcass. Even though you can use scraps for this dish, the salmon is the star here, so the rest of the ingredients should be cut smaller to showcase it; be sure to use the highest-quality, freshest salmon you can find. The sugar kelp flakes add a wave of briny flavor. Serve the ceviche as a dip with chips or crackers.

MAKES APPETIZERS FOR 10

¼ cup fresh lime juice

½ medium red onion, finely diced

2 tablespoons finely diced red bell pepper

1 to 2 jalapeños, finely diced

½ bunch cilantro, finely chopped, plus more for garnish

½ avocado, cut into small cubes

Salt, to taste

Hot sauce, to taste

1 pound clean raw salmon, cut into medium cubes

¼ cup dried and flaked sugar kelp blades

Put the lime juice in a large bowl and add all the ingredients except the salmon and kelp. This mixture can be held for up to a day.

Add the salmon pieces to marinate for five to ten minutes before serving.

Arrange the ceviche in a serving bowl garnished with extra cilantro. Fill a small bowl with the dried sugar kelp flakes. Provide spoons, plus small bowls for guests to fill with ceviche. Place a pinch of kelp flakes on your spoon, mound on the ceviche, enjoy, and repeat. The layering of briny, salt-forward kelp and lime-bright ceviche will swim across your taste buds like a high tide of flavor!

Photo by Wendy Larson

SEA AND SUNSHINE COOKIES

Before I met Wendy Larson, I met Wendy Larson's *amazing* cookies at a party. They were so crispy, chewy, nutty, oaty, and cherry-delicious that I asked her if I could share the recipe here—with one addition: seaweed. She loved the challenge! After testing a couple of different seaweed amounts, she left samples on her porch for me to pick up. I confess, I ate two, three, four. . . of her fabulous cookies before arriving home—they were so delicious. Nutrient dense, they'll satisfy a sweet tooth as long as a kayak paddle. Try them on the sea, on mountain trails, or at home dunked in a glass of milk (my grandboys' favorite).

MAKES 4 DOZEN COOKIES

¾ cup unsalted butter

1 cup packed brown sugar

½ cup granulated sugar

1 egg

3 tablespoons water

1 teaspoon vanilla

1 cup all-purpose flour

2 tablespoons dried sugar kelp or nori, finely crumbled

1 teaspoon cinnamon

Preheat the oven to 350 degrees F and line two baking sheets with parchment paper, or grease the sheets with butter or nonstick spray.

In a small bowl, cream together the butter and both sugars.

Add the egg and blend thoroughly, then mix in the water and vanilla. Set aside.

In a large bowl, combine the flour, seaweed, cinnamon, salt, and baking soda. Add the oats, cherries,

½ teaspoon salt

½ teaspoon baking soda

2 cups oats

1 cup dried cherries, chopped

1 cup dried apricots, chopped

½ cup coconut flakes
(unsweetened)

¼ cup raw sunflower seeds

¼ cup raw pumpkin seeds

¼ cup raw pecans, chopped

apricots, coconut, sunflower seeds, pumpkin seeds, and pecans, and mix well.

Add the wet ingredients to the dry ingredients in the large bowl and stir well, until all ingredients are moist.

Use a spoon to scoop about 2 tablespoons of dough into your hand. Shape a small ball and place on a baking sheet. Flatten each ball with your palm; you can moisten your palm with water to reduce stickiness. Place a dozen cookies on each baking sheet.

Bake for fifteen to twenty minutes, until cookies are golden brown.

Let cool slightly and then move the cookies while still warm to cooling racks or parchment paper. Allow to cool completely before transferring them to an airtight container.

Note: Make this recipe your own by adding more seaweed to taste, up to double the amount. Swap out the cherries and apricots for raisins, dried cranberries, or dried apples, or replace the pecans with almonds, walnuts, or hazelnuts. Other flours can be substituted for part of the all-purpose flour, including whole wheat, spelt, almond, or hazelnut flours.

HAPPY CRITTER BISCUIT CHEWS

Chris initially came up with this recipe to please the family pooch—a sweet, adopted black Lab–greyhound mix with a toothy grin. But Chris discovered he and our grandkids liked them as much as the dog did. He uses all organic ingredients—including mineral-rich kelp—and makes a batch every other month to stay in the dog's good graces.

MAKES ABOUT 100 BISCUITS

1 large sweet potato, grated

1 large beet, grated

1 large carrot, grated

3½ cups spelt flour, plus more as needed

1½ cups oat bran

½ cup molasses

½ cup canola or avocado oil, plus more as needed

½ cup nutritional yeast

1 tablespoon dried kelp powder

Preheat the oven to 275 degrees F.

In a large metal mixing bowl, combine all the ingredients. The dough should be pliable but not sticky. If it's thin and sticky, add additional flour to stiffen it. Too stiff? Add additional oil and some water to soften it.

On a lightly oiled baking sheet dusted with flour, roll the dough until it is ¼ inch thick. Cut into 1-inch squares. Bake for about one and a half hours, or until firm. For the last fifteen minutes, check the underside of the biscuits; if they're not browning slightly, flip and cook with bottom sides up, until slightly golden brown. Finished biscuits should be mildly chewy, not bone dry.

Cool completely and store one week's worth of biscuits in a glass jar. Freeze the remaining biscuits in a sealed tin or other suitable container with a tight-fitting lid for up to three months. Replenish your biscuit jar as needed. Watch out—you will find yourself snacking on biscuits along with the pooch!

SWEET AND SOUR FUCUS

SGang Gwaay, Dolly Garza, Haida and Tlingit, is a revered seaweed aficionado who would love for people to eat more nutritious fucus ("rockweed"). Robust in briny flavor, amped in minerals including iodine, and accessible at most low tides, fucus is featured here as a side dish that goes nicely with fish, fowl, and veggie stir-fries. This recipe is reprinted with permission and a salty thumbs-up from Dolly, who is the author of several of my favorite foraging books. Each book is large in wisdom yet small enough to tuck in your dry bag or backpack for easy reference.

This recipe is from *Common Edible Seaweeds in the Gulf of Alaska*. Dolly grew up harvesting with her family on the beaches of Ketchikan and Craig, Alaska. A retired professor of fisheries at the University of Alaska, Dolly now resides on Haida Gwaii, where she sustainably gathers spruce root and cedar bark for her traditionally woven spruce-root hats and baskets. For the apples, Granny Smith and Pink Lady varieties work well.

**MAKES 4 SERVINGS
AS A SIDE DISH**

4 tablespoons sunflower seeds

3 tablespoons oil

2 cups rockweed (fucus), cut into strips

2 cups peeled and sliced tart apples

¼ cup raisins

2 tablespoons honey

1 teaspoon cinnamon

In a large skillet, sauté the sunflower seeds in oil over medium heat until slightly brown, three to five minutes. Add the rockweed and sauté until tender. Add the apple slices, raisins, honey, and cinnamon.

Turn the heat down to low and simmer for a few minutes, or until the apples are soft. Serve as a side dish.

POPCORN SEA-SONINGS

Nothing is as fun to eat, or as messy, as popcorn at our house. Our grandboys love to pour the kernels into our air popper and hit the switch. Soon the kernels are revving around in a happy dance as Briar, the dog, stands by to wolf up nibbles. The maple sugar–sugar kelp version is a sticky-finger favorite created by our grandson "Sweet-Tooth" Talus.

THAI CURRY-CHILI-LIME POPCORN

1 teaspoon curry powder

1 teaspoon ground dried makrut lime leaves (see Notes)

1 teaspoon ground dried sugar kelp

¼ teaspoon garlic powder

Pinch of salt

Pinch of cayenne

CHEESE-SEA POPCORN

4 tablespoons cheddar cheese popcorn seasoning

2 teaspoons roasted dulse seaweed flakes (see Notes)

¼ teaspoon garlic powder

HIPPY DUST POPCORN

2 tablespoons nutritional yeast

1 teaspoon ground nori flakes

1 teaspoon ground winged kelp (wakame)

¼ teaspoon salt

Pinch of cayenne (optional)

MAPLE SUGAR–SUGAR KELP POPCORN

2 teaspoons maple syrup powder (see Notes)

1 teaspoon ground dried sugar kelp

¼ teaspoon pink Himalayan salt

For each seasoning option, mix the listed dry ingredients ahead of time. When the popcorn is ready, first toss with 1 to 2 tablespoons of melted butter, coconut oil, or mild-tasting olive oil (or you won't have a good stick-to-it-ness), then add seasoning and toss well to incorporate any flavor gems in the bottom of the bowl.

Each recipe supplies enough seasoning to lightly coat about 5 cups of popped corn (made from ¼ cup of kernels).

Notes: Find dried makrut lime leaves at an Asian market or online. To grind, tear out the tough stem and midvein, crumble the leaves into small bits, whir in a clean coffee or herb grinder to a dust, and strain through a sieve. You can also grind the leaves by hand in a mortar and pestle, though it's difficult to grind them all into a powder. Strain and save larger lime flakes for a Thai soup or rice dish.

Dulse flakes can be purchased in many health food stores, food co-ops, and online. Dry-roast dulse flakes in a small pan over low heat, stirring until they exude an aroma and turn a slightly darker red. Watch 'em like a hungry raven! They can turn from roasted to smoking and charred in a few blinks.

Maple syrup powder is available at some health food stores and food co-ops, as well as online.

GARLIC SPOT PRAWNS WITH NORI

Divinely succulent and sweet, spot prawns are dubbed the "lobster of the North Pacific" and are the largest prawn (females are ten inches long) on the West Coast. Kimber Owen of Gustavus, Alaska, a forager, kayaker, and owner of Sea Wolf Adventures, pairs spot prawns with fresh nori. Kimber gets her fresh prawns from her fisherfolk neighbors and harvests black seaweed from the beach that she dries on cloth sheets in her yard on sunny days. Spot prawns have a unicorn-horn spike to deter predators, like us, from snacking too easily. So it takes a bit of care to behead and shell spot prawns without getting poked.

Pour a glass of wine or a mocktail for yourself and your dinner guest, pull up a chair to the table with your bowl of whole prawns, and clean them together. Save their beautiful pink-orange shells with white moons for stock.

Here's a superpower tidbit about spot prawns. They are born male, then switch sexes to hide as females, 240 feet down in the darkness of the rocky seafloor, tending broods of up to 3,900 tiny eggs for five months. Somehow, that helps me appreciate these delicious morsels even more—for all they've survived! Kimber suggests serving spot prawns sprinkled over lemon basmati rice seasoned with Pickleweed Salt (see recipe, earlier in this section).

MAKES 2 SERVINGS

2 cloves garlic, crushed

1 tablespoon extra-virgin olive oil

1 tablespoon salted butter

1 handful dried nori seaweed, snipped into ½-inch pieces

12 to 16 spot prawns, heads and shells removed

In a large sauté pan, heat the olive oil and garlic over medium heat until the garlic starts to turn golden, about one minute.

Add the butter. As soon as the butter bubbles and froths, add the seaweed in crumpled bits.

Toss the prawns into the pan. Leave sizzling in the pan for thirty seconds, then flip over quickly and cook for another thirty seconds.

As soon as the prawns turn from clear to solid pink with a curl in the tail, pull them out of the hot pan and onto a plate. Don't overcook these tender morsels! The prawns will continue to cook on the plate. Serve immediately.

SMOKY SEA BACON

This easy recipe makes a handful of crispy faux-bacon for crumbling onto a BLT (a.k.a. DLT, for the dulse), baked potatoes, beer-steamed mussels with thyme, potato salad, hummus spread, maple-pecan ice cream, creamy carbonara, sheet-pan Brussels sprouts—in other words, try it on anything you'd anoint with bacon. Liquid smoke comes in bottles from various brands in some grocery stores. This recipe makes enough for two DLTs or salads.

MAKES 1 LARGE HANDFUL

½ cup dried dulse

1 teaspoon maple syrup

¼ teaspoon liquid smoke

Powdered nutritional yeast, to taste

½ tablespoon canola oil

In a medium bowl, toss the dried dulse with the maple syrup and liquid smoke. Add a few shakes of nutritional yeast and mix thoroughly.

In a small skillet, heat the oil to bubbling over medium-high heat. Add the dulse and fry quickly on one side, flip over, and fry the other side. Cook one to two minutes. The dried dulse will change color from burgundy to light brown.

Set on paper towels to cool. Crumble and use immediately for best flavor. Or store in an airtight jar for up to a week at room temperature. Adding a desiccant pack keeps the sea bacon crisp.

CHOCOLATE OCEAN PUDDING IN A NUTTY SHELL

This is my all-time *favorite* beach dessert! What could be more romantic on a beach camping trip than serving your beloved a beautiful clamshell filled with a chocolate ganache pudding amid a nutty crust? Watch out—whoever you serve this to may fall in love! Cleaned butter clamshells work great for individual portions; horse clam shells are ideal for a twosome.

Thanks to Sarah Spaeth—forager, tracking expert, and chef—for the crust recipe. I bring the nuts, coconut, and spice mixture (preground) from home and mix in the honey and vanilla at the beach. Vary the roasted almonds and pecans in the recipe by substituting macadamia nuts, hazelnuts, or even a store-bought nut mix. Garnish the pudding with chilled strawberries to speed up the gelling process. Try mixing in espresso powder or ¼ cup ground rose petals with ½ teaspoon of sugar. Orange zest is also lovely.

MAKES 8 BUTTER CLAM HALVES OR RAMEKINS, 4 HORSE CLAM HALVES, OR 1 (8-TO-9-INCH) PIE

RAW NUT CRUST
- 2 cups almonds
- 2 cups pecans
- 1½ cups unsweetened coconut flakes
- ½ cup honey, plus more as needed
- 1 teaspoon vanilla
- ½ teaspoon cinnamon

CHOCOLATE OCEAN PUDDING
- 4 cups full-fat coconut milk or half-and-half
- 1 cup Turkish towel, Turkish washcloth, or rainbow leaf, rinsed
- 2 cups semisweet chocolate chips
- 1 teaspoon vanilla extract
- 1 tablespoon unsweetened cocoa powder, optional

Put all the crust ingredients into a food processor. Pulse until well ground and the mix holds together when squeezed or pressed. If it is too crumbly, add more honey. Set aside.

In a medium saucepan, bring the milk and Turkish towel to a boil, then reduce to a simmer for twenty minutes. The heat allows the seaweed to exude its natural thickener: carrageenan. Don't be tempted to stir it, or you will break the seaweed into little bits, making it harder to strain out.

While the seaweed is simmering, prepare the nut crusts. Take a handful of nut crust and push into your choice of serving container. Push firmly with your fingers to evenly cover the bottom and sides. Aim for ⅛ to ¼-inch thickness. Set aside.

After the seaweed has simmered for twenty minutes, remove the pan from heat and pour the mixture through a sieve into a medium bowl to remove the seaweed. Stir in the chocolate chips until melted. Stir in the vanilla.

Pour the warm chocolate pudding into the prepared crusts and place in the refrigerator for up to an hour or more. Be patient, seaweed enthusiasts! Chocolate Ocean Pudding will do its magic thickening as it cools.

If you're camping, you can carefully arrange the prepared shells on ice in a cooler. Ladle the pudding into the shells and close the cooler. Wait two hours or more; it depends on how warm the ambient temperature is and how much carrageenan is packed in the seaweed—which can vary with the season. The pudding is ready when you can scoop up a spoonful and it doesn't run or collapse but stands tall and firm like ganache.

VARIATION: RASPBERRY CHOCOLATE OCEAN PUDDING POPS

After plopping 6 to 8 frozen raspberries in a popsicle mold's bottom, pour the pudding mixture into the mold and place them in the freezer for five hours until frozen. Voilà! You have a summertime treat mildly reminiscent of the frosty fudge pops the ice cream truck hawked—but with a hint of the sea. This delicious discovery is the brainchild of Elizabeth Campbell, one of my "Seaweed Sisters," who adores harvesting rainbow leaf seaweed and ogling at its iridescent dance in coastal tide pools. "My girls absolutely love 'em!" Elizabeth says with a twinkle in her eye.

MARGARITA SORBET WITH DULSE

A refreshing margarita sorbet for a summer's day! An optional splash of your favorite tequila spirit helps the sorbet stay soft. Dulse adds a subtle tide of sea salt across your tongue. You can also dip a wine glass in lime juice, then "salt" the rim with dulse—for a margarita-esque theme!

MAKES 6–8 SERVINGS

4 cups raspberries or strawberries

1 cup sugar

1 cup water

3 tablespoons lime juice

1 tablespoon dulse flakes (size of dried basil flakes)

1 shot tequila (optional)

In a blender, puree the raspberries, sugar, and water until smooth, then sieve into a medium bowl to strain out the seeds. Use a rubber spatula to push the mix through the sieve and scrape the strainer's underside to get all the delicious berry mix. Stir in the lime juice, dulse, and tequila.

Set up an ice bath by filling a large bowl with water and ice. Set the bowl of raspberry puree in the ice bath and chill for twenty to thirty minutes.

When chilled (ideally to about 45 degrees F), remove the mixture from the ice bath and transfer to an ice cream maker. Follow the manufacturer's instructions.

If you don't have an ice cream maker, pour the mixture into a glass baking dish and freeze it for seven to eight hours. When firm, use a fork to chop it into tiny, slivery pieces for a granita-style dessert. Or blend it in a food processor for a silky-smooth sorbet.

Serve the sorbet in chilled bowls.

SEA LETTUCE BUTTER

This butter is delicious with steamed Dungeness crab, corn on the cob, pasta, or taters! If you're beach camping, you can use a quarter cup fresh minced sea lettuce stirred into a stick of melted butter. Rinse sea lettuce thoroughly in a bowl of seawater first, and check the sea lettuce blades for little snails and beach hoppers that like to hide in the folds. If you're making this butter at home, you can freeze it until you're ready to use it.

MAKES 4 OUNCES

½ cup butter, softened

4 teaspoons dried sea lettuce flakes

1 teaspoon lemon zest

1 clove garlic, minced

Salt, to taste

Cream the butter with an electric mixer or a fork and blend in the sea lettuce flakes, lemon zest, and garlic.

Shape into a log between parchment paper and chill for five hours.

Store the log tightly wrapped in the fridge for up to two weeks or in the freezer for up to two months. Slice into small rounds and use on potatoes, pasta, or corn on the cob, or melt it for dipping steamed crab.

BEET, APPLE, AND GINGER SEA SLAW

In my seaweed workshops, as the blue sleeve of the tide covers the beach rocks—where hours before we had gathered sea lettuce and winged kelp—I hold a glistening bowl of sea slaw up in thanks. It takes a bit of practice to work comfortably with fresh seaweed—but your awesome efforts will be highly rewarded! Be sure to rinse the blades well at the beach.

You can substitute a quarter cup of dried winged kelp (Pacific wakame) flakes for the fresh seaweed. Just soften in warm water for fifteen minutes, drain, and toss in the bowl with your land veggies—easy peasy!

MAKES 8 SERVINGS

1 cup chopped fresh sea lettuce or winged kelp blades or a mix of both, or ¼ cup dried winged kelp flakes

½ cup balsamic vinegar, plus more as needed

3 tablespoons mild olive oil

Juice and zest of 1 lemon

1 tablespoon maple syrup, plus more as needed

1 tablespoon grated fresh ginger root

2 large beets, grated

2 large carrots, grated

2 apples (Cosmic Crisp, Fuji, Gala, or Honey Crisp), grated

2 cups thinly sliced purple cabbage

1 cup dried cherries

To prepare the sea lettuce blades for the salad, rinse in a bowl of fresh water, then spread across a cutting board. Pat down the seaweed with your fingertips and check for tell-tale lumps: tiny snails, beach hoppers, and isopods. In my seaside kitchen, I reserve a bowl with seawater and seaweed scraps for critters. After checking the seaweed, I return the little guys to the beach. Chop the sea lettuce into 1-inch pieces or smaller. Set aside.

For the fresh winged kelp, blanch the brown blades by dipping in boiling water for seven to ten seconds until green. Cut out and save the midvein for salsa or pickling. Loosely roll up the two remaining "sides" of the blade. Press down by hand on half the rolled winged kelp. Cut off ¼-inch-wide-by-1-inch-long strips from the edge (not the open end of the roll—unless you want long noodles for a gluten-free fettucine). Set aside.

In a large bowl, combine the balsamic vinegar, olive oil, lemon juice and zest, maple syrup, and grated ginger, and mix well. Add and mix together the beets, carrots, apples, cabbage, cherries, and both seaweeds.

If needed, amplify the tang with more balsamic vinegar, or fire up the heat with additional grated ginger. Mix again before serving to distribute the flavorful marinade.

BEACH ASPARAGUS SEAFOOD SALAD

Kaasei Naomi Michalsen learned about sukka'adzi (Lingít for beach asparagus) as a teenager growing up in Klawock, Alaska. She began harvesting the greens regularly when she was a young mother, especially after two Haida Elders asked her to pick some for them when they weren't able to do it themselves anymore. She has prepared this dish for family dinners and cultural celebrations, and it's always a big hit. Her favorite way uses a mix of seafood, including fresh herring eggs, to take it to the top! Be sure to trim the beach asparagus (also known as pickleweed or sea bean) by snapping off any discolored sections and retaining the firm green upper sections that snap crisply.

MAKES 4 SERVINGS

- 2 cups fresh beach asparagus (firm green upper sections only), washed and drained
- 4 strips bacon (optional)
- 1 cup steamed scallops, cooked shrimp, or herring eggs
- ½ cup chopped yellow or sweet onion
- 2 hardboiled eggs, chopped
- 2 tablespoons mayonnaise

Bring a pot of water to boil. Blanch the beach asparagus by placing it in a long-handled strainer and lowering the strainer into the boiling water for only forty-five to sixty seconds. Remove and plunge into an ice water bath to stop the cooking process. Drain and set aside.

If you are using bacon, chop it into small pieces and fry until crisp. Remove from the pan and drain on paper towels.

In a large mixing bowl, combine the beach asparagus with the bacon, seafood, onion, hardboiled eggs, and mayo, and mix well.

Refrigerate for one hour or more before serving.

WILD BEACH GREENS STIR-FRY

Slightly salty and very crunchy, suktéitl' (Lingít for goosetongue) is a delicious and nutritious wild vegetable that can be eaten raw, sautéed in stir-fries, added to soups, and more! At the right time and in the right place, it grows perfect, thick, lance-shaped leaves. Pluck a few leaves here and there from several plants, using your hands to find the base of each plant to snap off individual leaves. This recipe, from Kaasei Naomi Michalsen, makes a delicious side dish to any fresh fish. She first learned about goosetongue from the late Esther Shea, a treasured Taantakwaan Tlingit Elder. You can substitute beach asparagus (pickleweed), green beans, broccoli, or asparagus for the goosetongue. For a vegetarian option, skip the bacon and toss in Smoky Sea Bacon (see recipe earlier in this section).

MAKES 4-6 SERVINGS

4 strips bacon

1 tablespoon vegetable oil, plus more as needed

½ cup chopped yellow or sweet onion

2 carrots, sliced into coins

2 tablespoons minced garlic

2 cups chopped red or green cabbage

2 cups chopped fresh goose-tongue or beach asparagus, washed and drained

Teriyaki sauce (optional; see Note)

Salt and pepper, to taste

Cooked soba noodles or brown rice, for serving

Cut the bacon into small pieces and fry in a large sauté pan or wok until crisp. Remove from the pan, saving the drippings in the pan. Set the bacon on paper towels to drain.

If needed, add 1 tablespoon of the oil to the pan. Stir-fry the onion and carrots over medium-high heat for two to three minutes; the onions should be al dente, not softened. Add the garlic and cabbage and stir-fry for a couple more minutes. If the vegetables are sticking, add a bit more oil to the pan as you go. Finally, stir-fry the beach greens for a few minutes.

Add the bacon bits back to the pan, then the optional teriyaki sauce, and cook for one more minute. Season to taste.

Serve a nutritious crown over soba noodles or brown rice.

Note: Dress it up with a simple homemade teriyaki sauce. In a small bowl, whisk together ¼ cup soy sauce or tamari, 2 tablespoons water, 1 tablespoon fresh grated ginger root, 1 tablespoon minced garlic, and 1 to 2 teaspoons of your favorite sweetener (sugar, maple syrup, birch syrup, agave syrup, or honey).

SHELLFISH

RAZOR CLAM CANTALOUPE CEVICHE

A refreshing taste of ceviche on a summer day is like a trip to the beach. This recipe takes its inspiration from Chef Christy of Sea Rocket Bistro in San Diego, California, who makes a local fish ceviche with cantaloupe. It works with mango or papaya too. Any way you cut it, the lime, melon, cilantro, and sweet clams are a fiesta in your mouth. All this razor clam ceviche needs is an ocean view and a side of surf! I like to use razor clams here, but horse clams or, if you happen to be a deep digger, geoduck siphons also work well. You can buy frozen razor clams online through Quinault Nation fisheries.

MAKES 4–6 SERVINGS

2 cups raw razor clams, minced

¼ cup diced red onion

2 scallions, sliced thin at an angle

½ cup lime juice, plus more if needed

Juice of 1 medium orange

1 jalapeño or habanero (seeds removed), minced

½ medium ripe cantaloupe, cut into ½-inch chunks

Salt and pepper

½ cup roughly chopped cilantro leaves

Tortilla chips, for serving

Avocado slices, for serving (optional)

In a medium bowl, mix the razor clams, onion, and scallions with the lime and orange juice. Stir to make sure all the clam pieces are bathing in juice; add more lime juice if needed to cover the clams.

Marinate for twenty minutes so the fruit acids can "cook" the clams and the flavors can meld.

Mix in the jalapeño, cantaloupe, and salt and pepper to taste. Cover and chill for one hour.

Add the cilantro and mix to distribute. Serve in small, chilled bowls, with crunchy tortilla chips and avocado on the side.

Photo by Ficus Chan

HORSE CLAM STIR-FRY

I met fisherman Ficus Chan at the Bellingham Dockside Market over his tables of neatly arranged iced Dungeness crabs, sushi-grade frozen tuna, and artisan sea salts. But we bonded over horse clams. Ficus, owner of Crab Bellingham and a wild food foraging teacher, loves digging clams. His earliest memory of a horse clam is simply a half shell perched on his grandma's windowsill, and he remembers the stories his uncles and aunts shared about their days clam digging in Boundary Bay in the late 1960s. Growing up in a Chinese family in Vancouver, British Columbia, he ate a wide diversity of foods.

Chan told me horse clam and geoduck siphons (necks) have a texture called song cheoi (Cantonese) or shuangcui (Mandarin), meaning "bright, clear, crisp." The best way to enjoy them, he said, is to slice them thin for sashimi, ceviche, poke, or crudo, or cook them as little as possible in a stir-fry. This stir-fry is bright, crisp, quick, and simple.

MAKES 2 SERVINGS

2 horse clam necks (siphons)

2 tablespoons canola or grape-seed oil

3 fresh ginger root "coins" sliced 3 mm thick

2 cloves garlic, smashed, skins removed

2 stalks celery, sliced thin at an angle

Salt and pepper, to taste

1 tablespoon rice wine or dry sherry

1 tablespoon cornstarch

Rice or noodles, for serving

Bring a small pot of water to a boil and blanch the horse clam necks by submerging them with tongs for six to eight seconds. Immediately transfer them to an ice bath or run under very cold water. This will stop the cooking process and loosen the outer skin. Peel off the tough, brown outer skin. Slice the necks in half lengthwise. Then slice each of the halves crosswise, at an angle, as thin as you can. Set aside.

Heat a wok or medium sauté pan over high heat. Add the oil, stir in the ginger, and heat for ten seconds to infuse the oil with ginger. Add the garlic and celery and stir-fry for ten seconds. Add the sliced horse clam and stir-fry for twenty seconds. Add salt and pepper to taste.

Splash in the wine and cook for another ten seconds. Mix the cornstarch with 2 tablespoons of water, and stir in the cornstarch slurry to thicken the sauce. Remove from heat and serve with rice or noodles.

GARLIC GLAZED GEODUCK

This deceptively simple recipe with a high tide of flavor comes from Alaska fisherman Brian Zwick and his wife, Michele, a Tlingit and Ojibwe artist, and calls for geoduck "bellies." What's a geoduck belly? Well, I didn't know for sure either until I asked Brian and Michele. It's the tender strip of meat protected by the clamshell and attached below the siphon. For cooking's sake, it does not include the gold apple-shaped globe, which, anatomically speaking, is the proper stomach. Best to remove and toss this organ, advises this Ketchikan duo, in case of potential toxins. Brian and Michele say they'll take bellies any day over the neck meat.

This approach comes as a surprise to many chefs, who consider geoduck siphon meat the best sashimi. When their neighbor, Chef Naomi Michalsen, tasted their prized caramelized garlic geoducks, she couldn't believe the flavor. "And it was so simple a recipe! Why didn't I come up with that? And why have I been tossing them into chowder all these years?"

MAKES 2–3 MAIN COURSE SERVINGS (APPETIZERS FOR 6)

2 to 3 geoduck bellies
1 tablespoon minced garlic
Olive oil, for sautéing

In a medium pan over medium-high heat, sauté the geoduck bellies and garlic in olive oil until caramelized and enrobed in a gloriously garlicky glaze, two to three minutes. Flip and cook the other side to golden perfection, another minute.

Use a sharp knife to cut the belly meat the long way into two strips, then slice each strip into ¼-inch slices. (You might get up to forty slices from one geoduck belly—depending on size.) Serve immediately.

Photo by Michele Laduke

DRUNKEN CLAMS

Give me a pot of clams by the sea, a bottle of wine, and a crusty chunk of bread to sop up the juices and I am ridiculously happy. For this recipe, you can go rustic—just toss twelve ounces of beer or wine in a cook pot, bring the elixir to a boil, dump in your clams, and wait nine minutes—or you can dawdle some, sautéing the shallots and garlic in butter as you watch the lingering sunset. Either way, top it off with a handful of chopped parsley and a pinch of hot pepper; it's clam nirvana.

MAKES 4 SERVINGS

3 tablespoons unsalted butter

1 tablespoon extra-virgin olive oil

1 shallot, thinly sliced

3 cloves garlic, minced

12 ounces dry white wine or American-style lager beer

4 pounds of littleneck clams in the shell, scrubbed clean

Handful of chopped fresh flat-leaf parsley, tarragon, or thyme

Pinch of red pepper flakes (optional)

Lemon wedges, for serving

Crusty bread, for serving

In a medium saucepan over medium heat, add the butter and olive oil and sauté the shallots and garlic for three minutes, until softened.

Pour in the wine and bring to a simmer for three to four minutes to concentrate the flavors.

Cover and bring to a boil, then add the littleneck clams. Cover with a tight-fitting lid, reduce the heat, and simmer for seven to ten minutes, or until the clams have opened.

Toss in a handful of fresh herbs and the red pepper flakes. Give the whole shebang a good stir to be sure all the clams are coated. Discard any clams that have not opened.

Serve with lemon wedges and crusty bread to sop up the broth.

ROSIE'S BUTTER CLAM FRITTERS

This recipe is provided by Rosie, a traditional knowledge keeper and Coast Salish Elder in the Samish Tribe. Rosie enjoyed a good belly laugh when she first told me about her famous recipe. "Some say it is so delicious, you will want to eat way too many clam fritters!" These quick and easy camp-style fritters are perfect for beach outings. In spring, Rosie adds steamed or dried nettles and minced garlic for extra flavor, or she uses cooked chopped camas bulbs in place of the onions.

For a fluffier, maltier batter, Rosie says you can substitute a quarter cup lager-style beer like Rainier for a quarter cup of the water. Where I grew up, in Milwaukee, Wisconsin, golden beer-battered fish was a popular citywide tradition every Friday. I still hanker for crispy whitefish. Rosie's clam fritters introduced me to a West Coaster's version. Clam Friday, anyone?

**MAKES ABOUT
5 LARGE FRITTERS**

1½ cups buttermilk pancake mix

¾ cup water (or ¼ cup lager plus ½ cup water)

¼ teaspoon ground black pepper

1 cup chopped fresh or frozen butter clams (cut into bite-size pieces; see Note)

⅓ cup diced yellow onion

½ to 1 cup salted butter

In a medium bowl, gently mix the pancake mix, water, and pepper until just combined, then fold in the clams and onion. The texture should be like thick pancake batter.

Melt a stick of butter in a large pan over medium-high heat. Ladle about ½ cup batter into the hot butter. Let the fritter cook until it's crispy golden brown and well set, about 3–4 minutes. Use a spatula to turn the fritter and press on the middle to release moisture. Keep turning and pressing until the fritter is golden brown and crispy on both sides and no more moisture is escaping, about 6–8 minutes total. Transfer fritter to a plate lined with paper towels.

Continue with the rest of the batter, adding more butter between batches to keep about ¼ inch of butter in the pan. Enjoy hot.

Note: Shuck raw butter clams by inserting a knife into the clam and cutting the adductor muscles. Remove the part of the stomach that contains the food and cut off the dark black tip of the siphon. Rinse clams well. Cleaned clams can be frozen for later use. If using frozen clams, you can chop them while partially thawed.

BUTTER-OF-THE-SEA CRAB BOWL

From an early age, Terry Phair, a Lummi Nation member, learned fishing and crabbing and gained wisdom from the Elders in his community. Now, as a commercial diver, he harvests seafood, including sea urchins, sea cucumber, and geoduck. His brainchild is the Lummi Seafood Market, where he brings Indigenous-caught products to the local community. Terry says, "Eating sea urchin roe and crab head butter is one of our tribal Elders' favorites. It teaches us younger folks to take only what you need and to limit food waste. It is rich and nutritious." The crab "butter" has a briny, umami-rich, nutty flavor prized in Asian and Lummi Nation traditional cuisine.

Using the upside-down crab shell as a bowl, Terry steam-poaches an egg from his own family's chickens right in the crab shell. Then he spoons on rice, a golden gravy of uni butter, flaky Dungeness crab, scallions, and a squeeze of lime. Honestly, this creation is mythic! It is one of the most fascinating dishes I've had the honor to enjoy. Terry, my hands are raised up to you, 'Hy'shqe.

MAKES 2 SERVINGS

2 whole Dungeness crabs

½ cup unsalted butter

4 ounces uni (sea urchin roe), fresh or frozen (unthawed)

2 eggs

1 cup cooked white or brown rice or quinoa

2 tablespoons thinly sliced green onions

2 tablespoons thinly sliced chives

2 tablespoons bacon bits (optional)

2 lemon wedges

Hot sauce, such as sriracha

Salt and pepper, to taste

Bring a large pot of salted water to a hard boil over medium-high heat. Use tongs to place the two crabs in the boiling water. Cook for up to twenty minutes. Remove cooked crabs with tongs and set aside until cool to the touch.

While the crab is cooking, make the uni butter: Add the butter and urchin roe to a small sauté pan over low heat and allow the butter to melt. Cook for a few minutes. Keep on very low heat until ready to use.

As you disassemble the crabs, be careful not to break or crack the central part of the body cavity, which you will reserve for a serving bowl. Remove all legs from the main body. Remove and discard the gills. Leave the crab "butter," the yellow-green substance, inside the shell.

Remove the meat from the legs and claws. Set aside.

Crack one egg into each of the upside-down crab shells and steam in a covered soup pot fitted with a steamer basket and an inch of water in the bottom. Cook the eggs to your liking in the natural crab butter/juice inside the shell. Terry recommends cooking the eggs

only until they are overeasy, showing a skim of white across the yolk but still runny underneath.

Spoon half of the cooked rice into each crab shell, atop the egg. Add a ½ to ⅔ cup of uni butter on top of the rice. Sprinkle with the cooked Dungeness crab meat, green onions, chives, and bacon bits.

Add a squeeze of lemon and hot sauce on top, along with a sprinkle of salt and pepper to taste.

Enjoy with a fork or chopsticks.

HOW MUCH URCHIN ROE IN AN AVERAGE SEA URCHIN?

You might wonder how many urchins you need to flavor a pasta dish or pizza. Recipes in this book use one-third to two-thirds cup (2.5 to 5 ounces) of sea urchin roe. OK, but how many giant red sea urchins is that?

"It's a bit of a shell game. Hard to say, really," said one of the two urchin roe processors I talked to. "It depends on the species, season, and urchin's food supply," said the other. I kinda knew that already.

Next I reached out to my foraging buddy Annette. She's a retired engineer who adores a technical challenge as much as she adores fresh uni. We embarked on a roe-collecting experiment. We cleaned six giant red urchins, dive-harvested by Lummi Nation fisherman Terry Phair during his winter season. I paid about eleven dollars per live red urchin. The average amount of roe per urchin (average body size three to four inches, excluding spines) was 2.2 to 2.6 ounces—about one-third cup. Before you say "ouch," keep in mind that processed uni (the Japanese word for sea urchin roe) is pricier yet. It's upward of five dollars an ounce—cleaned and packaged. But you don't need much uni for luxuriant flavor.

Green and purple urchins, however, are smaller. They could have a half tablespoon of roe each—or less. You may need more than eight times as many green or purple urchins to equal one giant red urchin. Granted, you could just buy uni fresh or frozen online from processors on the Pacific or Atlantic Coast, although shipping fresh seafood overnight isn't cheap. Either way, if you decide not to DIY (see the Harvest Guide for Sea Urchins), you are going to shell out dollars. So why not try urchin fishing? And remember, eating urchins may help sustain kelp forests (see the "Sea Urchins, Sea Stars, and Kelp, Oh My!" sidebar in the Sea Urchins listing).

But before you head out, be prepared for slippery, rocky shores and ocean waves. Take a buddy. Check your state or province's recreational sea urchin harvest rules for daily size and harvest limits, permitted species, and open or closed areas. In parts of California, for instance, purple urchin can be gathered year-round—no limit!

CONSUMMATE CRAB CAKES

Years ago, a few sea kayaking buddies and I gathered for a crab-cake cook-off. We cracked, mixed, sizzled, chewed, and voted on our favorite. Chef Judith Weinstock's recipe won! Judith is a consummate Northwesterner—crab fisher, storyteller, folk guitarist, forest pilgrim—and founder and former owner of two seasonal-organic eateries, Streamliner Diner on Bainbridge Island and Kingston Hotel Café. This recipe hails from my berry-stained, butter-spattered copy of *Kingston Hotel Café Cookbook*.

It is shared with openhearted permission from Judith, who says, "To me, crab symbolizes the decadent side of Northwest living. Although we have to put up with gray skies, rain, and long winters, one summer meal with fresh crab as the centerpiece makes it all worthwhile. Visions of pulling up the crab pots, hauling them home, putting your largest kettle full of water on to boil, dumping in the crabs, and setting out bowls of dipping butter are all you really need to feel once again at peace with where you live."

I like to serve these with Cucumber-Seaweed-Sesame Salad (see recipe in Seaweeds & Beach vegetables).

MAKES 4 SERVINGS

- 1 pound cooked crabmeat
- 2 eggs, beaten
- 1 cup finely chopped cilantro
- ½ cup bread crumbs
- ¾ cup unsweetened coconut milk
- 1½ tablespoons peeled and minced fresh ginger root
- 2 teaspoons minced fresh lemongrass
- 1 minced makrut lime leaf
- 1 teaspoon sugar
- ½ teaspoon hot chili oil
- 1 tablespoon canola oil, for cooking

Squeeze the crabmeat as dry as possible. Use a clean towel and wring it as tightly as you can, until the meat actually looks dry.

In a medium bowl, mix all of the ingredients except the canola oil until evenly combined. Shape into 8 equal-sized cakes. (At this point, you can cover the cakes tightly and refrigerate them overnight, for cooking the next day.)

In a lightly oiled nonstick skillet over medium-high heat, fry the cakes until golden brown on one side, approximately three minutes. Flip and brown the other side of the cakes. Serve immediately.

UNI CARBONARA

I was in my twenties, sailing up the Inside Passage with three wanderlust sailor friends, when I tried my first fresh, salt-licked urchin. We stuffed rocks into our wet suits (for weight) and sank down below the ocean's surface for thirty seconds to pull basketball-sized red urchins off a submerged cliff. We dumped the rocks and shot to the surface with the four giant red urchins in tow. That first amazing bite contained wild magic, I swear! I promised myself I'd return alone; nine years later, I did. On that solo kayak journey, I became adept at using my college-day field hockey skills to dislodge a giant red sea urchin with my paddle and pop it onto my spray-skirted kayak cockpit. I've also procured sea urchins at extreme low tides from tide pools I could access on foot.

This decadent, satisfying, and quick meal is from the land of slow food—Italy. This recipe requires roe from one giant red sea urchin to flavor the sauce; that's the "slow" part. Read How to Clean a Sea Urchin in the main Sea Urchins entry for tips. But don't be put off—practice makes perfect. It takes me five minutes to remove the five "tongues" of roe in a giant red! For thousands of years along this coast, fresh sea urchin, eaten right out of its natural bowl, was a "fast food" for coastal travelers.

MAKES 2 SERVINGS

6 ounces dry rotini pasta (about 2 cups)

1 shallot, minced

2 cloves garlic, minced

Generous pinch of red pepper flakes

1 tablespoon olive oil

¼ cup dry vermouth

½ teaspoon tarragon

½ cup heavy cream

⅓ cup (2.5 ounces) urchin roe

¼ cup grated parmesan

1 tablespoon chopped chives or parsley, for garnish

Bring a medium pot of salted water to a boil and cook the pasta just shy of al dente. It should have more tooth than you'd want in the finished pasta. Drain and set aside.

In a medium pan over medium heat, sauté the shallot, garlic, and red pepper flakes in the olive oil until the shallots are translucent, about three minutes. Add the vermouth and tarragon, bring to a simmer, and reduce by one-third, about three minutes.

In a small bowl, whisk the cream and urchin roe, and add to the sauté pan. Bring to a simmer and reduce by half, three to five minutes.

Add the pasta and stir to coat with the sauce. Garnish with a tasty snow of quality parmesan and the chives or parsley.

OPPOSITE: *Two ways to invite an urchin to dinner: Uni Carbonara (top) and Sea Urchin Pizza (bottom, p. 342)*

SEA URCHIN PIZZA WITH NORI SEA BACON

This pizza is inspired by our coastal kelp forests and my first coastal foraging buddies on the Inside Passage—Gene, Mac, Alan, Mark, Rick, Katy, Carl, and Chris. You'll need about one-third cup (2½ ounces) of fresh urchin roe for each serving of this pizza; that's about one giant red sea urchin or eight to ten green urchins worth, more for purple urchins. See How to Clean a Sea Urchin in the main Sea Urchins entry. You can also purchase this briny, fruity, creamy, sweet (and pricey) delicacy—called uni in Japanese—at some seafood stores. Look for firm, orange-gold (not brown) roe. For baking the pizza, a sheet pan works fine, but using a pizza stone yields an authentic stone-fired crust.

MAKES 2 SERVINGS

Fine cornmeal, for dusting

½ pound pizza dough

2 small red potatoes, boiled and cut into coins

1½ tablespoons olive oil, divided

¾ cup grated gruyere

½ cup grated mozzarella

¼ cup very thinly sliced red onion (sliced into crescents)

2 cups arugula

Juice of ½ lime

Pinch of sea salt

⅔ cup fresh urchin roe

Sea bacon (see Smoky Sea Bacon recipe), sea lettuce, or wild nori (optional)

1½ limes, sliced into 6 wedges

Preheat the oven to 450 degrees F.

Sprinkle a light dusting of cornmeal onto a baking sheet, or parchment paper if you're using a pizza stone. Roll the dough into a 10- to 12-inch circle and place on the sheet or paper.

Top the dough with the potato coins. Brush the entire pizza, including potato coins, with 1 tablespoon of olive oil. Sprinkle with the gruyere, mozzarella, and onion.

Bake for eight to ten minutes. The pizza is done when the crust begins to turn golden and the cheese is bubbly and just starting to brown.

While the pizza is baking, toss the arugula in a medium bowl with the lime juice and the remaining ½ tablespoon olive oil. Set aside.

Remove the pizza from the oven. Add the urchin roe, arranging large red sea urchin tongues in a flower-petal pattern or smaller pieces of roe in dots. Garnish with the arugula. I make a wreath of arugula encircling my sea urchin "flower." Scatter with sea bacon, and serve immediately with lime wedges.

ACKNOWLEDGMENTS

Acknowledgments are a tide pool of space for holding an ocean of gratitude. I am deeply indebted to many individuals, human and otherwise. First and foremost, I give thanks for the sacred alliances among all plants, animals, minerals, bacteria, fungi, and natural systems, which sustain us. The wide waters and lands where I live, sea kayak, harvest, research, and teach span the vast ancestral territory of hundreds of First Nation and Tribal communities from California to Alaska. I raise my hands to our First Nations knowledge holders—past, present, and over the horizon. Their earth-centered values and resource stewardship practices offer a compass bearing in a smoke-strewn era. Gunalchéesh and Mange tak ("thank you" in Lingít and Danish) for sharing innumerable seaweed-harvesting workshops and feasts in your beautiful traditional territories.

A book of this scope and nature is woven together over many seasons by many hands. A flood tide of gratitude to my coastal network of devoted, caring, and informed Indigenous knowledge keepers, western scientists, foragers, camp cooks, chefs of all apron strings, kitchen recipe testers, and friends who jumped in with shovels, buckets, bags, crab traps, tree taps, and a miscellany of harvesting know-how for foraging and feasting trips. I stand in thanks up to my rubber-boot tops.

A tsunami of thanks to the Mountaineers Books crew. From the get-go, editor in chief Kate Rogers envisioned a delicious foraging guide, woven through with natural and cultural history, that leans into responsible and honorable harvesting—as well as educating foragers on the challenges native plants and animals face in a fast-changing climate. Her creative team became my kelp forest of holdfasts in a rush of deadlines and scheduling to produce this book. Each person served in some way to anchor the project in real time. Raised mugs of fireweed tea to publisher Tom Helleberg, managing editor Janet Kimball, penultimate senior editor Laura Shauger, development editor Erin Cusick, copy editor Erin Moore, creative director Jen Grable, sales director Darryl Booker, publicists Marissa Litak and Kate Jay, and all the numerous folks I can't fit in my tide pool who made this book shimmer. Huge splashes of gratitude to my agent, Anne Depue, for coaching me through depressing climate research, reading drafts, and offering timely encouragement. Your well-chosen words rooted me to my desk.

I am wildly grateful for the enthusiastic and multi-talented students at Fairhaven College and Western Washington University who jumped wholeheartedly into my wild food course and, by twist of fate, this book. These devoted and enthusiastic research assistants dug clams; clipped nettles, seaweed, and invasive knotweed; boned up on natural and cultural history (including impacts of climate change) and tested recipes. Thanks to Aubree Radktke, Clara Wallner, Elizabeth Merritt, Emma Gelino, Izzy Graham, Kenny Jacoby, Levi Friedman, Maya Harrison, Mirabelle LeMieux, Morgan Nichols, Suleyma Nunez Cordoba, Naomi Tyler, Paul Helmich, Raven Taylor, Ruby Roebuck, Tess Reding Hoffart, and Sarah Sasek. Enormous thanks to my team of five Wild Food students who worked for months in independent studies on this book: Grace Meyer, head book research assistant, kept chaos at bay by wrangling computer files and Excel spreadsheets while combing through hundreds of scientific articles and experimenting with shrubs and preserves. A blast of ocean spray to Katherine "Kat" Palmer, photographer and photo editor. Waves of appreciation to Reid Riker, Betsy Knutson-Skinner, and Kate Teele for a sumptuous season of recipe development, testing, and book research. Thank you, Sarah Ellis, for superb office organization and recipe typing and Elysian Borrell for giving a hand.

To my husband and green man, Chris Moench, innumerable thanks for being as enthusiastic about harvesting oyster mushrooms as you are about pulling invasive "stinky Bob." You have been a nourishing presence and a quiet eye in the storm.

Deep gratitude to all the foragers who love the Pacific Northwest coast in the most intimate of ways: by inviting sustainable wild foods to their tables. You make the admirable choice of supporting appetites and ecosystems. You remind us that the shortest distance from earth to table is truly delicious. That includes you, Kimber Owen, Fran Kelso, and Audrey Benedict!

Thanks to Whiteley Center on San Juan Island for a retreat space to complete the final draft.

Raised paddles to Nancy J. Turner, whose dog-eared ethnobotany books and devotion to teaching carry the wisdom forward, for sharing her published articles related to sustainable harvesting. A bag of beach asparagus raised to Naomi Kaasei Michalsen, Jared Qwustenuxun Williams, and SGang Gwaay Dolly Garza for their enduring teachings of traditional and spirit-restoring foods.

A high tide of thanks to my Seaweed Sisters, Valerie Segrest, Elise Krohn, Elizabeth Campbell, Jamie Donatuto, Aleta Post, Vanessa Cooper, Jessie Newman, Fiona Devereaux, and Kristine Pearson. Mushroom caps off to Elder Florence Englebretson, my childhood neighbor, who knew secret things like where to find slippery jacks and—more amazing—how to cook them for lunch. Thanks to friend and mycologist Dr. Fred Rhoades of Mycena Consulting, for reviewing the mushroom chapter.

Kelp-horn toots to Lisa Harper, who tested maple tempura and dandelion root truffle recipes.

A bow to Taylor Shellfish and Andy Dewey for supplying a handsome geoduck for book photos. Gratitude to all the photographers—listed in the photo credits on the copyright page—who filled in missing photos.

To Katy Beck, for sharing seaweed soup, botanical wisdom, misadventures (the best kind), and friendship for four decades: a caribou bow. To Mac Smith, my Mariana-Trench-deep thanks for that life-changing seaweed class in the 1980s and for being a foraging friend for life. To my family clans of wild food aficionados—the Hahns, Smiths, Petersons, Gauvreaus, Moenchs, Pasches, Taylors, and Augustines—may we eat at the wild table together for years to come.

Last but not least, a jar of Wisconsin Northwoods blackberry jam raised to my single father, Bud Hahn, who during family camping trips served up Yellowstone Lake trout for breakfast, Washington razor clam chowder for lunch, and Maine blueberries for dessert. The wild crab apple falls not far from the tree.

Serviceberry is one of the earlier bloomers in northwest forests.

RESOURCES

FIELD GUIDES & GENERAL INTEREST BOOKS

Arno, Stephen F., and Ramona P. Hammerly. *Northwest Trees: Identifying and Understanding the Region's Native Trees*. 2nd edition. Seattle: Mountaineers Books, 2020.

Arora, David. *All That the Rain Promises and More*. Berkeley: Ten Speed Press, 1991.

———. *Mushrooms Demystified: A Comprehensive Guide to the Fleshy Fungi*. Berkeley: Ten Speed Press, 1986.

Benedict, Audrey D., and Joseph K. Gaydos. *Explore the Salish Sea: A Nature Guide for Kids*. Seattle: Little Bigfoot, 2018.

Beug, Michael. *Mushrooms of Cascadia: An Illustrated Key to the Fungi of the Pacific Northwest*. 2nd edition. Berkeley: Ten Speed Press, 2024.

Druehl, Louis, and Bridgette Clarkston. *Pacific Seaweeds: A Guide to Common Seaweeds of the Pacific Coast*. Updated and expanded edition. Madeira Park, British Columbia: Harbour Publishing, 2016.

Eaton, Janice Schofield. *Discovering Wild Plants: Alaska, Western Canada, the Northwest*. Portland: Alaska Northwest Books, 2011.

Garza, Dolores A. *Common Edible Seaweeds in the Gulf of Alaska*. 2nd edition. Fairbanks: Alaska Sea Grant College Program, University of Alaska Fairbanks, 2012.

Hahn, Jennifer Peterson. *Pacific Coast Foraging Guide: 40 Wild Foods from Beach, Field, and Forest*. Seattle: Skipstone, 2010.

Harbo, Rick M. *A Field Guide to Seashells and Shellfish of the Pacific Northwest*. Madeira Park, British Columbia: Harbour Publishing, 2009.

Laursen, Gary A., and C. Neil McArthur. *Alaska's Mushrooms: A Wide-Ranging Guide*. Portland: Alaska Northwest Books, 2016.

Lindeberg, Mandy R., and Sandra C. Lindstrom. *Field Guide to Seaweeds of Alaska*. Fairbanks: Alaska Sea Grant College Program, University of Alaska Fairbanks, 2010.

Lloyd, T. Abe, and Fiona Hamersley Chambers. *Wild Berries of Washington and Oregon*. Auburn, WA: Lone Pine Publishing, 2014.

MacKinnon, Andy, and Kem Luther. *Mushrooms of British Columbia*. Victoria: Royal British Columbia Museum, 2021.

Pojar, Jim, and Andy MacKinnon. *Plants of the Pacific Northwest Coast: Washington, Oregon, British Columbia, and Alaska*. Tukwila: Lone Pine Publishing, 2016.

Schofield, Janice J. *Alaska's Wild Plants: A Guide to Alaska's Edible and Plentiful Harvest*. Revised edition. Berkeley: Alaska Northwest Books, 2020.

Sept, J. Duane. *The New Beachcomber's Guide to Seashore Life of California*. Madeira Park, British Columbia: Harbour Publishing, 2023.

———. *The New Beachcomber's Guide to the Pacific Northwest*. Madeira Park, British Columbia: Harbour Publishing, 2024.

Siegel, Noah, and Christian Schwarz. *Mushrooms of the Redwood Coast: A Comprehensive Field Guide to the Fungi of Coastal Northern California*. Berkeley: Ten Speed Press, 2016.

Trudell, Steve. *Mushrooms of the Pacific Northwest*. Revised edition. Portland: Timber Press, 2022.

Turner, Mark, and Ellen Kuhlmann. *Trees and Shrubs of the Pacific Northwest*. Portland: Timber Press, 2014.

Using Alaska's Wild Berries & Other Wild Edibles. FNH-00120. University of Alaska Fairbanks Cooperative Extension Service in cooperation with the USDA. 2022.

Viereck, Leslie A., and Elbert L. Little. *Alaska Trees and Shrubs*. 2nd edition. Fairbanks: Snowy Owl Books, 2007.

Winkler, Daniel. *Fruits of the Forest: A Field Guide to Pacific Northwest Edible Mushrooms*. Seattle: Mountaineers Books, 2022.

FIRST NATIONS FOOD TRADITIONS IN THE PACIFIC NORTHWEST

Anderson, M. Kat. *Tending the Wild: Native American Knowledge and the Management of California's Natural Resources*. Berkeley: University of California Press, 2013.

Fienup-Riordan, Ann, Alice Rearden, Marie Meade, and Kevin Jernigan. *Yungcautnguuq Nunam Qainga Tamarmi (All the Land's Surface Is Medicine): Edible and Medicinal Plants of Southwest Alaska*. Fairbanks: University of Alaska Press, 2021.

Jones, Anore. *Plants That We Eat: Nauriat Niġiñaqtuat*. Fairbanks: University of Alaska Press, 2010.

Luschiim Arvid Charlie, and Nancy J. Turner. *Luschiim's Plants: Traditional Indigenous Foods, Materials, and Medicines*. Madeira Park, BC: Harbour Publishing, 2021.

Turner, Nancy J. *Ancient Pathways, Ancestral Knowledge: Ethnobotany and Ecological Wisdom of Indigenous Peoples of Northwestern North America*. Volumes 1 and 2. Montreal: McGill-Queen's University Press, 2014.

———. *Food Plants of Coastal First Peoples*. Victoria Royal British Columbia Museum, 2007.

Turner, Nancy J., and Richard J. Hebda. *Saanich Ethnobotany*. Victoria: Royal British Columbia Museum, 2012.

FOOD PRESERVATION

Ball Home Canning Test Kitchen. *Ball Canning Back to Basics: A Foolproof Guide to Canning Jams, Jellies, Pickles and More*. New York City: Time Inc. Books, 2017.

Bell, Mary T. *The Essential Guide to Food Drying: A Fun Guide to Creating Snacks, Meals, and Crafts*. New York City: Skyhorse Publishing, 2022.

Kingry, Judi, and Lauren Devine. *Ball Complete Book of Home Preserving: 400 Delicious and Creative Recipes for Today*. Toronto: Robert Rose, 2024.

National Center for Home Food Preservation. *Complete Guide to Home Canning*. USDA et al. 2023. www.nifa.usda.gov/about-nifa/blogs/usdas-complete-guide-home-canning.

Parrish, Emillie. *Fermenting Made Simple: Delicious Recipes to Improve Your Gut Health*. Victoria: TouchWood Editions, 2022.

University of Alaska Fairbanks, Cooperative Extension Service, www.uaf.edu/ces/publications/database. Web-based learning modules for canning, pickling, and making jerky, plus other information about bullwhip kelp, morel mushrooms, fireweed, Alaska's wild berries and other wild edibles, backyard birch tapping, and preserving Alaska's bounty

NATIVE PLANT SOCIETIES

Increase your appreciation of native plants and habitats by joining a native plant society in your state or province. Local chapters sponsor field trips and educational events or projects while working to protect the Northwest's rich native plant heritage.

Alaska Native Plant Society
PO Box 141613
Anchorage, AK 99514
https://aknps.org
admin@aknps.org

California Native Plant Society
2707 K Street, Suite 1
Sacramento, CA 95816
www.cnps.org
cnps@cnps.org
(916) 447-2677

Native Plant Society of Oregon
PO Box 902
Eugene, OR 97440
www.npsoregon.org
info@npsoregon.org

Washington Native Plant Society
6310 NE 74th Street, Suite 215E
Seattle, WA 98115
www.wnps.org
info@wnps.org
(206) 527-3210

FORAGING GUIDELINES

"Respectful Harvesting Guidelines" by Kayaaní Sisters Council, Kaasei Indigenous Foodways, and Seventh Generation Fund for Indigenous Peoples. Available at www.kaasei.com.

The Cedar Box Experience: Harvest Ethics. An interactive, educational web resource that draws from the "Tend, Gather, and Grow Teaching Toolkit," the "Cedar Box Toolkit," and the Swinomish 13 Moons Curriculum. Visit
https://cedar-box.webflow.io.

COMMERCIAL WILD FOOD SOURCES

Birch Syrup and Birch Tapping Supplies
Kahiltna Birchworks, Alaska Birch Syrup and Wild Harvest Products
Talkeetna, AK 99676
www.alaskabirchsyrup.com
(907) 373-1309

MUSHROOM CLUBS

Join a local mushroom club, usually called a "mycological society" or "mycological association." Learn from the experts during field trips and monthly programs. Find affiliated clubs in your area, such as the Puget Sound Mycological Society at the North American Mycological Association (NAMA) website, www.namyco.org, which catalogs more than seventy-five clubs across the US and Canada.

MUSHROOMS

These sources offer wild, farmed, and grow-your-own options.

Cascadia Mushrooms

Oyster mushrooms (dried) and growing kits, plus recipes by myco-farmer Alex Winstead and Isabel Machuca-Kelley, based in Bellingham, Washington. Visit https://cascadia mushrooms.com.

Pacific Northwest Mushrooms

Morels and chanterelles (fresh), plus porcini powder, provided by a small family team in southern Oregon. Visit https://pnwmushrooms.org.

Untamed Feast Wild Mushroom Products

Porcini, morels, and forest blend mushrooms, plus recipes by a couple who forage and make mushroom mixes with a small cadre of fungiphiles, based in Victoria, BC. Visit www.untamedfeast.com.

Wine Forest Wild Foods

Founded by Connie Green, an early wild mushroom purveyor to the Bay Area's top chefs. Based in Napa, California, they offer porcini, morels, chanterelles, yellow foots, and more, plus recipes. Visit https://wineforest.com, or call (707) 944-8604.

SEAWEED

BC Kelp

Wild-harvested bull kelp, bladderwrack (*Fucus*), *Alaria*, and giant kelp from northern British Columbia, plus recipes. Small family business founded by Louise Gaudet, based in Prince Rupert.
Visit www.bckelp.com, or contact bckelp@bckelp.com or (250) 622-7085.

Canadian Kelp Resources Ltd.

Sugar kelp, bull kelp, winged kelp (*Alaria*), Macro kelp blades, and more, from the outer coast of Vancouver Island. Founded by phycologist Dr. Louis Druehl, author of *Pacific Seaweeds* and Canada's kelp guru, and based in Bamfield, British Columbia. Visit www.canadiankelp.com or email canadiankelp@gmail.com.

Daybreak Seaweed Co.

Dulse, winged kelp, and more, sourced from small-scale West Coast seaweed farmers spread from Southern California to Alaska. Based in San Diego. Learn more at https://daybreakseaweed.com.

Mendocino Sea Vegetable Company

Bladderwrack (fucus), nori, etc., from the California coast. Based in Philo, California. Visit www.seaweed.net, or contact kombuko@seaweed.net or (707) 895-2996.

Ocean Harvest Sea Vegetable Company

Wakame, bladderwrack (fucus), nori, and other seaweeds from Mendocino, California. Learn more at www.seaweedmermaid.net, or contact ohveggies@pacific.net or (707) 694-9496.

Rising Tide Sea Vegetables

Wakame, dulse, nori, sea lettuce, and other seaweeds from Mendocino, California. Learn more at www.loveseaweed.com. Contact risingtide@mcn.org or (707) 964-5663.

Yemaya Seaweed Co.

Julie Drucker and team have sung to the sea before harvesting wild kelp, including nori, wakame, and bladderwrack (fucus) on the Mendocino, California, coast for the past two decades. Learn more at www.yemayaseaweedcompany.com.

INDEX

ABOUT THE AUTHOR

Photo by Abalone Annette Dong

Jennifer Hahn was born in the Great Lake states. At age four, on a family camping trip to Washington's Olympic Peninsula, she spooned up her dad's gritty, buttery clam chowder and transformed into a coastal forager.

Hahn earned two bachelor's degrees, in environmental studies and writing, from Western Washington University, where she studied with Pulitzer Prize–winning author Annie Dillard. Hahn later founded Elakah Sea Kayak Expeditions and has led tours in Washington, Canada, Alaska, and Baja Mexico. She is the author of *Spirited Waters: Soloing South Through the Inside Passage*, and *Pacific Feast: A Cook's Guide to West Coast Foraging and Cuisine*. Hahn has been featured on National Public Radio and toured with the Washington Commission for the Humanities's Inquiring Mind series.

Hahn earned a master's degree in seaweed toxicology from Western Washington University's College of the Environment. Her community-based research took her around the Salish Sea to gather seaweed with the help of eighteen First Nations and Tribes, the results of which were published in the international journal *PlosOne*.

With decades of wilderness travel under her boots and kayak hull, including thru-hiking the Pacific Crest Trail from Northern California to Canada and kayaking solo from Ketchikan, Alaska, to Washington, Hahn works as a wilderness guide and teaching professor at Fairhaven College. She approaches foraging as a way to nourish connection. Hahn lives in Bellingham, Washington, with her potter husband and family.

ABOUT SKIPSTONE

Skipstone guides explore healthy lifestyles, backyard activism, and how an outdoor life relates to the well-being of our planet. Sustainable foods and gardens; healthful living; realistic and doable conservation at home; modern aspirations for community—Skipstone tries to address such topics in ways that emphasize active living, local and grassroots practices, and a small footprint. Our hope is that Skipstone books will inspire you to celebrate the freedom and generosity of a life outdoors.

All of our publications, as part of our 501(c)(3) nonprofit program, are made possible through the generosity of donors and through sales of 700 titles on outdoor recreation, sustainable lifestyle, and conservation. To donate, purchase books, or learn more, visit us online:

www.skipstonebooks.org
www.mountaineersbooks.org

SKIPSTONE

LIVE LIFE

MAKE RIPPLES

YOU MAY ALSO LIKE

   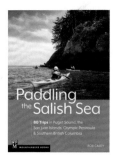